Joseph-Théophi

LIFE OF

Henri-Dominique LACORDAIRE, OP

BOOK 1

Translated by
George G. Christian, OP
and
Richard L. Christian

© 2014
Dominican Friars
Province of St. Joseph, USA

Vie du R. P. Lacordaire
Tome Premier
Joseph-Théophile Foisset

Paris
Librairie Jacques Lecoffre
Lecoffre Fils et Cie, Successeurs
20, rue Bonaparte

1870

Associate, cdt [C. D. Tansey]: Chap. 1-4.

TABLE OF CONTENTS

Table of Contents i

Declaration iv

Introduction 1

Chapter I: Education, Unbelief, Conversion 69

Chapter II: Early Years of Priesthood 110

Chapter III: *L'abbé* F. de la Mennais 146

Chapter IV: *L'Avenir* 195

Chapter V: Encyclical of 1832 230

Chapter VI: Fall of Fr. de La Mennais 261

Chapter VII: Conferences a Stanislaus College 307

Chapter VIII: First Conferences at Notre-Dame 340

Chapter IX: Letter to the Holy See -

                     Break with Bishop de Quélen 379

Chapter X: Series at Metz - Dominican Vocation 424

Chapter XI: La Quercia - Santa Sabina - San Clemente . 474

APPENDICES 514

Appendix I 514

Appendix II 515

Appendix III 519

Appendix IV 519

Appendix V 524

Appendix VI 524

Appendix VII 525

Appendix VIII 530

Appendix IX 530

Appendix X 532

Appendix XI 533

Appendix XII 536

Appendix XIII 538

Appendix XIV 544

Appendix XV 547

Appendix XVI 549

Appendix XVII 551

Appendix XVIII 559

Appendix XIX 560

Appendix XX 561

Appendix XXI 564

DECLARATION

This work was composed from memories and from correspondence. When I knew Lacordaire, he was seventeen years old, I was nineteen. Since then, I have not lost sight of him for even one day. Moreover, I had the good fortune that my memories — very strong indeed — were continually checked by the most undeniable of testimony: by letters written at the very moment when things were happening. In referring to those letters, I am very careful; I indicate the date and I name the persons to whom they were addressed. From them, I cite their most remarkable passages in quotation marks; but I must give notice that, having to meld into my report the facts that arose from the letters, I have had very few scruples about relating these facts without quotation marks, in the very words used by the author of the letter; I believed that, on this point, it was sufficient to indicate my sources at the bottom of the page. *[Changed to Endnotes - Trans.]*

With the same discretion, I have drawn from the admirable work that Father Lacordaire dictated on his deathbed.

Of all tasks, it has always been a delicate one to write a history of one's own times. And the task becomes even more difficult if the author publishes the work in his lifetime, if he leaves this work to the impassioned judgments of his contemporaries! Most men prefer to hear the praises of that which they love. What the Hebrews demanded of the prophet, that is what men demand of the historian: Tell us things that please us[1]. But history is history; it has no value except by way of truth.

I am not a eulogist, I am a witness. I come to relate what I saw, I can only relate it the way I saw it; I may have seen it imperfectly, but I am unable to lie.

I have written this book, as much as it was in me, in the presence of God, in a spirit of complete submission to His Church, the Catholic, apostolic, and Roman Church. For fifty years I have been on the ramparts for the defense of my faith. I pray that God will grant me the grace of dying as I have lived. Especially do I pray that the biography of Father Lacordaire will not be a contradiction to my rather long life, during which — I dare compliment myself here — I never for a single day wavered in fidelity to the Church and to the Holy See.

Joseph-Théophile Foisset

---

1. *Is* 30:10.

LIFE
of
Henri-Dominique LACORDAIRE, OP

INTRODUCTION

The decline of spiritual authority; causes of this decline — Anti-Christian sentiment of the eighteenth century and of the French Revolution — Sterility of error — Why Bonaparte created the Concordat — Organic Articles; supremacy of the State in matters of religion — Bishops, ecclesiastical prefects; humiliation of the Church of France — Attitude of certain Catholic writers — The University of the Empire — Imprisonment and suppression of Pius VII — The question of the institution of Bishops; Council of 1811; Concordat of Fontainebleau — The Church under the Restoration — Failure of the alliance between the throne and the altar — *The Émigrés* of the Church of France: Concordat of 1817 — The advanced age of the Bishops — Contrast with the vitality of France at that time — Lacordaire's frame of mind when he entered the seminary

One can hardly understand the life of a famous man without first having gained precise knowledge of the era in which God granted him to live. This is true for whomever appears in history, but how much more for Father Lacordaire! Who, more than he, was a man of his times? Who was involved earlier than he in the very muddled conflict of the nineteenth century? And so, before relating his life, I would like, if I may, to give readers a full understanding of the first years of that century, a period that influenced the childhood and adolescence of Lacordaire, and made him who he was. Before anything else, I would like explain the state of the Church, initially under the First Empire, then under the Restoration, when Henri Lacordaire entered the seminary. Finally, I would like to present an exact idea of the state of minds regarding religion and politics in both periods. But we need to start a bit farther back in time.

In the Middle Ages, the supremacy of religious authority generally prevailed in Christian Europe, although often astoundingly misunderstood. But in France, starting with Philip the Fair, a reaction of despotism mixed with violence and cunning, the jealousy and the excessive servility of legal counselors, the lack of forcefulness in the clergy, delivered the Church increasingly to him who was called the "Bishop from Without", that is to say, a master, "well armed and always present in its breast." Because of this, Catholic lifeblood was immediately and notably sapped. The Church would no longer see a St. Anselm, a St. Thomas Aquinas, a St. Bonaventure, nor a St. Bernard. The great schism of the West, the cries for reform in Constance and Basel, the rapid defection to Protestantism, not only of the three Scandinavian kingdoms but also of England, Scotland, and more than half of Germany, and finally, the eruption of Calvinism in the heart of France — all these factors shook the authority of the Holy See deeply everywhere. Later, the stubborn shrewdness of Jansenism, reinforced in the eighteenth century by parliamentary

Gallicanism, had in our daily lives practically ruined among us that sublime authority.

Then, and only then (let us not forget), did anti-Christian sentiments rear their head. Everything favored the ruin of souls: at court, the public scandals of the Regency and those of the overly-long life of Louis XV, the worldliness of the clergy, the almost universal dispersal of monks, the sophisticated disorders of the nobility, the Jansenistic and Gallican spite of the middle class, the eloquent sophisms of Rousseau, the literary eminence of Voltaire, and finally, the deplorable insufficiency of contemporary apologetics. Should we be surprised that from 1760 on, anti-Christian opinions burst like grape-shot in the innumerable pamphlets emanating from Ferney[1], endlessly filled with verve, that animation which makes impiety so contagious and so popular? The Jesuits were swept out like dust and scattered by the wind. Voltaire was carried in triumph in Paris. Anti-Christian sentiments reigned in all the salons, throned in all the academies; henceforth, or very nearly so, it will be the only topic in all the rostrums from Mirabeau to Robespierre. It is the anti-Christian views of the Constituent Assembly alone that explain why this Assembly, by set purpose, separated itself from the Church, whose writings were so favorable to the reform of abuses and to the development of civic freedoms. Anti-Christian feelings explain why the Church was despoiled, without taking into account the offers she had made to defray a large part of the debt of the State. It is anti-Christian views that allow us to understand why the Church was subverted from top-to-bottom when the State arrogated to itself the power to reconfigure dioceses, like the no less excessive right to abolish the Concordat of Francis I, and to transfer to non-religious electors the choice of bishops, bypassing altogether confirmation by the Pope. Incompetence was flagrant; the violation of freedom of religion, clear as day;

but, at all costs, it was necessary to portray the Church as incompatible with the Revolution, and the Revolution incompatible with the Church[2].

At the fall of Robespierre, it is true, the tide of anti-Christian feelings was stemmed, but it did not abandon the territory it had gained. For another eight years — and here, I let Father Lacordaire speak:

"The Church presented to angels and to men only extensive ruins. The remains of its hierarchy, decimated by a revolution which spared no virtue, wandered, for the most part, in exile. Its temples were converted to secular usages; some were destroyed; others closed and emptied; still others consecrated to the schism that had been inaugurated, under Louis XIV, by the men of Port-Royal, and which grown bigger by fear at the feet of the gallows, coveted the bloody heritage of the saints. The monasteries, with which the Church had peopled cities and wilderness areas, became factories, farms, prisons, or uninhabited places. The Church retained nothing of the heritage which it had acquired through centuries of charity. Since she herself was barren, no one could foresee her bringing about near the overturned altar such men who one day would be able to help their exceptional predecessors in rebuilding her from the debris.

"And yet, the Church of France, now impoverished and destitute, having scarcely a chalice from which to drink the blood of its Master — the Church of France had conquered its enemies. From that very powerful Revolution, which the human spirit had prepared by three centuries of labor and which had given birth to so many men and to so many extraordinary events, no belief was able to emerge. The Revolution had destroyed a monarchy, won battles, terrified Europe; it did everything except what could change the world. The limit had been crossed at which error had enough consistency to remain the common faith and bond between people; indeed the point had been reached at which error could no longer join two men together, and where it remained *as if overwhelmed by its triumph* [emphasis in original]. Although the Church in France had been disturbed by a stubborn schism [Jansenism] — which tore at it from within for one hundred fifty years — it was impossible for the Revolution to introduce a national religion. What saves and perpetuates error is that portion of truth mixed in it, and the authority thereby conferred on it. The more error increases, the more of truth it loses, and all the more does its authority diminish, because it disturbs ever increasingly the fundamental principles which it had retained in its understanding. Minds become amazed and follow error to the precipice where it is carried; but, as soon as they attempt to understand it, it fades away, it escapes their grasp very quickly, like a phantom whose reality disappears before those who attempt to touch it from close up. And then, all of a sudden, man finds himself alone, naked, without beliefs, gasping for breath in the face of truth.

"This is where France stood the day after its first Revolution. The sterility of error, unable in the midst of that universal upheaval to establish a belief and a church, revealed that its final hour had arrived. Napoleon understood it in the same way that, fifteen centuries earlier, Constantine had understood the fall of idolatry. When a sect of Deists approached him to ask him to recognize their religion as that of the State, he responded with the answer he already had in his thoughts for everyone who hoped to take advantage of the heritage of the Roman Church: 'There are only four hundred of you!' The Concordat of 1801, between the Holy See and the French Republic, was the outcome of the power that truth had gained in a struggle in which it seemed to have lost everything. A great captain, by the battles he had won, was elevated to be the head of the State; he tried to learn what kind of support he had in the human spirit, but found he had none, other than a ruined Church which, for a century, had become the folk tale of skeptics[3]."

Nonetheless, we should not exaggerate this victory.

True, in spite of the Revolution, Catholicism remained the religion of the vast majority of Frenchmen who had one. On those grounds, it remained a force, the liveliest and most potent of social forces. It is the eternal honor of the genius of Napoleon's government that, surrounded by Deists and atheists, it alone had a clear intuition of that significant fact, and took it seriously into account. From that came the Concordat of 1801, whose greatness should in no way be minimized nor its importance underestimated.

But the Catholic faith was not the rule of life for the First Consul; he was not a St. Louis[4], he was a politician. He was less resolved to serve Religion (this is a critical point) than to have Religion serve him.

No one could be mistaken, when on promulgating the Concordat, he seemed to have watered down this very solemn treaty by a long series of legislative directives, of which he was the sole author, and to which he gave the name, unknown until then, *Organic Articles*[5].

These marked the supremacy of the State in matters of religion. In proposing to the legislative body that it establish as law those leonine provisions, the most religious and the most moderate of Napoleon's councillors, Portalis the elder, expressed this principle: "Public power is nothing unless it is *everything*; the Ministers of Religion should not claim the ability to limit it.[6] These words need no comment.

The head of the Catholic Church was declared to be in a state of permanent suspicion; every act emanating from him was treated as void as regards France, unless it had been approved by the government[7]. The day was to come when, under threat of exile, all religious correspondence with him would be forbidden[8]. General Councils — those which represented the Church as a whole — were designated as *foreign* synods[9]. It was forbidden to publish their decisions in France without the express authorization of the political party in power. Interior synods, even purely diocesan ones, simple gatherings of priests with the bishop presiding, were proscribed[10]. The guardianship of the canons of the Church was entrusted to a council of laymen, named by the Prince and removable *ad nutum* [at will - Trans.], almost all of them chosen from among the sons of Voltaire. This council served as supreme judge in cases of abuse of power committed by clerics. Abuse was defined as "any procedure which, in the exercise of Catholic worship, could compromise the honor of citizens, trouble their conscience, degenerate into oppression against them, in injury or in public scandal[11]." That is to say, as Bentham wrote concerning the word *libel*: "whatever can displease whomever for any reason whatsoever."

All of Napoleon's correspondence shows that, in his eyes, the bishops (*his* bishops, he used to call them) were simply ecclesiastical monitors, charged with *managing* the clergy under the direction of the Minister of Worship[12], a title equally new and insignificant, used to designate the government's commissioner appointed to *supervise religions*[13]. Besides, even if there were still bishops, there was no episcopal body left. Indeed, the Minister of Worship had as his mission not only to see that the bishops refrained from any oral conference between each other, but also that they not consult each other in written letters (that would have been *to hold a council by correspondence*). Not only bishops, but all the pastors in primary centers headed by justices of the peace were to be named and approved by the Prince; moreover, they were to bind themselves by oath to report any incident that could endanger the State[14]. The easy removal of priests under the hand of the bishop, himself subject to even greater pressure, rounded out the system[15].

Even that was not enough. Every ecclesiastical establishment, other than the seminaries, was suppressed[16]. No group or association of men or of women was allowed *under pretext of religion* without express authorization from the government[17]. The rules governing the organization of seminaries were to be submitted for the Prince's approval. Concerning the theological limits of the spiritual power, the professors were held to teach the doctrines recommended by the secular power. Would you believe it? Every year, bishops were ordered to send to the Minister of Religions the names of the students in seminaries and to perform no ordinations until such time as the government had approved the number of candidates[18].

With that, the Church of France — I saw this with my own eyes — fell to an even lower condition than one could fully describe[19]. Emigrant priests were returning, no doubt under amnesty, but still suspect. Nonetheless, the clergy took up its ministry with no less zeal, and with an impartiality worthy of the Church's finest hours. Never were the episcopacy and the priesthood more exemplary in their morals, more irreproachably committed even to the most insignificant labors of their sacred ministry. But, at the same time, the clergy applied itself fully to obtain forgiveness for its resurrection. If, in the Church, the priestly virtues were not rare — this needs to be said: outstanding personalities were lacking. The monarchy of Louis XV had not formed any, and the long years of exile had not exhausted in the clergy the courage to suffer, but, rather, the courage to fight. Not one of those confessors of the faith yielded on the *Credo,* as did the clergy under Henry

VIII and Gustaf Wasa. Nonetheless, without sensing the accompanying humiliation, they were subjected to the law of the victor. Many of the *organic* charges had been in force under the *ancien régime*, such that they were not as outraged by them as we are today. They gave no thought to the fact that the *ancien régime* had been shattered and dishonored as despotic by the Revolution to such a degree that the heirs of the Revolution were not in a position, it seems, to restore the regime's tyranny and make it worse.

I say: *to make it worse.* Indeed, what had never been seen before, the pastoral letters of the bishops could no longer be published without the express permission of the prefect, who was sometimes Protestant, more often than not a non-believer. And this lasted until the censure of episcopal writings was concentrated in a special bureau in Paris, under the watchful eye of the First Consul, (and, later,) the Emperor[20]. Even more, the word of God was placed under police surveillance. Denis Frayssinous[21] was summoned by Fouché to include in some fashion, in the conferences which he gave on the existence of God in the Church of St. Sulpice, some praise of military conscription. The first time, a special report from Portalis to the Emperor was needed to quiet the storm[22]. The extremely careful moderation of the preacher's language was unsuccessful in having his conferences tolerated until the end of the series.

And yet, even in the neutralized position given it, the new episcopacy could still have maintained some of its dignified attitude, which, during the persecution, had gained the respect of Europe. It is painful for me to say this: the episcopacy did not know how to do so. It lavished too much incense on the new Cyrus. To be sure, legitimate recognition was due to Napoleon for having desired the Concordat of 1801. But in 1802, when the first provisions appeared, how can we not judge the author of the Concordat for the legislative dispositions he added to this great act, in glaring contempt of the Holy See? Obviously, praise was to be kept within certain limits. History would not be able to remain silent concerning the fact that the Holy See was not protected by many bishops. In this matter, some of them were short-sighted to the very end, even during the captivity of Pius VII[23].

At the same time, the writers who professed Catholicism had adopted, in the *Mercure de France* and the *Journal des Débats* (shortly *Journal de l'Empire*), a tactic which they felt was appropriate, as if something that was not respectable could nonetheless be resourceful for Catholics: they lauded Napoleon excessively so that he would allow them to scold the Revolution and Voltaire. The Master accepted their flatteries; but as for the rest, he rudely imposed silence on them[24]. Unfortunately, it so happened that many of them disgraced themselves to no purpose, not without compromising, to a certain degree, the cause they had intended to serve.

Fortunately, other Catholic writers were, in this respect, blameless. Everyone knows that the author of *Génie du Christianisme*[25] publicly and immediately broke away from the murderer of the Duke of Enghien. A man filled with faith, the poet Ducis, refused the functions of senator. Both of them fittingly represented Christian honor during those difficult days; I praise them for having stood tall in the presence of that giant of a man before whom all Europe knelt down.

Should I speak of the colleges of the First Empire? Here I touch the most painful wound of all. Those colleges are certainly far from us; but the institution to which they belonged survives. In what I have to say about the past, many will see an indirect attack against the present, an issue with which I need not concern myself. On this matter, it is painful for me to trouble many men whom I honor and cherish. But History is

History: its first law is to say nothing false; the second is not to keep silent about what is true[26]. Now, as to the truth, here it is.

While claiming for the State the duty of offering to everyone the benefit of public instruction, the Revolution, at least under the Consulate, respected the rights of families. The State opened schools, it did not impose them. Everywhere, it accepted the autonomous harmony of municipal teaching and of ecclesiastical teaching. As Emperor, Napoleon saw things differently. He abolished the freedom of instruction; the right of running schools became the exclusive monopoly of the State. The University of the Empire was created. It left Christian families with only one choice: either serfdom or *dechristianization* of their children. In effect, how to protect these children from the contagion of anti-Christianity, after they had been plucked from their families by a kind of annual pruning, to have them live for eight years, at the beat of the drum, in barracks that foreshadowed the military, helter-skelter with those in whom faith was completely dead? This was the conscription of souls, an unlimited and universal conscription, one that did not admit quality members. This is the nature of the institution, abstraction made of the men charged with following through. I am not judging; I am simply reporting.

To be sure, the choice of the Grand Master, de Fontanes[27], was pleasing to everyone; he knew how to find associates worthy of himself: Joubert, Gueneau de Mussy, Ambroise Rendu, and others, including many retired revolutionaries and scoundrels. It is only right to praise the considerable services of the righteous men whom I have just named. But could they see to it that France would no longer be what the eighteenth century and the Revolution had made of her? Could they turn away from the State schools the sons of Voltaire-tinged families? Could they require of teachers that they give their pupils open example of a serious practice of the

Catholic religion? No, they could not! No one in the world could have. Public behavior completely repudiated this. Such was the misfortune of the time, and that was not the fault of Mr. de Fontanes nor of his friends. Well, then, under these conditions, how to infuse public schools with the atmosphere of faith in which were born and reared the generations of previous centuries? That was a thousand times impossible; the consequences of this impossibility are evident: in all the colleges, without exception, an original clique of young people, with no Christian tradition and without innocence, tyrannically setting the law for their fellow students; mutual instruction in vice, with a precocious egoism and the hardness of heart which follows it; a spirit of permanent revolt against God and against teachers. The one who writes this history has seen these things happen; not one of his contemporaries will gainsay his testimony.

The remedy would have been free competition. This was forbidden. From 1 June 1809 on, every educational establishment, however little known, was to accept the official link to the Grand Master, or cease to exist. We can read in the correspondence of Father Jean de la Mennais with what merciless eagerness were pursued those humble priests who attempted to teach a little Latin to young Breton lads, whom they were preparing for the major seminary[28]. The boarding schools that clerical charity had established for that purpose were placed under the control of the University; either it chose their teachers or it approved of them. The children received in those houses, reduced to being simple boarding schools, had to attend college or *lycée* classes. Nay more, faculties of theology of purely civil creation were invented. Appointed by the Grand Master, these professors of theology swore obedience to him. This was an attempt to transfer higher instruction in theology from the Church to the University of the Empire, by conferring grades that were purported to be absolute requirements for ecclesiastical advancement. "A priest," the Emperor wrote, "who had depended on no other authority than his ecclesiastical superiors, will be unable to occupy high posts unless THE UNIVERSITY CONFERS THEM ON HIM! — which it could refuse to do if the priest were known to harbor ultramontane ideas or others dangerous to authority[29]." Is that not clear? Napoleon wanted to be the sole teacher: and how could one escape the imperial grasp when all careers were blocked to anyone who had not crossed the University's Thermopylae? Here was something without precedent in Europe, without precedent in ancient as well as in modern times. France was pushed to accept this by being persuaded that, without it, the Revolution and national unity were endangered.

I could not stress enough this package of imperial autocracy. It was a complete system, powerfully conceived, skillfully coordinated, the system of the Pharaohs, summarized by Moses in these terms: "Oppress with skill[30]." This oppression, I admit, weighed not only on the Catholic Church of France, but also on the Protestants and the Jews. The aim was to even out the creeds, to abase one by the other, by scrambling them[31]. Nonetheless, the Protestant or Hebrew consistories did not embarrass Caesar, they never offered him any resistance. Now the Catholic Church had a head who was not subject to Napoleon: as long as the Pope was not pliable like a glove in the hand of the dominator of the world, nothing could be done; the almighty power of Caesar had its limits. On the other hand, if and when the Sovereign Pontiff became a simple tool of government, manipulated at will by the successor of Charlemagne, immediately the will of Napoleon would become the voice of God, the living rule of the human conscience. God did not allow this to happen, but we will see that it would not have taken much for this monstrous dream to be fulfilled.

Before we return to the long duel of the greatest power there ever was and the conscience of an elderly captive, I pray allow me to note two facts. Many persons willingly persuade themselves that, if the Pope fell under the subjection of a government, in the present state of public opinion and behavior, that government would never think of attacking Catholic beliefs or morals. And yet, that is exactly what Napoleon Ist did on two occasions, which it is important to highlight.

Everyone knows the dogma: "Outside the Church there is no salvation." Well, Napoleon tried to suppress it by having it disappear from the catechism which he imposed on all the dioceses of France. The intervention of Cardinal Fesch[32] was needed to have those words reinserted in the imperial catechism. — From another angle, the Emperor ordered the insertion there of a long chapter on *love* for Napoleon (yes, *love*), commanded on pain of ETERNAL DAMNATION[33]. — At the same time, he kept in the civil code the right to divorce. Portalis *[see Note 7]* forbade priests from refusing to grant the nuptial blessing to those who remarried during the lifetime of their wife, after having divorced her[34]. With such recent examples at hand, how can it be claimed that Catholic dogma and morality have nothing to fear from subjection of the Pope to secular domination?

It is this subjection, not partial but total, that was to be the supreme goal of Napoleon's politics. As early as 1806, the Pope was nothing but *Bishop of Rome*[34]*; Caesar is its Emperor*[35]. Notes were exchanged; Pius VII recalls his ministers as often as Napoleon demands; but the Pope nonetheless retains his free choice. Then, events keep happening. Captured in Rome, Pius VII is thrown into prison; his States are confiscated, and all exercise of his spiritual power is SUPPRESSED IN FACT, up to the fall of the Empire. This is not ancient history; what I have said, I have seen happen.

Only one issue embarrassed the Emperor. With the person of Pius VII placed under interdict, Napoleon counted on substituting the action of the bishops to that of the Pope. But death was decimating the episcopate, and how to create Catholic bishops while bypassing the Pope? In order to help him resolve the question, the Emperor assembled in Paris his subjects, the *monsignori* of France and of Italy. In his omnipotence, he decorated this assembly with the title of *national council*, and proposed that — since, in the past six months, the Pope had not consecrated the men chosen by the Emperor — the assembly should decree to have the metropolitan make them bishops. How more openly could the Church be placed into the hands of Caesar?

A commission of the bishops, charged with writing a report on the imperial proposition, struggled to gain some time; in a timid conclusion, it sought to confer with the Pope on the project of the decree[36]. Would you believe that on this simple motion of delay by the Commission, without even giving the assembled prelates time to discuss the issue, Napoleon declared the council dissolved. Three members of the Commission, seized during the night, were held at Vincennes until they handed in their resignations from their respective sees. Terrified by these measures, the other bishops were summoned one by one by the Minister General of the Police; in the latter's hands, each one in turn bound himself to turn over the hierarchy to the imperial omnipotence. Once more assembled, even when the Emperor did not bother to revoke the decree of dissolution of the council, they confirmed the will of the Master. In truth, they were told that the Pope had given his consent; after this, in order to discourage Pius VII's resistance, he himself was led to believe that the bishops had abandoned him.

Is that all? Absolutely not! Surrounded by traitors from the early days, weakened by a habitual if not constant secrecy, during four years, one moment fascinated by a skillfully prepared meeting with Napoleon's upward rise — more so by his sweet talk than by his threats — Pius VII signed the suicide of the papacy, at Fontainebleau, on 25 January 1813. It was a repetition of the downfall of Pascal II[37]. An unforgettable example of the danger which the religious independence of the Holy See risks when it is no longer protected by a temporal barrier. No doubt Pius VII hastened to retract an action so forced or unexpected. As anticipated, this retraction was ignored; Napoleon considered it as absolutely not having been received. As a general answer, he had included in the *Bulletin des lois de l'Empire* [Bulletin of the Laws of the Empire] what he called the concordat of Fontainebleau[38]. Supported by the signature of the Pope, what resistance could he have met in the Church of France if God had not intervened at Leipzig[39]? Who does not know that the students at the Seminary of Ghent, numbering 236 — among whom were 40 deacons or subdeacons — having refused to attend the Mass of an intruder whom the Emperor had named bishop of that diocese, were abducted and incorporated into a regular army regiment, in which they served until the fall of Napoleon[40]?

These things have been forgotten to a great degree, and too few persons today realize how little it would have taken for the Russian Church to serve as the type of Church which, from the straits of Messina up to the Elbe, would have continued to call itself Roman Catholic. Moreover, who does not sense that, if once this crime had been committed, it would have marked the end of the conscience of the human race? How long would it have held off the bondage and the perversion of the Catholic priesthood? "The princes who lust for spiritual authority," said Lacordaire, "never dared to take it onto the altar of their hands. They realize all too well that in this lies a greater stupidity even than sacrilege. Incapable as they are of being *directly* recognized as the source and the regulators of Religion, they seek to become its masters through the intermediary of some clerical body, fashioned to their wills. Once there, these high priests without a mission, usurpers of truth itself, dole out to the people only that amount of truth which they judge sufficient to curb revolt. They make of the blood of Jesus Christ an instrument of moral servitude and of political calculation, up to the day when they are warned by terrible catastrophes that the greatest crime of sovereignty against itself and against society is the impious touch on Religion[41]."

It is understandable that the Church welcomed the Restoration as a deliverance. Not only did this place her outside of imperial clutches, but also for the first time since the Revolution, it was treated with respect by the public power; on every step of the throne, the Church saw princes who believed what she believed, and by whom she was loved. As a gift for this joyous event, Louis XVIII, in his constitutional charter, proclaimed the Catholic religion the religion of the State. The violation of Sunday rest was prohibited by a law. Divorce disappeared from the civil code. Bishops obtained the freedom to manage their minor seminaries. Even more, the administration of primary instruction was placed in their hands. The Ministry of Religion was abolished. A bishop was at the same time Minister of Ecclesiastical Affairs and of Public Instruction. Legislation encouraged religious congregations of women. Residences of men were looked upon favorably by the government. A law was even passed for the punishment of sacrilege. The King, Charles X, his son, the Dauphin, the Prime

Minister Mr. de Villèle, most of the latter's colleagues, all the Directors General, all the heads of services, all prefects, all the higher level magistrates — all of them were sincerely Catholic. All the other functionaries leaned in that direction. Intense works of evangelization were undertaken by the missionaries of France and by the Jesuits in all quarters of the kingdom.

It has to be said, because it is true: the lack of success of all that was enormous. The only result was to make Religion detestable and powerless to an almost unbelievable degree.

The law about Sunday observance, while openly observed in cities by the closing of stores, met in France, as the Revolution had, a determined opposition that could not be overcome. Voltaire and Rousseau had not been reprimanded even once under the Empire; from 1817 to 1824, twelve editions of the first, and thirteen of the second were published. Helvetius, Diderot, d'Holbach, Dupuis, Volney, came out of their tombs. A long procession of the dead (the expression is from Lacordaire) was evoked with fanaticism against the Church, and, taking into account the passions of the day, all these departed men appeared to be alive. The scurrilous platitudes of Pigault-Lebrun[42] were spread in 32,000 copies; the songs of Béranger[43] gained influence. Everywhere the Church found adversaries without number against her: not only the fanatics of the secret societies, and behind them, the avowed followers of Voltaire, but also the volatile mass, frightened by the phantom of the *ancien régime*. Raised to the religion of the State, Catholicism was one of the facets of that regime and the most detested one of all.

Indeed, the eighteenth century was still alive. In 1802, Jesus Christ returned to His temples: but He did not enter the souls which anti-Christian feelings had taken away from Him. At the time, in practically all of France, most of those who exercised a liberal profession were without religion; not only did they abstain from all worship, but on every occasion in their daily conversations, anti-Christian hostility overflowed. Article 6 of the Charter of Louis XVIII seemed to be a declaration of war against the unbelief practiced by the French bourgeoisie. But what becomes influential is whatever is practiced in morals and not what is written in laws. France being what it was in 1814, Article 6 of the Charter could only be the legal constitution of a kind of official hypocrisy, something deeply repugnant to the character of the nation, and rightly so. Indeed, and above all, it is of the essence of religion to be sincere; to practice, one must believe. And so, when in the hearts of people, contrary religious beliefs meet, like two enemy armies on the same battlefield, when in public morals this antagonism has roots that are three-fold secular and recognized as complex, and to go further, when I do not say the Catholic faith but the *Christian* faith is in the numerical minority of the classes who dominate and teach others — all that is indeed a great catastrophe. For the nation, it is a significant moral diminution; and yet, any pressure, even indirect, exercised by secular authority to arrange religious demonstrations where faith is absent would only make the evil more intense and more profound.

We can see this in 1830 and 1831. The passions stored up deep in souls by the open alliance of the throne and the altar, exploded with rage. The crosses of mission, planted with such brilliance under the Restoration, were everywhere overthrown. Saint-Germain-l'Auxerrois Church was vandalized; the archbishop's residence in Paris was destroyed by savages, under the indifferent eyes of the armed National Guard. Would those excesses have been possible in 1814, at the downfall of the oppressor of Pius VII? Did they come to anyone's mind in 1848, with the disappearance of a government notoriously unfavorable to the Church? After

1830, it took three years before clerical dress could reappear in the streets of Paris, while in 1848, it did not hide itself even for one day. These are not theories, they are facts, and they are as bright as the sun; they are unassailably true.

Under the Restoration, many Catholics were already aware of the delusion of most bishops of France concerning the importance given to religion from the King's "protection," in the word of the time. But those Catholics were ignored, and that is understandable; experience had not yet spoken out. Unfortunately, the Church of France also had its emigrants.

These were the bishops named by Louis XVI, who had not reentered France until with Louis XVIII. By a two-fold sensibility (monarchical and Gallican), these bishops had refused the Pope's request for them to give up their sees and had protested against the Concordat of 1801, which took account of them as having resigned. Their notable fidelity to the House of Bourbon made of them, in matters of religion, the natural councillors of the restored monarchy.

First of all, the bishops led the monarchy in a dangerous direction, in difficult and complicated negotiations with the Holy See, to obtain the annulment of the great act of 1801. In their thinking, nothing that had been done in France during the absence of the legitimate king was to survive after his return. Pius VII resisted for a long time; we can understand that he found it repugnant that he himself repeal the act which had crowned his pontificate. Nonetheless, in 1817 he ended up signing the reestablishment of the concordat between Leo X and Francis I. This was to turn back three centuries earlier and it was enough to bring together against the treaty all of the new France. Dioceses were increased from fifty to ninety-two; this meant that forty-two new sees had to be financed. The support of the Chambers was necessary; it was quickly evident that no such help would be forthcoming. The situation was thus found to be singularly unreal: the King had given his solemn word to the Holy See, yet he could not keep it. A compromise was finally reached: the Concordat of 1817 was not abrogated, it was side-stepped. In a Consistory, the Pope declared that the new agreement with France could not be executed; nonetheless, he accepted it as the base for a general rearrangement of the boundaries of the dioceses of France, whose number was raised to eighty.

As a result, there was in the kingdom a surplus of thirty bishops. Because of them, the church of France could be renewed, but only on one condition: that the bishops would take their times into account and be both men of government and men of the apostolate. No such idea had entered anyone's mind. The point was simply to *clean up* the episcopate, that is to say, to set up as bishops those gentlemen or those promoted to nobility who still remained in the ranks of the priesthood[44]. Most of those chosen were elderly; their advanced age was compensated for by no other recommendation than that of their birth. Consequently, a senile and impotent breath spread over the Church. Everywhere, the most sterile remembrances of the past; understanding of the present, nowhere to be found. A pious and enlightened bishop, somewhat overpraised by the public, but too undervalued since by those who did not know him, Father Frayssinous[1] had the notion of restoring the ancient Sorbonne University, "the permanent council of the Gauls." In the eighteenth century, especially in the second half, the Sorbonne had really lost its reputation; it was fading away like all the *ancien régime*. At length, it was able to raise itself up and resume growth. There was room for all kinds of improvements. It was an endeavor similar to founding in Paris, in our day, a center of ecclesiastical studies superior to those commonly found in seminaries. Nonetheless, the idea of Father Frayssinous, perhaps a bit limited, amounted to nothing. Father de la Mennais found him dangerous, as if stained with Gallican after-thoughts. Moreover, feebly received by the bishops, this idea definitely disappeared before the pretensions of the archbishopric of Paris.

Now at the time of which I speak, in contrast to that senility, to that insufficiency on which I painfully had to insist, an energy of unexpected exuberance was circulating in minds. Under the two-fold excitement of peace and political freedom, the youth in the schools unfurled their sails; with unlimited ardor, they aspired to new shores, to new horizons. The old leaven of revolution fermented in some, enthusiasm for the unknown in others. But everyone felt that the future did not belong to the elders, and that, while remaining faithful to the Church, which belongs to all times, she had to be seen as separate from the men of the *ancien régime*, who were mortal. Truth persists while men pass on, and with them the garb of the day with which they had clothed the truth.

Such was Henri Lacordaire's state of mind when he entered the seminary. No doubt the situation had its dangers, but it also had its limits. Whatever enthusiasm and boldness of intellect the young lawyer who was becoming a seminarian could have had, we will see that docility of heart and filial piety toward the Church had always been stronger. Nonetheless, when we consider his thinking about the conduct of Napoleon I, especially with regard to the Church, we have no problem explaining the persistent horror Lacordaire had for despotism.

When we realize the ravages of religion in France brought about by the so-called protection of King Charles X, we are less astounded at the attitude taken in 1830 by the man who was called by God to establish, five years later, the work of the Conferences of Notre-Dame in Paris and to re-inaugurate, on this side of the Alps, the Order of St. Dominic.

ENDNOTES

1. Ferney: a chateau on Lake Leman where Voltaire lived for a while. - Trans.
2. The same Machiavellianism is exercised in Italy in our day. The clergy of the Piedmont was generally favorable to the Statute of Charles Albert; it was cast, willy nilly, into the opposition by gladly breaking ties with the Pope.
3. *Considérations sur le système philosophique de M. de la Mennais* (préface).
4. Louis IX, King of France (1226-1270) - Trans.
5. As everybody knows, Pius VII protested strongly against these articles in the Consistory of 24 May 1802. (Author)
6. Rapport de Portalis sur les *Articles organiques* (Disc., rapp. et trav. inédits sur le Concordat de 1801, p. 87.
— Jean-Étienne-Marie Portalis: French lawmaker (1746-1807), compiler of the Civil Code - Trans.
7. Loi du germinal, an X, art. 1er.
8. Code pénal, art. 208.
9. Loi du 18 germinal, art. 6.
10. Loi du 18 germinal, art. 4.
11. Loi du 18 germinal, art. 6. — Jeremy Bentham, English philosopher (1748-1832); honorary French citizen. - Trans.
12. See Appendix I, page ...: letter of Napoleon to Portalis, 21 May 1804.
13. These are the terms of the Penal Code, art. 207.
14. Art. 6 & 7 of the Concordat. - See Appendix II, page ..., how Napoleon understood that oath.
15. Law of 18 germinal, art. 31.

16. Law of 18 germinal, art. 11.
17. Decree of 3 messidor, year XII.
18. Law of 18 germinal, art. 23 to 26.
19. See Appendix III, page 475.
20. L'Église romaine et le Premier Empire, par d'Haussonville, t. 1, p. 272-276.

I take this opportunity to explain myself without straying to this book. The author is favorable to the separation of Church and State; I condemn this separation as leading to the total de-christianization of society. But the work of Haussonville, insofar as it deals with the actions of Napoleon against Pius VII and against the Church, is no less damning, and in its totality, very conclusive.

21. Frayssinous: Denis count of Frayssinous (1765-1841). Bishop of Hermopolis; Grand Master of the University, Minister of Ecclesiastical Affairs. Writer of *Defense of Christianity*, and *Gallican Liberties*.

- Fouché: (1759-1820); Minister of Police. - Trans.
22. See Appendix IV, page .....
23. This excess of praise on the part of bishops shocked even Napoleon (Testimony of de Broglie, bishop of Ghent, in a conversation with the Prefect of Police, Réal). It increased his contempt for men. After his downfall, it was a simple pleasure to insert in the *Biography of Contemporaries* the names of the bishops, along with fragments of their mandates in honor of the Emperor. The Voltaire disciple Beuchot published a funeral oration of Napoleon composed solely of snips from these mandates. The effect of that work was not favorable to the episcopate.
24. See Appendix V, page ...
25. Chateaubriand: Vicomte François-René Chateaubriand; (1768-1848). French writer. - Trans.

26. *Quis nescit primam esse Historiae legem ne quid falsi dicere audeat; deinde, ne quid veri non audeat?* (Cicero: *de Oratore*, II, 15).
27. Fontanes: Jean-Pierre Louis de Fontanes (1752-1921), French poet and writer. - Trans.
28. Lettres de M. de la Mennais à M. Brulé. Bray, Paris 1865. — Brulé died as Bishop of Vincennes (Indiana, USA).
29. Notes pour le Ministre des Cultes (Saint-Cloud, 30 juil. 1806. *Corres. de Napoleon 1er*, t. XIII, p. 15.
30. *Opprimamus eos sapienter.* [Exodus 1:10]
31. De Maistre: *Corres. diplomatique*, II, 182.
32. Card. Fesch : Joseph Fesch (1763-1839). Napoleon's uncle; bishop of Lyons, Grand Almoner of the Empire.
33. See Appendix VI, page 480.
34. Lettre de Napoléon au cardinal Fesch, 7 janv. 1806. *Corres. de Napoleon*, t. 11, 528.
35. Lettre de Napoléon à Pie VII, 22 févr. 1803. *Corres. de Napoléon*, t. XII, 38.
36. It is sad to realize that, in a first exchange all the members of the Commission faltered, except for d'Avian, archbishop of Bordeaux, and de Broglie, bishop of Ghent. But on the following day, the majority found itself strong. Among the weak ones, one could not help but be surprised to find cardinals Spina and Caselli, both negotiators of the Concordat.
37. Pascal II: pope, 1099-1118; during his entire reign, he fought against Henry V but could not prevent him from invading Italy.
38. See Appendix VII, page . . .
39. Leipzig: campaign of October 1813. Decisive defeat of Napoleon and his return to France. Forced to abdicate; exiled to Elba in May 1814.
40. See Appendix VIII, page . . .
41. *Lettre sur le Saint Siège.*

42. Pigault-Lebrun: Charles-Antoine Guillaume de Lespinoy, dit Lebrun (1753-1835). French writer.
43. Béranger: Pierre-Jean de Béranger (1780-1837). Popular song-writer and singer. Celebrated the Napoleonic legend and fought against the Restoration.
44. Lettre de l'abbé de La Mennais à M. Brulé (Paris, 6 août 1817). — The compliant testimony of Picot could not prevail over this very confidential letter, coming from a man well-informed, and *therefore* a capable judge. - It dealt only with the choices of 1817.

Chapter 1

Education—Unbelief—Conversion

Early years — Family — School — Law school — La Société d'Études of Dijon — Training at the bar in Paris — Conversion — Entering seminary.

Jean-Baptiste Henri Lacordaire was born in Recey, a small town in the hills of Burgundy, set on a slope by the edge of a river called the *Ource*, which flows into the Seine.

It was on the 12th of May, 1802, at the same period of time when churches were opening again in all of France; but the church in Recey was still closed. Henri Lacordaire was baptized in a neighboring town, Lucey, by the priest serving that area. The humble priest had no way of foreseeing what this child would one day become in God's Church[1].

Lacordaire's birthplace was in the ancient duchy of Langres, Bussières-les-Nonnes, so named because of the neighboring Cistercian abbey, contemporaneous with Saint Bernard.[2] In an unusual configuration, found also in Domremy, the birthplace of Joan of Arc, a stream divided Bussières between two provinces: the section of Bussières on the stream's right shore belonged to Burgundy; that on the left shore, to Champagne. The house in which Henri Lacordaire's father was born was in the Burgundian section.

Monsieur Nicolas Lacordaire, Lacordaire's father, was a director of surgery, following in the footsteps of some family members before him. Madame Lacordaire had been orphaned; she was born the daughter of a lawyer in Dijon's parliament. Her eminently respected father was a man of greater probity than wealth.

When Henri Lacordaire was four years old, his father died. His mother resettled in Dijon, her birthplace, for the education of her four sons, of whom Henri was the second.

This education was rigorous. Madame Lacordaire was a woman of forceful character, sound and steadfast in mind, her faith simple and strong. Forced to sell the house in which her children had been born, she made a point of letting them know that they were of limited means and that in later life they would have to count only on themselves.

From 1806 to 1809, Henri resided in Brussières[3], at the home of his father's older brother. He cherished the memory of this stay, which always remained sacred to him: the view of the woods, as well as the frugal customs of the countryside at the beginning of this century.

When he was seven years old (*the age of discretion*, as our fathers used to say), his mother brought him back to Dijon to have him begin classical studies. Faithful to all the good traditions, she also led him to the parish priest to make his first confession. "I crossed the sanctuary," he said. "I found alone in the beautiful and vast sanctuary a dignified elderly man, gentle and welcoming. It was the first time that I had approached the priest; until this point, I had never seen him except at the altar, amid pomp and incense. Father Deschamps (that was his name) sat on a bench and motioned for me to kneel next to him. I do not remember what I said to him or what he said to me, but this first meeting between my soul and God's representative made an unblemished and deep impression on me. To this day, I have never entered into the sacristy of Dijon's Church of Saint-Michel without being reminded of my first confession as represented by that wonderful elderly man and the openness of my own childhood. Everyone in that church, moreover, exhibited a spirit of piety; I never saw that place again without experiencing a certain emotion that no other church has been able to inspire in me. My mother, Saint-Michel, and the religion of my birth created in my soul a kind of structure, the first, the most moving and durable of all[4]."

It would not be long, however, before this impression would fade more than we could express. In 1812, three months before the end of the academic year, Henri Lacordaire entered, with a half-scholarship, as a boarding student at the *lycée impériale* of Dijon; he was ten years old[5].

It was this time that provided a remembrance which would never leave his memory, an experience typical of the behavior customary among students of that era. "From the very first day," he said. "my fellow students took me for some sort of plaything; I could not take a step without their brutality finding a way to target me. For several weeks, I was deprived by violence of all nourishment except my soup and my bread. To escape from this mistreatment, I went to the study room during recess when possible. I hid there under a bench from the fellow students who were coming after me. There, helpless, abandoned by all, I shed tears before God, offering my suffering as a sacrifice, praying and lifting my heart to the cross of His Son through a loving union that, later, I was perhaps never to experience to the same degree. . . . This torture ceased during vacation as well as when school reopened, either because they had tired of pursuing me, or perhaps because I had deserved a certain reprieve on account of some degree of innocence[5]."

This was hardly an isolated occurrence; France allowed students to be brought up in this way. Should anyone be surprised that more than one fully grown man remembers having had a similar experience?

At the age of twelve, Henri made his first communion. "It was," he continued, "my last joyful experience of religion. Soon the shadows thickened around me; a cold night surrounded me on all sides, and in my conscience, I no longer had any sign of God's presence[6]."

What to say about his studies? A good student — although not particularly outstanding in the elementary grades — year by year, he rose higher and higher in rankings of fellow students, up to the end.

In the beginning, Henri had a piece of very good luck. Three months after he entered the school, there arrived from the *École Normale* a young professor, twenty-two years old. In the autumn of 1812, "the child with black eyes and long eyelids" immediately pleased this Monsieur Delahaye. Humbly assuming responsibility for overseeing the elementary class, he felt, it seems, a bit constricted in his task as grammarian. He frequently enjoyed inviting several students to his room to develop their memories by having them recite the poetry of La Fontaine. Henri Lacordaire distinguished himself immediately in this exercise: no effort, no uneasiness, a remarkable memory, clear and easy articulation. He recited the words as if he had written them himself. He did not try to create any special effect. Self-consciousness seemed foreign to him; one would have said he forgot himself entirely. One sensed that a gentle and calm feeling animated him from within. "I did not know," wrote his venerable teacher fifty years later, "I did not know where he had found this calm, this gentleness, under which one could clearly see a strong and resolute will[7]."

Charmed by these talents, Delahaye requested permission to have Henri work directly alongside him during part of the study hours; this initiative lasted three years. Racine succeeded La Fontaine, then Voltaire, some of whose entire tragedies the young student learned by heart; during a recess period, he was learning one act of *Athalie*[8]. Certainly Delahaye did not surmise the genius of his pupil. But Lacordaire always attributed his subsequent successes in secondary school not only to Delahaye's diligent attention at that time, to the careful and freely given counsel he received from him later, but also to the elevated sentiments that had inspired him in their conversations. "As one who loved literature," said Father Lacordaire on his deathbed. "Delahaye sought to inspire in me a taste for literature; an upright and honorable man, he strove to make me gentle, chaste, sincere, and generous, and to tame my high-spirited nature, so lacking in docility. Religion was foreign to him; he never spoke of it to me, and I maintained the same silence about it.... He therefore allowed me to slip down the slope that carried my fellow students far from all religious faith; but he kept me on the high summits of literature, and of honor, upon which he had established his own life. The events of 1815 took him from me prematurely. He entered the field of law and became advisor to the court in Rouen. I have always associated the memory of him with everything good that occurred to me."

On his death-bed, Father Lacordaire accused himself of not having been obedient enough in school. This brings to mind the judgment passed on Crébillon[9] by his teachers: *A shrewd boy, but an extraordinary rascal.* Perhaps at times Henri Lacordaire deserved this judgment; but he was generally very docile. The "testimony" of his close friends among his fellow students, in agreement with that of Delahaye, leave no doubt in this regard. But in a contrast so characteristic of him, this habitual docility coexisted with something impetuous and ardent; and his young will revealed itself to be at once unmanageable and resolute. From this perspective, he was more than once a cause for despair among his teachers, whose supervision he frustrated by the most daring of student tricks.

In these early years of his academic life, Henri Lacordaire did not work a great deal, except for the last three months of an academic year (in order to be able to reap a harvest of awards to take back to his mother). He went along with being taken for lazy, but not with being thought of as incompetent. Receiving a low grade in mathematics was enough to drive him to win the first prize in that course the following year. He bet himself that he could do it and he won.

Moreover, it was not only in the field of public speaking, despite what Lacordaire has said about it, that the literary seeds planted by Delahaye began to germinate in his young mind; his grades in *troisième* and *seconde,* which I have before me, also belie this opinion. It was not only in public speaking, I recognize, that he took flight like an eagle. At this juncture, he not only surpassed, but eclipsed, his fellow students. The school in Dijon did not have another example of such stunning superiority. This excellence had such an impact that, from that time forward, the name of Henri Lacordaire gained a kind of celebrity throughout his province. I remember that he who bore that name already seemed to us crowned with glory, when he came and sat next to us on the benches of the School of Law in Dijon, in November 1819.

At this moment, a new horizon opened before him. Meanwwhile, his mode of life changed. "On entering the School of Law," he said, "I returned to my mother's small house and rediscovered the endless charm of domestic life, so tender and modest. In that house, there was nothing superfluous, only a rather austere simplicity, a strict economy, the scent of a bygone age, and something of the sacred, associated with the virtues of a widowed mother of four children, seeing them around her as adolescents already, and predicting that she would leave behind her a generation of honest and perhaps even distinguished men[10]."

Father Lacordaire spoke of his law studies in far too modest terms; it would be wrong to take this modesty at face value. My memories as a fellow student and the academic records of the Faculty of Law protest loudly against the idea that Lacordaire the priest held concerning himself as Henri Lacordaire the lawyer. It was not in him, despite what he himself has said, to be mediocre in anything; there are in our ranks some rivals, but he was always the first among the first.

He had as his teacher of civil law Proudhon[11], a man of some intellectual vigor, but more remarkable for the clarity of his lectures. Unfortunately, the professor was a man of his time. The days of Grotius, of Domat, and of Daguesseau[12] were long gone; the field of law had lost its majesty and grandeur. No more sweeping perspectives, no more natural law, no more public law, not even a trace of the philosophy of law; no mention of its history, and, consequently, no in-depth knowledge of Roman law. It was, in effect, a technical exegesis of law articles simply listed one after the other, with no perspective on the past, no introduction to the eternal profundities of the law, no regard for the general laws of human society. It was a form of teaching suitable for producing tradesmen, but incapable of forming great legal minds, great magistrates, and genuine citizens[13].

Should anyone be surprised that an intelligence as superior as Lacordaire's held this damaged discipline in only lukewarm esteem? His lack of attraction to positive law[14], to private law, and to business law, would bear fruit later on.

"Fortunately, among the 200 students who participated in his courses, he encountered a dozen or so who wanted to become something other than real estate lawyers, and for whom country, glory, and the civic virtues were a more powerful inspiration than the opportunity to amass a vulgar fortune. They recognized each other very quickly through the mysterious sympathy that joins vice with vice, mediocrity with mediocrity, but which also draws together souls of a higher nature, who seek a higher goal. Almost all these young people owed their superiority to Christianity. Even though I did not share their faith, they very much wanted, to include me in their group. Soon, intimate gatherings and long promenades involved us in the greatest issues of philosophy, of history, of politics, and of religion[15]."

Dare I say it? These gatherings, these walks, shaped Henri Lacordaire's destiny. They determined the direction of his spirit and of his will for the rest of his life[16].

In Switzerland, said a traveler, between Neufchâtel and Geneva, there is a fountain whose water separates and flows partly to the north, and partly to the south. The northern waters join up with a stream that ends up in Lake Neufchâtel, whose flows eventually lose themselves in the Rhine and in the North Sea. The southern waters enter into Lake Geneva, which is to say the Rhone, which in turn runs toward the Mediterranean Sea. This fountain is the place that marks the separation of the two rivers. In the same way, the moment I am describing was the point at which Lacordaire's own life changed course. Until then, he had followed the common slippery slope that carried along with it the crowd of our fellow students far — very far — from all religious faith. It seemed, therefore, that he would naturally slide faster and faster down this slope. But Providence had other plans for him. In a bold exercise of his own free choice, Lacordaire threw himself resolutely into the counter-current, without knowing — and neither did we — that by the power of truth, he would be led logically one day to what he earlier had desired least — to the Catholic religion, to the priesthood, to the cloister.

It was 1821. After twenty-two years of war[17], France

35

rejoiced in peace the way one might normally rejoice in a conquest. It was no longer that heroic fervor that was so fruitlessly extravagant in so many battles under the Empire. It was of another, perhaps no less generous, kind: the fervor that creates poets, orators, and genuine citizens. Everything was coming back to life at the same time: institutions, literature, history, philosophy. The public square had de Serre and Lainé, and it would in the future have Berryer and Guizot[18]. Counted among the journalists of the time were Chateaubriand, Bonald, and La Mennais. Lamartine[19] had just published his first *Meditations,* Victor Hugo[20] his first *Odes;* Shakespeare, Schiller, Goethe, Byron, Walter Scott, all suddenly adopted by the French as one of their own, seemed to open to us limitless perspectives, horizons that were both unknown yet attainable. Guizot was preparing the history of the English Revolution, Thiers [21] that of the French Revolution; Augustin Thierry, in labors that eventually cost him his eyesight, created for us a sense of the historical truth about the Dark Ages and the Middle Ages. Cousin dethroned sensualism while translating Plato. It was said[22] that this was like an *instauratio magna* [great restoration] of the human spirit.

Moreover, what sincerity, what disinterestedness in our studies! The young people of that time (I am speaking of those of a certain quality) had a zeal for something greater than obtaining employment or accumulating wealth: they had a passion for what is true, for what is beautiful — a passion for the ideal in everything. Certainly they did not lack illusions, but these were generous illusions. Assuredly, they raised many more problems than they were capable of solving. They tackled many books and many problems that were beyond their abilities, the greatest monuments, certainly, as Father Lacordaire said, the most lofty problems of the human spirit. But one has to believe that some of this remained with them, and that the young people who leafed through, even superficially, Plato, Aristotle, Cicero, Descartes, Grotius, Montesquieu[23], Pascal, Bossuet, Leibnitz, were able later to call on what they had gleaned from their exposure to these great minds. These were the men with whom Lacordaire associated at age twenty. Who would dare to say that these readings, however rapid and incomplete as they were, did not leave in his mind, so quick to understand and appreciate, an enlightening and fertile impression? As for me, who knew Henri at this period of his life and since then have never lost sight of him for a single day, I do not hesitate to affirm that in politics, philosophy, history, literature, what the *Société d'Études* of Dijon had made him remained with him always up to the end. It was only about religion that he changed, and this was shortly after the sweep that I am discussing and through a kind of personal incubation period of the seeds that the *Société d'Études* had planted in his mind.

This *Société* was divided into four sections: Philosophy, History, Public Law, and Literature. Lacordaire enrolled in all four sections and managed all these studies simultaneously; from the first days, he showed himself peerless in creativity and in writing ability.

The writer in him was the first to become apparent. Twice a month, the four sections, whose particular conferences occurred weekly, came together in a general assembly to listen to literary essays being read aloud.

I will never in my life forget the impression produced in our midst by Lacordaire's first reading. In this albeit youthful composition, his magnificent imagination shone with such splendor that from that day on, we felt his thoughts inhabited a realm superior to ours; his thoughts were clothed in a brilliance that, up to that time, Chateaubriand's prose had only hinted at[24].

In the conferences, he surprised us even more. Each section had a specific program of study. Every week, the agenda addressed one of the program's questions. A member designated in advance, read a report, which introduced and opened the discussion. More than anyone among us, Lacordaire jumped into the fray. The ideas the rest of us held were different from his own. After the report, he often felt the need to protest. It was like the eruption of a volcano. Never since have I encountered anywhere such promptness, such spontaneity, such rich creativity. The flow of ideas and images was to be envied. One would have said that the sentences were already preformed in his mind. *Plenus sum sermonibus, et coarctat me spiritus uteri mei: loquar et respirabo paululum*[25]. This verse from Job gives an accurate picture of Lacordaire at age twenty. He spoke almost as if to deliver himself of a demon from within, and therefore there was an abundance of arguments, a fiery spirit, an incomparable originality and suitability of expression. Ideas and images flowed in an abundance to be envied. Nonetheless, let us restate what characterized this youthful eloquence above all; it was a marvelous but rare gift among the children of Northern France: it was its colorfulness, it was its brilliance.

"We still hear," wrote a member of the *Société d'Études* twenty-five years later, "we still hear these informal speeches full of flashes of inspiration, those spirited arguments filled with unexpected resources, with nimbleness and wit; we still see that sparkling and fixed gaze, penetrating and inscrutable; we still hear that voice—clear, vibrant, trembling with emotion, out of breath—carried away by its own dynamism, hearing only itself, and abandoning itself unreservedly and without constraint to an inexhaustible eloquence of the richest kind. O those beautiful years that went by so quickly, o those precious and magnificent workings of the mind, which foretold an incomparable athlete in God's cause[26]!"

I said previously that the current of ideas among us was not his. Allow me to explain.

Lacordaire graduated from secondary school at the age of seventeen. His faith was destroyed — as he himself said so many times — but he was honest, open, spontaneous, honorable, deeply taken with the humanities and with beautiful things, *having before him, as the guiding torch in his life, the human ideal of glory*[27]. His love of study and the lofty nature of his feelings had saved him from common unruliness. He had remained relatively chaste, without contact with women, as did Euripides' Hippolytus, however without prudery one guesses, and lending his ear to the more-or-less liberal confidences of his friends from school, but disapproving of easy loves, for which he forgave no one.

In his mind as in his heart, Christianity was deficient, lacking its North Star. Therefore, as an adventure, he read everything that came into his hands, with an eagerness that lacked direction; less attracted to the Ancients, as was true of many of his contemporaries, than to the Moderns; less attracted to the seventeenth century than to the following one. It was thus that he devoured the *Contes* of Voltaire[28], and his *Dictionnaire philosophique*. But early on, Jean-Jacques Rousseau[29] attracted his convictions no less. The confession of faith in Voltaire's *Vicaire Savoyard* became his religious gospel, and the Social Contract of Rousseau as his political gospel.

Henri had not experienced in his family, nor had he himself ever known, the feeling that attributes the qualities of majesty and sacredness to royalty. With the exception of his mother, all of his paternal and maternal forebears grieved for the Empire. All had witnessed the Restoration[30] with sorrow.

Not that Napoleon was popular in 1813; quite the contrary. But in 1814, the presence of foreigners [i.e., troops from other French Provinces – Trans.] had excited to the highest pitch in the invaded provinces, such as Burgundy and Champagne, the pain of being a humiliated country. People no longer wondered who had provoked these reprisals from Europe, who had drawn them, armed, to our nation's soil. People felt themselves trampled under the enemy's feet; people hoped fervently to drive them back outside our borders; they ardently wished the man who held the sword of France to be triumphant. And, when these wishes were disappointed, even the immense act of generosity that peace represented, due to the return of the Bourbons, did not console Henri Lacordaire for his disappointed hopes. His patriotic imagination took fire, as Lorain has said, on behalf of the exalted person, now vanquished. He found himself, therefore, quite naturally a Bonapartist, and, when opposition to the Restoration by Bonapartists became liberal, he became a liberal; indeed, he was one already, like all of us, because of his classical education. "I naturally found myself a liberal by instinct," he himself wrote. "And as soon as I heard the echo of public events, I was indeed a man of my times in my love of liberty, as I was in my ignorance of God and of the Gospel[31]."

However, let us say right at the start that this liberty which he always loved was never a revolutionary liberty, the freedom to destroy for the sake of destroying, an anarchic freedom; rather, it was an ordered liberty, a regulated and tempered liberty, a liberty represented at that moment by the Duc de Richelieu[32], Lainé, de Serre, and, in the opposition, Camille Jordan and Royer-Collard. Henri Lacordaire was horrified by [the Terror] of 1793. His heroes were not the heroes of the French Revolution — Mirabeau[33], Barnave, Vergniaud — but those of Ancient Greece and Rome, who seemed like giants to us, as were those of Homer. This was the fault of our education more than of our judgment. It was good, to be sure, to have us admire that which was admirable in Greece and Rome; but the error of our teachers was not to make us realize at the same time that there was something missing in pagan cultures — so exclusively vaunted —, and to neglect to make us appreciate everything that makes the superiority of Christian civilization incontestable.

The liberty about which Henri Lacordaire dreamed in 1821 was at the same time too abstract — like the liberty of the Social Contract — and too pagan. But it was not full of hatred, and that statement is enough to show how it differed radically from the liberalism of the Revolution. It was to Lacordaire's credit, in his youth as well as in his maturity, to love liberty without a spirit of domination, without partisanship; to love liberty for its own sake, as one loves moral excellence, truth, and justice; to love it also for the benefits it provides; to love it because it fills a deep need in the human spirit and gives dignity to human life.

We understand now what we had in common with Henri and what separated us. We loved liberty as much as he did and for the same reasons; but we did not conceive of liberty as he did. The young people who in 1821 established Dijon's *Société d'Études* were strongly in support of the Restoration, and most of them were Catholic, but they did not wish to make a particular point publicly about this; they depended solely on themselves. No affiliation attached them either to the Congregation, as it was called[34], nor to the *Société des Bonnes Lettres* nor to that of *Good Studies* [unable to detail either one - Trans.], nor to a single one of the works of monarchical or religious proselytizing of the era. All spirit of exclusion was foreign to them, and the proof is, that, from the first day of its existence, the *Société d'Études* included Henri

Lacordaire in its ranks.

Nevertheless, however tolerant it was, the majority of the members were royalist and Catholic: royalist, not separating national law from royal law; and Catholic, without ostentation and without shame, without the spirit of domination and without servile and pusillanimous concessions, without indifference as without bitterness. In the end, however, it must be said that this majority was clearly royalist and clearly Catholic.

As a result, it did not accept the eighteenth century as an authority at all, and in this regard, I dare say, it was far ahead of contemporary youth.

I am not looking at this history through a prism; I am not writing solely from memory; the minutes of the meetings of Dijon's *Société d'Études* still exist, and I have them at hand.

As far as philosophy goes, starting in 1821, Condillac[35] was clearly regarded among us as a superficial thinker. Not a single one of us, not Lacordaire any more than the others, defended his doctrine. The less advanced members followed the teaching of Laromiguière, who ascribed to the activity of the soul, as is well known, a completely different role than did his teacher. Opposition to this point of view was based on Reid's book concerning the human spirit[36]; this alone indicates the pioneering quality that animated our group, because who else in the provinces had heard of Reid? (The lessons of Royer-Collard[37] on philosophy in Scotland and Jouffroy's translation of Reid were not published until 1828.) Even Kant, although still not translated [into French], was not entirely unknown to us. Other fellow students boldly went back as far as Bossuet (*De la connaissance de Dieu et de soi-même*) [On the knowledge of God and of oneself][38]. Whatever else was said about him by a writer of great authority — who was, however, of a generation that did not understand ours — in fact, we needed to defend ourselves a lot more from the excessive ideas of de Bonald,[38] de Maistre,[40] de la Mennais[41] than from those of the Encyclopedists, particularly discredited in our eyes by the destruction they had wrought.

Consequently there was nothing commonplace in the current of ideas that swept us along; without doubt we were men of our time, but we were also independent of our time.

In literature, we devoured Madame De Staël's l'*Allemagne* [Germany][42], Guizot's [translations of] Shakespeare, de Barante's translations[43] of the dramatic works of Schiller, Schlegel's *Cours de littérature dramatique* [Study of dramatic literature]. While we were inspired by this breath of fresh air from abroad, we sacrificed neither Racine nor Molière to these foreign gods.

Our History section was a reaction against [Voltaire's] *Essai sur les mœurs* [An essay on morality][28]. But if we did not disdain or hate the past, we did not worship it either. We applied ourselves to understanding the older France, not to decry it, but rather to understand it better and the better to serve the France of today. Through a wide range of eras and customs, we assiduously studied the history of our country's interests and opinions; we admired above all the great examples of civic heroism: Juvénal des Ursins[44], la Vacquerie, Achille de Harlay, Matthieu Molé — examples that pagan antiquity did not surpass and that had impressed us very little when we were in school. In a word, we rounded out our philosophical, literary, historical, and political education to the degree that we could.

In Public Law, our gaze was not directed backward to the *ancien régime;* we wanted the Charter of 1814, but supplemented with the legal projects we discussed and deliberated on with all the passion and confidence of youth — projects whose liberalism certainly was not lacking in either sincerity or boldness.

It was in the midst of these heated discussions that, on 5 March 1822, Lacordaire, who usually was the only leader of the whole *Société d'Études*, asked to speak. He renounced the political doctrine of Rousseau as *leading straight to social suicide,* and declared that, persuaded by four months worth of debates, he, too, henceforth was on the side of the Restoration, if it were brought to fulness by liberty, according to the Charter. The acclamation was unanimous. The session was momentarily disrupted; as if propelled by an electrical surge, all the members who were present threw themselves one after the other into Lacordaire's arms. In its eleven years of existence, Dijon's *Société d'Études* had never experienced a day like this one.

Henceforth, Henri was a constitutional royalist, the term used at that time. His attitude toward the place of religion was modified in a marked fashion. Until that point, he had professed Deism, at times with a sharp touch of Voltairian mockery. Even if he did not become a believer immediately, at least the social side of the religious question, the evidence of the good that religion accomplished for man, its actions so manifestly helpful and salutary to people, had an increasing impact on him. His liberalism was frightened by Voltairian thought. "Impiety," he wrote, "leads to depravity. Corrupted morals give birth to corrupting laws. And license leads people in the direction of slavery without their having the time to utter a cry of protest."

He did not stop there. Among the members of the *Société d'Études*, there was one with whom he asked to converse three times a week on the subject of religion up to the end of the school year. He to whom this request was made is still living. He has declared that he had never seen a commitment to the art of discussion equal to that of

Lacordaire[45]. Henri put forth his objection with his natural superiority; then he would listen to the response without interrupting. To be sure, it was rare that he gave up unexpectedly, given the many internal resources he had with which to reply. But at the next encounter, if reflection had convinced him, he never missed saying spontaneously: "I was wrong to object to what you said the other day. Let us no longer discuss that matter. But I have another difficulty to propose to you," and he would start to debate a new point.

It was his way of considering every angle before reaching a conclusion. However, a great point had been won: Lacordaire had stopped looking down upon Catholic doctrine. From that time onward, this very lively intellect was at work on the religious question. It does not seem rash to think that the spirit of doubt in him gradually lost ground during this prolonged, amicable controversy, which lasted five months.

Such were his leanings, still uncertain in the realm of religion, when he left Dijon to go to the capital to train for the bar. On 30 November 1822, he took the oath as lawyer before the Paris court[46].

A good and fair man, President Riambourg[47], honorary member of the *Société d'Études*, had recommended Henri Lacordaire to his colleague, Alexandre Guillemin, lawyer to the Councils and to the Appeals Court. Guillemin received the young trainee with open arms. After having praised his protégé, Riambourg wrote that nothing more was needed than to set him on an appropriate path in Paris. Guillemin decided that the first guidance he owed to Henri was to suggest his going regularly to a confessor. Guillemin was astonished when he heard this response: "Oh, sir, I don't do that[48]!"

It was in Henri's character to take seriously

everything he did: he gave himself unreservedly to his new situation, attended the conferences of lawyers, and strove to set literature aside in order to focus completely on the study of law. He knew that, in sending him to Paris, his mother had taken on a financial sacrifice above and beyond her resources; it took a while before Lacordaire could lighten the burden by depositing in her hands his first attorney fees. Unfortunately, he was only twenty and a half years old, and a recent ordinance prohibited appearance before the bar under the age of twenty-two[49]. True, this did not bother him greatly. "If I were cited before the disciplinary council," he wrote on 18 January 1823, "it would be an occasion to make a good speech, nothing more. A young lawyer who is condemned for pleading a case with talent before the permissible age could turn this condemnation into honor."

Accordingly, he entered the legal profession full of confidence. He was poor but cheerful, assured as he was that his poor student quarters would one day be visited by glory. To get a picture of Henri Lacordaire at this time, one must reread this page that captures him so well, by the best informed of his biographers, Lorain: "Henri's character and talent burst forth in singular contrasts. This spontaneous spirit was capable of sustained, painstaking, continuous, daily, and persistent work. His energetic nature was patient, anger tamed by gentleness. His impatient and sovereign imagination was capable of detailed, long-term planning. He expressed his viewpoints readily, but also engaged in steadfast reflection and constant adjustment. In his blossoming adolescence, all the seriousness of a mature man was already evident. A mad gaiety, sometimes approaching the buffooneries of a child, was mixed with the meditativeness of a deep thinker. With this passionate temperament, he had a natural attention to detail, a simple elegance; he prized appropriateness and accuracy. When a friend's gaze fell on his work room, he found only careful and balanced arrangement. No disorder among the books, the papers, the writing desk, the pens, even the penknife, placed with a kind of artfulness on the little black table, everything visually pleasing. The same regularity, the same neatness in his manuscripts, in his handwriting, in everything he did, in all he touched." As he was at the age of twenty, so he remained until the end. We have in our possession the erasures of Bossuet and those of Buffon; we will never see those of Lacordaire.

We have already seen that Guillemin treated him as a father would a son. He immediately assigned him some cases from his old law office in the royal court, among others, an important affair of state, in which one of the greatest names in the First Empire was found compromised, and in which Tripier was his adversary. Lacordaire (we shall see why) was never to take on this high-profile case. But meanwhile he appeared several times, always successfully, before the tribunal of the Seine and the bar of the Court of Assizes. The legal briefs that he composed drew attention. Guillemin presented him to the Attorney General of the Appeals Court, Mourre, whose niece Guillemin had married, and this eminent magistrate charged the young trainee with preparing draft indictments. Need we say more? The day that Lacordaire had the good fortune of pleading a case before Berryer, the great lawyer was so impressed that he immediately invited him to visit the following day, conversed with him for an hour, and then said: "You can consider yourself in the top ranks of the bar." (What an impressive prediction, especially from such an eminent source!) "But," he continued, "you have some great pitfalls to avoid, among them the abuse of your facility with words[50]."

Before entering the seminary, Lacordaire confided to me that had only this one conversation with Berryer, whose exact date I have, 8 February 1824. We have just seen in what

47

terms the conversation in question was summarized two weeks later by Lacordaire himself. Thirty-seven years later, the facts were transformed in Berryer's memory. The illustrious orator believed that even then, he had predicted Henri Lacordaire's prominence as an orator in the Notre-Dame Conferences. Accordingly, in receiving Father Lacordaire into the French Academy, Guizot felt justified in attributing these words to Berryer: "Become a priest, and you will become an eminent preacher." I can attest that, the very next day after Father Lacordaire's induction into the Academy, 25 January 1861, Father Lacordaire assured me in the most decisive way that Berryer had never said anything to him remotely resembling this.

This was Henri Lacordaire's situation at the Law Court at the beginning of 1824.

His state of mind at this time is not any less known to us. He exaggerated on his deathbed his differences of opinion with the other young people who belonged to the *Société des Bonnes Études* in Paris. He described himself more accurately in a letter that slightly predated this period[51]: royalist in politics, "without associating to it that harshness and narrowness of vision which dishonors the truth." All of his most intimate correspondence at this moment of his life was written in this vein. These were his political views all the way to the Revolution of 1830. His royalist sympathies were simply an intellectual decision, while the sympathies of the other members were driven by deep feelings. For the most part, they were inclined to exaggerations that he could not subscribe to, and it is the remembrance of that aspect of his relationship to them that stayed with him. Hence the statement in the *Notice* to which I alluded here.

As for religion, Henri loved it already, without exactly admitting it. "I have a soul very much inclined to religion," he added, "and a very unbelieving spirit; since it is in the nature of the mind to allow itself to be subjugated by the soul, it is likely that one day I will be a Christian[52]. I am able to live in solitude but also to hurl myself into the vortex of human affairs, loving calmness when I think about it, and loving bustle when I am living in the midst of it, sometimes taking rest in the country as if I were visiting my favorite castle, yet easily bidding adieu to it when I walk over the Pont Neuf in Paris. I am confirmed in my logical conviction that to try everything and to change one's location do not change one's nature and that there are needs in the soul which this world cannot satisfy. I am restless and come to conclusions so quickly that I am often misled. I have loved some men; but I have not yet loved any women, and I will never love them as they really are[53]."

Nothing, however, outwardly betrayed this early disenchantment. "Everyone in the world predicted a great future for me," Lacordaire said. And indeed he did have choices open to him. He could choose between the bar, which was opening up to him very promising possibilities, or work as a public prosecutor, which was more suited, perhaps, to his talents, and where the patronage of Mourre would not be lacking. But an inner voice was telling him that his calling did not lie there. Indeed, an indefinable malaise (let us allow one of his confidantes to speak of this), a "deepening sense of sadness and the majesty of Christian thought silently rocked the foundation of this soul that could be satisfied by nothing else. For him, society had few charms. He was bored by the theater. He was 'lost, discouraged, alone in the midst of 800,000 men, *weary of everything without having known anything.*' These bouts of melancholy foretold the day of divine matters[54]."

What changes had occurred within him?

He had arrived in Paris at the end of 1822, admiring and loving the ethics of the Gospel (these were the words he used), respecting its ministers, because their influence was beneficial to society. But he had not yet taken a step, it seems, beyond the profession of faith of the Savoyard vicar[28]. However, his mind was preoccupied by religious questions and his conscience troubled by these questions more than he wished to admit to his unbelieving friends. The latter, consumed by the defiant attitude of the times, would not concede that one could have an untainted bond to Catholicism. They also were watching with unconcealed anxiety this disciple of Jean-Jacques [Rousseau] coming under the influence of Riambourg and receiving the patronage of Guillemin.

Henri did his best to reassure them. But it was not in his nature to hamper either the free flight of his intellect in its search for truth, nor the sincerity of his communication. During his long evenings in solitude, the conversations on religious topics in Dijon during the summer of 1822 came back to mind. Once again he tackled the lofty questions that have always preoccupied the greatest intellects. He meditated on them deeply in the secret of his conscience without confiding in anyone about them; it was in this sense that he could truthfully say that no living person had played a role in his conversion. Gerbet, with whom the members of Dijon's *Société d'Études* had corresponded, had welcomed him warmly when he arrived in Paris, but their relationship was never close, and they did not speak at all about religion when they were together. Lacordaire repeatedly confirmed this. The work of God was nonetheless operating in this noble soul.

In 1823, he spent vacation with his family, keeping his secret. From that point on, he was profoundly transformed: the prejudices in his mind against the Catholic faith that had accumulated over many years had melted like the snow under the sun. "I did not really have any objections," he said to me later, "but I was not yet entirely sure that this would be the definitive state of my mind. I dreaded that doubts would once again arise someday. I was," he added, "like the Austrian army in 1813, on the opposite side of the Rhine[55]; not a single French bayonet opposed their passage, but the Austrians did not trust them, and they were there for six weeks without crossing over. And so, before declaring my conversion, even to my mother, I let six months go by."

This moment is so significant in the life of Father Lacordaire, that I can do no better than to let him speak in his own words up to his entrance into the seminary.

Once converted, he began to think, naturally, of gradually preparing his friends for this news — friends who had remained skeptics or Deists. On 7 February 1824, he wrote to one of them, "Would you have believed that I am becoming a Christian day by day? It is a remarkable thing, this gradual change in my point of view. I have been brought to the point of faith, and at the same I have never been more of a philosopher. 'A little philosophy can distance one from religion; a lot of philosophy, however, brings one back.' An important truth[56]."

Then, on 22 February:

"Yes, my dear Lorain, I do believe. I quibble with one phrase in your letter where you doubt my sincerity and good faith. If my letter were not so wild (this is an allusion to several jokes that preceded this passage), I would speak to you about my beliefs, and what led me to this point. How did it come to be that my friends do not understand me? They were skeptical about my political conversion and saw it as a skillful calculation; now they mock my religious conversion and invite me to wait for the Jesuits to overthrow the *Université*[57]."

Finally, on 15 March:

"I have been struck in recent days by an idea even more extraordinary than this. Let me be nailed live to a wooden cross—if I have not thought seriously about being a village pastor. Illusions of the moment! Phantoms that disappear so quickly! The need to shake oneself up in life's Mount Etna!

"You ask me to share my thoughts on religion. But I do not have space in this letter today. I will say only that *I have arrived at my religious beliefs through my social convictions,* and that today, nothing seems to me more demonstrable than the fact that society is a basic necessity. Consequently, Christianity is divinely inspired, because it is the only means capable of bringing society to its perfection. It transforms man with all his weaknesses and it also transforms the social order in all its various conditions[58].

"My dear friend, I have always searched for truth in good faith while leaving aside all pride — which is the only way to find truth. If my opinions owed something to the circle of friendships in which I moved (a reference to the walks of the summer of 1822), it is at the same time true that I never submitted to any but my own reflections and I arrived at insights independently."

A bit later, when the truth was completely out, Lacordaire confided in a letter to another friend:

"My religious sacrifice doubtless surprised you, because it hit you like a thunderbolt for which nothing had prepared you; because you knew me as I was when I left Dijon, and not as the man I had become. But my thinking developed over a period of eighteen months."

"It is not, my dear friend, that I have read many works to form my conviction; I did not touch a single one. It is not that I experienced a gradual and imperceptible seduction by the people around me. Not even four times have people talked to me about religion[59]. I found faith more as a memory than as a new gift, as a consequence of principles already acquired than as a new creation of my thinking. I remember one night reading the Gospel of St. Matthew, and I wept: when one weeps, one believes not long after[60]."

In his correspondence with Lorain, he went into more depth:

"When I examine the course of my thoughts over the past five years[61], the point where I began, the degrees and latitudes which my mind traveled, the definitive result of this slow progress bristling with obstacles, I am astonished and feel moved to the adoration of God.

"My dear friend, this makes no sense except for him who has passed from error to truth, who is aware of all the previous ideas he had seized upon, came to understand their connections, the strange alliances, the gradual linking as he now ties them to the different stages in his move toward certainty. A sublime moment it is, when the last trace of light penetrates into the spirit, and attaches to a common center the truths which are scattered there. There is always such a distance between the moment that follows and the moment that precedes, between what one was previously and what one is after, that the word *grace* was created to express this miraculous turn of events, to express this illumination from above. It is like watching a man move forward haphazardly, blindfolded; as the blindfold is loosened bit by bit, he catches a glimpse of daylight, and, in the instant that it falls from his face, he finds himself facing the sun[62]."

This is the very language we hear from the lips of Father on his deathbed:

"No book, no man, was God's instrument in my regard. No Christian sermon captured my attention. After eighteen months, I was alone in Paris as I had been on the first day, a stranger to all parties, with no tide to sweep me along, with no particular influence to enlighten my mind. . . . Without doubt, I was suffering from a difficult and total isolation; but this was part of the divine perspective concerning me. Painfully, I crossed this desert of my youth, not knowing that it would have its Sinai, its flashes of light and its taste of water.

"It is impossible to say on what day, at what hour, and how, my faith that had been lost ten years earlier, reappeared in my heart like a torch that had never been extinguished. Theology teaches us that there is another light than that of reason, another impetus other than nature. 'The spirit of God,' says the apostle John, 'blows where it wills, and you do not know whence it comes, or whither it goes[63].' An unbeliever the night before, a Christian the following morning, certain with an invincible certainty, this was not a rejection of reason, suddenly enchained in an incomprehensible servitude. Rather, it was the expansion of reason's clarities, a view of everything under a more extended outlook and a more penetrating light. Neither was it the submissive abasement of character under a strict and frozen rule, but the development of its energy through an action whose origins lay beyond nature. Neither was it, finally, the abnegation of the heart's joys, but rather their fulness and increase. Man in his fullness remained intact; moreover, no one other than God did this.

"Whoever has not known such a moment has not known the life of man. All Christians are more or less familiar with this state; but it is never more vivid and more gripping than on a day of conversion[64]."

For the first time, we have just embraced one by one, with a single glance, all the levels of the wonderful change that was coming to an end . Make no mistake: man acts in full freedom; but God leads him. It was God, who had given Lacordaire a Christian mother. It was God who introduced him, at age eighteen, to an organization of young Christians, intelligent men, who did honor to their faith by their behavior and their character. It was God who later created for him, in the middle of Paris, a solitude of mind and heart, completely receptive to memories of the domestic hearth, of maternal tenderness, and of the joys of the first communion, as *an historical and social manifestation of Christianity*[65]. Finally, it was God who struck the rock and caused to spring from it life-giving water.

The miracle was not to end there.

For someone who rediscovers Christianity, what could be more logical than to devote his entire being to the apostolate of the reclaimed truth! As it happens, one of the gifts Lacordaire had received from God was an ardent sense of logic which rushed forward in a single bound to the very conclusion of a situation, to the heart of a feeling or of an idea. As Lorain said, for Lacordaire, being a Christian was to be a priest; and being a priest was later to be a monk. Lacordaire was aware that, to a man, all his family would be against this decision, along with his unbelieving friends (and perhaps others also) — finally, maybe, even his mother. None of this could stop him.

"Once a Christian," said Father Lacordaire, "the world did not vanish from view, but rather it grew larger even as I did. Instead of a vain drama and short-lived ambitions that were disappointed or satisfied, I saw the world as a great invalid in need of help, and to me there was nothing comparable to the joy of serving it under the watchful eye of God, with the Gospel and the Cross of His Son." In short, Lacordaire saw himself as called from above. "The desire for the priesthood," he said, "overwhelms me as a natural consequence of my own salvation. The desire was strong, passionate, spontaneous, and unshakable. Not once in forty years, through all the vicissitudes of a turbulent life, did I have feelings of regret for it[66]."

That is the truth. The whole truth. In this account, one can tell there is not an iota of fiction. And, in fact, before entering Saint-Sulpice [seminary], Henri Lacordaire had loved no woman other than his mother. Many of his fellow students and his contemporaries outlive him; not one of them will contradict this: *He who saw it has borne witness — his testimony is true*[67]. In giving himself to the Church, Henri Lacordaire brought to God a passionate soul, but also unblemished morals, an ascetic youth and a virgin heart.

Having made the resolution, all that remained was to obtain his mother's consent. Henri sought this toward the end of March[68]. But Madame Lacordaire had placed other hopes in her son. She was not lacking in ambition for this son, who for a long time had been the pride of the family. Her dreams for Henri included assuming the mantle of Daguesseau; she counted on him for honor and for security and peace in her old age. She feared the possibility of his carrying the Gospel to regions where she could not follow. Unprepared for the prospect of his leaving the world, resigning herself to this idea was all the more difficult because she felt justified in questioning a vocation that seemed all too suddenly arrived at and insufficiently tested. She wrote him six letters, suffused with both joy at the conversion of her Augustine[69] and sadness at the prospect of losing him. But in the final analysis, she was *Christian, courageous and strong.* Not wanting to interfere with the call of Providence, after five weeks she agreed to the wishes of her son[70].

In the meantime, Lacordaire informed Guillemin of his desire to enter the seminary of Saint-Sulpice and of his hope in obtaining a half-scholarship to defray as long as he could the expenses to his mother, who up until now had made so many sacrifices on his behalf (they seemed a loss at this point). Guillemin led him to one of the Grand Vicars of the archdiocese of Paris, Borderies, who later became the bishop of Versailles. Borderies, of holy memory, was a congenial individual. According to Guillemin, Borderies took Lacordaire aside, doubtlessly for a more thorough questioning, and brought him back "with the joy of a good pastor; a joy that was shining forth in the midst of tears[71]." Borderies lodged at the archbishop's palace, a magnificent residence that was savagely destroyed in full view of the armed National Guard, on 13 February 1831[72]. He immediately introduced Lacordaire to the archbishop, Msgr de Quélen. The prelate received the young neophyte with kindness and good grace. "He asked me," said Father Lacordaire, "what diocese I was from, and whether it was indeed my will to join his. When I responded in the affirmative, he said he would write the bishop of Dijon, and also invited me, for my part, to do the same. Then he added: 'At the bar you were defending perishable causes; in the future you will be defending causes of eternal justice. You will see justice appraised inconsistently by men; but above, there is a court of appeals where justice will be definitively served[73].'"

The archbishop of Paris could not afford to cover the costs of the ecclesiastical education of a young man destined for another diocese. So, before allowing Lacordaire to leave, Borderies, without losing a moment, had Lacordaire write a letter whose contents he dictated. In the most simple terms, the letter asked the bishop of Dijon for his release on the grounds that the signatory, born in Recey-sur-Ource, "had obtained from the kindness of the archbishop of Paris a half-scholarship to the seminary of Saint-Sulpice[74]." The point of this maneuver was obvious. We do not know what postscript the archbishop of Paris had written in his own hand; but it is safe to presume that he wrote in a manner that would ensure success — which, moreover, came without delay. De Quélen, enjoyed the highest authority at the heart of the French Church. The bishop of Dijon, de Boisville, happy to have this opportunity to please the archbishop, sent his *exeat* without asking for any further information. The prelate, who had not taken possession of his diocese until after Henri had left for Paris, and who, moreover, lived among us in a rather patrician setting, had never heard Lacordaire's name before; he did not for an instant doubt that this man was but an obscure cleric, born in a remote corner of his diocese, but reared in Paris at the expense of archiepiscopal charity. "What else would you expect?" he said, later excusing himself for this perception. "He wrote me a letter in which the only things lacking were spelling errors; I took him to be the greatest simpleton of my diocese[75]."

ENDNOTES

Attention: Original footnotes of the author in this (38) and other chapters were transformed into endnotes. Additional endnotes by the translators are noted by bold-faced numerals.

---

1. See the official registration of his baptism in Appendix IX, page 531.
2. Today Bussières-les-Belmon.
3. *Notice sur le rétablissement en France de l'Ordre des Frères Prêcheurs.* [The final testament of Father Lacordaire, dictated on his deathbed — See Internet: www.worksoflacoraire.com: "Overview of the Order of Friars Preachers..." Referred to as *Notice* in notes.
4.- French educational system . . .**Primary**, 5 levels; **middle**

school ["collège"],4 levels [called 6th form, 5th form, 4th form, 3rd form = British style]; **lycée**: last three years of secondary education [3 levels, called 2nd, 1st, and terminal]. - See Internet for more details.

5. *Notice.*

6. *Notice.*

7. Letter from Delahaye, 20 March 1862.

8. Testimony of Guérard, of the Institute, one of Henri's fellow students at the school in Dijon.

9. Crébillon, Claude (1707-1777): capable writer but his works were excessively licentious. – Son of Prosper Jolyot dit Crébillon.

10. *Notice.*

11. Pierre Joseph Prudhon (1809-1865), socialist and author of famous theories about property and founder of an insurance system. He criticized communism, the sovereignty of the state, the economic system, the proletariat,

12. Grotius, Hugo (1583-1645): Dutch scholar and statesman; founder of modern science of international law.

    Domat, Jean (1625-1696); law scholar.

    Daguesseau: lawyer.

13. *Notice.*

14. As opposed to natural law, positive law studies the laws of a particular time, place, and culture.

15. *Notice.*

16. "These minds whose thinking transformed my own, and *which led me to where I am.*" — Lacordaire, letter of 29 December 1829 to Foisset.

17. That is, the series of Napoleonic wars.

18. De Serre, Olivier (1539-1619); founder of French agronomy.

    Berryer, Antoine (1790-1868); top-notch lawyer. Opposed to the Second Empire.

Guizot, François (1787-1874); statesman, French historian, Minister. Led to the 1848 Revolution.
19. Chateaubriand, François René de C. (1764-1848); vicomte, illustrious writer. Later, Minister of Foreign Affairs.

Bonald, Louis de B. (1754-1840); vicomte; writer and philosopher; defender of the monarchy and of religion.

La Mennais, Félicité Robert de L. (1782-1854); French philosopher and theologian; brilliant writer. Originally taught that the Church was the depository of all truth; later condemned by the Church. - See website: www.worksoflacordaire.com, Reflections on the Philosophical System of Father de La Mennais.

Lamartine, Alphonse Marie-Louis de Prat de L. (1790-1869); poet and politician.
20. Hugo, Victor (1802-1885); illustrious French write, poet, defender of democracy.

Scott, Sir Walter (1771-1832); writer.
21. Thiers, Adolphe (1797-1877); French historian, statesman, minister. In and out of government.

Thierry, Jacques Nicolas Augustin (1795-1856); French historian; promoter of historical studies.

Cousin, Victor (1792-1867); philosopher and politician; member of the Eclectic School.
22. Caro, *Revue des Deux-Mondes*, 15 March 1865. — Article entitled *"De 1820 à 1830."*
23. Montesquieu, Charles de Secondat, baron La Brède et de M. (1689-1755); celebrated French author, philosopher. Supported the separation of powers, and brought moderation to the passion of progress.

Leibnitz, Gottfried Wilhelm (1646-1716); illustrious German philosopher and genius; mathematician.

Pascal, Blaise (1623-1662); French thinker; illustrious mathematician and scientist. Follower of Jansenius at Port

Royal.

24. Chateaubriand, vicomte François-René de C. (1768-1848); writer of novels, painter, poet. Great influence on nascent Romanticism. [See 19, above.]

25. *I am full of words, the spirit within me constrains me!. . . I must speak, that I may find relief* (Job 32:18, 20). Herbert G. May and Bruce M. Metzger, eds. The Oxford Annotated Bible, Revised Standard Version (New York: Oxford University Press, 1977). Unless otherwise noted, all scriptural passages in English are quoted from this source. [cdt].

26. Lorain, *Le R. P. Lacordaire*, p. 12.

27. *Notice*.

28.Voltaire, François-Marie Arouet dit V. (1694-1778); writer, literary critic. Looked to the past. Open enemy of the Church. In his Essay on morals, he propounded religious tolerance, liberty of conscience, and improvement of social life. — In his "Savoyard vicar": Voltaire approved of the vicar's profession of faith only on the pages devoted to the definition of natural religion [involving the mind and the heart].

29. Rousseau, Jean-Jacques (1712-1778); romantic and controversial writer; social theorist. Source of French Romanticism; looked to the future. Wrote the *Social Contract*. His view of the excellence of nature was a chimera. Inaugurated the French Revolution.

30. "Restoration" refers to the period 1814-1830, when the Bourbons were restored to the throne of France. "The nation at large received them with reluctance, chiefly for three reasons: 1. because they had been placed on the throne by foreign arms (Louis XVIII openly acknowledged that he owed his throne to the English; 2. because, while they had been absent from France, it had undergone a total change, and they had thus become strangers to the country in which the principles of the Revolution were permanently established; 3. because they

brought back with them an obsolete *noblesse*, opposed to the whole spirit and tendency of modern French politics." Quotation from "History of France, from the Restoration of the Bourbons, to the Declaration of Louis-Philip, King of the French; from 1814 to 1830," *Enclyclopædia Americana: A Popular Dictionary of Arts, Sciences, Literature, History, Politics, and Biography*, volume 5, ed. Francis Lieber (Philadelphia: Desilver, Thomas & Co., 1836), p. 219. Accessed 5 February 2011, at
http://books.google.com/books?id=HtcuAQAAIAAJ&pg=PA219&dq=restoration+france+bourbons&hl=en&ei=RG5NTdWXJ8v2gAev0KzhDw&sa=X&oi=book_result&ct=result&resnum=3&ved=0CDEQ6AEwAg#v=onepage&q=restoration%20france%20bourbons&f=false. [cdt]

31. *Notice.*

32. Richelieu, Armand-Jean du Plessis, duc de R. (1585-1642); cardinal, statesman, Prime Minister; skilled politician. Reformed the finances, the army, the legislature. Supported royal absolutism. Founded the French Academy [the Forty Immortals].

Jordan, Camille (1771-1823): writer, politician. Doctrinaire under the Restoration.

Royer-Collard, Pierre-Paul (1768-1845); philosopher, political orator. Also, doctrinaire under the Restoration.

33. Mirabeau, Honoré-Gabriel (1749-1791); French orator. Led a troubled life. His character was inferior to his talent.

Vergniaud, Pierre Victurien (1752-1793); skilled orator and politician.

Barnave, Joseph (1761-1793); orator the Constituent Assembly.

34. Congregation: a society founded in 1801 to intensify religious life, under the Restoration. It fell with the fall of

Charles X.

35. Condillac, Étienne Bonnal de C. (1715-1780); philosopher of the Sensualist School [knowledge based on the senses].

Laromiguière, Pierre (1756-1837); one of the founders of Eclecticism.

36. Reid, Thomas (1710-1796); philosopher in Scotland; held that knowledge arose from internal experience and common sense.

37. Royer-Collard, Pierre-Paul (1768-1845); philosopher, political orator. Also, doctrinaire under the Restoration.

Jouffroy, Théodore (1796-1842); French spiritualist philosopher. Introduced Scottish philosophy to France.

38. Bossuet, Jacques-Bénigne (1627-1704); illustrious French orator and writer.

39. Viscomte Louis de Bonald (1754-1840) was a significant figure in the Bourbon Restoration and also a counter-Revolutionary theorist.

40. Joseph-Marie, Comte de Maistre (1753-1821) was a lawyer, diplomat, and philosopher who believed in the hereditary monarchy. — A writer; supported both civil and religious authority.

41. De La Mennais: see 19, above.

42. Mme de Staël, Anne-Louise-Germaine Necker (1766-1817). Noted for her intellect and her writings. Disciple of J. J. Rousseau.

43. Barante, baron Guillaume-Prospère Bruguière de B. (1782-1866); historian and statesman.

Schiller, Johann Christoph Freidrich von S. (1759-1805); writer, tragic poet, historian. Of rare originality and lively imagination.

44. Juvenal des Ursins [Jean 1er] (1360-1431). Claimed descent from the Orsini family in Italy. French judge.

Vacquerie, Auguste (1819-1895); writer, journalist,

drama writer of the Romantic School.

Harlay, Achille de H. (1536-1619); first President of the Paris Parliament; supporter of royalty.

Molé, Matthieu (1584-1656), son of Edward. President of the Parliament. Held an important role in the *Fronde* ["slingshot"], a civil war, 1648-1653, regarding the financial policies of Cardinal Mazarin.

45. Monsieur Guillemin gave the same testimony about him (*Souvenirs du Ciel*, p. 249): "Monsieur Lacordaire had an admirable way of discussing religion; he forgot himself completely in search of truth alone."

46. Letter to Lorain, 2 December 1822.

47. Riambourg (Jean-Baptiste-Claude), born in Dijon in 1776. He was one of the first to enter the *École Polytechnique* after it was established. But as an orphan, without fortune, the sole source of support for his family, he was forced to give up mathematics and turn his sights to the bar. Law was not yet taught in a systematic way, and thus he was forced, as were all his contemporaries, to supplement with his vigorous intelligence courses that were incomplete and improvised. It was in them that his penetrating mind and the power and rectitude of his judgment burst forth. He had the gift of elevating the questions that he touched upon, and the balance of all his faculties was not any less marvelous than their breadth. Also his reputation grew rapidly, and, when he became counselor to the court of Dijon in 1812, public opinion ratified this choice. However, indignant about the return of Napoleon in 1815, without any fanfare he sacrificed his position to his political convictions, even though he had not received any favors from the Restoration. Named Attorney General on account of his good example, albeit unwittingly, his allegiance was to the purest form of royalism, tempered by an independence conformed to the firmness of his character just

as to the incomparable docility of his virtue. In this battle post, he could not bend to political exigencies, and it was felt necessary to appoint him to the chair of President of the Chamber in 1818. One might say that this was his natural place, so much was he born the judge, so much did he seem called to these austere functions by the superior rectitude of his judgment, his boundless zeal for the good and the just — shining qualities that were joined to an exquisite tact that always emphasized the positive. At the accession of the royalist ministry of 1822, he refused to take any steps to regain his position as Attorney General. In 1830, he decided he could not take a new oath.

No issue was foreign to President Riambourg—in science, in jurisprudence, even in the arts. However, he preferred philosophy, in which he showed great superiority. His works, put in order after his death by the author of this book, appeared in a second edition in 1850: a volume in- 4° * in the Migne** collection. Deeply imbued with Christian principles, a good mathematician, a consummate logician, he found quick and sure ways to demonstrate through philosophy the great truths of Catholicism. His treatise, *Du Rationalisme et de la Tradition* [Rationalism and Tradition], was welcomed by the religious world with great acclaim.

In Dijon, he was known for his boundless kindness, particularly as regards youth; for this, he was revered. However, Monsieur Riambourg's way of expressing himself, always clear and judicious, essentially lacked scope. His imperturbably calm conversation lacked warmth. As a result the true superiority of his mind — which was overly-controlled — escaped the notice of many people.

* In 4° [in-quarto]: format of a book whose pages are folded into 4 sheets, forming 8 pages. - A book in this format.

** Migne, abbé Jacques-Paul (1800-1875). Founder

of the journal *Univers*; editor of theological encyclopedias.

48. This answer was given to me in these very words by Guillemin, in Dijon, several days later.

49. Royal ordinance of 20 November 1822.

50. Letter to Lorain, 23 February 1824.

51.To Fontaine, 10 November 1823. - No clarity found concerning the two societies: *Bonnes Lettres* and *Bonnes Études* and their relationship.

52. From that time forward, he was more [of a Christian] than he wished to admit; perhaps it would be more accurate to say that this was already an admission of sorts.

53. Letter to Fontaine, a lawyer in Paris, 17 November 1823. This letter is cited in its entirely by Father Chocarne. The friendship would develop no further because Lacordaire entered the seminary six months later.

54. Lorain, pp. 16-17.

55. Battle of Dresden, 1813, during which Napoleon was forced to retreat. Paris was captured in March 1814.

56. *Letter to Lorain* — Who does not know the statement by Bacon (1561-1626) to which Lacordaire makes allusion here: *Parvi haustus philosophiæ faciunt incredulum magni christianum.* In Bacons' s words: "A little philosophy inclineth man's mind to atheism, but depth in philosophy bringeth man's mind about to religion."

— Roger Bacon (1561-1626) espoused the method of experimentation, in an attempt to put science back into philosophy. — Latin source: *Parvi haustus philosophiae faciunt incredulum magni christianorum.*

57. The University: The body of administrators appointed by the state to oversee the entire educational system. - This is the body Lacordaire fought against in his "Freedom of Instruction."

58. Letter to Lorain. — The idea is barely sketched but I

believe in the concluding syllogism: If society is from God, and if Christianity is the only religion that civilizes, how could Christianity not come from God? All the religions that man has devised for himself: polytheism, mohammedanism, led to the degradation of man. If this is not the case with Christianity is that not proof that it does not come from man but from God? On this point, who would have known the conditions of the genuine civilization of man if not the One Who made man?

Moreover, when Lacordaire announced his conversion to an unbelieving royalist friend, he had to present the truth to him in a most appropriate [and personal] way. "One finds it unusual," he told him later, "that I was led to religious ideas through political ones; the more I grow, the more I discover the appropriateness of that path. Besides, one can arrive at Christianity through all the paths, because it is the center of all truth."

59. This has been completely confirmed by the witness of Guillemin: *Le Père Lacordaire*, pp. 78-79. See also p. 8.

60. Letter to Boissard, 22 May 1824. — Note: This letter has also been attributed to Chateaubriand.

61. Since his entrance in the School of Law.

62. Letter of 11 May 1824.

63. Full text of John 3:8 reads: "The wind blows where it will, and you hear the sound of it, but you do not know whither it goes; so it is with every one who is born of the Spirit."

64. *Notice.*

65. See *Considerations sur le système philosophique de M. de La Mennais*. – See endnote 19, above: Reflections on the Philosophical System of Father de La Mennais.

66. *Notice.*

67. John 19:35.

68. Letter to Foisset, 2 May 1824.

69. In the *Notice,* Father [Lacordaire] describes his mother's

opposition as occurring after his contacting the archdiocese about entering the priesthood. On this point, his memory in 1861 was incorrect, as is proven by this phrase in a letter he wrote to Foisset on 2 May 1824: "I informed my mother about my project at the end of March." Besides, I have here a letter from Madame Lacordaire to her son, dated 31 March 1824, responding to the first confidences about his vocation. Certain of his mother's eventual consent, he did, however, write to the bishopric of Dijon before obtaining her official approval.

70. St. Augustine (354-430): after a stormy childhood, and following years of his mother's tears and prayers, he was converted by St. Anselm. Religious apologist; philosopher: worked to reconcile faith and reason. Mentioned his mother, St. Monica, in his *Confessions*.

71. *Souvenir du Ciel*, by Guillemin, p. 253.

72. See www.worksoflacordaire.com on web: Fundraising for the rebuilding of the Archbishop's residence in Paris.

73. *Notice*.

74. *Souvenir du Ciel*, by Guillemin, p. 253.

75. "He had a right to feel that way," said Father Lacordaire, with a smile, at the *Institut de Sorèze*. "Think about it, I started my letter using the present participle."

Chapter 1

Education—Unbelief—Conversion

Early years — Family — School — Law school — La Société d'Études of Dijon — Training at the bar in Paris — Conversion — Entering seminary.

Jean-Baptiste Henri Lacordaire was born in Recey, a small town in the hills of Burgundy, set on a slope by the edge of a river called the *Ource*, which flows into the Seine.

It was on the 12th of May, 1802, at the same period of time when churches were opening again in all of France; but the church in Recey was still closed. Henri Lacordaire was baptized in a neighboring town, Lucey, by the priest serving that area. The humble priest had no way of foreseeing what this child would one day become in God's Church[1].

Lacordaire's birthplace was in the ancient duchy of Langres, Bussières-les-Nonnes, so named because of the neighboring Cistercian abbey, contemporaneous with Saint Bernard[2]. In an unusual configuration, found also in Domremy, the birthplace of Joan of Arc, a stream divided Bussières between two provinces: the section of Bussières on the stream's right shore belonged to Burgundy; that on the left shore, to Champagne. The house in which Henri Lacordaire's father was born was in the Burgundian section.

Monsieur Nicolas Lacordaire, Lacordaire's father, was a director of surgery, following in the footsteps of some family members before him. Madame Lacordaire had been orphaned; she was born the daughter of a lawyer in Dijon's parliament. Her eminently respected father was a man of greater probity than wealth.

When Henri Lacordaire was four years old, his father died. His mother resettled in Dijon, her birthplace, for the education of her four sons, of whom Henri was the second.

This education was rigorous. Madame Lacordaire was a woman of forceful character, sound and steadfast in mind, her faith simple and strong. Forced to sell the house in which her children had been born, she made a point of letting them know that they were of limited means and that in later life they would have to count only on themselves.

From 1806 to 1809, Henri resided in Brussières, at the home of his father's older brother. He cherished the memory of this stay, which always remained sacred to him: the view of the woods, as well as the frugal customs of the countryside at the beginning of this century.

When he was seven years old (*the age of discretion*, as our fathers used to say), his mother brought him back to Dijon to have him begin classical studies. Faithful to all the good traditions, she also led him to the parish priest to make his first confession. "I crossed the sanctuary," he said. "I found alone in the beautiful and vast sanctuary a dignified elderly man, gentle and welcoming. It was the first time that I had approached the priest; until this point, I had never seen him except at the altar, amid pomp and incense. Father Deschamps (that was his name) sat on a bench and motioned for me to kneel next to him. I do not remember what I said to him or what he said to me, but this first meeting between my soul and God's representative made an unblemished and deep impression on me. To this day, I have never entered into the sacristy of Dijon's Church of Saint-Michel without being reminded of my first confession as represented by that wonderful elderly man and the openness of my own childhood. Everyone in that church, moreover, exhibited a spirit of piety; I never saw that place again without experiencing a certain emotion that no other church has been able to inspire in me. My mother, Saint-Michel, and the religion of my birth created in my soul a kind of structure, the first, the most moving and durable of all[3]."

It would not be long, however, before this impression would fade more than we could express. In 1812, three months before the end of the academic year, Henri Lacordaire entered, with a half-scholarship, as a boarding student at the *lycée impériale* of Dijon; he was ten years old[4].

It was this time that provided a remembrance which would never leave his memory, an experience typical of the behavior customary among students of that era. "From the very first day," he said. "my fellow students took me for some sort of plaything; I could not take a step without their brutality finding a way to target me. For several weeks, I was deprived by violence of all nourishment except my soup and my bread. To escape from this mistreatment, I went to the study room during recess when possible. I hid there under a bench from the fellow students who were coming after me. There, helpless, abandoned by all, I shed tears before God, offering my suffering as a sacrifice, praying and lifting my heart to the cross of His Son through a loving union that, later, I was perhaps never to experience to the same degree. . . . This torture ceased during vacation as well as when school reopened, either because they had tired of pursuing me, or perhaps because I had deserved a certain reprieve on account of some degree of innocence[5]."

This was hardly an isolated occurrence; France allowed students to be brought up in this way. Should anyone be surprised that more than one fully grown man remembers having had a similar experience?

At the age of twelve, Henri made his first communion. "It was," he continued, "my last joyful experience of religion. Soon the shadows thickened around me; a cold night surrounded me on all sides, and in my conscience, I no longer had any sign of God's presence[6]."

What to say about his studies? A good student — although not particularly outstanding in the elementary grades — year by year, he rose higher and higher in rankings of fellow students, up to the end.

In the beginning, Henri had a piece of very good luck. Three months after he entered the school, there arrived from the *École Normale* a young professor, twenty-two years old. In the autumn of 1812, "the child with black eyes and long eyelids" immediately pleased this Monsieur Delahaye. Humbly assuming responsibility for overseeing the elementary class, he felt, it seems, a bit constricted in his task as grammarian. He frequently enjoyed inviting several students to his room to develop their memories by having them recite the poetry of La Fontaine. Henri Lacordaire distinguished himself immediately in this exercise: no effort, no uneasiness, a remarkable memory, clear and easy articulation. He recited the words as if he had written them himself. He did not try to create any special effect. Self-consciousness seemed foreign to him; one would have said he forgot himself entirely. One sensed that a gentle and calm feeling animated him from within. "I did not know," wrote his venerable teacher fifty years later, "I did not know where he had found this calm, this gentleness, under which one could clearly see a strong and resolute will[7]."

Charmed by these talents, Delahaye requested permission to have Henri work directly alongside him during part of the study hours; this initiative lasted three years. Racine succeeded La Fontaine, then Voltaire, some of whose entire tragedies the young student learned by heart; during a recess period, he was learning one act of *Athalie*[8]. Certainly Delahaye did not surmise the genius of his pupil. But Lacordaire always attributed his subsequent successes in secondary school not only to Delahaye's diligent attention at that time, to the careful and freely given counsel he received from him later, but also to the elevated sentiments that had inspired him in their conversations. "As one who loved literature," said Father Lacordaire on his deathbed. "Delahaye sought to inspire in me a taste for literature; an upright and honorable man, he strove to make me gentle, chaste, sincere, and generous, and to tame my high-spirited nature, so lacking in docility. Religion was foreign to him; he never spoke of it to me, and I maintained the same silence about it. . . . He therefore allowed me to slip down the slope that carried my fellow students far from all religious faith; but he kept me on the high summits of literature, and of honor, upon which he had established his own life. The events of 1815 took him from me prematurely. He entered the field of law and became advisor to the court in Rouen. I have always associated the memory of him with everything good that occurred to me."

On his death-bed, Father Lacordaire accused himself of not having been obedient enough in school. This brings to mind the judgment passed on Crébillon[9] by his teachers: *A shrewd boy, but an extraordinary rascal.* Perhaps at times Henri Lacordaire deserved this judgment; but he was generally very docile. The "testimony" of his close friends among his fellow students, in agreement with that of Delahaye, leave no doubt in this regard. But in a contrast so characteristic of him, this habitual docility coexisted with something impetuous and ardent; and his young will revealed itself to be at once unmanageable and resolute. From this perspective, he was more than once a cause for despair among his teachers, whose supervision he frustrated by the most daring of student tricks.

In these early years of his academic life, Henri Lacordaire did not work a great deal, except for the last three months of an academic year (in order to be able to reap a harvest of awards to take back to his mother). He went along with being taken for lazy, but not with being thought of as incompetent. Receiving a low grade in mathematics was enough to drive him to win the first prize in that course the following year. He bet himself that he could do it and he won.

Moreover, it was not only in the field of public speaking, despite what Lacordaire has said about it, that the literary seeds planted by Delahaye began to germinate in his young mind; his grades in *troisième* and *seconde,* which I have before me, also belie this opinion. It was not only in public speaking, I recognize, that he took flight like an eagle. At this juncture, he not only surpassed, but eclipsed, his fellow students. The school in Dijon did not have another example of such stunning superiority. This excellence had such an impact that, from that time forward, the name of Henri Lacordaire gained a kind of celebrity throughout his province. I remember that he who bore that name already seemed to us crowned with glory, when he came and sat next to us on the benches of the School of Law in Dijon, in November 1819.

At this moment, a new horizon opened before him. Meanwwhile, his mode of life changed. "On entering the School of Law," he said, "I returned to my mother's small house and rediscovered the endless charm of domestic life, so tender and modest. In that house, there was nothing superfluous, only a rather austere simplicity, a strict economy, the scent of a bygone age, and something of the sacred, associated with the virtues of a widowed mother of four children, seeing them around her as adolescents already, and predicting that she would leave behind her a generation of honest and perhaps even distinguished men[10]."

Father Lacordaire spoke of his law studies in far too modest terms; it would be wrong to take this modesty at face value. My memories as a fellow student and the academic records of the Faculty of Law protest loudly against the idea that Lacordaire the priest held concerning himself as Henri Lacordaire the lawyer. It was not in him, despite what he himself has said, to be mediocre in anything; there are in our ranks some rivals, but he was always the first among the first.

He had as his teacher of civil law Proudhon[11], a man of some intellectual vigor, but more remarkable for the clarity of his lectures. Unfortunately, the professor was a man of his time. The days of Grotius, of Domat, and of Daguesseau[12] were long gone; the field of law had lost its majesty and grandeur. No more sweeping perspectives, no more natural law, no more public law, not even a trace of the philosophy of law; no mention of its history, and, consequently, no in-depth knowledge of Roman law. It was, in effect, a technical exegesis of law articles simply listed one after the other, with no perspective on the past, no introduction to the eternal profundities of the law, no regard for the general laws of human society. It was a form of teaching suitable for producing tradesmen, but incapable of forming great legal minds, great magistrates, and genuine citizens[13].

Should anyone be surprised that an intelligence as superior as Lacordaire's held this damaged discipline in only lukewarm esteem? His lack of attraction to positive law[14], to private law, and to business law, would bear fruit later on.

"Fortunately, among the 200 students who participated in his courses, he encountered a dozen or so who wanted to become something other than real estate lawyers, and for whom country, glory, and the civic virtues were a more powerful inspiration than the opportunity to amass a vulgar fortune. They recognized each other very quickly through the mysterious sympathy that joins vice with vice, mediocrity with mediocrity, but which also draws together souls of a higher nature, who seek a higher goal. Almost all these young people owed their superiority to Christianity. Even though I did not share their faith, they very much wanted, to include me in their group. Soon, intimate gatherings and long promenades involved us in the greatest issues of philosophy, of history, of politics, and of religion[15]."

Dare I say it? These gatherings, these walks, shaped Henri Lacordaire's destiny. They determined the direction of his spirit and of his will for the rest of his life[16].

In Switzerland, said a traveler, between Neufchâtel and Geneva, there is a fountain whose water separates and flows partly to the north, and partly to the south. The northern waters join up with a stream that ends up in Lake Neufchâtel, whose flows eventually lose themselves in the Rhine and in the North Sea. The southern waters enter into Lake Geneva, which is to say the Rhone, which in turn runs toward the Mediterranean Sea. This fountain is the place that marks the separation of the two rivers. In the same way, the moment I am describing was the point at which Lacordaire's own life changed course. Until then, he had followed the common slippery slope that carried along with it the crowd of our fellow students far — very far — from all religious faith. It seemed, therefore, that he would naturally slide faster and faster down this slope. But Providence had other plans for him. In a bold exercise of his own free choice, Lacordaire threw himself resolutely into the counter-current, without knowing — and neither did we — that by the power of truth, he would be led logically one day to what he earlier had desired least — to the Catholic religion, to the priesthood, to the cloister.

It was 1821. After twenty-two years of war[17], France rejoiced in peace the way one might normally rejoice in a conquest. It was no longer that heroic fervor that was so fruitlessly extravagant in so many battles under the Empire. It was of another, perhaps no less generous, kind: the fervor that creates poets, orators, and genuine citizens. Everything was coming back to life at the same time: institutions, literature, history, philosophy. The public square had de Serre and Lainé, and it would in the future have Berryer and Guizot[18]. Counted among the journalists of the time were Chateaubriand, Bonald, and La Mennais. Lamartine[19] had just published his first *Meditations,* Victor Hugo[20] his first *Odes;* Shakespeare, Schiller, Goethe, Byron, Walter Scott, all suddenly adopted by the French as one of their own, seemed to open to us limitless perspectives, horizons that were both unknown yet attainable. Guizot was preparing the history of the English Revolution, Thiers [21] that of the French Revolution; Augustin Thierry, in labors that eventually cost him his eyesight, created for us a sense of the historical truth about the Dark Ages and the Middle Ages. Cousin dethroned sensualism while translating Plato. It was said[22] that this was like an *instauratio magna* [great restoration] of the human spirit.

Moreover, what sincerity, what disinterestedness in our studies! The young people of that time (I am speaking of those of a certain quality) had a zeal for something greater than obtaining employment or accumulating wealth: they had a passion for what is true, for what is beautiful — a passion for the ideal in everything. Certainly they did not lack illusions, but these were generous illusions. Assuredly, they raised many more problems than they were capable of solving. They tackled many books and many problems that were beyond their abilities, the greatest monuments, certainly, as Father Lacordaire said, the most lofty problems of the human spirit.

But one has to believe that some of this remained with them, and that the young people who leafed through, even superficially, Plato, Aristotle, Cicero, Descartes, Grotius, Montesquieu[23], Pascal, Bossuet, Leibnitz, were able later to call on what they had gleaned from their exposure to these great minds. These were the men with whom Lacordaire associated at age twenty. Who would dare to say that these readings, however rapid and incomplete as they were, did not leave in his mind, so quick to understand and appreciate, an enlightening and fertile impression? As for me, who knew Henri at this period of his life and since then have never lost sight of him for a single day, I do not hesitate to affirm that in politics, philosophy, history, literature, what the *Société d'Études* of Dijon had made him remained with him always up to the end. It was only about religion that he changed, and this was shortly after the sweep that I am discussing and through a kind of personal incubation period of the seeds that the *Société d'Études* had planted in his mind.

This *Société* was divided into four sections: Philosophy, History, Public Law, and Literature. Lacordaire enrolled in all four sections and managed all these studies simultaneously; from the first days, he showed himself peerless in creativity and in writing ability.

The writer in him was the first to become apparent. Twice a month, the four sections, whose particular conferences occurred weekly, came together in a general assembly to listen to literary essays being read aloud.

I will never in my life forget the impression produced in our midst by Lacordaire's first reading. In this albeit youthful composition, his magnificent imagination shone with such splendor that from that day on, we felt his thoughts inhabited a realm superior to ours; his thoughts were clothed in a brilliance that, up to that time, Chateaubriand's prose had only hinted at[24].

In the conferences, he surprised us even more. Each section had a specific program of study. Every week, the agenda addressed one of the program's questions. A member designated in advance, read a report, which introduced and opened the discussion. More than anyone among us, Lacordaire jumped into the fray. The ideas the rest of us held were different from his own. After the report, he often felt the need to protest. It was like the eruption of a volcano. Never since have I encountered anywhere such promptness, such spontaneity, such rich creativity. The flow of ideas and images was to be envied. One would have said that the sentences were already preformed in his mind. *Plenus sum sermonibus, et coarctat me spiritus uteri mei: loquar et respirabo paululum*[25]. This verse from Job gives an accurate picture of Lacordaire at age twenty. He spoke almost as if to deliver himself of a demon from within, and therefore there was an abundance of arguments, a fiery spirit, an incomparable originality and suitability of expression. Ideas and images flowed in an abundance to be envied. Nonetheless, let us restate what characterized this youthful eloquence above all; it was a marvelous but rare gift among the children of Northern France: it was its colorfulness, it was its brilliance.

"We still hear," wrote a member of the *Société d'Études* twenty-five years later, "we still hear these informal speeches full of flashes of inspiration, those spirited arguments filled with unexpected resources, with nimbleness and wit; we still see that sparkling and fixed gaze, penetrating and inscrutable; we still hear that voice—clear, vibrant, trembling with emotion, out of breath—carried away by its own dynamism, hearing only itself, and abandoning itself unreservedly and without constraint to an inexhaustible eloquence of the richest kind. O those beautiful years that went by so quickly, o those precious and magnificent workings of the mind, which foretold an incomparable athlete in God's cause[26]!"

I said previously that the current of ideas among us was not his. Allow me to explain.

Lacordaire graduated from secondary school at the age of seventeen. His faith was destroyed — as he himself said so many times — but he was honest, open, spontaneous, honorable, deeply taken with the humanities and with beautiful things, *having before him, as the guiding torch in his life, the human ideal of glory*[27]. His love of study and the lofty nature of his feelings had saved him from common unruliness. He had remained relatively chaste, without contact with women, as did Euripides' Hippolytus, however without prudery one guesses, and lending his ear to the more-or-less liberal confidences of his friends from school, but disapproving of easy loves, for which he forgave no one.

In his mind as in his heart, Christianity was deficient, lacking its North Star. Therefore, as an adventure, he read everything that came into his hands, with an eagerness that lacked direction; less attracted to the Ancients, as was true of many of his contemporaries, than to the Moderns; less attracted to the seventeenth century than to the following one. It was thus that he devoured the *Contes* of Voltaire[28], and his *Dictionnaire philosophique*. But early on, Jean-Jacques Rousseau[29] attracted his convictions no less. The confession of faith in Voltaire's *Vicaire Savoyard* became his religious gospel, and the Social Contract of Rousseau as his political gospel.

Henri had not experienced in his family, nor had he himself ever known, the feeling that attributes the qualities of majesty and sacredness to royalty. With the exception of his mother, all of his paternal and maternal forebears grieved for the Empire. All had witnessed the Restoration[30] with sorrow. Not that Napoleon was popular in 1813; quite the contrary. But in 1814, the presence of foreigners [i.e., troops from other French Provinces – Trans.] had excited to the highest pitch in the invaded provinces, such as Burgundy and Champagne, the pain of being a humiliated country. People no longer wondered who had provoked these reprisals from Europe, who had drawn them, armed, to our nation's soil. People felt themselves trampled under the enemy's feet; people hoped fervently to drive them back outside our borders; they ardently wished the man who held the sword of France to be triumphant. And, when these wishes were disappointed, even the immense act of generosity that peace represented, due to the return of the Bourbons, did not console Henri Lacordaire for his disappointed hopes. His patriotic imagination took fire, as Lorain has said, on behalf of the exalted person, now vanquished. He found himself, therefore, quite naturally a Bonapartist, and, when opposition to the Restoration by Bonapartists became liberal, he became a liberal; indeed, he was one already, like all of us, because of his classical education. "I naturally found myself a liberal by instinct," he himself wrote. "And as soon as I heard the echo of public events, I was indeed a man of my times in my love of liberty, as I was in my ignorance of God and of the Gospel[31]."

However, let us say right at the start that this liberty which he always loved was never a revolutionary liberty, the freedom to destroy for the sake of destroying, an anarchic freedom; rather, it was an ordered liberty, a regulated and tempered liberty, a liberty represented at that moment by the Duc de Richelieu[32], Lainé, de Serre, and, in the opposition, Camille Jordan and Royer-Collard. Henri Lacordaire was horrified by [the Terror] of 1793. His heroes were not the heroes of the French Revolution — Mirabeau[33], Barnave, Vergniaud — but those of Ancient Greece and Rome, who seemed like giants to us, as were those of Homer. This was the fault of our education more than of our judgment. It was good, to be sure, to have us admire that which was admirable in Greece and Rome; but the error of our teachers was not to make us realize at the same time that there was something missing in pagan cultures — so exclusively vaunted — and to neglect to make us appreciate everything that makes the superiority of Christian civilization incontestable.

The liberty about which Henri Lacordaire dreamed in 1821 was at the same time too abstract — like the liberty of the Social Contract — and too pagan. But it was not full of hatred, and that statement is enough to show how it differed radically from the liberalism of the Revolution. It was to Lacordaire's credit, in his youth as well as in his maturity, to love liberty without a spirit of domination, without partisanship; to love liberty for its own sake, as one loves moral excellence, truth, and justice; to love it also for the benefits it provides; to love it because it fills a deep need in the human spirit and gives dignity to human life.

We understand now what we had in common with Henri and what separated us. We loved liberty as much as he did and for the same reasons; but we did not conceive of liberty as he did. The young people who in 1821 established Dijon's *Société d'Études* were strongly in support of the Restoration, and most of them were Catholic, but they did not wish to make a particular point publicly about this; they depended solely on themselves. No affiliation attached them either to the Congregation, as it was called[34], nor to the *Société des Bonnes Lettres* nor to that of *Good Studies* [unable to detail either one - Trans.], nor to a single one of the works of monarchical or religious proselytizing of the era. All spirit of exclusion was foreign to them, and the proof is, that, from the first day of its existence, the *Société d'Études* included Henri Lacordaire in its ranks.

Nevertheless, however tolerant it was, the majority of the members were royalist and Catholic: royalist, not separating national law from royal law; and Catholic, without ostentation and without shame, without the spirit of domination and without servile and pusillanimous concessions, without indifference as without bitterness. In the end, however, it must be said that this majority was clearly royalist and clearly Catholic.

As a result, it did not accept the eighteenth century as an authority at all, and in this regard, I dare say, it was far ahead of contemporary youth.

I am not looking at this history through a prism; I am not writing solely from memory; the minutes of the meetings of Dijon's *Société d'Études* still exist, and I have them at hand.

As far as philosophy goes, starting in 1821, Condillac[35] was clearly regarded among us as a superficial thinker. Not a single one of us, not Lacordaire any more than the others, defended his doctrine. The less advanced members followed the teaching of Laromiguière, who ascribed to the activity of the soul, as is well known, a completely different role than did his teacher. Opposition to this point of view was based on Reid's book concerning the human spirit[36]; this alone indicates the pioneering quality that animated our group, because who else in the provinces had heard of Reid? (The lessons of Royer-Collard[37] on philosophy in Scotland and Jouffroy's translation of Reid were not published until 1828.) Even Kant, although still not translated [into French], was not entirely unknown to us. Other fellow students boldly went back as far as Bossuet (*De la connaissance de Dieu et de soi-même*) [On the knowledge of God and of oneself][38]. Whatever else was aid about him by a writer of great authority — who was, however, of a generation that did not understand ours — in fact, we needed to defend ourselves a lot more from the excessive ideas of de Bonald[38], de Maistre[40], de la Mennais[41] than from those of the Encyclopedists, particularly discredited in our eyes by the destruction they had wrought.

Consequently there was nothing commonplace in the current of ideas that swept us along; without doubt we were men of our time, but we were also independent of our time.

In literature, we devoured Madame De Staël's l'*Allemagne* [Germany][42], Guizot's [translations of] Shakespeare, de Barante's translations[43] of the dramatic works of Schiller, Schlegel's *Cours de littérature dramatique* [Study of dramatic literature]. While we were inspired by this breath of fresh air from abroad, we sacrificed neither Racine nor Molière to these foreign gods.

Our History section was a reaction against [Voltaire's] *Essai sur les mœurs* [An essay on morality][28]. But if we did not disdain or hate the past, we did not worship it either. We applied ourselves to understanding the older France, not to decry it, but rather to understand it better and the better to serve the France of today. Through a wide range of eras and customs, we assiduously studied the history of our country's interests and opinions; we admired above all the great examples of civic heroism: Juvénal des Ursins[44], la Vacquerie, Achille de Harlay, Matthieu Molé — examples that pagan antiquity did not surpass and that had impressed us very little when we were in school. In a word, we rounded out our philosophical, literary, historical, and political education to the degree that we could.

In Public Law, our gaze was not directed backward to the *ancien régime;* we wanted the Charter of 1814, but supplemented with the legal projects we discussed and deliberated on with all the passion and confidence of youth — projects whose liberalism certainly was not lacking in either sincerity or boldness.

It was in the midst of these heated discussions that, on 5 March 1822, Lacordaire, who usually was the only leader of the whole *Société d'Études*, asked to speak. He renounced the political doctrine of Rousseau as *leading straight to social suicide,* and declared that, persuaded by four months worth of debates, he, too, henceforth was on the side of the Restoration, if it were brought to fulness by liberty, according to the Charter. The acclamation was unanimous. The session was momentarily disrupted; as if propelled by an electrical surge, all the members who were present threw themselves one after the other into Lacordaire's arms. In its eleven years of existence, Dijon's *Société d'Études* had never experienced a day like this one.

Henceforth, Henri was a constitutional royalist, the term used at that time. His attitude toward the place of religion was modified in a marked fashion. Until that point, he had professed Deism, at times with a sharp touch of Voltairian mockery. Even if he did not become a believer immediately, at least the social side of the religious question, the evidence of the good that religion accomplished for man, its actions so manifestly helpful and salutary to people, had an increasing impact on him. His liberalism was frightened by Voltairian thought. "Impiety," he wrote, "leads to depravity. Corrupted morals give birth to corrupting laws. And license leads people in the direction of slavery without their having the time to utter a cry of protest."

He did not stop there. Among the members of the *Société d'Études*, there was one with whom he asked to converse three times a week on the subject of religion up to the end of the school year. He to whom this request was made is still living. He has declared that he had never seen a commitment to the art of discussion equal to that of Lacordaire[45]. Henri put forth his objection with his natural superiority; then he would listen to the response without interrupting. To be sure, it was rare that he gave up unexpectedly, given the many internal resources he had with which to reply. But at the next encounter, if reflection had convinced him, he never missed saying spontaneously: "I was wrong to object to what you said the other day. Let us no longer discuss that matter. But I have another difficulty to propose to you," and he would start to debate a new point.

It was his way of considering every angle before reaching a conclusion. However, a great point had been won: Lacordaire had stopped looking down upon Catholic doctrine. From that time onward, this very lively intellect was at work on the religious question. It does not seem rash to think that the spirit of doubt in him gradually lost ground during this prolonged, amicable controversy, which lasted five months.

Such were his leanings, still uncertain in the realm of religion, when he left Dijon to go to the capital to train for the bar. On 30 November 1822, he took the oath as lawyer before the Paris court[46].

A good and fair man, President Riambourg[47], honorary member of the *Société d'Études*, had recommended Henri Lacordaire to his colleague, Alexandre Guillemin, lawyer to the Councils and to the Appeals Court. Guillemin received the young trainee with open arms. After having praised his protégé, Riambourg wrote that nothing more was needed than to set him on an appropriate path in Paris. Guillemin decided that the first guidance he owed to Henri was to suggest his going regularly to a confessor. Guillemin was astonished when he heard this response: "Oh, sir, I don't do that[48]!"

It was in Henri's character to take seriously everything he did: he gave himself unreservedly to his new situation, attended the conferences of lawyers, and strove to set literature aside in order to focus completely on the study of law. He knew that, in sending him to Paris, his mother had taken on a financial sacrifice above and beyond her resources; it took a while before Lacordaire could lighten the burden by depositing in her hands his first attorney fees. Unfortunately, he was only twenty and a half years old, and a recent ordinance prohibited appearance before the bar under the age of twenty-two[49]. True, this did not bother him greatly. "If I were cited before the disciplinary council," he wrote on 18 January 1823, "it would be an occasion to make a good speech, nothing more. A young lawyer who is condemned for pleading a case with talent before the permissible age could turn this condemnation into honor."

Accordingly, he entered the legal profession full of confidence. He was poor but cheerful, assured as he was that his poor student quarters would one day be visited by glory. To get a picture of Henri Lacordaire at this time, one must reread this page that captures him so well, by the best informed of his biographers, Lorain: "Henri's character and talent burst forth in singular contrasts. This spontaneous spirit was capable of sustained, painstaking, continuous, daily, and persistent work. His energetic nature was patient, anger tamed by gentleness. His impatient and sovereign imagination was capable of detailed, long-term planning. He expressed his viewpoints readily, but also engaged in steadfast reflection and constant adjustment. In his blossoming adolescence, all the seriousness of a mature man was already evident. A mad gaiety, sometimes approaching the buffooneries of a child, was mixed with the meditativeness of a deep thinker. With this passionate temperament, he had a natural attention to detail, a simple elegance; he prized appropriateness and accuracy. When a friend's gaze fell on his work room, he found only careful and balanced arrangement. No disorder among the books, the papers, the writing desk, the pens, even the penknife, placed with a kind of artfulness on the little black table, everything visually pleasing. The same regularity, the same neatness in his manuscripts, in his handwriting, in everything he did, in all he touched." As he was at the age of twenty, so he remained until the end. We have in our possession the erasures of Bossuet and those of Buffon; we will never see those of Lacordaire.

We have already seen that Guillemin treated him as a father would a son. He immediately assigned him some cases from his old law office in the royal court, among others, an important affair of state, in which one of the greatest names in the First Empire was found compromised, and in which Tripier was his adversary. Lacordaire (we shall see why) was never to take on this high-profile case. But meanwhile he appeared several times, always successfully, before the tribunal of the Seine and the bar of the Court of Assizes. The legal briefs that he composed drew attention. Guillemin presented him to the Attorney General of the Appeals Court, Mourre, whose niece Guillemin had married, and this eminent magistrate charged the young trainee with preparing draft indictments. Need we say more? The day that Lacordaire had the good fortune of pleading a case before Berryer, the great lawyer was so impressed that he immediately invited him to visit the following day, conversed with him for an hour, and then said: "You can consider yourself in the top ranks of the bar." (What an impressive prediction, especially from such an eminent source!) "But," he continued, "you have some great pitfalls to avoid, among them the abuse of your facility with words[50]."

Before entering the seminary, Lacordaire confided to me that had only this one conversation with Berryer, whose exact date I have, 8 February 1824. We have just seen in what terms the conversation in question was summarized two weeks later by Lacordaire himself. Thirty-seven years later, the facts were transformed in Berryer's memory. The illustrious orator believed that even then, he had predicted Henri Lacordaire's prominence as an orator in the Notre-Dame Conferences. Accordingly, in receiving Father Lacordaire into the French Academy, Guizot felt justified in attributing these words to Berryer: "Become a priest, and you will become an eminent preacher." I can attest that, the very next day after Father Lacordaire's induction into the Academy, 25 January 1861, Father Lacordaire assured me in the most decisive way that Berryer had never said anything to him remotely resembling this.

This was Henri Lacordaire's situation at the Law Court at the beginning of 1824.

His state of mind at this time is not any less known to us. He exaggerated on his deathbed his differences of opinion with the other young people who belonged to the *Société des Bonnes Études* in Paris. He described himself more accurately in a letter that slightly predated this period[51]: royalist in politics, "without associating to it that harshness and narrowness of vision which dishonors the truth." All of his most intimate correspondence at this moment of his life was written in this vein. These were his political views all the way to the Revolution of 1830. His royalist sympathies were simply an intellectual decision, while the sympathies of the other members were driven by deep feelings. For the most part, they were inclined to exaggerations that he could not subscribe to, and it is the remembrance of that aspect of his relationship to them that stayed with him. Hence the statement in the *Notice* to which I alluded here.

As for religion, Henri loved it already, without exactly admitting it. "I have a soul very much inclined to religion," he added, "and a very unbelieving spirit; since it is in the nature of the mind to allow itself to be subjugated by the soul, it is likely that one day I will be a Christian[52]. I am able to live in solitude but also to hurl myself into the vortex of human affairs, loving calmness when I think about it, and loving bustle when I am living in the midst of it, sometimes taking rest in the country as if I were visiting my favorite castle, yet easily bidding adieu to it when I walk over the Pont Neuf in Paris. I am confirmed in my logical conviction that to try everything and to change one's location do not change one's nature and that there are needs in the soul which this world cannot satisfy. I am restless and come to conclusions so quickly that I am often misled. I have loved some men; but I have not yet loved any women, and I will never love them as they really are[53]."

Nothing, however, outwardly betrayed this early disenchantment. "Everyone in the world predicted a great future for me," Lacordaire said. And indeed he did have choices open to him. He could choose between the bar, which was opening up to him very promising possibilities, or work as a public prosecutor, which was more suited, perhaps, to his talents, and where the patronage of Mourre would not be lacking. But an inner voice was telling him that his calling did not lie there. Indeed, an indefinable malaise (let us allow one of his confidantes to speak of this), a "deepening sense of sadness and the majesty of Christian thought silently rocked the foundation of this soul that could be satisfied by nothing else. For him, society had few charms. He was bored by the theater. He was 'lost, discouraged, alone in the midst of 800,000 men, *weary of everything without having known anything.*' These bouts of melancholy foretold the day of divine matters[54]."

What changes had occurred within him?

He had arrived in Paris at the end of 1822, admiring and loving the ethics of the Gospel (these were the words he used), respecting its ministers, because their influence was beneficial to society. But he had not yet taken a step, it seems, beyond the profession of faith of the Savoyard vicar[28]. However, his mind was preoccupied by religious questions and his conscience troubled by these questions more than he wished to admit to his unbelieving friends. The latter, consumed by the defiant attitude of the times, would not concede that one could have an untainted bond to Catholicism. They also were watching with unconcealed anxiety this disciple of Jean-Jacques [Rousseau] coming under the influence of Riambourg and receiving the patronage of Guillemin.

Henri did his best to reassure them. But it was not in his nature to hamper either the free flight of his intellect in its search for truth, nor the sincerity of his communication. During his long evenings in solitude, the conversations on religious topics in Dijon during the summer of 1822 came back to mind. Once again he tackled the lofty questions that have always preoccupied the greatest intellects. He meditated on them deeply in the secret of his conscience without confiding in anyone about them; it was in this sense that he could truthfully say that no living person had played a role in his conversion. Gerbet, with whom the members of Dijon's *Société d'Études* had corresponded, had welcomed him warmly when he arrived in Paris, but their relationship was never close, and they did not speak at all about religion when they were together. Lacordaire repeatedly confirmed this. The work of God was nonetheless operating in this noble soul.

In 1823, he spent vacation with his family, keeping his secret. From that point on, he was profoundly transformed:

the prejudices in his mind against the Catholic faith that had accumulated over many years had melted like the snow under the sun. "I did not really have any objections," he said to me later, "but I was not yet entirely sure that this would be the definitive state of my mind. I dreaded that doubts would once again arise someday. I was," he added, "like the Austrian army in 1813, on the opposite side of the Rhine;[55] not a single French bayonet opposed their passage, but the Austrians did not trust them, and they were there for six weeks without crossing over. And so, before declaring my conversion, even to my mother, I let six months go by."

This moment is so significant in the life of Father Lacordaire, that I can do no better than to let him speak in his own words up to his entrance into the seminary.

Once converted, he began to think, naturally, of gradually preparing his friends for this news — friends who had remained skeptics or Deists. On 7 February 1824, he wrote to one of them, "Would you have believed that I am becoming a Christian day by day? It is a remarkable thing, this gradual change in my point of view. I have been brought to the point of faith, and at the same I have never been more of a philosopher. 'A little philosophy can distance one from religion; a lot of philosophy, however, brings one back.' An important truth."[56]

Then, on 22 February:

"Yes, my dear Lorain, I do believe. I quibble with one phrase in your letter where you doubt my sincerity and good faith. If my letter were not so wild (this is an allusion to several jokes that preceded this passage), I would speak to you about my beliefs, and what led me to this point. How did it come to be that my friends do not understand me? They were skeptical about my political conversion and saw it as a skillful calculation; now they mock my religious conversion and invite me to wait for the Jesuits to overthrow the *Université*[57]."

Finally, on 15 March:

"I have been struck in recent days by an idea even more extraordinary than this. Let me be nailed live to a wooden cross — if I have not thought seriously about being a village pastor. Illusions of the moment! Phantoms that disappear so quickly! The need to shake oneself up in life's Mount Etna!

"You ask me to share my thoughts on religion. But I do not have space in this letter today. I will say only that *I have arrived at my religious beliefs through my social convictions*, and that today, nothing seems to me more demonstrable than the fact that society is a basic necessity. Consequently, Christianity is divinely inspired, because it is the only means capable of bringing society to its perfection. It transforms man with all his weaknesses and it also transforms the social order in all its various conditions[58].

"My dear friend, I have always searched for truth in good faith while leaving aside all pride — which is the only way to find truth. If my opinions owed something to the circle of friendships in which I moved (a reference to the walks of the summer of 1822), it is at the same time true that I never submitted to any but my own reflections and I arrived at insights independently."

A bit later, when the truth was completely out, Lacordaire confided in a letter to another friend:

"My religious sacrifice doubtless surprised you, because it hit you like a thunderbolt for which nothing had prepared you; because you knew me as I was when I left Dijon, and not as the man I had become. But my thinking developed over a period of eighteen months."

"It is not, my dear friend, that I have read many works to form my conviction; I did not touch a single one. It is not that I experienced a gradual and imperceptible seduction by the people around me. Not even four times have people talked to me about religion[59]. I found faith more as a memory than as a new gift, as a consequence of principles already acquired than as a new creation of my thinking. I remember one night reading the Gospel of St. Matthew, and I wept: when one weeps, one believes not long after[60]."

In his correspondence with Lorain, he went into more depth:

"When I examine the course of my thoughts over the past five years[61], the point where I began, the degrees and latitudes which my mind traveled, the definitive result of this slow progress bristling with obstacles, I am astonished and feel moved to the adoration of God.

"My dear friend, this makes no sense except for him who has passed from error to truth, who is aware of all the previous ideas he had seized upon, came to understand their connections, the strange alliances, the gradual linking as he now ties them to the different stages in his move toward certainty. A sublime moment it is, when the last trace of light penetrates into the spirit, and attaches to a common center the truths which are scattered there. There is always such a distance between the moment that follows and the moment that precedes, between what one was previously and what one is after, that the word *grace* was created to express this miraculous turn of events, to express this illumination from above. It is like watching a man move forward haphazardly, blindfolded; as the blindfold is loosened bit by bit, he catches a glimpse of daylight, and, in the instant that it falls from his face, he finds himself facing the sun[62]."

This is the very language we hear from the lips of Father on his deathbed:

"No book, no man, was God's instrument in my regard. No Christian sermon captured my attention. After eighteen months, I was alone in Paris as I had been on the first day, a stranger to all parties, with no tide to sweep me along, with no particular influence to enlighten my mind. . . . Without doubt, I was suffering from a difficult and total isolation; but this was part of the divine perspective concerning me. Painfully, I crossed this desert of my youth, not knowing that it would have its Sinai, its flashes of light and its taste of water.

"It is impossible to say on what day, at what hour, and how, my faith that had been lost ten years earlier, reappeared in my heart like a torch that had never been extinguished. Theology teaches us that there is another light than that of reason, another impetus other than nature. 'The spirit of God,' says the apostle John, 'blows where it wills, and you do not know whence it comes, or whither it goes[63].' An unbeliever the night before, a Christian the following morning, certain with an invincible certainty, this was not a rejection of reason, suddenly enchained in an incomprehensible servitude. Rather, it was the expansion of reason's clarities, a view of everything under a more extended outlook and a more penetrating light. Neither was it the submissive abasement of character under a strict and frozen rule, but the development of its energy through an action whose origins lay beyond nature. Neither was it, finally, the abnegation of the heart's joys, but rather their fulness and increase. Man in his fullness remained intact; moreover, no one other than God did this.

"Whoever has not known such a moment has not known the life of man. All Christians are more or less familiar with this state; but it is never more vivid and more gripping than on a day of conversion[64]."

For the first time, we have just embraced one by one, with a single glance, all the levels of the wonderful change that was coming to an end. Make no mistake: man acts in full freedom; but God leads him. It was God, who had given Lacordaire a Christian mother. It was God who introduced him, at age eighteen, to an organization of young Christians, intelligent men, who did honor to their faith by their behavior and their character. It was God who later created for him, in the middle of Paris, a solitude of mind and heart, completely receptive to memories of the domestic hearth, of maternal tenderness, and of the joys of the first communion, as *an historical and social manifestation of Christianity*[65]. Finally, it was God who struck the rock and caused to spring from it life-giving water.

The miracle was not to end there.

For someone who rediscovers Christianity, what could be more logical than to devote his entire being to the apostolate of the reclaimed truth! As it happens, one of the gifts Lacordaire had received from God was an ardent sense of logic which rushed forward in a single bound to the very conclusion of a situation, to the heart of a feeling or of an idea. As Lorain said, for Lacordaire, being a Christian was to be a priest; and being a priest was later to be a monk. Lacordaire was aware that, to a man, all his family would be against this decision, along with his unbelieving friends (and perhaps others also) — finally, maybe, even his mother. None of this could stop him.

"Once a Christian," said Father Lacordaire, "the world did not vanish from view, but rather it grew larger even as I did. Instead of a vain drama and short-lived ambitions that were disappointed or satisfied, I saw the world as a great invalid in need of help, and to me there was nothing comparable to the joy of serving it under the watchful eye of God, with the Gospel and the Cross of His Son." In short, Lacordaire saw himself as called from above. "The desire for the priesthood," he said, "overwhelms me as a natural consequence of my own salvation. The desire was strong, passionate, spontaneous, and unshakable. Not once in forty years, through all the vicissitudes of a turbulent life, did I have feelings of regret for it[66]."

That is the truth. The whole truth. In this account, one can tell there is not an iota of fiction. And, in fact, before entering Saint-Sulpice [seminary], Henri Lacordaire had loved no woman other than his mother. Many of his fellow students and his contemporaries outlive him; not one of them will contradict this: *He who saw it has borne witness — his testimony is true*[67]. In giving himself to the Church, Henri Lacordaire brought to God a passionate soul, but also unblemished morals, an ascetic youth and a virgin heart.

Having made the resolution, all that remained was to obtain his mother's consent. Henri sought this toward the end of March[68]. But Madame Lacordaire had placed other hopes in her son. She was not lacking in ambition for this son, who for a long time had been the pride of the family. Her dreams for Henri included assuming the mantle of Daguesseau; she counted on him for honor and for security and peace in her old age. She feared the possibility of his carrying the Gospel to regions where she could not follow. Unprepared for the prospect of his leaving the world, resigning herself to this idea was all the more difficult because she felt justified in questioning a vocation that seemed all too suddenly arrived at and insufficiently tested. She wrote him six letters, suffused with both joy at the conversion of her Augustine[69] and sadness at the prospect of losing him. But in the final analysis, she was *Christian, courageous and strong.* Not wanting to interfere with the call of Providence, after five weeks she agreed to the wishes of her son[70].

In the meantime, Lacordaire informed Guillemin of his desire to enter the seminary of Saint-Sulpice and of his hope in obtaining a half-scholarship to defray as long as he could the expenses to his mother, who up until now had made so many sacrifices on his behalf (they seemed a loss at this

97

point). Guillemin led him to one of the Grand Vicars of the archdiocese of Paris, Borderies, who later became the bishop of Versailles. Borderies, of holy memory, was a congenial individual. According to Guillemin, Borderies took Lacordaire aside, doubtlessly for a more thorough questioning, and brought him back "with the joy of a good pastor; a joy that was shining forth in the midst of tears[71]." Borderies lodged at the archbishop's palace, a magnificent residence that was savagely destroyed in full view of the armed National Guard, on 13 February 1831[72]. He immediately introduced Lacordaire to the archbishop, Msgr de Quélen. The prelate received the young neophyte with kindness and good grace. "He asked me," said Father Lacordaire, "what diocese I was from, and whether it was indeed my will to join his. When I responded in the affirmative, he said he would write the bishop of Dijon, and also invited me, for my part, to do the same. Then he added: 'At the bar you were defending perishable causes; in the future you will be defending causes of eternal justice. You will see justice appraised inconsistently by men; but above, there is a court of appeals where justice will be definitively served[73].' "

The archbishop of Paris could not afford to cover the costs of the ecclesiastical education of a young man destined for another diocese. So, before allowing Lacordaire to leave, Borderies, without losing a moment, had Lacordaire write a letter whose contents he dictated. In the most simple terms, the letter asked the bishop of Dijon for his release on the grounds that the signatory, born in Recey-sur-Ource, "had obtained from the kindness of the archbishop of Paris a half-scholarship to the seminary of Saint-Sulpice[74]." The point of this maneuver was obvious. We do not know what postscript the archbishop of Paris had written in his own hand; but it is safe to presume that he wrote in a manner that would ensure success — which, moreover, came without delay. De Quélen, enjoyed the highest authority at the heart of the French Church. The bishop of Dijon, de Boisville, happy to have this opportunity to please the archbishop, sent his *exeat* without asking for any further information. The prelate, who had not taken possession of his diocese until after Henri had left for Paris, and who, moreover, lived among us in a rather patrician setting, had never heard Lacordaire's name before; he did not for an instant doubt that this man was but an obscure cleric, born in a remote corner of his diocese, but reared in Paris at the expense of archiepiscopal charity. "What else would you expect?" he said, later excusing himself for this perception. "He wrote me a letter in which the only things lacking were spelling errors; I took him to be the greatest simpleton of my diocese[75]."

ENDNOTES

Attention: Original footnotes of the author in this (38) and other chapters were transformed into endnotes. Additional endnotes by the translators are noted by bold-faced numerals.

---

1. See the official registration of his baptism, Appendix IX, page 534.
2. Today Bussières-lès-Belmon.
3. *Notice sur le rétablissement en France de l'Ordre des Frères Prêcheurs*. [The final testament of Father Lacordaire, dictated on his deathbed — See Internet: www.worksoflacoraire.com: "Overview of the Order of Friars Preachers..." Referred to as *Notice* in notes.

4.- French educational system . . .**Primary**, 5 levels; **middle school** ["collège"],4 levels [called 6th form, 5th form, 4th form, 3rd form = British style]; **lycée**: last three years of secondary education [3 levels, called 2nd, 1st, and terminal]. - See Internet for more details.

5. *Notice.*

6. *Notice.*

7. Letter from Delahaye, 20 March 1862.

8. Testimony of Guérard, of the Institute, one of Henri's fellow students at the school in Dijon.

9. Crébillon, Claude (1707-1777): capable writer but his works were excessively licentious. – Son of Prosper Jolyot dit Crébillon.

10. *Notice.*

11. Pierre Joseph Prudhon (1809-1865), socialist and author of famous theories about property and founder of an insurance system. He criticized communism, the sovereignty of the state, the economic system, the proletariat,

12. Grotius, Hugo (1583-1645): Dutch scholar and statesman; founder of modern science of international law.

   Domat, Jean (1625-1696); law scholar.

   Daguesseau: lawyer.

13. *Notice.*

14. As opposed to natural law, positive law studies the laws of a particular time, place, and culture.

15. *Notice.*

16. "These minds whose thinking transformed my own, and *which led me to where I am.*" — Lacordaire, letter of 29 December 1829 to Foisset.

17. That is, the series of Napoleonic wars.

18. De Serre, Olivier (1539-1619); founder of French agronomy.

   Berryer, Antoine (1790-1868); top-notch lawyer.

Opposed to the Second Empire.

Guizot, François (1787-1874); statesman, French historian, Minister. Led to the 1848 Revolution.

19. Chateaubriand, François René de C. (1764-1848); vicomte, illustrious writer. Later, Minister of Foreign Affairs.

Bonald, Louis de B. (1754-1840); vicomte; writer and philosopher; defender of the monarchy and of religion.

La Mennais, Félicité Robert de L. (1782-1854); French philosopher and theologian; brilliant writer. Originally taught that the Church was the depository of all truth; later condemned by the Church. - See website, www.worksoflacordaire.com, Reflections on the Philosophical System of Father de La Mennais

Lamartine, Alphonse Marie-Louis de Prat de L. (1790-1869); poet and politician.

20. Hugo, Victor (1802-1885); illustrious French write, poet, defender of democracy.

Scott, Sir Walter (1771-1832); writer.

21. Thiers, Adolphe (1797-1877); French historian, statesman, minister. In and out of government.

Thierry, Jacques Nicolas Augustin (1795-1856); French historian; promoter of historical studies.

Cousin, Victor (1792-1867); philosopher and politician; member of the Eclectic School.

22. Caro, *Revue des Deux-Mondes*, 15 March 1865. — Article entitled "*De 1820 à 1830.*"

23. Montesquieu, Charles de Secondat, baron La Brède et de M. (1689-1755); celebrated French author, philosopher. Supported the separation of powers, and brought moderation to the passion of progress.

Leibnitz, Gottfried Wilhelm (1646-1716); illustrious German philosopher and genius; mathematician.

Pascal, Blaise (1623-1662); French thinker; illustrious

mathematician and scientist. Follower of Jansenius at Port Royal.

24. Chateaubriand, vicomte François-René de C. (1768-1848); writer of novels, painter, poet. Great influence on nascent Romanticism. [See 19, above.]

25. *I am full of words, the spirit within me constrains me!... I must speak, that I may find relief* (Job 32:18, 20). Herbert G. May and Bruce M. Metzger, eds. The Oxford Annotated Bible, Revised Standard Version (New York: Oxford University Press, 1977). Unless otherwise noted, all scriptural passages in English are quoted from this source. — Associate's *Note* [cdt].

26. Lorain, *Le R. P. Lacordaire*, p. 12.

27. *Notice*.

28. Voltaire, François-Marie Arouet dit V. (1694-1778); writer, literary critic. Looked to the past. Open enemy of the Church. In his Essay on morals, he propounded religious tolerance, liberty of conscience, and improvement of social life. — In his "Savoyard vicar": Voltaire approved of the vicar's profession of faith only on the pages devoted to the definition of natural religion [involving the mind and the heart].

29. Rousseau, Jean-Jacques (1712-1778); romantic and controversial writer; social theorist. Source of French Romanticism; looked to the future. Wrote the *Social Contract*. His view of the excellence of nature was a chimera. Inaugurated the French Revolution.

30. "Restoration" refers to the period 1814-1830, when the Bourbons were restored to the throne of France. "The nation at large received them with reluctance, chiefly for three reasons: 1. because they had been placed on the throne by foreign arms (Louis XVIII openly acknowledged that he owed his throne to the English; 2. because, while they had been absent from France, it had undergone a total change, and they had thus become strangers to the country in which the principles of the Revolution were permanently established; 3. because they brought back with them an obsolete *noblesse*, opposed to the whole spirit and tendency of modern French politics." Quotation from "History of France, from the Restoration of the Bourbons, to the Declaration of Louis-Philip, King of the French; from 1814 to 1830," *Enclyclopædia Americana: A Popular Dictionary of Arts, Sciences, Literature, History, Politics, and Biography*, volume 5, ed. Francis Lieber (Philadelphia: Desilver, Thomas & Co., 1836), p. 219. Accessed 5 February 2011, at http://books.google.com/books?id=HtcuAQAAIAAJ&pg=PA219&dq=restoration+france+bourbons&hl=en&ei=RG5NTdWXJ8v2gAev0KzhDw&sa=X&oi=book_result&ct=result&resnum=3&ved=0CDEQ6AEwAg#v=onepage&q=restoration%20france%20bourbons&f=false. [cdt]

31. *Notice*.

32. Richelieu, Armand-Jean du Plessis, duc de R. (1585-1642); cardinal, statesman, Prime Minister; skilled politician. Reformed the finances, the army, the legislature. Supported royal absolutism. Founded the French Academy [the Forty Immortals].

Jordan, Camille (1771-1823): writer, politician. Doctrinaire under the Restoration.

Royer-Collard, Pierre-Paul (1768-1845); philosopher, political orator. Also, doctrinaire under the Restoration.

33. Mirabeau, Honoré-Gabriel (1749-1791); French orator. Led a troubled life. His character was inferior to his talent.

Vergniaud, Pierre Victurien (1752-1793); skilled orator and politician.

Barnave, Joseph (1761-1793); orator the Constituent Assembly.

34. Congregation: a society founded in 1801 to intensify religious life, under the Restoration. It fell with the fall of Charles X.
35. Condillac, Étienne Bonnal de C. (1715-1780); philosopher of the Sensualist School [knowledge based on the senses].
   Laromiguière, Pierre (1756-1837); one of the founders of Eclecticism.
36. Reid, Thomas (1710-1796); philosopher in Scotland; held that knowledge arose from internal experience and common sense.
37. Royer-Collard, Pierre-Paul (1768-1845); philosopher, political orator. Also, doctrinaire under the Restoration.
   Jouffroy, Théodore (1796-1842); French spiritualist philosopher. Introduced Scottish philosophy to France.
38. Bossuet, Jacques-Bénigne (1627-1704); illustrious French orator and writer.
39. Viscomte Louis de Bonald (1754-1840) was a significant figure in the Bourbon Restoration and also a counter-Revolutionary theorist.
40. Joseph-Marie, Comte de Maistre (1753-1821) was a lawyer, diplomat, and philosopher who believed in the hereditary monarchy. — A writer; supported both civil and religious authority.
41. De La Mennais: see 19, above.
42. Mme de Staël, Anne-Louise-Germaine Necker (1766-1817). Noted for her intellect and her writings. Disciple of J. J. Rousseau.
43. Barante, baron Guillaume-Prospère Bruguière de B. (1782-1866); historian and statesman.
   Schiller, Johann Christoph Freidrich von S. (1759-1805); writer, tragic poet, historian. Of rare originality and lively imagination.

44. Juvenal des Ursins [Jean 1er] (1360-1431). Claimed descent from the Orsini family in Italy. French judge.

Vacquerie, Auguste (1819-1895); writer, journalist, drama writer of the Romantic School.

Harlay, Achille de H. (1536-1619); first President of the Paris Parliament; supporter of royalty.

Molé, Matthieu (1584-1656), son of Edward. President of the Parliament. Held an important role in the *Fronde* ["slingshot"], a civil war, 1648-1653, regarding the financial policies of Cardinal Mazarin.

45. Guillemin gave the same testimony about him (*Souvenirs du Ciel*, p. 249): "Monsieur Lacordaire had an admirable way of discussing religion; he forgot himself completely in search of truth alone."

46. Letter to Lorain, 2 December 1822.

47. Riambourg (Jean-Baptiste-Claude), born in Dijon in 1776. He was one of the first to enter the *École Polytechnique* after it was established. But as an orphan, without fortune, the sole source of support for his family, he was forced to give up mathematics and turn his sights to the bar. Law was not yet taught in a systematic way, and thus he was forced, as were all his contemporaries, to supplement with his vigorous intelligence courses that were incomplete and improvised. It was in them that his penetrating mind and the power and rectitude of his judgment burst forth. He had the gift of elevating the questions that he touched upon, and the balance of all his faculties was not any less marvelous than their breadth. Also his reputation grew rapidly, and, when he became counselor to the court of Dijon in 1812, public opinion ratified this choice. However, indignant about the return of Napoleon in 1815, without any fanfare he sacrificed his position to his political convictions, even though he had not received any favors from the Restoration. Named Attorney

General on account of his good example, albeit unwittingly, his allegiance was to the purest form of royalism, tempered by an independence conformed to the firmness of his character just as to the incomparable docility of his virtue. In this battle post, he could not bend to political exigencies, and it was felt necessary to appoint him to the chair of President of the Chamber in 1818. One might say that this was his natural place, so much was he born the judge, so much did he seem called to these austere functions by the superior rectitude of his judgment, his boundless zeal for the good and the just — shining qualities that were joined to an exquisite tact that always emphasized the positive. At the accession of the royalist ministry of 1822, he refused to take any steps to regain his position as Attorney General. In 1830, he decided he could not take a new oath.

No issue was foreign to President Riambourg—in science, in jurisprudence, even in the arts. However, he preferred philosophy, in which he showed great superiority. His works, put in order after his death by the author of this book, appeared in a second edition in 1850: a volume in- $4°$ * in the Migne** collection. Deeply imbued with Christian principles, a good mathematician, a consummate logician, he found quick and sure ways to demonstrate through philosophy the great truths of Catholicism. His treatise, *Du Rationalisme et de la Tradition* [Rationalism and Tradition], was welcomed by the religious world with great acclaim.

In Dijon, he was known for his boundless kindness, particularly as regards youth; for this, he was revered. However, Monsieur Riambourg's way of expressing himself, always clear and judicious, essentially lacked scope. His imperturbably calm conversation lacked warmth. As a result the true superiority of his mind — which was overly-controlled — escaped the notice of many people.

* In 4° [in-quarto]: format of a book whose pages are folded into 4 sheets, forming 8 pages. - A book in this format.

** Migne, abbé Jacques-Paul (1800-1875). Founder of the journal *Univers*; editor of theological encyclopedias.

48. This answer was given to me in these very words by Guillemin, in Dijon, several days later.

49. Royal ordinance of 20 November 1822.

50. Letter to Lorain, 23 February 1824.

51. To Fontaine, 10 November 1823. - No clarity found concerning the two societies: *Bonnes Lettres* and *Bonnes Études* and their relationship.

52. From that time forward, he was more [of a Christian] than he wished to admit; perhaps it would be more accurate to say that this was already an admission of sorts.

53. Letter to Fontaine, a lawyer in Paris, 17 November 1823. This letter is cited in its entirely by Father Chocarne. The friendship would develop no further because Lacordaire entered the seminary six months later.

54. Lorain, pp. 16-17.

55. Battle of Dresden, 1813, during which Napoleon was forced to retreat. Paris was captured in March 1814.

56. *Letter to Monsieur Lorain* — Who does not know the statement by Bacon (1561-1626) to which Lacordaire makes allusion here: *Parvi haustus philosophiæ faciunt incredulum magni christianum*. In Bacons's words: "A little philosophy inclineth man's mind to atheism, but depth in philosophy bringeth man's mind about to religion."

— Roger Bacon (1561-1626) espoused the method of experimentation, in an attempt to put science back into philosophy. — Latin source: *Parvi haustus philosophiae faciunt incredulum magni christianorum*.

57. The University: The body of administrators appointed by the state to oversee the entire educational system. - This is the

body Lacordaire fought against in his "Freedom of Instruction".

58. Letter to Lorain. — The idea is barely sketched but I believe in the concluding syllogism: If society is from God, and if Christianity is the only religion that civilizes, how could Christianity not come from God? All the religions that man has devised for himself: polytheism, mohammedanism, led to the degradation of man. If this is not the case with Christianity is that not proof that it does not come from man but from God? On this point, who would have known the conditions of the genuine civilization of man if not the One Who made man?

Moreover, when Lacordaire announced his conversion to an unbelieving royalist friend, he had to present the truth to him in a most appropriate [and personal] way. "One finds it unusual," he told him later, "that I was led to religious ideas through political ones; the more I grow, the more I discover the appropriateness of that path. Besides, one can arrive at Christianity through all the paths, because it is the center of all truth."

59. This has been completely confirmed by the witness of Guillemin: *Le Père Lacordaire*, pp. 78-79. See also p. 8.

60. Letter to Boissard, 22 May 1824. — Note: This letter has also been attributed to Chateaubriand.

61. Since his entrance in the School of Law.

62. Letter of 11 May 1824.

63. Full text of John 3:8 reads: "The wind blows where it will, and you hear the sound of it, but you do not know whither it goes; so it is with every one who is born of the Spirit."

64. *Notice.*

65. See *Considerations sur le système philosophique de M. de La Mennais.* – See endnote 19, above:

Reflections on the Philosophical System of Father de La Mennais.

66. *Notice.*
67. John 19:35.
68. Letter to Foisset, 2 May 1824.
69. In the *Notice,* Father [Lacordaire] describes his mother's opposition as occurring after his contacting the archdiocese about entering the priesthood. On this point, his memory in 1861 was incorrect, as is proven by this phrase in a letter he wrote to Foisset on 2 May 1824: "I informed my mother about my project at the end of March." Besides, I have here a letter from Madame Lacordaire to her son, dated 31 March 1824, responding to the first confidences about his vocation. Certain of his mother's eventual consent, he did, however, write to the bishopric of Dijon before obtaining her official approval.
70. St. Augustine (354-430): after a stormy childhood, and following years of his mother's tears and prayers, he was converted by St. Anselm. Religious apologist; philosopher: worked to reconcile faith and reason. Mentioned his mother, St. Monica, in his *Confessions.*
71. *Souvenir du Ciel,* by Guillemin, p. 253.
72. See www.worksoflacordaire.com on web: Fundraising for the rebuilding of the Archbishop's residence in Paris.
73. *Notice.*
74. *Souvenir du Ciel,* by Guillemin, p. 253.
75. "He had a right to feel that way," said Father Lacordaire, with a smile, at the *Institut de Sorèze.* "Think about it, I started my letter using the present participle."

Chapter II

Early Years of Priesthood

Seminary — First indications of a monastic vocation; thoughts of becoming a Jesuit — priestly ordination and the refusal of the position of auditor of the Roman Rota — Plan to emigrate to the United States — The spirit of the French clergy under the Restoration.

On 12 May 1824, Henri Lacordaire's twenty-second birthday, Gerbet[1], the bishop of Perpignan (now deceased), and de Salinis, the archbishop of Auch (also deceased), took him to Issy, a branch of the Major Seminary in Paris, directed, as the Major Seminary itself was, by the Society of Saint-Sulpice. The Sulpicians received Lacordaire cooly, perhaps to test his vocation, but perhaps also because of the two individuals who introduced him, were widely known to be associated with Father Félicité [Félix] de La Mennais. The Sulpicians had little taste for either La Mennais' philosophical ideas, or for his extreme political and religious convictions[2]

The new seminarian did not pay any heed to this reception. He was content no longer to be breathing the air of the world, and he felt renewed physically and spiritually in the midst of the beautiful countryside, screened by the wooded heights of Meudon, of Bellevue, of Sèvres, and of Saint-Cloud. Issy reminded him of Brussières. His life of twenty-two years was in blossom. He was beside himself with the joy at the implementing of his sacrifice[3].

At the same time, he tried increasingly to have his friends understand and accept what he had just done. "Once my religious beliefs were crystallized, without my saying anything to anyone," he wrote on 22 May, "I felt movements within me that were carrying me away from the world. At first, I resisted easily enough; I was in a contented mood; my name was already known among those new to the bar; small successes had augured greater successes. But self-love kept me tied to the earth. However, the *interior voice* that called me suddenly became more insistent, yet at the same time more muffled. This driving force had a quality of gentleness and tenderness, a vague premonition of the delights of solitude and the service of God. Note, my dear friend, that this could not have been the result of the difficult isolation that a young man often experiences in Paris. I lived at that time with one of our compatriots, who was no stranger to me and to the memories of my childhood, nor to the more recent memories of my foray into the world[4].

"His character was somewhat similar to mine, and the differences added a certain charm to our relationship, the longevity of which was particularly welcome in Paris, that abyss where people seem only to catch a glimpse of each other. I was no longer alone either during my walks or during my meals, neither was I alone at the hour when one retires, nor at the hour when one gets up to go about one's everyday activities. For all that, this union, which warmed two hearts once again, did not prevent the discomfort from worsening; I became more and more confused and finally at peace when my sacrifice was implemented."

"My friend, I have not fled from other people and the repellent aspects of society. I am well aware that one cannot flee them because they are omnipresent. But I stripped them of everything that could make them bitter to the taste. Pride is the center of everything in the world. It disturbs the world and poisons its joys — to our torment. This passion causes man more suffering than joy. This burden was lifted from me by that influence that one accepts only in the innermost sanctuary of the heart. You may feel that this was only a secondary motive, but I am speaking to you about this because our friends in common have mentioned this to me.

"You do not know, my dear friend, how sweet my solitude is. You should not suspect me of wanting to mislead you and conversing with you about a happiness that I do not truly feel. It is only in the world that we put on a smile while there are tears in our heart. Well! My character—which heretofore has been melancholy, serious—has faded away as I experience the peace of this house. The only reason I realized I was filled with joy was that everyone has remarked on it. Here is a source of happiness that will last for three years."

In fact, theological studies lasted only three years. But Lacordaire did not want to throw himself into these studies without preparation. And, besides, would it have been wise for him to rush into the middle of a course that had already been in process for the previous six months? He wanted instead to complete his philosophical studies. During the five months that remained before the next academic year, he sacrificed vacation and rest to devote himself in solitude to the basics of theology. He had returned to Issy on 12 May. On 12 June, the evening preceding the feast of the Holy Trinity, he received the tonsure, and he wrote to a friend: "This is forever!"

All of his letters from this period reveal a deep and radiating joy.

"Do you know," he writes, " what one of my joys is? It is to relive my youth again, but now with the resources that generally belong to someone who is more mature. In secondary school, one is very much a child. He does not understand the value of man or of things. He lacks the necessary thought structure to know how to choose friends properly. Then, when he is thrust out into the world, he is no longer equal to the task of forming solid relationships, whether it was because men no longer live in close relationship, or whether it is because self-interest and self-love slip into the most unsullied relationships, or whether it is because the heart is less at ease in the midst of noise and social activity. Friendship has more of a grip when there are one-hundred forty young people who see each other incessantly, whose lives overlap in all ways, who all seem like blossoms that are specially chosen and set apart[5]."

These words have much truth to them. Very few people have brought to friendship the infinite tenderness of soul that Lacordaire brought — a tenderness all the more uncontaminated and exquisite for its freedom from the yoke of the senses. De Montalembert[6] described monastic friendship. He translated, with exquisite charm, some wonderful passages written by Saint Anselm about a monk who was dear to him. But I dare say that there was nothing in these passages more tender and better expressed than two letters written at the age of twenty-three by Lacordaire to a fellow students at Saint-Sulpice— the first to try to keep him in the seminary, the other beseeching him to remain faithful to God after he had decided to leave the seminary.

At Issy, Lacordaire charmed all his rivals. He enjoyed being well-liked; he retained some of the congeniality of the world, and he still exhibited many of the social graces that had disappeared during that century. More outgoing, more communicative than he had been before his state of life changed, satisfied with his future, whatever it turned out to be, dreaming of a life of poverty the way he used to dream of a life of acclaim, he lived quietly and contentedly both with his colleagues and with himself. How happy he felt that few things distracted him but that little nothings could warm his heart! What joy he took in his cherished solitude! How he delighted in the gardens of the Seminary!

"When I walk in the fresh air of the morning, I enjoy thinking about the progress of the fruits that I have seen the previous evening and will see again the following day. The cherries no longer show me their red heads peeking through the green of their leaves. It is now the turn of the plums, the apricots, the peaches, which are beginning to take on a slight hue. Above all, I like the vegetable garden; seeing a simple leafy plant is for me a great pleasure. I can see the greens, very small, arranged in staggered rows, in a visually appealing way. They increase; the large green leaves are tied close together with strands of straw. They turn yellow, and a few days later, there is nothing left for them—neither dew nor sunlight.

"In the midst of this varied contemplation, which gently distracts me from more serious thoughts, I feel drawn upwards by admiration and love toward the mysterious intellect which revealed itself to us by such a magnificent creation, and which has placed in the smallest leaf of a tree marvels that are inaccessible to man's powers of reasoning.

"The memory of my father is associated with all these feelings. My father, who loved gardens very much, handed down that taste to me[8]."

Who could mistake the intimate serenity of these tones? When one has read similar letters, how could one doubt the sincerity, the purity of sentiment that inspired them? How would it be possible to doubt for an instant the supernatural vocation of the man who wrote them?

Nonetheless, the seminary can have its trials. Lacordaire, as we have seen, passed from the life of his century into that of the sanctuary with no preparation for the transition, with no one to initiate him into the set of serious attitudes and strict habits that constitute the Sulpician life. He had not sufficiently divested himself of the older man so that, without his wishing it and without his even being aware, his demeanor stood out markedly from that of the other seminarians. Thus, for example, giving in to a very lively inclination of his, he sought out particular friendships, sensibly prohibited by Olier[9]. In periods of recreation, he loved noise, lots of movement, two things contrary to the taste of the Society of Saint-Sulpice. His gaiety at times seemed even eccentric. During class, it was completely different. The strict jouster of Dijon's *Société d'Études* reappeared in full force, entering into a one-on-one confrontation with the confounded professor, pushing him, pressing him, overwhelming him, as if in a boxing match in ancient Rome[10]. One senses that the struggle had nothing pedantic about it. There was in this novice theologian almost as much inadequacy as genius. But it was an incessant stream of fire and smoke, a vigor, a burst of argumentation that dazzled the other students and astonished the teacher. Thus, the roles were reversed: the student seemed to be teaching the lesson and the teacher to be absorbing it.

One also sensed that things could not continue for long in this vein. But as Fénélon[11] said, there is nothing more protective than Saint-Sulpice. Made aware of what was happening, the superior of the Society, the venerable and wise Garnier, wanted to observe Lacordaire from close up, in order to judge for himself about Lacordaire's vocation. "My dear friend," he said to him, "Please come to the house in Paris. I will appoint you to lead conferences there, because you must learn theology thoroughly. I will also appoint you to be one of the catechists in the parish of Saint-Sulpice, so that you can sharpen your talent for public speaking." Then, placing his hand paternally on Lacordaire's shoulder, "Come," he added,

"I would like to be your confessor." This happened at the end of January 1826.

Restrained by this disturbing experience, Henri contained his natural petulance, in periods of recreation as well as in class. In his academic work, he stayed silent when he was not specifically questioned. But he did not succeed in countering the original impression that he had made at Issy — that he had not shown sufficient self-control to rein in the outbursts of his intelligence, that he had argued too many theses before entering the seminary[12]. However, in response to this, he did not reproach anyone. He even defended the Sulpician mode of teaching theology against friends from outside the seminary. In the end, however, he was not the Sulpician type, and the irrepressible sincerity of his nature prevented him from concealing this. He himself admitted that his character was not flexible. The son of a century that hardly knew the meaning of obedience, *independence had been his social rank and his guide.* He had some excessive ideas on the subject, which he maintained with a delicate susceptibility, which Saint-Sulpice nevertheless should have understood, without necessarily having to admit to it openly. He did nothing about it. Sure of the sincerity of the inspiration that had led him to the seminary, ready to give his blood for the Church, sincerely enamored of obscurity, Lacordaire nevertheless was not perceived as pious, because his piety did not fit the mold envisioned by Olier. In addition, his liberal opinions, which he never hid, were a veritable scandal to Garnier, an inexplicable anomaly. On all these grounds, his teachers questioned his vocation.

God forbid I should ever take anything away from the veneration due to the Society, which saved the spirit of the priesthood in France and which has given to the Church Olier, Tronson[13], Émery[14]! Father Lacordaire would not allow any criticism — he, who on his deathbed, rendered to the men of Saint-Sulpice this expression of gratitude: he called them "upright, pious men, removed from all intrigue and ambition, honorable in their talents as in their virtue[15]." Certainly, he was thinking above all about the seminarians at Saint-Sulpice when he uttered these perhaps too absolute words: "A priest who has never gone to the seminary will never have an ecclesiastical spirit." But history has its own laws, and it should be permitted to the historian to say that the Sulpician type, as respectable as he may be, is not the only exemplar of the Catholic priesthood. Even in the seventeenth century, if there were not a more holy priest than Olier, certainly there were some of a more imposing and impressive nature. In addition, since Olier's tenure, the Society of Saint-Sulpice was itself unable to escape from the general weakening of character and mind in the eighteenth century as well as in our own. The Society was always prudent; it has now become somewhat timid.

Father Lacordaire's superiors did the following: they allowed two and one-half years to pass without calling him to holy orders[16]. The young Levite was not passive in the face of this. His perseverance was not shaken. He did not hesitate at all in his aspirations for the priesthood. He only wondered whether he was not being called to a more complete self-sacrifice. It is not certain whether he was thinking at that time of committing himself to the foreign missions. I have in hand an entire letter, a fragment of which, cited separately by Lorain, seemed to betray a thought [about the foreign missions]. I believe a meaning has been attributed to this letter that is not supported. However, in thinking about the mistrust that he was subject to in the seminary, it seemed to Lacordaire that a will superior to his own was pushing him into the desert. And, as there were at this time no other religious in France than the sons of Saint Ignatius, he had the thought of entering into this valiant militia, which had just received into its ranks a brilliant deserter from the public prosecutor's office in Paris, Gustave de Ravignan[17].

Like most men of his time, Henri Lacordaire had great prejudices against the Jesuits. "But," he said in 1826, "the business of this century is to save religion. Thus, the only means, setting aside divine action, is religious education. What are the priests doing in the parishes? They maintain the knowledge and the practice of Christian truths in women, in some men, in some young people. At times they pull back from error some souls in whom faith is reawakening, and that is all. Closed in the sanctuary, where they hold vigil over the structures that remain, they cannot defend them from outside attack. Sometimes, they look down from their position high up on the walls of Zion, and they see that the number of those who are laying siege is growing all the time. And, descending back into the interior of the temple, they talk about what they have seen in sad and eloquent words, which touch only the hearts that have no need of hearing the words. Only education seizes the human race, and the Jesuits alone are capable of making education what it needs to be for the salvation of religion. If the Jesuits were not here, to whom would we entrust this? Look around and search [18]."

He was frightened above all by the lack of initiative in the clergy of that time. The bishops named under the Empire and the Restoration were, as was previously noted, older men with little energy left, who breathed only the air of the past. Assuredly, the sap of the Church in France was far from exhausted. For example, Frayssinous[19], under the Empire, had started to teach apologetics from the pulpit of Saint-Sulpice, an idea well received by all, until he was gagged in a wretched manner by Fouché's police[20]. Unfortunately, however, Frayssinous did not resume the apologetics course to a sufficient degree when, under the Bourbons, when freedom of speech was granted to him once again. Still, this paved the way for a kind of catechism of perseverance, which forged the well-justified reputations of de Quélen[21], Borderies[22], Letourneur, Feutrier[23], and Gallard[24]. They were later placed in leadership positions in the most prominent dioceses in the French Church. It was in this way that the idea of undertaking missions within France was conceived by Forbin-Janson[25] and Rauzan. Much zeal and talent were brought to this work, unfortunately and awkwardly compromised by an imprudent mélange of political propaganda and the apostolate. Aside from these attempts — the value of which should be recognized, even though they did not originate from the episcopacy — no other effort was made to ensure that the nineteenth century did not proceed as had the eighteenth century. On the contrary, the Jesuits took some initiative, although they had only recently come back to life[26] and still were of the old school. Not only did they preach and hear confessions, not only did they engage in missions, but they wrote scholarly books and founded secondary schools. At the same time, they created the commendable Institute of the Ladies of the Sacred Heart for the education of girls. Father Lacordaire was struck by all of this. "They chose," he added, "a certain number of their students, and they immersed them in the study of the hard sciences; every day, the professors at the *École Polytechnique* came to teach them and encourage their progress, with the goal that, at the end of a certain number of years, they would have produced experts capable of holding their own against adversaries working in the schools, in the academies, in newspapers, and in scientific publications[27]."

I am emphasizing purposely this wound of inertia, which was so lethal to the Church in France during the time. All the young Levites who had the life sap in them were suffering somewhat at the spectacle of this inertia, of seeing everything done by rote, a situation described by Jouffroy as like watching a decrepit body in the process of slowly dying. As a result of this suffering, young people came to hold the bishops in disdain, and quickly moved on to experiment with other ventures. It was as a result of this that of ten seminarians for whom many held high hopes, nine threw themselves at the feet of La Mennais, who alone among the secular clergy promised actually to do something. The immense fascination that he held for the young clergy was due mainly to this cause. It was this that at a certain moment was to deliver to him Father Lacordaire himself.

Father Lacordaire said with his customary eloquence: "At every available opportunity, the Church must think of restoring the religious sciences—at the risk of shirking her duty. And, if it fails to do this, the Church is exposed to the greatest risk. A multitude of drifting spirits who have no idea how to direct their leisure or their activities are introduced into the heart of the Church. Unskilled in the sacred ministry because God has inspired in them a different vocation, they search in vain for the hearth where their passion will be looked after, purified, put to use through shared work with others on the path of Catholicism. *They languish while they are carried away in isolation.* They feel they are perishing without having contributed to God's plan. The loss of so many individuals with the potential to act on behalf of the good is a profound misfortune. However, one never stops without penalty souls engaged in a movement that carries them to their goal. Spirits who have not been given a structured outlet will encounter each other sooner or later in their sorrowful search, *joining together in a disordered joy,* upset by the recognition of how numerous they are, by the memory of their own inaction. And this society without rules will fall one day, like lightning that has gathered for a long time in the clouds, right on top of a Church that no longer has theologians[28].

But we are getting ahead of ourselves. In 1826, as we will see later, Lacordaire was summarily rejecting the overtures of La Mennais [to join his circle of students and associates]. His need for activity and for the apostolate led him in the direction of the Institute of Saint Ignatius. Only one objection made him hesitate: It was what was called the alliance of the Jesuits — who counted among their numbers many émigrés — with what was called the party of the *ancien régime*[29]. Listen carefully to these words: the *ancien régime;* it was not only the absolute monarchy, it was above all the narrowness, weakness, and irrelevance to which the *ancien régime* had succumbed. At the same time, impatience and a need to take action brought him to the Jesuits. Lacordaire ended up putting this objection out of his mind, and asked de Quélen for permission to join the Jesuits in Montrouge[30].

The archbishop refused. He had a deep affection for Lacordaire; he regarded him as one of his personal victories; he was not unaware of the honor that this young priest could bring to his episcopacy. Naturally, he did not hide from the Sulpicians this step that the young seminarian had taken to commit himself to the Society of Jesus. Father Duc de Rohan[31,] who later became a cardinal, had served as the enthusiastic intermediary for Lacordaire. The duke had seen Lacordaire during his frequent visits to Saint-Sulpice, and he was impressed by the superior gifts that seemed to radiate from the young Levite. As a result of this clear expression of the predilections of his exceptionally gifted student, Garnier finally lowered the barriers that he had put up previously. On Christmas Eve 1826, Father Lacordaire was ordained sub-deacon, and on 25 September 1827, he wrote: "What I wanted to do, is done. I have been a priest for three days: *Thou art a priest forever, after the order of Melchizedek*[32].

At that moment, one of the directors of Saint-Sulpice, Boyer, wished to point out Lacordaire to his relative and friend, Frayssinous, Minister of Ecclesiastical Affairs, for the role of auditor of the Rota in Rome. But Lacordaire, without hesitating, declined this offer, which held promise of a successful ecclesiastical future.

Then something happened that reflected badly, it appears, on the administrative abilities of de Quélen: Once Father Lacordaire had become a priest, his bishop was not sure what to do with him. At first he wished to associate him with the Church of Saint-Sulpice, as priest-administrator, or to give him a position as one of the clergy at the Church of La Madeleine. Obstacles (the nature of which are unknown to me) were making it impossible for the archbishop to succeed in this. Then there was the question of whether to name Lacordaire assistant chaplain at the *Collège Henri IV*[33]. But he refused, with a generosity that was characteristic of him, because he knew his predecessor had been moved out of this position against his will. Four months went by. At the end of February 1828, the archbishop placed Father Lacordaire in the position of chaplain at the Convent of the Visitation, lost on the edges of Paris, on one of the narrow, winding streets near the *Jardin des Plantes*. There, his duties included teaching catechism classes to thirty boarding students ranging in age from twelve to eighteen[34].

I paid a visit to him in his solitude. I can still see his little room, neat, but largely empty, with no other furniture than a very simple bed, a few chairs, a table, a desk; moreover, I can attest to the fact that he was happy living there. His mother came to live with him. He aspired to nothing more than obscurity.

Preoccupied from that time forward with renewing Christian apologetics[35], he had embarked on an immense project of philosophical and theological studies. It was at this point that he read all of Plato, part of Aristotle, all of Descartes, and that he re-read — still without approving of them — the works of La Mennais. At the same time, he was studying the history of the Church. He used primary sources in his theological studies: Holy Scripture and the writings of the fathers of the Church. "Strength is in the primary sources," he correctly observed," and I want to go to those sources." It was Saint Augustine with whom he became most familiar. He devoured Augustine's works with the same passion that Ezekiel [devoured the scroll of wisdom in the Hebrew scriptures][36].

At the end of one year, de Quélen added to this small duty at the Visitation that of assistant chaplain at the *Collège Henri IV*, an offer which, for the reasons noted earlier, Lacordaire had turned down the previous year. He no longer had any objections; this time, he accepted.

The responsibilities of a chaplain seemed, in fact, tailor-made for him. As a student who had been in the *Université*[37] system, who knew better than he the seriousness of the wound he must heal? How to speak about it, and yet, how to leave it unsaid? He had been a boarding student at a *collège*. He had endured as we all did the routine of living in what were essentially barracks instead of with our own families. There, he learned moral insularity, a precocious egoism, the loss of innocence, and hardness of heart, the last of which is, in short, the result of losing innocence. And, finally he learned the spirit of pride and rebellion against God and authority. And he always retained the impression of an unspeakable distaste, tempered by a passionate commiseration with the victims of our public education. These are not the verbiage of a particular political party. These are facts. Lacordaire did not attack the leaders of the *Université,* most of whom at that time were worthy to be esteemed by everyone, but he did attack a more powerful influence, alas, than men. He attacked the general state of society, which was devastated by the spirit of doubt and indifference. He was attacking the institution per se, which was conscripting souls into service. He was attacking [society's] incision, which — lethally, inexorably, blindly — cut children off from their Christian families, to have them live for eight years pell-mell with the children of families in whom all faith had been extinguished. Father Lacordaire was under no illusions that he would be able to stop this torrent on his own. However, as a chaplain, he hoped to have some hold on at least some of these young minds, on some of these young hearts. He thought he knew the students well. He knew how much he cared for them and with what a sincere passion he generally loved the things that the best among his students loved: eloquence, poetry, science, liberty, honor. However modest his hopes might have been (who can understand this?), they were crushed. All of his youthfulness of spirit, all of his enthusiasm, all of his eloquence, were not able to influence hearts that had withered before their time and minds that had lost the capacity to be receptive to the supernatural, and even, from many points of view, that had lost *the intellectual benefits of the mind*, as the poet says.[37] What sorrow this caused Father Lacordaire! There was a memorable moment in the midst of this. It was the report that he wrote for the archbishop of Paris on the religious and moral state of the *collèges* of the city, and that was signed by nine chaplains of these *collèges* on 6 July 1830. Here follows the report, which gives insight into Lacordaire's state of mind and the approach he would take a bit later in a great struggle:

"By decree of the Honorable Minister of Ecclesiastical Affairs and Public Instruction, dated 15 June 1830, having designated a commission to examine, among other topics, the religious and moral state of the royal *collèges* of Paris, the chaplains of these institutions have believed it necessary to share humbly with the authorities everything they know and everything they can say about this very serious subject.

"They have not heretofore done so because they had never been directly requested to do so.

"They are doing so today to unburden their consciences, fearing that, if they were to remain silent in the context of a publicly sanctioned inquiry, their silence would be interpreted in the eyes of the authorities and of the families as a sign of approval and as grounds for feeling that all is well.

"They have worked together on this document because they share the same responsibilities as well as the same difficulties, and because the thoughts that preoccupy them do not involve a particular problem, nor a particular royal *collège*.

"Convinced that the misfortunes of religion in the *Université* system are due to general causes, the undersigned do not associate themselves with any local or personal considerations. They limit themselves, according to the terms of the decree, to indicating the religious and moral condition of the royal *collèges* of Paris, always keeping in mind the barriers that the most holy ministry which they are privileged to serve forbids them from crossing. It is by reason of conscience, and to remain within the set limits, that they present to the authorities the general outline that follows. Yet it must be said that this is only a faint picture of the sad state of religion in the *collèges*.

"The chaplains are in a state of profound despondency and dismay to which no words can do justice on account of the almost absolute impotence of their ministry, although they have not spared any care, or any avenue of study, to make their ministry fruitful.

"The children in their care have hardly entered the state-run *Université* preparatory school, when the good sentiments that they have learned from their families begin to change. They evince a marked boredom when performing the simplest exercises, the most necessary of Christian life. And at the time of their first communion, it seems like a significant achievement if one is able for a few days to lead them out of the mechanical state they have gotten in the habit of assuming during their religious duties. If there are among them any who remain faithful to their early religious sentiments, they seek to hide this fact like a deadly secret. One can see them affecting a cavalier attitude, begging in a thousand ways to be thought of more highly by their fellow students. This seeking after human approbation wears out these delicate souls. It is a silent and continuous persecution, sometimes even a vocal one. The idea of the good seems associated with the idea of shame. They dare to pray only with their prayer books closed. The sign of the cross for them is an act of courage. If a stranger came upon the scene of these many children gathered together to worship God, unless the stranger looked at the altar, he would never suspect that these children were Christians.

"Their faith has not altogether perished at this point; but, a bit later, between the ages of fourteen and fifteen, our efforts become useless. We lose all religious influence over them. In each *collège*, if one counts the classes in mathematics, philosophy, and rhetoric, and the students in *seconde,* only seven or eight of the eighty or one-hundred students attend Mass on Sundays.

"As it happens, indifference and the passions are not alone responsible for this widespread and early obliviousness to God, but so is an active lack of belief. How, in fact, could they have faith, when they see around them so much disdain for religion, hearing consistently so much contradictory discourse, when they can find Christianity nowhere but in a chapel, and there they find only an empty Christianity, which offers nothing more than official formalities? We ourselves, we sense it disappearing as we speak to them; we sense the holy courage and boldness of the faith disappearing. No longer do we represent to them the ministers of Jesus Christ; to them, we are merely teachers of philosophy. Our claims on them are limited to tossing a few doubts into their souls, to making them think about the fact that perhaps it may be possible that the Gospel is the work of God, and we unfortunately do not always succeed in providing them even with this resource to combat the prejudices to which they are exposed.

"So here they are at fifteen years of age, without any internal rule or discipline for their thoughts, with no restraint on their actions, except that of an external discipline that they hate, or of teachers whom they consider to be mercenaries. The fear of punishment and ambition for the future are the only things that give a semblance of submission to the spirit of rebelliousness with which they are imbued. Worn out by a life that religion has not softened, they view the *collège* as a prison, and youth as a time of misfortune.

"Finally, when they have completed their course of studies, among those who graduate in rhetoric or philosophy, need one say how many still have their faith and practice it? *Approximately one each year in each collège.*

"So a chaplain who devotes eight years of his life to the system of the *Université,* can hope during this interval to produce eight or ten Christians, and if he has colleagues, of which we each have several, even this glory will be shared. Thus, out of the four hundred students sent to our establishments for eight years of education, only eight or ten of them will be able to keep their faith. The rest of the students conspire against those students who have faith. Which is to say, out of four hundred possible opportunities, there are three-hundred ninety that are threatening the ability of a child to become a man of religion. Those are the hard numbers that represent hope; and those hard numbers are the final result of our labors. This can be further confirmed by noting that, in *écoles speciales*[39] of all types, the number of students who practice their religion is small. And yet, this small group, with few exceptions, was not educated in the system of the *Université*.

"We vouch for all this; it is with great regret that we have stated these things, and that we have described in such an unfavorable light children whom we cherished from the very first day they were entrusted to our care. We console ourselves concerning this sad duty with the idea that today we give them the greatest proof of affection that they have ever received from us. Besides, who will not admit that these children are more to be pitied than condemned?

"The facts that we have just laid out are already known to the headmasters of secondary schools and lay civil servants, responsible for oversight by the *Université*; we have said nothing that is not consistent with their private misgivings. The only possible difference between their opinions and ours, is that they believe the root problem to lie in our century, and that there is no way to reform it. It is true that this sense of discouragement seems justified, especially when one considers that, in all times, under all political systems, after multiple reforms, the *Université* has always borne the same fruits. Several of us spent our youth in the same environment. What they formerly saw as its students, today they see as its civil servants. They never remember their education without a limitless ingratitude, just as they will never remember current public service with anything but sorrow. It is also true that the experience of the *Collège Royal de Saint-Louis*, whose establishment represented the most brilliant effort by the *Université* on behalf of religion[40], nonetheless offers no certainty for the future. Nor de we have any confidence in what could be done when continuing to follow in the path that has been followed up until now.

"The undersigned stop here. It is up to the authorities to go further, *and to determine whether*, after so many fruitless efforts, *the most efficacious course might not be the EMANCIPATION OF TEACHING, which has been requested so often,* and which would appear to flow logically from the institutions established in France by the wisdom of our kings. The undersigned add that they cannot allow themselves to believe that Christianity — which has led so many people in France from childhood to adulthood — has been denied the gift of raising generations in the fear of God, and that, once its legitimate liberties are restored, Christianity cannot accomplish its noble and divine mission."

Admittedly, the report we have just read, and the bitter disappointment whose cry it is, shine much light on the desire that, as we shall see, was driving the disheartened Lacordaire to leave France for America. But there was another reason for this desire.

For most people, study is a means to an end, not an end in itself. Without doubt, there are some men whose natures make them what I would call Benedictines at heart, for whom prayer and study in God's presence are sufficient. But there are also souls that God created for the apostolate, and who suffer as long as their vocation is not fulfilled. These expansive souls who are ready to fight for their cause must spread their wings in the external world; action is necessary. Father Lacordaire was one of these souls. In becoming a monk, he did not expect to be confined in a desert, but rather to play a role — which involved a more comprehensive and practical commitment —

in addressing the double issue that concerned us throughout our adolescence: the harmony of faith and reason; and the confrontation of the two realms — the spiritual realm and the political realm. In seminary, no day passed without Lacordaire having this thought. After he had become a priest, the thought continued to occupy him at every moment. All of his reading, all his meditations centered on this critical question: *"The world being what it is . . .* what should a priest think about the relationship between religion and the social order[41]?"

The world being what it is . . . The question was perfectly articulated. It focused less on doctrine than on fact. But the focus on fact implied a question of conduct. In a country where the unity of faith was shattered without remedy as it had been in France for three centuries, where the equality of religions before the law had been absorbed in the habits of the nation long before it had been [expressed] in public laws, where consequently all doctrines had their say, everywhere and anytime, without any restraint; in a country where public instruction, which is to say the education of every new generation, is in the hands of the state, or, to put it another way, in the hands of those with political power (who were indifferent, even hostile, to the beliefs of the majority of citizens), what can be done to safeguard as well as possible religious truth and public morality?

That is the question[42].

The Restoration thought it had solved the problem: It had, within the limits of what was possible for it, placed public power in the service of truth. It had declared that the Catholic religion was the state religion. The king, his family, his ministers, civil servants of all ranks, consistently set a pious example, or, at least, showed respect for the sacred. A law of reparation outlawed divorce; another law required observance of rest on Sundays; a third punished sacrilege. Religious communities were encouraged and protected. Minor seminaries were established. The responsibility for primary education was given over completely to the bishops. One of them even was appointed to be Grand Master of the *Université*. Priests and lay persons of proven faith directed all the *collèges;* all professors who were anti-Christian were excluded from teaching.

Well! Let us say it again, there was widespread public opposition to all of this. In spite of all these purges, all the state schools were lacking in piety. No doubt, opposition to the Bourbons, the alarmist influence of interests born out of the Revolution, a fear of a return to the *ancien régime,* a mourning over the end of the Empire, the mirage of the Republican utopias, figured greatly in this uprising of spirits. All these were so many circumstances aggravating the situation. But the situation existed independently of these circumstances because it would have existed under Napoleon had he attempted to do for religion what the Restoration had attempted to do. Not a single human power would have been capable of seeing to it that the eighteenth century and the Revolution were as if they had not happened; — that their influence had not planted in [the nation's] priorities, morals, and opinions, profound roots, unable to be eradicated, swift arousal of strong objections, and a mocking all adverse precautions.

The world being what it was, what to do? What should one wish for, protection or neutrality from those in public power? What to think, moreover, of the Charter of Louis XVIII[43], when weighed on the scale of the sanctuary, which is to say, seen from the point of view of the interests of religion?

The French clergy previously had faith (the word is not too strong) in the Bourbons. They cherished them; they were content with the influence they were able to wield through them. Alas! They exaggerated the Bourbons' effectiveness. The royal prerogative, from this point of view, was dear to them.

And the restrictions imposed on that prerogative received no sympathy from the ministers of the altar; there had been little change on this point between 1791 and 1814[44].

Father Lacordaire was not like this. The liberal royalism that he adopted in 1822 was not the mannered and empty royalism he had experienced at Paris's *Bonnes Lettres* and *Bonnes Études*. Neither was it a royalism hostile to the Charter, which unfortunately characterized most emigrés and priests in France. Accusing them of not cherishing institutions that reminded them of the bloody past, Lacordaire believed firmly that these institutions, already corrected through experience, and open to being corrected a great deal more, had a raison-d'être in meeting the obvious needs of the times. Had not limited monarchy been public law in France since time immemorial? How could anyone, therefore, make the French people, the new France, accept the autocracy of the Bourbons, an autocracy suspected of bringing back a regime of the privileged? Above all, the France of the Restoration needed to be protected against the reappearance of ancient abuses. A compromise, therefore, was thoroughly indispensable, and this compromise could be none other than the Charter. Who was it that dreamed of reestablishing the Three Orders, the Estates General, the Parliaments[45]? Moreover, how to moderate royalty effectively, once it had been freed from those secular counterweights that had been decisively destroyed? In order to go forward, what control could be put in place other than that of the two chambers created by the Charter? With Lacordaire as with many individuals of his generation, this was not an opinion. It was a deeply held belief, (I came close to calling it a political religion).

But this isolated him immeasurably from his contemporaries in the seminary, and even more from those who had gone before them in the priesthood. "I remained a liberal when I became Catholic," he himself said. "In entering Saint-Sulpice, I abandoned none of my own opinions, since freedom of opinion is allowed to all Christians. Moreover, I did not know how to hide everything that separated me, in this regard, from the clergy of my time. I was alone in these convictions, or at least I never encountered (in the clergy) a single person who shared them. The cause of Christianity, linked to the cause of the Bourbons, was also linked to their fate, and the priest who was not under the Bourbon flag seemed an enigma even to the most moderate. To the most passionate, he seemed a traitor. My mother was alarmed by my isolation. She said to me several times with a certain sadness: 'You have no friends!' In point of fact, I had none[46]."

This situation was not without courage and dignity, but neither was it without its sadness. In the long run, such a situation weighs very heavily on a sensitive spirit; Lacordaire's correspondence attests to this. Should one be surprised that, undergoing a trial of this magnitude for two years, discouraged inexpressibly by the fruitlessness of his zeal at the *Collège Henri IV*, he began to listen to the offers made to him in 1830 to go the United States of America, where he would find what was missing in France: a Church that is truly free, a clergy as liberal as it was orthodox, an unlimited field for the apostolate?

The Catholic Church in the United States has a curious history.

In 1633, under Charles I, a Catholic peer from Great Britain, Lord Baltimore, landed in America on the Chesapeake Bay. He disembarked there, accompanied by two-hundred families, who came to seek, on the opposite side of the Atlantic, the freedom to continue to serve God as all of England had served God from the time of Augustine of Canterbury all the way up to the time of the divorce of Henry VIII. An English Jesuit was with them. They established

133

themselves in virgin country that they called Maryland (the land of Mary), in honor of the Mother of God. It is worthy of mention that while all around them the numerous sects issuing forth from the Reformation were banishing one another ceaselessly, the young Catholic colony of Baltimore, directed by the Jesuits, gave the New World a unique example. It offered the shelter of its territory and the fairness of its laws to the oppressed of all Christian communions. This was not rewarded. Nonconformists took refuge in Maryland in such great numbers, that within at least twenty-five years, they had enough strength to isolate the Catholics, to outlaw their priests, and to impose on the introduction of a new Irish Catholic the same tax that was imposed on the importation of a black [slave][47]. Things remained this way until the War of Independence.

To resist Great Britain, the Anglo-Americans needed all their strength, and the Catholics would not spend a long time coming to an agreement about this. Thus, Maryland's representative to the Continental Congress, Charles Carroll of Carrollton, was a fervent Catholic, and few men [other than he] rendered such great service to the American cause. In addition, a Jesuit from Maryland of the same name, Father Carroll, was delegated with [Benjamin] Franklin by the Congress of 1776 to dissuade the Canadians from joining the English cause. More fortunate than their [Catholic] brothers of the Low Countries [the Netherlands], who, after spilling their blood against Philip II for the Dutch Protestants, were not able to obtain from them freedom of worship, the Catholics in the United States were treated as brothers by their fellow citizens. Not only were the minor edicts against them repealed, but, for them as for the other Christian communions, the equality of religions before the law became in the United States a reality. And, in one of those coincidences that is not rare in the history of the Church, at the very moment when the public practice of religion in France receded into darkness for ten years, the Catholic hierarchy was officially established in the American republic. On 6 November 1789, a date to be remembered, Pius VI established an episcopal see in Baltimore and appointed Father Carroll bishop of the United States.

France, which had fought to such an extent for the political emancipation of the Anglo-Americans, could not do less through the apostolate for the young American Church. A man whose name is very often associated with all judicious and courageous action on behalf of the good at the end of the last century, Émery, Superior General of Saint-Sulpice, had the excellent idea of searching in the United States for a refuge for the Society during the schism that was beginning to take place in France. In August 1790, he offered the new bishop of Baltimore the prospect of establishing in his episcopal city another Sulpician seminary, which would train new laborers in the field of evangelism throughout the United States. And such was God's blessing on Émery's idea that, from one sole bishopric with twenty-two missionaries and 24,500 lay people in the Catholic Church in the American Union of 1791, [the Church has grown to] encompass forty-three episcopal sees and four-and-a-half million faithful today.

This was the work to which Father Lacordaire urgently wished to devote his life. He knew (and he was proud of this) that in order for this wonderful expansion of Catholicism in the United States to take place, France had sacrificed some of its greatest individuals. The Fénelon of our age, Cheverus[48], who served as archbishop of Bordeaux, and the cardinal, Dubourg[49], who died as archbishop of Besançon, had been bishops—one of Boston, the other of New Orleans. Many of the apostle-bishops who established Anglo-American catholicity, Flaget[50], Maréchal[51], Bruté[52], Loras[53,] Odin[54],

Portier[55], and de la Hailandière[56], were Frenchmen. And it was in France that Dubois[57], Bishop of New York, perhaps more energetically than anyone, made an appeal to Lacordaire in January 1830 to be his principal cooperator in the largest diocese of the United States.

By virtue of its commercial importance and its large population, New York was indeed the preeminent city in the American Union. The city had 200,000 inhabitants at that time; today it has a million and a quarter, of whom 400,000 are Catholics. As it happened, when the first bishop of this large city, Connelly[58], took possession of his episcopal see in 1816, there were in his diocese only three churches and four priests for sixteen thousand faithful[59]. His successor, Dubois, who died in 1842, was a long-time Sulpician. He had left France in 1791, had established in the Diocese of Baltimore a significant educational institution, the minor seminary at Emmittsburg, since transformed into a "secondary school." In addition, he in cooperation with a great soul, Mrs. Seton[60], created in America the institute of the Daughters of Charity, since incorporated into the admirable family of the Daughters of Saint Vincent de Paul. In 1830, he was sixty-seven years old. Always indefatigable and having only eighteen priests to evangelize 180,000 Catholics, he did not hesitate to travel back across the ocean to France to recruit more missionaries.

Father Lacordaire had been brought to his attention. As early as 1826, when he was still a simple seminarian, Lacordaire was inspired, as are all great hearts, by the miracles of conversion brought about by missionaries working in distant countries. "Their history is testimony," he wrote. "The heart of man knows well that the principal source of their success, apart from what God has done, is the certitude of their faith, proved by the exile they have willingly condemned themselves to, and by their amazing work, which brings no visible recompense.

The more good one wishes to accomplish in religion, the more one must give people proof of one's faith through the holiness and self-denial of one's life. As a great orator robed in purple, I would be accomplishing nothing. As a simple missionary, without talent, clothed in rags, and three thousand leagues from my native country, I could move kingdoms[61]."

These sentiments were always present in his mind. However, the overtures that the bishop of New York made to Lacordaire had a completely different character. The offer did involve Henri's leaving his mother behind, separating himself from France, and moving far away. But it did not involve risking his life, either in barbarous countries as did the martyrs of Tonkin[62] and those of Japan[63]. Nor did it involve risking his life as did the martyrs of Guyana, in an environment that seemed to devour human beings. The United States represented an exile, but it was an exile from one civilization to another. At first, Lacordaire was not drawn to this prospect. He did not have much taste for "this nation of business men, who believe themselves wise because they are skillful, who believe themselves to be virtuous because they are tidy[64]."

He did not hurry to make a decision. He mulled it over for six months. However, the persistent lack of fruitfulness of his ministry at the *Collège Henri IV*, an impatience to spread the fire [of faith] that was consuming him, the sense that was growing every day of the French clergy's inertia and its aversion to liberal ideas, drove Lacordaire toward America. There was another decisive reason: the great problem of the relationship between religion and political and civil society had been resolved in the United States in a way different from that of the system of concordats that had prevailed in Europe, and it was worth studying firsthand over there [in America] the experience of a whole new mode of existence for the Catholic Church.

"Spiritual society and material society," wrote Lacordaire to a friend, "should subsist together without destroying one another. There are only three ways they can coexist: the superiority of one over the other; the absolute independence of one from the other; and their enmeshment through a series of mutual concessions. Now, this last method does not work because, in all times—above all in times when faith is weak—the Church is at the mercy of material society, which in the final analysis makes decisions on its own while claiming these decisions are mutual."

This last approach makes people perceive the Church as fearful, as opposed to liberty. This ends sooner or later in a national church. In contrast, the second way, which has been established today in the United States, raises the Church significantly in the esteem of the people. It allows the Church to be vital, very adapted to an era of popular liberty."

This is not to say that Father Lacordaire thought this was the ideal mode of existence for the Church. "Such a solution divides up the world," he wrote on 19 July 1830. "It is metaphysically so *false*, that never would people of faith individually have the thought of adopting it: it is a sublime remedy, but it is only a remedy."

This demonstrates that he believed at that time that spiritual society was superior to material society. This solution, according to him, which places the spirit above the flesh, unified society into an organic whole. He found this mode of existence to be so simple, such a moderating influence on people and on power, that a truly Christian nation had never known any other way and that it chooses this [system], he said, without giving it a second thought. Nonetheless, he felt that this system could not be reborn except in a manner other than previously practiced, and only when people and kings begged for it on both knees. In the meantime, what to do? Take the

Church out of its state of enmeshment and place it in a state of absolute independence[64]. Where to find absolute independence, other than in America?

Once he arrived at this conclusion, Father Lacordaire ceased feeling distaste for the United States. He accepted the twofold responsibility of Vicar General of New York and superior of the seminary, which placed in his hands the oversight of ecclesiastical studies and all of the young clergy of the diocese. La Mennais was to have a significant impact on this decision.

What was the story behind Father Félicité [Félix] de La Mennais? And how did it happen that, after rejecting him for such a long time, Lacordaire devoted himself to him completely? This is important enough a question to merit in-depth study.

ENDNOTES

Some 40 footnotes by author, converted to endnotes. Additional notes added by translators.

1. Note—The relationship between Lacordaire and Gerbet was described on page 1, above. Salinis, inseparable from Gerbet, not surprisingly, found himself an outsider in these relations. They offered Lacordaire the opportunity to meet their old teachers, and he accepted.

On de La Mennais, see Chapter III, below. See also Internet: www.worksoflacordaire.com: *Reflections...*

2. Letter of 29 July 1824 to Lorrain.

3. Hippolyte Régnier, of Dijon's *Société d'Études*, died very

early after having written in 1824 a prospectus in favor of the Jesuits, and later the *Essai d'histoire du clergé de France pendant la Révolution* (Paris, Bricon, three volumes). He had come to share room and board with Henri Lacordaire during February 1824. He was the older brother of Father Joseph Régnier.

4. Letter to Lorrain, 31 January 1825.

5. Montalembert: Charles Forbes, conte de Montalembert. French publisher and politician. Founded *L'Avenir* newspaper with Lacordaire. Noted defender of liberal Catholicism. After his condemnation by Rome, he recanted and took up defending ultramontanism.

6. See these two letters, Appendix X, page 533.

7. Letter to Lorrain, 29 July 1824.

8. Olier, Jean-Jacques (1608-1657): founded of the Society of Saint-Sulpice and of its seminary. Its purpose was the education of priests.

9. [Virgil's] *Aeneid,* Book V [chapter 17], lines 456-460:
> Impetuous he drives Dares full speed all round the ring. . . . . No stop or stay gives he. . . . so from each huge hand the champion's strokes on dizzy Dares fall.

Theodore C. Williams, trans., *Aeneid* (Boston: Houghton Mifflin Co. 1910). Accessed 7 December 2010, at
http://www.perseus.tufts.edu/hopper/text?doc=Perseus%3Atext%3A1999.02.0054%3Abook%3D5%3Acard%3D421. [cdt]

10. Fénelon: François de Solignan de la Mothe F. (1651-1715). Archbishop of Cambrai. Capable diplomat, preacher, and knowledgeable about arms. Tutor of the Duke of Burgundy. Although he had aristocratic tendencies, he was opposed to the absolutism of the Great King, Louis XIV. Condemned by Rome for his Quietism, he submitted.

11. *Notice.*

12. Tronson; Guillaume Alexandre Tronson de Coudray (1750-1798). French lawyer and politician. Defender of Marie-Antoinette. Deported to Guyana for opposing the *Directoire*.
13. Émery: Michel Particelli, dit Émery (c. 1595-1650). Superintendent of Finances under Mazarin. His unpopular financial edicts contributed to the *Fronde*. Mazarin had to depose him.
14. *Notice*.
15. The year 1825 passed without Lacordaire's being called to the minor orders. He would have had to advance to that stage by Christmas 1825, then to the subdiaconate during the Feast of the Holy Trinity 1826, in order to become a deacon at Christmas that same year, and a priest during the Feast of the Holy Trinity 1827. Therefore, when he did not receive any call during Christmas 1825, nor on Trinity Sunday 1826, he could only conclude that he had been rejected by his superiors.
16. Ravignan left the world (April 1822) to enter Issy, where he spent six months before presenting himself to the noviitiate of the Jesuits in Montrouge.
17. Letter to Foisset, 25 April 1826.
18. Frayssinous, Denis-Antoine-Luc, Comte de Frayssinous (1765-1841): Grand Master of the University. French politician, orator, writer, Peer of the realm. Bishop, wrote in support of the Gallican Church.
19. Fouché, Joseph (1759-1820); promoted to Duke of Otrante by Napoléon who also appointed him Minister of Police. He left Napoléon, changed parties, and eventually became a citizen of Austria.
20. De Quélen: Hyacinthe-Louis, conte de Quélen (1778-1839). Member of the French Academy, 1824. Archbishop of Paris.
21. Borderies, Jean-François-Étienne (1764-1832): theologian, bishop of Versailles. Left France at the time of the Civil

Constitution of the Clergy, when priests had to swear allegiance to the government. He returned to his country later.

22. Feutrier, François-Hyacinthe (1765-1830). Peer of the kingdom. Bishop of Beauvais.

23. Gallard: doctor of the Sorbonne; at one point, he refused the chair of Sacred Eloquence.

24. Probably Forbin-Janson, Charles Auguste (1785-1844).

25. Starting in the mid-eighteenth century, the Jesuits were suppressed in Europe an account of a series of political and economic struggles. They were suppressed once again under Napoleon. However, with the Restoration in 1815, the Jesuits were able to become an active presence once again in Catholic countries.

26. Letter of April 1826.

27. *Considérations sur le système philosophique de M. de La Mennais,* pp. 28–29. - For translation in English, see: www.worksoflacordaire.com on the Internet: *Reflections...*

28. *Ancien régime* [former system]: the political and social system of France prior to the Revolution. Everyone was a subject of the King of France as well as a member of an estate and of a province.

29. Montrouge was the place the Jesuits had their novitiate at that time.

30. Louis-François-Auguste de Rohan-Chabot (1788-1833). Former cavalry colonel; Napoleon's chamberlain. Cardinal. Refused to support Louis-Philippe.

31. Hebrews 7:17.

32. *Collège*: public colleges were founded and supported by the township, although they may have received funds from the State. On the contrary, *lycées* were owned and operated by the State. There were also private colleges. The College of France, established by Francis I, was given autonomy, outside of the University control.

33. Letter to Foisset, 22 February 1828.
34. Letter to Lorain, 14 November 1827.
35. Ezekiel 3:1-3. *And he said to me, "Son of man, eat what is offered to you; eat this scroll, and go speak to the house of Israel."/ So I opened my mouth, and he gave me the scroll to eat./ And he said to me, "Son of man, eat this scroll that I give to you and fill your stomach with it." Then I ate it: and it was in my mouth as sweet as honey.*
36. The University: a body of state-appointed officials who were charged with full control of all education, from primary grades to university.
37. *Che han perduto il ben dell' intelletto.* [Dante Alighieri, *Inferno*, Canto III, verse 16. English text quoted from Seth Zimmerman, trans., *The Inferno of Dante Alighieri* (2003). Accessed 7 December 2010, at http://home.earthlink.net/~zimls/HELLIII.html.
38. Specialized private institutions of higher education.
39. The Royal College of Saint-Louis was given full autonomy, thereby having been placed outside of the University control.
40. Letter to, 19 July 1830. [cdt]
41. William Shakespeare, *Hamlet*, act III, scene I.
42. Charter of 1814, granted by Louis XVIII (Louis-Stanislas-Xavier): the "Desired" one of the House of Bourbon. Established a constitutional monarchy. For more details, see *Wikipedia* on the Internet.
43. National Convention (1792-1795) held all executive powers. It brought about many successful and beneficial changes. Under Napoleon, the Convention was replaced by the Directory.
44. The three Orders (social classes) were:

    1st :Lords Spiritual (clergy)

    2nd: Lords Temporal (nobility)

    3rd: The Commons (bougeoisie)

- Later: 4th: journalists
- The Estates General was the legislature of France before 1789. Clergy, nobility, and bourgeoisie sent representatives to them.
- Parliaments: Any of several high courts of justice in France before 1789.

For additional information, see the Internet at: Answers.com.

45. *Notice*.

46. The Law of 1704 stipulated that a tax should be levied on every Irish servant imported to America.

47. Cheverus: Jean-Louis Lefebvre de Cheverus (1768-1836). First bishop of Boston, Massachusetts. Talented, charitable, holy. Nursed the stricken in two yellow fever epidemics. Charmed non-Catholics. Later, in France, named Cardinal.

48. Dubourg: Louis-Guillaume-Valentin Dubourg (1760-1833). Second bishop of Louisiana-the Floridas. A Sulpician; formerly taught at Georgetown College.

49. Flaget: Benedict-Joseph Flaget (1763-1850). First bishop of Bardstown, Kentucky. A Sulpician. The see was later transferred to Louisville, KY.

50. Maréchal, Ambroise (1764-1821): Sulpician.

51. Bruté, Simon Gabriel Bruté de Rémur: first bishop of Vincennes (Indiana); seat later moved to Indianapolis.

52. Loras, Pierre-Joseph-Matthieu "Mathias (1792-1858); bishop and builder of the diocese of Dubuque, Iowa.

53. Odin, John M. (1805-1870), a Lazarist [Vincentian]; first bishop of Galveston, Texas.

54. Portier, Michael (1795-1859): first bishop of Mobile, Alabama.

55. Hailandière, Célestin Laurent Guynemer de la Hailandière (1798-1882): second bishop of Vincennes (Indiana).

56. Dubois: Jean-Antoine "John" (1764-1842). Third bishop of New York.

57. Connolly: Dominic John (1750-1825). Second bishop of New York. A member of the Dominican Order.

58. In 1840, the Catholic population of the diocese consisted of 200,000 souls, of whom 90,000 were in the City of New York and its environs.—Letters of Father Hughes, Archbishop of New York, *Annales de la Propogation de la Foi,* volume XIII, 132. In 1866, the *Catholic World,* a monthly magazine published in New York, counted 400,000 Catholics in the city, which had a total of one million inhabitants.

59. Elizabeth Ann Bayley Seton (1774-1821). Widow, foundress of Sisters of Charity (Emmitsburg, MD). Canonized in 1875.

60. Letter to Lorain, 21 October 1826.

61. Also known as the Vietnamese Martyrs.—*Translator's Note.* — Feast 24 November.

- Martyrs of Japan: especially in Nagasaki 1597 and 1616. See Catholic Encyclopedia for more details.

62. Gustave de Beaumont, *Marie ou L'Esclavage aux États Unis.*

63. All of this argumentation has been taken directly from a letter from Lacordaire written on 19 July 1830. I call the attention of all my readers to the undeniable testimony of his true sentiments with regard to the relationship between Church and state.

Chapter III

Father F. de La Mennais

Education —Unbelief—Conversion.—First writings—The Essai sur l'indifférence—The prodigious success of volume I; reaction against the second volume—The author's internal rebellion—First trip to Rome—Direction given by La Mennais to religious polemics—Anti-Gallicanism—La Mennais breaks with the Bourbons—His evolution toward support of modern liberties—His modes of action, as varied as they are numerous—La Chênaie and Malestroit—Proposals made by Father Gerbet to Father Lacordaire; the longtime and persistent refusal of the latter—How he finally ceded.

Félicité Robert de la Mennais[1] was seven years old when he lost his mother in 1789. Brought up in the old Catholic and monarchical faith (in Brittany, these were all of a piece), and just barely out of childhood, he risked his life many times under the Terror by attending furtive Masses celebrated at midnight in a garret. Therefore, it was natural that he grew up completely horrified by those who hunted down priests like wild beasts, and that, early on, he took the oath of Hannibal[2] against the Revolution.

How could his education not be imbued with the misfortunes of the times? *Féli*—that was how his family referred to him right up to the end—had no teachers, properly speaking, other than himself.

Unfortunately, he would never accept other teachers. To tame this stubborn character, his uncle, Monsieur Robert de la Saudrais, had the idea of trying to contain him, in a manner of speaking, within [the confines of] his library—a fatal prison, which pleased Féli so much that he spent all his time there[3]. In this place, a fired-up imagination, an unrestrained curiosity, drove this spirit relentlessly to readings of the most divergent and questionable sort. Pell-mell, he devoured languages and books, with no structure or plan, and, consequently, without developing areas of knowledge that were related and solidly integrated. In addition, far from being, as has been written about him, one of the most well-rounded men of his time, he never became either a humanist, or a philosopher, and certainly not a theologian. One thing seemed certain: lost in this chasm of incoherent reading, where the writings of the eighteenth century played a prominent role, Féli de la Mennais experienced a loss of the faith and the innocence of his earlier years[4].

However, there was a guardian angel in his family, his brother Jean-Marie, who was two years older. He was also a member of the élite, and he was a priest. Won back to God through his brother's tenderness, Féli made his first communion in 1804, at the age of twenty-two. Not long after, he wrote his *Réflexions sur l'état de l'Église en France.*

Written in the solitude of La Chênaie, in the middle of the woods—a place that was not well known then, but very famous today[5]—this book indicated that the Church had a champion worthy of Her. The author has many insights. He groaned loudly about the insufficiency of ecclesiastical training, above all in the areas of biblical Exegesis and Eastern languages. Furthermore, he demanded the right to hold provincial councils, diocesan synods, ecclesiastical retreats, conferences for priests on doctrine, communal life in presbyteries, the restoration of priestly education through the teaching congregations, the evangelization of parishes by missionaries, and the entrusting of education to women's and men's [religious] institutes. Haven't we seen efforts in this regard ever since, efforts which have had only partial success?

The style of *Réflexions,* perhaps a bit overworked, and perhaps too rigid, nevertheless demonstrates solid mastery of the subject matter. But it shows no trace of original talent. The author was very careful (this was generally expected) to tip his hat in passing to the "man of genius who had just *reestablished* in France the monarchy of religion." Vain precaution! This was 1808 (General Mollis was already occupying Rome)[6]. Fouché[7], who was in charge of the police for the Empire, mercilessly banned the work. It is true that the book did say, "The provincial councils could not inspire the slightest mistrust in a prince who did not have the *secret intention* of taking over spiritual authority."

Féli de la Mennais had been warned. It is a profound mystery that, based on texts collected by his brother, he drafted a second work of critical importance in the crisis in which the convocation of the so-called council of 1811 had engaged the Episcopacy[8]: *Tradition de l'Église sur l'institution des Évèques*[9].

Nothing at this point presaged the La Mennais of *L'Avenir*. No harsh tones, no acerbity. At this time the man arguing the cause of religion was full of moderation and the writer was accurate, irreproachable; however, his style was stilted and completely lacking in eloquence. These early years of La Mennais are a genuine revelation: although in later life he was capable of so many passions, he was at the age of thirty-two still utterly the master of himself and very tempered [in his approach to controversy].

Four years later, the name that no one had known previously was the greatest name in the French Church; the first volume of *l'Essai sur l'indifférence en matière de Religion* had just been published (1818).

How to explain this sudden transformation of the writer, and above all, how to explain his sudden glorification?

Without doubt the times had changed. Instilling in France an unrest that was inexpressibly profound, the return of Napoleon in 1815 had revived to the highest pitch passions that were thought to have been extinguished forever. Naturally, those passions provoked and inflamed contrary passions. I am not saying these things at random; I am describing and confirming what I saw with my own eyes. In addition, having been ordained to the priesthood at the age of thirty-four, on 9 March 1816, La Mennais thought himself to be a new man: the sacerdotal flame burned in his soul, and it had sparked eloquence in his soul as well[10]. This explains the transformation of La Mennais into a writer, but it is not enough to understand fully his extraordinary success. Who will reveal the mystery to us? Let us listen to Father Lacordaire:

"One-hundred-fourteen years had passed since the death of Bossuet, seventy-six since that of de Massillon[11]. Accordingly, there were seventy-six years without a single Catholic priest in France gaining renown as a writer or a superior man. La Mennais appeared with all the more impact because the eighteenth century had taken up its arms once again. His *Essai sur l'indifférence* was an admirable return of logical arguments proving to men the necessity of faith, arguments given life once again by their application to errors that were more extensive than they had been in previous eras. Except for certain phrases where excessive imagination belied a certain youthfulness — which actually added more depth to the work — everything was simple, true, vigorous, engaging. It was traditional Christian eloquence, *a bit severe sometimes;* however, error had done so much damage, it had spread with so much insolence despite its offenses and its invalidity, that it was pleasing to witness it being chastised by ironclad logic. It aroused boundless enthusiasm and gratitude. Truth had been waiting for so long for an avenger! In a single day, La Mennais — unknown the day before — found himself invested with the authority of Bossuet[12]."

There is no exaggeration in these words.

"Europe," continued Lacordaire, "was waiting for the continuation of La Mennais' work[12]. The author had at this point established only the importance and necessity of faith. But what was the true religion? By what method could one discern it? What kind of authority did human reason have in the ordering of life? These were the questions that remained to be resolved.

"After waiting two years, the second volume of the *Essai* was published. It is impossible to describe adequately the sense of shock it caused. From the heights of the ancient defense of the faith, La Mennais had descended into dry discussions of philosophy. The solution he proposed violently produced a divided people."

How could it not have been otherwise? In his second volume, La Mennais, this absolute defender of the faith, began by sharing common cause with the skeptics. As they did — and for the same reasons they did — he challenged all the conventional arguments for belief; for him, there was no authority except that based on the common consensus of the human race.

How strange! He did not realize that it was precisely common consensus that condemned him; because all the reasons for belief that the *Essai* rejected, the human race, as we all know, has always accepted.

Besides, who can not see that the assumptions of the human race at times can be challenged? In fact, was not the human race almost universally polytheistic for centuries? La

Mennais would not cede his point in the slightest. He resolutely denied that the world was ever polytheistic and he wrote two volumes in an effort to prove it. His admirers were so fascinated with him that these two volumes — today largely unread — seemed extraordinary to them. It is such a sacrifice to burn the idols that we have adored[13].

On the other hand, there was an immense uprising in opposition. Saint-Sulpice and all the seminaries in France protested as one voice. The bishops joined ranks in great number against the Mennaisian theories. Note that the innermost soul of La Mennais is revealed here: we see him capable of everything except submission. From this time forward, he will be ripe for disaster.

In fact, frightened by the raging fury from all quarters, his spiritual director, the pious Father Carron, begged him not to publish anything more on such serious matters without having first consulted established theologians. "If my theses are rejected," answered La Mennais, I do not see that there is ANY firm way to defend religion. Besides, I asked Rome to examine my book. Moreover, if the judgment is negative, I have decided I will not write anything further[14]."

Is it clear what La Mennais is doing here? On the one hand, his theories imply that never before him had religion been firmly defended. All the Fathers, all the Doctors of the Church were guilty in a fundamental way because all of them accepted the reasons for belief that the *Essai* had repudiated. On the other hand, La Mennais had recourse to the judgment of Rome; but, if Rome did not agree with him, he would not retract anything he had said. He would simply put down his pen. Is that not precisely what he did twelve years later? The La Mennais of 1820 was already the man of 1832. It is enough to make one tremble. Basically, he had no humility.

Whatever else may be said, the author of the *Essai*

was finally in his element. He knew how to move and persuade others. He understood very well that young people and women supported him, and he could do with them as he wished. In addition, he was certain that he could attract passionate men as easily as those of more narrow intelligence, precisely through all that tends toward the absolute in the mind and in language. He knew that only the minds of the élite grasp nuances. The majority of men see in black and white.

La Mennais was also aware that he was not in an isolated position. He was no longer — as he had been in 1818 — a simple apologist for religion; he had become a political writer, and, as such, the idol of an entire party, the party in power in France at the time, and also powerful in Europe as a whole, on account of the power of the absolute monarchy. Bonald, Maistre were his allies[15]. In fact, after having fought brilliantly in the *Le Conservateur*[16] (1818–1820), La Mennais remained in the arena even after Chateaubriand[17] withdrew because he would not accept the censorship[18]. He wrote, therefore, with Bonald in *Le Défenseur;* then he wrote in *Le Drapeau Blanc,* a daily paper more impassioned than any other. Had he not proven how his bitter and burning words could at will shake the very fibre of those who were Catholic and royalist? Unbelievable! One would soon see an ordinary priest in sovereign control of the minds of the French Catholic Church, completely independent of and in spite of the episcopacy. And, to add to the singularity of this situation, the apostle owed this influence to the steadfast application of the most anti-theocratic principle on earth — the principle of freedom of the press. Remove that freedom (at that time, as in 1782 and 1789, Gallicanism[19] had the only word), and La Mennais would have been impotent.

La Mennais did not truly gain sway over public opinion until the end of 1824 (although it had been his to seize six years earlier), when he returned from Rome, where he had been showered with the kindness of Leo XII[20]. At that time, he was — or at least he seemed to be — the greatest athlete for God not only in the French Church, but also in the entire Catholic Church. The story was told a bit later that in his study, facing the crucifix, the Sovereign Pontiff would allow only two images: that of the Holy Virgin and the portrait of the author of the *Essai*.[21] It was commonly assumed for a long time, until recent denials, which I am not in a position to verify[22], that, had it not been for Villèle[23] — who did not think that a Frenchman could be clothed in crimson except under the auspices of the King — Leo XII would have appointed La Mennais a cardinal[24].

In any case, from the time of his return from Rome, the author of the *Essai* would listen to no points of view other than his own. More importantly, no one savored with so much delight the pleasure of defiance. From this point of view, he had no equal. The bitterness of his language soon became contagious. It spread more and more each day through the *Mémorial Catholique,* a monthly journal established under his patronage by two young priests, Gerbet and Salinis, with the assistance of Count O'Mahoney, a spirited man with a vigorous and merciless sense of irony. An upheaval had occurred in the tone of religious debate. To be sure, in the period of Bossuet in the seventeenth century, religious argumentation did not lack for vigor and power. But what a sense of moderation in language, even on the subject of Luther and Calvin! Émery[25] in the eighteenth; Frayssinous[26] in the nineteenth, even La Mennais himself in his *Tradition de l'Église,* all followed this example. But the *Essai sur l'indifférence* was written in a completely different tone. The debate became aggressive, haughty, provocative, filled with bitterness and irony. At first, it was more often than not just a reprisal against individuals who respected nothing, fanatical enemies of God, and the people who insulted the Church. But in *Défense de l'Essai* and in the *Mémorial,* all La Mennais' adversaries, wherever they were, above all Catholic adversaries, were pilloried repeatedly. It is difficult to do justice to the dilettantism with which all forms of derision were exhausted. Guizot[27] testified correctly that Catholicism is a great school of respect. No one deserved less than La Mennais to be the object of this praise[28].

Besides, his polemics varied little; he had only two answers, consistently supported by his adoring public. Of the Jesuits, who were suspicious of his philosophy, he said: "You don't understand anything about it." To Saint-Sulpice and the Gallicans, he answered: "You are Gallicans." His tactic, new at that time, was to crush all opposition while finding shelter under the name of the Pope. As soon as he was contradicted, he attributed it to Gallicanism, and this answer, always at the ready, freed him from the obligation of any further argument or any proof. The power words can have is a given; Gallicanism was like the head of the Medusa. On the lips of La Mennais and his friends, the evocation of the specter of Gallicanism had the virtue of magically causing people to recoil.

This is understandable.

Jansenist[29] and parliamentary [i.e., legally defined] Gallicanism[30] led to the schism of 1791[31]. After that time, the schism inspired the Organic Articles of 18 germinal 1802 [32] and laid the foundation for the so-called Concordat of Fontainebleau[33]. Under any name, it was odious. Purely theological Gallicanism became equally suspect to genuine Catholics, and justifiably so, considering the craftiness with which Napoleon, suddenly breaking with the Pope, rushed to codify into state law the Declaration of 1682[34], and to use it to create his great war machine against the liberty of the Church. It was this climate of opinion that in 1819 created the success

— impugned at first — of the book, *Du Pape,* by the Comte de Maistre[35].

But without reforming Gallicanism (which had its extenuating circumstances during the great Schism of the West[36] and during the *Ligue*[37], something too often forgotten today), history must realize that Saint-Sulpice was not favorable to the Declaration of 1682. Even if the well-established opposition of the Society to this act did not reach the point of heroism, one can never praise enough the courage above and beyond the call of duty in Émery during the critical trials of 1811[38]. At the time, was it not as a punishment for its exceptional fidelity to the Holy See that the Society of Saint-Sulpice had been dissolved and dispersed? La Mennais should have remembered that. Accordingly, it is certain that he was not at all justified in denouncing the Sulpicians as the personification of Gallicanism[39].

It was true that Saint-Sulpice rejected the *Éssai*'s doctrine on certainty. It was also true that La Mennais, "that great immoderate mind[40]," was not at all of the Sulpician temperament. Finally, it was also true that, without being champions of Bossuet[41], the successors of Émery found that the ultramontanism[42] of the author of the *Essai* went too far: for their part, they held to Gosselin's more qualified commentaries on papal power in the Middle Ages[43], and to those of Frayssinous on the true principles of the Gallican Church[44]. One could refute them, but was it appropriate to humiliate them publicly? After all, of the four famous articles drafted reluctantly by Bossuet, only one — that which sanctioned the independence of kings — had the unreserved agreement of the Sulpicians. Was that justification for covering them pell-mell with the shame of being schismatics? For a long time, had not La Mennais himself formally exempted from his reprobation this first article[45]?

Once set on a certain path, however, the author of the *Essai* could not but pursue it to its very end: finally, he did lash out against the first article as passionately as he had against the three others.

In 1826, he mounted the most provocative challenge on this point[46]. He maintained that, *without becoming exiled from God,* one could not refuse to the Pope the right to depose kings.

Should he have been allowed to go on expressing these ideas? The government made no judgment on this issue.

It is important to recognize that the situation was fairly complicated. What today would have involved no danger at that time entailed much peril. It was a moment when the piety of Charles X was seen in all quarters as delivering the state into the hands of the Church. One party that had influence in France exploited this accusation with frightening success. Important men, who were neither revolutionary nor impious, Royer-Collard[47], Lainé[48], de Montlosier[49], shared these anxieties among themselves and then, with all sincerity of intention, spread these concerns to others[50]. Presided over by Séguier, an old émigré from a family of the *parlement*[51], (it must be said), the court of Paris on 3 December 1825 had just solemnly acquitted a newspaper (*le Constitutionnel*), which had been indicted for manifesting irreligion. The court declared it acquitted — not as innocent, but justifiably excused on account of the risk that was being posed to Gallican liberties. All of this undermined the throne, and it is incontestably under the suspicion of conspiring with theocracy that Charles X's reign toppled a little bit later[52]. Given this situation, how to prevent La Mennais, an ultramontane, from seeming to be the bull-horn for the clergy, and how to prevent Villèle — if he was allowed to continue asserting his ideas with impunity — from being viewed as his collaborator.

Therefore, what was required was a disavowal that would be above all suspicion. What was required was a law suit. That is why the government thought it necessary to take off its gloves. It would have nothing to celebrate. Summoned before the tribunal of the *police correctionelle,* but defended by Berryer, La Mennais, sentenced with a perfunctory thirty francs in fines, emerged victorious from the struggle.

He was not any less outraged by the prosecution initiated against him in the name of the King, and his bitterness remained implacable. From that day forward, he considered the links that connected him with the Bourbons as broken, and there was no going back. "The state marches to its destruction," he wrote. "The Kings stumble along, their empty thrones no longer mean anything. Well! I ally myself with what remains, with what will endure, with that which will never be conquered: the cross of Jesus of Nazareth[53]."

That was a turning point in the life of La Mennais. Up to this time, he had said: "God and King." In one fell swoop, he would retract half of his motto. Henceforth, he would say: "God without the King," until one day he would finally say in his heart: "Neither God[54] nor King."

From this moment, the inevitable and irrevocable fall of the Bourbons was in his view a Providential fact (I almost said a *fait accompli*). A witness to this is still living; to him La Mennais said these very words on Easter day 1827: "What is being done to the Bourbons is definitive for all time; and I would like everything to be accomplished tomorrow; *What you are going to do, do quickly*[55]." Thirty months later, when Berryer urged him to defend the legitimists[56], who had just found refuge in the arms of old political friends of La Mennais, he responded using the words that had been used about Lazarus, who had been dead for four days: *There is an odor*[57].

In the meantime, public events took their course.

Frayssinous, Minister for Ecclesiastical Affairs, a man universally and justifiably revered, but cut out for less difficult times, vainly tried to weaken the party whose stance the enemies of religion and of the king managed to cobble together from the La Mennais position — the only fully sincere expression, they said, of the innermost thoughts of the Church in France. The prelate vainly requested the bishops in Paris to sign a public declaration of their sentiments on 3 April 1826. This unsystematic declaration only put into high relief all the ground Gallicanism had lost at the heart of the episcopacy. In fact, while disavowing La Mennais as an "official without portfolio," and while maintaining without specifying "the *accepted* wisdom of the French Church," the signatories refrained carefully from officially sanctioning the Declaration of 1682. They were content with affirming in the temporal order "the full and absolute independence of rulers from the authority, either direct *or indirect,* of any ecclesiastical power." It was under similar constraints, perhaps even more accentuated, that the other bishops individually allied themselves to the Act of 3 April. All of it lacked clarity, vigor, accent. Frayssinous had not attained the goal he had sought.

In addition, far from ceasing, anticlerical fears took flight. A longtime member of the right in the National Constituent Assembly, the Comte de Montlosier[58], had just published his famous *Mémoire à consulter contre le parti-prêtre*[59]. He showed himself to be all-powerful, absolute leader of the King's council and of the chamber of deputies, sovereign dispenser of all employment, impatient to reestablish the *billets de confession*[60] and to organize public suppression of individual conscience. France, according to him, was being governed without its knowledge by a secret society, the *Congrégation,* under the close supervision of the Jesuits, whom Montlosier denounced as having a fraudulent existence in the kingdom, citing prominently the parliamentary[61] [i.e., court] decrees[62] and the edict of Louis XV[63]. According to him, one could not sound the alarm loudly enough against such a conspiracy and such a danger[64].

What truth was there to these accusations?

It is known that the brief of Clement XVI[65], which dissolved the Society of Jesus, was not accepted by Catherine II; she preserved the Jesuits in the part of Poland that she took control of in 1772. Later, in 1801, Pius VII, canonically recognizing this situation, had approved the existence of the Jesuits in Russia; in 1814, he reestablished the Society throughout the world.

As it happens, there were in France a certain number of priests who, during the emigration, were taken by a desire for a higher perfection, and devoted themselves to a religious life according to the rules and spirit of Saint Ignatius, but without entering into communication with the Jesuits in Russia. Upon their return to their country, they opened secondary schools there under the name, "Fathers of Faith." Dealt a blow by the dispersion that resulted from the decree of 3 Messidor, Year XII[66], they were reunited once more, after the fall of the Empire, under the direction of their superior, Father Varin, and it was only then that they were individually accepted for the first time into the Society of Jesus. Obviously, they brought to the Society hardened political opinions for which the Society itself was in no way responsible.

Three months later, they were able, under the authority of the bishops, to open five *grands collèges* that were known as minor seminaries. Eight of them were in operation in 1826.

One can see in La Mennais' *Réflexions sur l'Église* the regrets felt in France and the prestige later associated with their name.

All the works of zeal were soon spontaneously entrusted to them. Among these works, one—the *Congrégation*—was made famous on account of the hate it inspired in one party.

Long before the Revolution, *Congrégation* was the name that pious associations, formed under the direction of the sons of Saint Ignatius, took throughout the world. At the end of the Revolution, an old Jesuit, then seventy years old, Father Delpuits, gave — in a sense, bestowed — this name on a group of young Christian students that he was supervising in Paris. They gathered each Sunday, heard the Mass and a lecture from their instructor, and visited the poor. During the captivity of Pius VII[67], the *Congrégation* came under suspicion, and gatherings were prohibited. But the *Congrégation* subsisted under the direction of one of the holiest priests of that time, Father Legris-Duval, who, in 1815 handed over control of the *Congrégation* to the fathers of the Society of Jesus.

All of this was innocence itself. But the founders of the Fathers of the Faith, as was previously noted, were émigrés. The spirit of emigration was prevalent among them, and moderate royalists, as well as those who sympathized with the Revolution, were in agreement in their perception of the French Jesuits as political adversaries; in spite of themselves, they overestimated Jesuit power and ability. At the same time, it happened to be the case that the young members of the *Congrégation* were for the most part royalists by birth, naturally inclined by the political loyalties of their families to put their trust in the Restoration; as a result, many of them gained positions in the civil service.

Soon, the opposition was moved to see in the *Congrégation* only careerists and hypocrites, affiliated with a secretive government that entangled all of France in its nets.

In fact, this was a huge exaggeration. I do not deny that there were at that time political intrigues, and that two or three priests, such as Liautard[68], were mixed up in them; and that vile souls, as there are in every age, were spying under religious cover. What I do deny is that the *Congrégation* was established with this goal in mind. I deny even that it slid down that slope as much as has been said; and finally, I deny that it ever possessed or exercised the influence that has been attributed to it. In 1826, when Montlosier stirred up public opinion against *the black spectre*[69], not a single minister, even Frayssinous, belonged to the *Congrégation,* and the man who was second in command in the Cabinet, Corbière, was openly opposed to it.

Indeed, there existed in France at that time, in families that had especially suffered during the Revolution, an outbreak of ideas that were excessive and, as is said of our time, profoundly reactionary. These are the ones, who, jeopardized for a long time by events, created an explosion in the Chamber session of 1815, and to whom indignation, aroused by the assassination of the Duc de Berry[70] (1820), had suddenly restored their influence. But the *Congrégation* played no role in this. Only the clergy, under the Restoration, made the mistake of associating, through its wishes as well as its actions, in the reaction that I just described — and La Mennais, by the way, more ardently, more imperiously, than all of the priests and bishops put together. Let us add, in the interest of full truth, that the French Jesuits were not distinguishable from the old clergy in this regard.

However, it was a French Jesuit, also an old émigré, an old Father of the Faith, but stationed in Rome on account of his responsibilities as Assistant General for France, inspired by the very source of the spirit of his Order — it was, I said, a French Jesuit, Father de Rozaven, who wrote these wise words in 1825:

"La Mennais seems to be *always overstepping* the truth. I read his opinions on the law of sacrilege, on the law regarding religious communities; I read his latest work[71]. His caustic tone, his constant denunciations, his grim predictions, do not convince me, but rather leave me only with a feeling of darkness in the soul. The government can answer: 'Give me a Christian people,' and I will give them laws conforming to the 'perfection of the Gospel.' Instead of shouting at the governments, the Apostles worked to convert the people. And that is, I believe, the path that needs to be taken in France, all the more since the Ministry appears to encourage the missions and all works that promote the good of society. Instead of shouting so loudly against the Ministry, which accomplishes nothing but only adds new obstacles to the good they wish to achieve, would it not be reasonable for everyone who is wise and well-intentioned to come together to support it, encourage it, to praise the little bit of good that it can do and to excuse even its faults? Bitter zeal does nothing but persuade evil and make the good more difficult to achieve... It is not the government that can render a people Christian; this is the duty of those who labor for the Gospel. All that one can expect from the government is that it encourage this enterprise[72]."

But prejudice does not view things objectively. The Society of Jesus remained the scapegoat for the political hatreds and irreligious passions of the moment. Montlosier called first and foremost for the vengeance of the law courts on the Jesuits. Then he brought his denunciation before the Chamber of Peers, which, with a majority of 113 to 73, sent it to the government, so that the latter would enforce what were called *the laws of the kingdom*. Finding himself cornered, Villèle, who was representing the Ministry and could create a bold diversion, proposed a law establishing the freedom of instruction. I should acknowledge that no one was prepared for this. The Premier Minister preferred to try to overwhelm the opposition by pouring into the Upper Chamber seventy-six new Peers who were sympathetic to his politics. At the same time, in 1827, he engineered the dissolution of the other chamber [Chamber of Deputies] to bolster up the waning authority of his majority through the popularity of a new mandate. But the casting of ballots defeated his expectations, and Charles X was forced to change his Cabinet. The King entrusted the seals to Portalis, whose report was the basis upon which the Chamber of Peers received favorably Montlosier's petition. Wasn't this to announce ahead of time the death sentence for the Jesuits?

Charles X did not intend this at all. All he wanted was to gain some time. He was under the illusion that moving Villèle aside would be sufficient to appease people. Five months passed before the new Ministers overcame his misgivings. He did not give in until after Leo XII declared that, if for motives based in political necessity — a necessity of which the King was the sole judge — it was thought necessary to close the Jesuit *collèges*, it would be inappropriate to say that this measure was objectionable[73].

Necessity, strictly speaking, did not exist at all. Who would be convinced by the argument that France dethroned Charles X only to escape the danger the kingdom faced on account of eight *collèges* run by the Jesuits? But the truth is that the situation as presented was false. What was at the root of all this? A new chamber of deputies, elected under the influence of a strong political bias. It was believed that the King was under the yoke of the clergy; it was widely believed that the clergy was hostile to the Charter and taking directions from the Jesuits. The general consensus was that the King should vigorously shake off the yoke. The Ministers demanded this, as an unequivocal measure of the monarch's support for their government. They threatened to resign en masse if this demonstration of support was not forthcoming. It was thus that they obtained the ordinances of 16 June 1828[74].

The bishops objected from all quarters. As Gallicans had always done in similar situations, Portalis did not miss the opportunity to resort to the Holy See. A letter from Cardinal Bernetti, Secretary of State, urged the bishops to trust in the wisdom of the King. At the very point when the Ministry thought the debate had been resolved, La Mennais entered the arena.

But here the *état légal* of that time needs to be described briefly.

Public law under the Empire, maintained at this point by the Restoration, was that public instruction emanated from the state. One law delegated teaching to a group that was called the *Université,* which was similar only in name to the old universities of England, Germany, and Italy. It was not at all like them; it was, in fact, a corporation with its own intrinsic life and independence. The French *Université* was nothing more than a branch of the government; all its members were chosen by the government and most could be fired at its will. At the same time, as was noted in the Introduction, it held in its hands the key to all academic careers; it was a form of centralization, and also one of its potent forces.

One of the first acts of reparation by Talleyrand's provisional government in 1814[75] was to respond to the public outcry by placing the authority and direction for education into the hands of individual families[76]. On 5 October 1814, a further step was taken in this direction: the minor seminaries, freed from any jurisdictional control by the *Université,* were placed completely in the hands of the bishops. Eight prelates took advantage of this freedom to teach the Jesuits in their own homes. It was in this that Portalis saw a double fraud in the law, which admitted no exception to the monopoly of the *Université* except in obvious ecclesiastical vocations, but which, on the other hand, did not allow any title or under any pretext the right of association and common life of men who had made the vow of chastity, obedience, and poverty, unless authorized by the state.

In the presence of a similar thesis put forth by a minister of Charles X, there was not a single outcry from Catholic families. La Mennais seized the opportunity provided by the public distress. Six thousand copies of his book, *Des Progrès de la Révolution et de la guerre contre l'Église* [The progress of the Revolution and the war against the Church] were snapped up in less than two weeks.

One could have foreseen from him this declaration of war. In fact, the *Université* did not have an adversary that was older or more enlightened [than the Church]. La Mennais had played a role at certain times in the long struggles of the *Université's* predecessor, disputing every inch of the terrain in his Brittany that was claimed by the Imperial *Université* of 1808 and of 1809. Féli had branded this *Université* with a hot iron in his first diatribe in 1814. In 1817, he took up the charge again. The following year, he published a third manifesto, *De l'Éducation dans ses rapports avec la liberté* [The relationship of education with liberty]. Finally, on 22 August 1823, he released his famous *Lettre au Grand-Maître* (the Grand Master being at that time Frayssinous). But all of this did not compare to his final work, which appeared at the beginning of 1829.

All the same, the ordinances of 1828 were but the occasion for the work. Basically, the work had its roots in something entirely different. Notwithstanding its title (*Des Progrès de la Révolution et de la guerre contre l'Église*), a title calculated to attract men rooted in the past, La Mennais was bringing about through it a change in the direction of modern political trends — a change that was indeed unforeseen and not well understood.

As early as the book's third page, one reads the following words: "We ask for the Catholic Church the liberty promised by the Charter to all religions, the liberty that Protestants and Jews enjoy, that the Muslim and Buddhist would enjoy if they lived in France. . . . We demand freedom of conscience, freedom of the press, freedom of education. The Belgian Catholics, like us, are demanding the same things, oppressed as they are by a mistreating government."

The entire agenda of *L'Avenir* is already present in these few words. La Mennais did not go so far as to advocate openly an alliance with liberalism, as he did after the Revolution of 1830. But from that time forward, as we can see, he consistently extolled the Belgian Catholics, who had begun actively to put this alliance into action. On this last point, he was more explicit in his letters[77].

Is it necessary to explain this evolution? Since his trial, as has been noted — that is to say, for the last three years — La Mennais had ceased to be a royalist. Nevertheless, he had remained, I concede, more pessimistic, more alarmist, more anti-liberal than ever[78]." But two significant popular movements, taking place outside of France, to the benefit of Catholicism, opened to the author of the *Essai* entirely new horizons. It was the era when the voice of a great leader, Daniel O'Connell, forcing open the doors of the British Parliament and, with the assistance of the Irish people, was able to bring about the emancipation of Catholics in the three kingdoms. It was also the time when the ordinances against the Jesuits appeared in France, when freedom of education was violated in Belgium by the Calvinist king of the Low Countries. That was enough. The protest of Catholic Belgians, passionate admirers of the great Irish activist, called forth, from the solitude of La Chênaie, a reverberation as powerful as it was unexpected. The events just described profoundly altered La Mennais' point of view.

Starting with the month of July 1828, in the wake of the ordinances of Portalis[79], the *Mémorial Catholique,* the monthly organ of the Mennaissian school, thundered against both persecutions, the one in Belgium and the one in France.

In a few more months, La Mennais would confidently write these very words: "An immense liberty is indispensable in order for the truths that save the world, *if indeed it ought to be saved,* to evolve as they should[80]." And not long thereafter: "*Everything must be accomplished through the people,* which is to say, a new people, formed gradually through the influence of a better-conceived Christianity, in the midst of the ruined nations[81]. . . When the Catholics join in the cry for *liberty,* many things will change[82]."

Are we not increasingly finding ourselves on the path toward *L'Avenir?*

It was not that La Mennais abjured his utopian theocracy for this. Far from it. He only was changing the means by which this would be accomplished: losing hope in the kings, he began to place hope in the people. "Is it the case," he wrote, "that French Catholics, who number more than twenty-five million, will not end up asking themselves whether, when the question is reduced to sheer strength, they will not count for something in this issue?" But the people, like the kings, should always remain the ministers and soldiers of the Church. "In my view," wrote the author of l'*Essai,* "Society is *one.* Temporal sovereignty is nothing other than the duty imposed on those in power to maintain the spiritual society, *the only true society,* submitting the forces of rebellion to the commandments of God, of which society is henceforth the *minister of the Good,* as the Apostle said. As soon as the forces in power turn their actions against the spiritual society, they are no longer sovereign. The Church, in this case, does not *take away* the sovereignty, but only declares that it no longer exists; She resolves an issue of conscience for her subjects[83].

It did not occur to La Mennais to wonder whether this theory had a chance of being accepted. "What does it matter?" he wrote. "One owes it to men to speak the truth; one must speak it to the every end, even when they can no longer hear it: some to life, others to death." Extravagant minds have never had any other language but this.

However, the time had come for La Mennais to become a pragmatic man. He no longer limited himself to writing; he wished to act. In response to the ordinances of Portalis, an association was formed for the defense of religion. La Mennais consistently claimed the credit for this idea[84]. De facto, it removed the direction of the Catholic opposition from the Bishops and placed it squarely in the hands of the Mennaisians[85].

But the Association[86] was far from producing what the head of the Mennaisian school had promised. Largely composed of friends of the Jesuits and of men who adhered to the politics of the extreme right, the Association found itself at the opposite pole from the ideas and sentiments of the author of *l'Essai*. The administration, as Mennaisian as it was, was under pressure to take into account the Association's composition.

Thus, in spite of La Mennais, the membership allowed the Association to establish *Le Correspondant*, under the secondary influence of Bailly (who applied tenacious and incessant pressure). *Le Correspondant* was at first a semiweekly folio, destined to be the counterpart to a similar publication, *Le Globe*, created by Pierre Leroux and Dubois (from the Loire-Inférieure[87]), and which had become under the direction of the latter the most important mouthpiece for the anti-dynastic and anti-Christian opposition[88]. The *Le Correspondant*[89], in turn, would soon confound the expectations of its founders. Entrusted to the youthful elite from *Bonnes Études,* the journal remained royalist, and, in this regard, as well as in its moderation, it displeased La Mennais, who never was able to tolerate it. But the publication was of its time, and from this perspective, it was not at all influenced by the throwback ideas of its owners.

Another of La Mennais' ideas did hold promise. Early on, he thought of making la Chênaie a Catholic Port-Royal[90], a center for religious studies that would be totally independent of Episcopal direction. From 1825 on, he attracted to that place a man of some very real distinction in certain areas — Gerbet : of a delicate character, a somewhat laconic nature, a weak will, the soul of a poet, an exquisitely elevated intelligence, suave, adroit, tentative, it must be said, like the author of *Maximes des Saints*[91]. The salient feature of Gerbet was gentleness. His voice was weak, but saturated with honey, as Lacordaire described it. The gift of improvisation and spontaneity had not been granted to him. Yet he possessed another kind of gift, which was even more rare in the Mennaisian school: the gift of gracefulness. No one contributed more than he to charm the evening readings and the walks at Brittany's Port-Royal. He believed himself called to be the Ignatius of Loyola of the nineteenth century. He wished to establish a religious institute that would supplant and replace that of the Jesuits, which, according to him, was now but a shadow of its former self[92]. He even informed Pope Leo XII of his project, but the Pope issued a dilatory and evasive response[93].

La Mennais followed through on this plan. Under his brother's name as the ostensible head of the new religious institute, he acquired in Malestroit[94], in the diocese of Vannes, a house where he established the seminary for his project, which he called the Congregation of Saint Peter. Malestroit was only three leagues from Ploërmel, the center for the Institute of the Brothers of Christian Instruction, of which Father Jean de La Mennais was the founder and the Superior General. In addition, he belonged to the community of missionaries in the diocese of Rennes, who directed the major and the minor seminaries[95]. It is clear that there was quite a large network that encompassed not only the diocese of Rennes, but all of Brittany.

La Chênaie, where Father Féli resided, was a kind of vestibule for Malestroit. The teacher set about to gather around himself those of his followers who had not yet taken the step of becoming involved in the Congregation of Saint Peter.

The study of living languages flourished there, and Féli himself gave lessons in Italian and English, delighting in reading texts with his students in the original language, whether it was [Dante Alighieri's] *The Divine Comedy* or [John Milton's] *Paradise Lost*.

The halo that crowned the author of *l'Essai sur l'Indifférence* attracted men of real merit to that place. As has been noted, Gerbet lived at La Chênaie. The Superior of Malestroit was Blanc, author of a remarkable history of the Church; and the director of studies was Rohrbacher, who needs no further introduction[96]. Included among the teachers was Hercé, previously a member of the House of Deputies during the Restoration, who, at the time of his death, was Bishop of Nantes (chosen by Louis-Philippe). Numerous young people rushed there — whether to Malestroit or to La Chênaie — filled with energy and fervor. Included among them was Eugène Boré[97], known for his chivalrous journey into Persia, for his wide-ranging studies in many disciplines, and for the eminent services he rendered to the Church in Constantinople. In addition to him, there were many individuals of superior intellect. However, there were also romantics among them, men incapable of accommodating themselves to the exigencies of real life. Maurice de Guérin[98] was one of these.

From the beginning, the Mennaisian school had reached out to Lacordaire. Before leaving Dijon, Henri had served as Secretary for External Relations for the *Société d'Études,* which had Gerbet as its representative in Paris. Naturally, the latter received Lacordaire with flourish and introduced him to La Mennais in the spring of 1823. The young Burgundian lawyer was not at all impressed. The following is Lacordaire's description of the great writer, after their first encounter: "He is a small, wizened man, with a thin and yellowish face, simple in his ways, razor-sharp in his conversation, *which focused primarily on his book.* Nothing about him bespoke his genius. If one were to place him among other men of the Church, with this brown frock coat, his short trousers, and his black silk stockings, one could easily mistake him for a parish sacristan[99]."

Lacordaire was more impressed by Gerbet. The day preceding the publication of *Mémorial Catholique* (December 1823), the Father's overtures becoming increasingly insistent, he obtained from Henri — already won over in the secrecy of his heart — the promise of collaboration, which finally shrank down to the writing of one article[100]. Three months later, as he was entering the seminary, Lacordaire asked Gerbet and Salinis to be his sponsors. In January 1825, Gerbet stepped down from his position as assistant chaplain of the Collège Henri IV and renounced the prospect of a quiet life with Salinis to give himself completely to La Mennais and to join his associates at La Chênaie. He spoke about Lacordaire to the Teacher [La Mennais], and the Teacher could not but yearn for such a disciple. On 4 March, Gerbet wrote to Henri, to plead with him (it was in fact too late) not to be incorporated into the diocese of Paris until he had received information "that concerned the good of the Church." On 8 May, he announced to Lacordaire that a visit from La Mennais was imminent. It never took place.

During the month of September of that same year, Gerbet warmly invited Lacordaire to spend the rest of his vacation at La Chênaie. "This concerns critically important issues, that cannot be explained except in person, issues that without doubt have been arranged by Providence, and that could result in a great Good, to which you could make a significant contribution[101]." Lacordaire was not moved by this appeal. "I like," he wrote, "neither the philosophical system of La Mennais, which I believe to be untrue, nor his political opinions, which I find to be excessive. Nor do I like his attitude, which it seems to me robs talent of a great part of what it could accomplish for the Good. I have decided not to be part of any coterie, however illustrious it may be. I want to belong only to the Church[102]." There could be no more elevated sentiment nor verbal expression.

The following year, the overtures were redoubled, with no greater success. A bit later, La Mennais, hounded, as previously noted, by the *police correctionelle,* was reprimanded by the bishops of France, by the Sulpicians, by the Jesuits. "He would be alone in the world," said Lacordaire. "which for him was an infallible sign that he was right[103]."

In 1829, during the month of July, the distance Lacordaire kept from La Mennais was still in full force. "What is your opinion of the book, *Progrès de la Révolution* [104]? Does it not seem to you to be an exaggeration of the ideas of Maistre? It has often occurred to me that this writer does not come up with his own ideas. He simply parrots the ideas of his predecessors, while inflating them out of proportion. I feel as if I were watching a painter recreating Poussin's *Déluge* in a 100- by 100-foot size[105]." But a bit later in that same year, as was noted earlier, during the idleness of vacation, a terrible storm brewed in Father Lacordaire's soul. Without sustenance from without, this flame devoured itself. It was not without reason that God said: "It is not good for man to be alone[106]." - "I have no companions in any sphere of my life," we read in one of his letters in the month of September. "My room no longer knows the footsteps of friends. In my studies for the priesthood, I found not a single soul with whom I could lose myself in true communication. Such an individual is far from me. I have banished all the unmindful ones, to whom I have nothing to say. My friends for all time (those from Dijon) still have all my affection, and the memories of them are the only thing on Earth that moves me. I will not try to give you as proof a pouring out of doctrines and projects; my thoughts and I, we live too much day to day, and rarely does the sun rise for us in the same place as on the preceding day[107]."

"God has indeed changed me. He has created a thousand deserts around me. I am transformed into something different every day[108]."

Not only did he suffer from his isolation; but also from the inaction and passivity of the clergy which weighed on him terribly; he felt he was suffocating, like a bird on the receiving end of pneumatic machinery[109]. "How is it possible to think, when there is no longer any Catholic thought? How to speak, when all of Israel sleeps[110]?"

Everything was lacking all at once. He wished that God would send France a great statesman. Mockery! The Richelieu of that time was Polignac[111]. "I await our liberator," Lacordaire wrote, "And all I see is the sun covered in dust." He had thought himself called to the apostolate in the *collèges,* but how could he not have been appalled by the fruitlessness of his ministry at [*Collège*] Henri IV? At the same time, he continued to be the recipient of the most tender solicitations from La Chênaie[112]. Affected by these incessant requests, as if under the influence of deluded ethical motives, the young chaplain reread the works of La Mennais, especially those that discussed the relationship of religion to the political order. As a result, he came to the point of persuading himself that he had misjudged the lone wolf of La Chênaie[113]. His interior dispositions had changed. Thus tested and thus tempted, how could Lacordaire not have felt a deep need, a passionate need, to attach himself to someone, to join someone on a project, to end his sterile existence by joining his efforts to those of others? In one of the sudden decisions that were not uncommon in his life, he turned toward the young republic of the United States and toward the only school of Catholic thought that had any real vigor, any semblance of a future. In order no longer to be alone and ineffective, he wished to bring to the New World the prestige and influence of this school, which, at least was not somnolent — one which aspired to new and vibrant studies, and that above all would henceforth be a friend of liberty.

"It is La Mennais," he wrote, "who will be the founder in France of a Christian *and American* liberty[114]." — "To lift the Church out of the state of entanglement it is in at home, to place it in a state of absolute independence such as the Church in America has: this is what must be done first and foremost. Once I came to this conclusion, I went to La Chênaie[115]."

Indeed he went there during the month of May 1830, at the instigation of Jules Morel, a young Mennaisian priest, with whom he had become friends at Saint-Sulpice and who was to travel with him to America. On his deathbed, Lacordaire judged himself severely for this decision. Let us hear him in his own words:

"Two months before the Revolution of 1830, convinced that my priestly vocation in France would never be able to develop freely, I decided to seek in the United States of America a theater of action more in line with the ideas that preoccupied me. Once this decision was made, the idea took hold of me to become better acquainted with La Mennais and to pay him a visit in Brittany, in his house at La Chênaie. I had seen him only twice, very briefly. But, after all, he was the only man of great stature in the French Church, and the few clergymen that I knew well were his friends.

"Once I arrived in Dinan, I plunged alone along dark paths through the woods. After asking directions several times, I found myself facing a somber and isolated house, whose mysterious fame not a single noise disturbed. It was La Chênaie.

"La Mennais, alerted ahead of time by a letter that announced my visit and my support, received me cordially. Near him was Gerbet, his closest disciple, and a dozen young people, whom he had gathered in the shadow of his glory, as the seed of the future for his ideas and projects. Early the following day, he had me summoned to his chambers and wished that I listen to two chapters of a philosophical theology that he was preparing, one on the Trinity, the other on creation. These two chapters, very eccentric and full of generalizations, were the basis of his work. I heard the reading with astonishment: his explanation of the Trinity struck me as incorrect, and that of the creation more so.

"After dinner, we gathered in a clearing, where all the young people amused themselves happily with their Teacher. In the evening, everyone gathered in an old undecorated living room. La Mennais was semi-reclined on a chaise longue, with Gerbet seated on the end, and the young people gathered in a circle around them. The conversation and the general attitude were infused with a certain idolatry, the likes of which I had never witnessed before. The four-day visit, while surprising me more than once, did not break the bond that had just been formed with the illustrious writer. His philosophy had never been clear in my mind; his absolutist politics had always repelled me; his theology had just thrown me into doubt regarding his very orthodoxy. Nevertheless, it was too late: I had allied myself, without enthusiasm, but of my own will, to the School, which up to this point, had been unable to gain either my sympathy or my beliefs. This erroneous step, difficult to understand, was to determine my fate[116]."

It was basically a mistake, but the attenuating circumstances are self-evident. Is it not obvious that the parties involved were unequal? Lacordaire, young, unknown, unsure of himself, was seeking his own voice. La Mennais had found his, he knew what he wanted, he had the double advantage of age and of renown. How could he not have dominated in the relationship with Lacordaire, given the prominence fame had given him? In addition, his winning point with regard to Lacordaire was his political conversion. It was from this perspective, in the eyes of Lacordaire, that La Mennais made up for his weaker points, and gained credibility. "He was a Druid revived in Armorique[117]," said Henri, "who sings of liberty in a voice that is somewhat primitive. The heavens are blessed! The word *liberty* is eloquent on every lyre, even when there is only one string of the instrument left, as in Sparta[118]."

In addition, there was in the very person of the author of the *Essai* a seemingly limitless seductiveness. Cardinal Wiseman gave testimony to this, in the following portrait that he sketched from memory thirty years later:

"It is difficult to say how he was able to gain such a great influence over others. His air and his facial expression were little suited to commanding respect; he lacked stature, had an authoritative attitude, and not a single external grace. Several times, in different periods of his life, I had lengthy conversations with him. He was always the same: head bent over, holding his hands folded together in front of him, or rubbing them slowly one against the other; In answering a question, he could express himself in a single wave of thoughts flowing spontaneously and seamlessly. He was able to embrace the subject as a whole and at the same time to divide it into its different points, as symmetrically as did Fléchier[119] or Massillon. All of this was carried out in a tone that was monotonous, but gentle. His reasoning was so air-tight, and at the same time so polite and elegant, that if one closed one's eyes, one could imagine listening to a finished book being read aloud[120]."

No fireworks, it is true. But also no dressing up, no grandiosity, no charlatanism. This frail being, sickly, suffering, who spoke in such a modest and coherent way, could win one over quickly through his very simplicity. The more as writer he had aggrieved anyone through his acerbity and condescension, all the more as man could he overtake, penetrate, and charm in his moments of simplicity, gentleness, and spontaneity. It is impossible to convey how good, affectionate, and even tender he could be toward those he hoped to win over. Lacordaire agreed completely with him on the direction of the clergy of the United States. "La Mennais," he wrote, "knows about the Bishop of New York's proposal; he approved it. *We have associated this proposal to great plans,* and several of us, friends, will leave together next spring[121]."

ENDNOTES

- Originally 58 footnotes, changed to endnotes. New endnotes by translators are in bold face numbers.

1. It seems that in Breton [a Celtic language spoken in Brittany—*Trans.*] "menez" means "mountain." The small La Mennais farm is located in the township of Trigavou, in the district of Dinan (Côtes-du-Nord).
2. Hannibal (B. C. 247–183), a hero of the second Punic War, held an oath from the age of nine on to wreak vengeance on the Romans who had taken possession of lands belonging to Carthage.
3. De La Gournerie: Introduction to the Correspondence between La Mennais and Bruté.
4. In a letter from Féli to Bruté (17 February 1809), one reads: "When I reflect on my past life, on this life *filled with offenses,* the most rigorous self-denial, the severest and most drawn-out penances would not be enough to expiate it." Féli, born 19 June 1782, was then about twenty-seven years old.
5. Located in the township of Plesder, district of Saint-Malo, eight kilometers from Dinan.
6. Pope Pius VII (1742–1823) refused to enact Napoleon's Continental System, which involved a trade embargo on Great Britain and Ireland. In an effort to force the pope to accede to his wishes, Napoleon ordered General Mollis (2 February 1808) to occupy Rome. Source: *Hansard's Parliamentary Debates: Third Series, Commencing with the Accession of William IV, Comprising the Period From the Tenth Day of August to the Fifth Day of September, 1848* (London: G. Woodfall and Son, 1848), p.210. Accessed 2 October 2010, at http://books.google.com/books?id=FcE9AAAAcAAJ&pg=PA209&lpg=PA209&dq=general+mollis+rome+1808&source

=bl&ots=IZpi-71oPL&sig=dctRkQTwAOo8voyr7o1NzVj Kybg&hl=en&ei=1sinTKSdMis01QeNh4XvDA&sa=X&oi =book_result&ct=result&resnum=1&sqi=2&ved=0CBQQ6 AEwAA#v=onepage&q=general%20mollis%20rome%2018 08&f=false. [cdt]

7. Joseph Fouché (1759–1820), Napoleon's Minister of Police.

8. Through the council of 1811, Napoleon sought a way to bypass the influence of the pope and to assume administrative control of the French and Italian dioceses. *The Catholic Encyclopedia,* Volume X, ed. George G. Herbermann et al. (New York: The Encyclopedia Press, Inc.: 1913), p. 696. [cdt]

9. "I came to Paris for the printing of *our* work: *La Tradition,* etc., which will appear in the next three weeks or later." —Letter from Féli, 24 July 1814 (*Corresp. Bruté,* p. 99).—"*La Tradition* is MY work, and I based it COMPLETELY on the texts that Jean collected" (Ibid., p. 95).

10. Recent discoveries have indicated that, when ordination was imminent, terrible scruples shook the soul of La Mennais, and that he was ordained a priest in spite of himself. I believe there is no conclusion one can draw from this passing crisis: many excellent priests have experienced a similar one.

La Mennais became a subdeacon at the age of thirty-three, a priest at thirty-four. He was a good priest for a long time (See a letter from Father Gerbet about the illness of his teacher in 1827.—*Corresp. de La Mennais,* volume I, p. 270).

11. Jacques-Bénigne Bossuet (1627–1704) and Jean-Baptiste de Massillon (1663–1742) were celebrated French bishops and preachers.

12. *Considérations sur le système philosophique de M. de La Mennais,* p. 35 and following. - See also the Internet: www.worksoflacordaire.com, under: *Reflections...*

13. "Clovis (c. 466–511), the first Catholic king to rule over Gaul (France), was converted as an adult to Catholicism by

Saint Remigius and received into the Church at Rheims. At his baptism, St. Remigius held up the cross and said: 'Adore that which you have hitherto burned, burn the idols that you have hitherto adored.'" Quotation from *The Age of Hildebrand: Introduction to the Rise of the Papal Supremacy,* Third Millennium Library. Accessed 7 October 2010, at http://www.third-millennium-library.com/ MedievalHistory/Age_of_Gregory_VII/INTRODUCTION/2.html. [cdt]

14. Letter to Father Carron, 1 November 1820. — *Corresp. de La Mennais,* volume I, pp. 39 and 90. — Submitted in confidence by Father de La Mennais to Joseph de Maistre, this inclination toward a recourse to Rome was not followed up on. — [Joseph de Maistre (1753–1821) supported the restoration of the House of Bourbon and of the Roman Catholic Church as the official religion of France.]

15. Louis de Bonald (1754–1840), like Joseph de Maistre (see footnote 14), supported the restoration of the House of Bourbon and of the Roman Catholic Church as the official religion of France.

16. A newspaper published by ultra-royalists, supporters of Charles X.

17. François-René, vicomte de Chateaubriand (1768–1848), a royalist and devout Catholic, was a writer, politician, and diplomat. He was the author of the famous *Le Génie du Christianisme* (1802).

18. Perhaps this refers to a process to insure that the contributors to the paper "toed the line."

19. "Gallicanism, a complex of French ecclesiastical and political doctrines and practices advocating restriction of papal power .... Despite its several varieties, Gallicanism consisted of three basic ideas: independence of the French king in the temporal order; superiority of an ecumenical council over the

pope; and union of clergy and king to limit the intervention of the pope within the kingdom." Quotation from "**Gallicanism**," *Encyclopædia Britannica*, 2010. Accessed 3 October 2010, at <http://www.britannica.com/EBchecked/topic/224387/Gallicanism>. [cdt]

20. On 10 October 1824, La Mennais wrote to de Croÿ, the Grand Almoner of France: "Three weeks ago, the Sovereign Pontiff asked me insistently to accept lodgings in the Vatican." — FORGUES, *Notes et Souvenirs*, p. 40.

21. *Corresp. de La Mennais*, volume II, p. 49.

22. Monsieur CRÉTINEAU-JOLY, volume II, pp. 339–340 of his book, *L'Église romaine en face de la Révolution*.

23. Jean-Baptiste de Villèle (1773–1854), French statesman and ultra-royalist.

24. Cardinal Wiseman (*Recollections of the last four Popes*, part II, chapter VII) reported the language used by Pope Leo in his Consistory speech in which he declared a cardinal reserved *in petto:* "an accomplished writer whose works have not only rendered a great service to religion, but have delighted and surprised Europe." These statements, Wiseman acknowledged, described La Mennais more accurately than anyone else.

25. Sulpician superior (d. 1811).

26. Denis de Frayssinous (1765–1841) is known primarily for his conferences at Notre-Dame de Paris, which attempted to reinvigorate religious belief after the Revolution.

27. François Pierre Guillaume Guizot (1787–1874), French orator, historian, and politician.

28. See Appendix XI, page 533.

29. "Jansenists called for ecclesiastical affairs to be regulated by a general council of the church. Conciliarist anti-papalism was combined with a call for a more democratic power-structure within the church." Quotation from Colin Jones, *The Great Nation: France from Louis XV to Napoleon* (New York:

Columbia University Press, 2002), p. 99. Accessed 3 February 2011, at

http://books.goonepagem/books?id=auSg60LiOvkC&printsec=frontcover&dq=The+Great+Nation:+France+from+Louis+XV+to+Napoleon&hl=en&ei=TPNKTaf-LtPngQfIn5H-Dw&sa=X&oi=book_result&ct=result&resnum=1&ved=0CCkQ6AEwAA#v=onepage&q&f=false. [cdt]

30. "Parliamentary Gallicanism, a position of the *parlements*, advocated the complete subordination of the French Church to the state and even the government's intervention in financial and disciplinary matters." Quotation from William J. Roberts. *France: A Reference Guide from the Renaissance to the Present.* (New York: Facts on File, Inc., 2004), p. 300. Accessed 3 October 2010, at

http://books.google.com/books?id=ogdZu2l2CYkC&pg=PA300&dq=jansenist+parliamentary+gallicanism&hl=en&ei=bMSoTNKkFoGBlAeN3KjXDQ&sa=X&oi=book_result&ct=result&resnum=1&ved=0CCcQ6AEwADgK#v=onepage&q&f=false. [cdt]

31. The schism of 1791 occurred between juring and non-juring priests (i.e., those who agreed to abide by regulations exerting the state's control over religion, and those priests who refused to do so).

32. The Organic Articles of 1802, promulgated by Napoleon and opposed by Pope Pius VII, greatly increased the power of the state in matters of religion.

33. The Concordat of Fontainebleau was signed by Napoleon and Pius VII on 25 January 1813. In it, the Pope gave up his temporal authority and part of his religious authority. This marked the rupture of the union of Church and State.

34. The Declaration of the Clergy of France Concerning Ecclesiastical Power (1682) officially articulated the four key principles of Gallicanism. "According to the Gallican theory,

... the papal primacy was limited, first, by the temporal power of princes, which, by the Divine will, was inviolable; secondly by the authority of the general council and that of the bishops, who alone could, by their assent, give to his decrees that infallible authority which, of themselves, they lacked; lastly, by the canons and customs of particular Churches, which the pope was bound to take into account when he exercised his authority." Quotation from "Gallicanism," *The Catholic Encyclopedia*, Volume VI, p. 352. [cdt]

35. In *Du Pape,* Joseph de Maistre (1753–1821) asserts, among other ideas, the sovereignty of the pope and the infallibility of papal teaching. Source: "Joseph-Marie, Comte de Maistre," *The Catholic Encyclopedia*, Volume IX, p. 554. [cdt]

36. The Great Western Schism (1378-1417 [or 1430]). This was marked by political intrigue and created a pontifical crisis: one Pope elected in Rome, another in Avignon. Here are to be found the roots of Gallicanism. It also marked the dissolution of feudal society.

37. The Catholic League, formed in 1576 by the Duc Henri de Guise aimed, among numerous other goals, to stem the rising tide of Protestantism.

38. In 1811, Napoleon ordered the suppression of the Society of Saint-Sulpice. Source: Charles George Herbermann, *The Sulpicians in the United States* (New York: The Encyclopedia Press, 1916), p. 197. Accessed 4 February 2011, at http://books.google.com/books?id=678QAAAAIAAJ&printsec=frontcover&dq=The+Sulpicians+in+the+United+States&hl=en&ei=4_JLTeXTKsnZgAfDsLH9Dw&sa=X&oi=book_result&ct=result&resnum=1&ved=0CCcQ6AEwAA#v=onepage&q&f=false. [cdt]

39. See his Report to Leo XII, *Œuvres inédites,* published by Blaize, volume II, p. 330.

40. Sainte-Beuve.

41. Bossuet was a principal architect of the Declaration of the Clergy of 1682.

42. A point of view in the Roman Catholic Church that supports the supremacy of papal power.

43. Jean-Edmé-Auguste Gosselin (1787–1858), superior of the Sulpician seminary from 1831 to 1844. His most famous work is *Pouvoir du Pape au moyen âge* (1839).

44. *The True Principles of the Liberty of the Gallican Church (1818).*

45. See his *Tradition de l'Église,* introduction, p. 72; above all, his *Observations sur la promesse d'enseigner les quatre articles de 1682,* published in May 1824: "I don't claim to take sides for or against the four articles; I EVEN DECLARE TO HOLD AS MUCH AS ANYONE TO THE FIRST (p. 9). . . . The doctrine of the power of popes over the temporal sovereignty of kings no longer has support, even "across the mountains" [this term probably refers to Rome—*Translator*] . . . the independence of sovereigns in the temporal order *being universally recognized,* one sees no reason to proscribe the teaching of the first article (p. 25)."

46. *La Religion considérée dans ses rapports avec l'ordre politique et civil* (second part). — A letter from the author to the Count de Senfft (26 February 1826) left no doubt about his plan to defy the government on this point (*Corresp.,* volume I, p. 162).

47. Pierre-Paul Royer-Collard (1763–1845), philosopher and politician. He was a member of the French Academy starting in 1827.

48. Lainé: supporter of Gallicanism. See note 50.

49. François Dominique de Reynaud, Count of Montlosier (1755–1838). In 1791, he was elected to the National Constituent Assembly, where he sat on the royalist side.

50. The following is an account of the arguments of these and

other men against the power of religion over the state: "Casimir Perier, Royer-Collard, Pasquier, and Lainé, in accusing the government of culpable complaisance, appealed to the nation with all the authority of their talents and character, against the theocratic principle which threatened religion and society alike, against a theocracy more political than religious, which in the words of Royer-Collard 'has all the appearance of a Counter-Revolution.' With greater violence Montlosier denounced before the Royal Courts of Justice the encroachments of the Clergy and prophesied a speedy return to the tumults and bloodshed of the *Ligue*." Quotation from Émile Bourgeois, *History of Modern France: 1815–1913* (Cambridge, U.K.: Cambridge University Press, 1919), p. 84. Accessed 4 February 2011 [by cdt], at http://books.google.com/books?id=j01LAAAAMAAJ&pg=PA84&dq=Royer-Collard,++Lain%C3%A9++de+Montlosier&hl=en&ei=zwFMTYCSCYjVgAeerawu&sa=X&oi=book_result&ct=result&resnum=1&ved=0CC4Q6AEwAA#v=onepage&q&f=false.

51. The *parlement* was "the supreme court under the *ancien régime* in France. It developed out of the Curia Regis (King's Court), in which the early kings of the Capetian dynasty (987–1328) periodically convened their principal vassals and prelates to deliberate with them on feudal and political matters. It also dealt with the few legal cases submitted to the king as sovereign judge." Quotation from "Parlement," *Encyclopædia Britannica*, 2011. Accessed 4 February 2011, at <http://www.britannica.com/EBchecked/topic/444192/Parlement>. [cdt]

52. Some caricatures depicted Charles X celebrating Mass in his private apartments. These caricatures were widely believed. (Gerbet, letter of 18 February 1827 — *Corresp. de La Mennais,* volume I, p. 226).

Charles Philippe, Charles X (1757-1836), was "the Beloved" of the Bourbon family.
- "Prosecution" refers to filing a law suit.
53. To the Countess of Senfft, 24 April 1826.—He had been sentenced on the 22nd.
54. In the *Esquisse d'une philosophie,* La Mennais is pantheist, which is indisputably one of the forms of atheism.
55. The Bourbon dynasty, which had been overthrown in the July Revolution of 1830. During the Restoration, they were referred to as the "ultra-royalists."
56. The text in italics quotes Jesus' words after Satan has entered into Judas (John 13:27).
57. Source: John 11:39b. After Jesus asks Martha to take away the stone covering the entrance to the cave where Lazarus had lain dead, Martha says: *"Lord, by this time there will be an odor, for he has been dead four days."*
58. 1 March 1826.
59. Francois Dominique de Reynaud, Comte de Montlosier (1755–1838). In 1791, he was elected to the National Constituent Assembly, where he sat on the royalist side.
60. The *billets* were papers affirming submission to a bull (issued by Pope Clement XI), which suspected Jansenists were ordered to sign. (Source: **"Billets de confession**." *Encyclopædia Britannica.* 2010. Encyclopædia Britannica Online. 02 Oct. 2010
<http://www.britannica.com/EBchecked/topic/65386/**billets-de-confession**>.) [cdt]
61. *Arrêts* were final decisions made through royal power, expressing "the king's law with incontestable authority." Quotation from "**arrêt**," *Encyclopædia Britannica,* 2010. Accessed 2 October 2010 [cdt], at
http://www.britannica.com/EBchecked/topic/36076/arret>.

62. The *parlement* was historically the supreme court in France. See note 51, above.

63. "European monarchs, like Louis XV (1715–1774) wanted more control over church affairs. In 1762, Louis expelled the Jesuits out of France and confiscated all their property." Quotation from "Rise and Fall of the Jesuit Order," 101.com, 2010. Accessed 2 October 2010, at http://www.suite101.com/content/the-jesuits-a44644. [cdt]

64. The *Denuntiation* of Montlosier against the Jesuits was filed with a clerk of the Court of Paris on 16 July 1816.

65. The Brief of Suppression (1773).

66. Year XII of the Republican calendar is 1804, when a decree during the Empire suppressed congregations that had still managed to come into being in spite of previous laws outlawing religious life.

67. (1809–1814).

68. An ultra-royalist sympathizer.

69. A pejorative term for Jesuits, presumably on account of their black religious habit.

70. The Duc de Berry was born in 1778, and had spent his youth and early manhood in exile. . . . The French nobility of the old *régime* looked upon him as the hope of the Bourbon dynasty." Quotation from Francis Johnson, *Famous Assassinations of History* (Chicago: A.C. McClurg & Co., 1903), pp. 332–333. Accessed 3 February 2011, at http://books.google.com/books?id=kloWAAAAYAAJ&printsec=frontcover&dq=Famous+Assassinations+of+History&hl=en&ei=Qh1LTZGpKJD1gAf90OEy&sa=X&oi=book_result&ct=result&resnum=3&ved=0CDkQ6AEwAg#v=onepage&q&f=false. [cdt]

71. *La Religion considerée dans ses rapports avec la société* [Religion in its relation with society.]

72. Letter of 24 July 1825, addressed to Mme Swetchine.

73. *Père de Ravignan,* by Poujoulat, p. 206, according to notations made by Frayssinous, one of the three French prelates that were then consulted by Charles X; the two others were the Archbishop of Paris (de Quélen) and the Archbishop of Bordeaux (Cheverus).

74. Poujoulat, work previously cited.—These ordinances took away from the Jesuits the eight educational institutions that they had previously directed, and to prevent them from returning to them, required the superiors of minor seminaries to declare that the institutions did not belong to any religious congregation.

75. Tallyrand-Périgord, Charles Maurice T-P, Prince de Bénévent. (1754-1838). Former bishop. French diplomat; great skill and spirit, but no morality.

76. Decree of 8 April 1814. This decree could not have had any other motive than that of satisfying public opinion.

77. "Liberty, whether possessed or sought after, is today the most important need of the peoples, *and the indispensable requirement for their redemption"* (letter to the Comte de Senfft, 11 January 1829).

"If only people would wake up! The Belgian Catholics are in this regard far more advanced than we are; They sensed the necessity of healing themselves of *this terrible malady* called *royalism.* It is time for a new spirit to rise up in the peoples. Without this, there is no salvation either for them or for the sovereigns" (to the Countess of Senfft, 30 January).

"I cannot conceive of the possibility of a return to order except through the means used by the Belgians. Liberalism frightens people; if one imbues liberalism with Catholicism, society will be reborn" (*Correspondance,* volume II, pp. 103 and 105).

78. "I have certain knowledge that, more than ever, Protestantism is desired, and that it is firmly believed that it

will be established." (La Mennais to Salinis, 7 January 1828).

"It will be said that the *Roman* priests turn people away from obedience to the law and so *bloody* laws will be enacted against them. This is what we are destined to see, and many other things also." (From the same writer to the Marquis of Coriolis, on the same date.)

"It will be said that it is the government of Charles, the office of Portalis-Martignac, that seek *Protestantism* and *bloody* laws against the Roman priests!"

79. "The Ordinances of the 16th of July, 1828 aimed at regulating the small seminaries, institutions where, in every diocese, the young men destined for the priesthood were prepared for their office. . . . The Ordinances placed the seminaries under the control of the University." Quotation from *The Fortnightly* 71:1899, p. 576. Accessed 17 October 2010, at http://books.google.com/books?id=uQweAQAAIAAJ&pg=PA576&dq=france+ordinances+of+1828&hl=en&ei=PAu7TLuPGoOKlwfx77TTDA&sa=X&oi=book_result&ct=result&resnum=2&ved=0CDEQ6AEwAQ#v=onepage&q=france%20ordinances%20of%201828&f=false. [cdt]

80. To the Comtesse de Senfft, 14 November 1828.
81. To the Comtesse de Senfft, 11 January 1829.
82. To the Comtesse de Senfft, 5 January 1829.
83. To the Baron de Vitriol's, 6 April 1829.
84. To the Baron de Vitrolles, 6 April 1829.
85. Letter to the Comte de Senfft, 21 February 1829. —*Correspondence,* volume II, p. 17, line 3.
86. The Association had as its ostensible president a man of the law court, the Duc d'Havré: he was a name, and nothing more. The Association had a general council, but it met only sporadically. All activity was concentrated under the direction of five individuals: Father Perreau, Vicar General of the

Grande Aumônerie, an elderly individual of little consequence; Father Desgenettes, a parish priest of great piety from Paris; Cauchy, a gifted surveyor, but in everything else simple like a child; Laurentie, stripped of his function as *inspecteur général des études* on account of his adherence to Mennaisian doctrines; and finally, de Salinis, a dynamic person, an accomplished diplomat, of impartial mind, having all that was required to lead others in a tactful manner. The essential figure in this project was Bailly, a loyal retainer, completely suited to playing a secondary role. They encountered numerous obstacles, and, in his letters, La Mennais complained about it loudly. However, Salinis and Laurentie were the unmistakable leaders. Earlier — starting in 1827 — they had already seized control of the *Société Catholique des Bons Livres*. [Foisset]

87. A department on the West Coast of France, now known as the Loire-Atlantique.

88. It is curious that the idea for creating *le Globe* was suggested to P. Leroux by the establishment of the *Mémorial Catholique* (Sainte-Beuve, *Causeries,* volume VI, p. 213). I do not know of any other examples in current times where in external matters, the initiative of the children of the time has unremittingly outpaced the Sons of the Light. [Foisset]

89. In this first phase, *Le Correspondant* was principally written by de Cazalès, the son of the nobility's great orator in 1789 [Jacques Antoine Marie de Cazalès (1758–1805)], and by de Carné, today a member of the *Académie Française,* with the participation of Franz de Champagny, who since has become an historian of the Caesars and the Antonines. — De Champagny was a historian with a specialty in ancient Rome who wished to demonstrate the social utility of Christianity. His *L'Histoire des Césars* began appearing in installments in the *Revue des Deux Mondes* starting in 1836; His *Antonyms* appeared in 1863. Source: Frederic Eugene Godefroy, *Histoire*

de la Littérature Française au Dix-Neuvième Siècle, Bibliophile, n.d., pp. 193–195. Accessed 3 February 2011, at http://books.google.com/books?id=5euyfzeySRsC&pg=PA1 95&dq=historien+des+C%C3%A9sars+et+des+Antonins&h l=en&ei=ebbWTNz4D4KdlgfV0pCQAw&sa=X&oi=book_ result&ct=result&resnum=6&ved=0CEIQ6AEwBQ#v=onep age&q=historien%20des%20C%C3%A9sars%20et%20des %20Antonins&f=false. [Foisset]   [cdt]

90. Prominent and intellectually capable men were gathered together at Port-Royal. Unfortunately, its convents and schools became intimately associated with Jansenism. La Mennais wanted to set up a similar gathering of minds, but one orthodox in religion.

91. François Fénelon, Archbishop of Cambray (1651–1715).

92. To the Marquis de Coriolis, 31 January 1828.

93. Forgoes has provided the Italian text of this response. But he thought it wrong to assume that the Pope's response had anything to do with the Association for the Defense [of Religion]. The dates offer decisive evidence. The response in question is dated 30 June 1828, and the Association for the Defense of Religion was not formed until the month of July.—The letter of Waille, cited by Forgoes (*Notes et Souvenirs,* p. 71), and dated 7 June, should certainly be dated 7 July; the Association was formed in response to the Ordinances of 28 [*sic*] June, before which time the Association had no reason for existing. [Foisset]

94. A town in southeastern Brittany.

95. The minor seminary, which was also a coeducational *collège,* was established in Saint-Méen (Ille-et-Vilaine).

96. René-François Rohrbacher (1789–1856), author of *Histoire Universelle de l'Église Catholique.*

97. Eugène Boré (1809–1878). Linguist and missionary. Recipient of the Cross of the Legion of Honor for his service to the French nation. Elected Superior General of the Congregation of the Mission, 11 September 1874. Source: *The Catholic Encyclopedia,* Vol. XVI (Index), p. 11.

98. Maurice de Guérin (1810–1839) was a poet of noble descent.

99. To Brossard, 3 June 1823.

100. *Du Droit Public (Mémorial,* February 1824, pp. 149–155).

101. Letter of 7 September 1825.

102. To Lorain, 7 June 1825, on the subject of Gerbet's initiative [described in his letter] of 8 May.

103. To Foisset, 25 April 1826.

104. Published in 1829.

105. To Foisset, 19 July 1829.

106. Genesis 2:18.

107. To Lorain, 22 September 1829.

108. To Foisset, 29 December 1829.

109. In traditional physics experiments designed to prove the necessity of air for respiration, birds exposed to the compressed air of a pneumatic machine would soon become agitated and then expire. Source: Messrs Monge et al., *Dictionnaire de Physique,* Volume I (Paris: Hotel de Thou, 1793), p. 133. Accessed 12 November 2010, at http://books.google.com/books?id=MHdBAAAAcAAJ&pg=PA133&dq=comme+l%E2%80%99oiseau+sous+le+r%C3%A9cipient+d%E2%80%99une+machine+pneumatique&hl=en&ei=ImfdTJiXFsSqlAev6JHbDA&sa=X&oi=book_result&ct=result&resnum=2&ved=0CCoQ6AEwAQ#v=onepage&q=comme%20l%E2%80%99oiseau%20sous%20le%20r%C3%A9cipient%20d%E2%80%99une%20machine%20pneumatique&f=false.   [cdt]

110. To Foisset, 13 April 1830.

111. Jules Auguste Armand Marie, Prince de Polignac (1780

–1847). Charles X named him foreign minister in August 1829 and prime minister in November 1829. De Polignac was opposed to the liberal tendencies of the Charter of 1814. Source: William J. Roberts, *France: A Reference Guide from the Renaissance to the Present* (New York: Facts on File Library of World History, 2004), p. 482. Accessed 12 November 2010, at

http://books.google.com/books?id=ogdZu2l2CYkC&pg=PA482&dq=Jules+Auguste+Armand+Marie,+Prince+de+Polignac&hl=en&ei=4mrdTJD4L8KclgflwvGNDQ&sa=X&oi=book_result&ct=result&resnum=1&ved=0CCoQ6AEwAA#v=onepage&q=Jules%20Auguste%20Armand%20Marie%2C%20Prince%20de%20Polignac&f=false. [cdt]

112. These solicitations no longer came from Gerbet, but from a Polish individual, Father Kamienski, who admired Lacordaire deeply and whose devotion to La Mennais was only as a last resort.

113. "Recently, I have spent much time rereading his works, and *they brought me back in his direction,* especially those that discussed the relationships between religion and the political order" (letter to Foisset, 25 May 1830).

114. To Lorain, 2 July 1830.

115. To Foisset, 19 July 1830.

116. *Notice,* chapter II.

117. The ancient name for Brittany.

118. Letter of 25 May 1830 to Lorain.

In a speech given at the *Athénée* in Paris in 1819, Benjamin Constant (1767 –1830), the French writer and politician, discussed the strict control of religion and family life by authorities in ancient times. A quote from his speech: "Among the Spartans, Therpandrus could not add a string to his lyre without causing offense to the ephors." (The ephors were Spartan magistrates.) — Source: *The Political Writings*

of Benjamin Constant, ed. Bianca Maria Fontana (Cambridge, U.K.: Cambridge University Press, 1988), p. 311. Accessed 14 November 2010, at
http://books.google.com/books?id=wW9vx_fjZ3IC&pg=PA311&dq=therpandrus&hl=en&ei=z_beTLuFLcTflge-3cjdAw&sa=X&oi=book_result&ct=result&resnum=3&ved=0CC8Q6AEwAg#v=onepage&q=therpandrus&f=false. [cdt]
119. Esprit Fléchier (1632–1710), famous orator and Bishop of Nimes.
120. *Souvenirs sur les quatre derniers Papes,* p. 315 in the translation.
121. 19 July 1830, to Foisset.—The bishop of New York was not at La Chênaie when Lacordaire went there. At that time, the prelate was in Rome. I am not saying this at random, but on the basis of letters that I have in hand. "I have received some more letters from the bishop of New York, including descriptions of his projects and the means of carrying out these projects, in comprehensive detail. On another matter, Providence recently opened some paths that will facilitate the participation that he *requests of us.*" (La Mennais to de Salinis, 20 May 1830). [Foisset]

Chapter IV

L'Avenir

Fall of Charles X: Lacordaire's observations — Establishment of L'Avenir — Difficulties — La Mennais' extreme ideas — Montalembert; his friendship with Lacordaire — The association for religious liberty — Political trials — The free school — The impetus given by L'Avenir — Civil damages and the voluntary suspension of the publication — La Mennais, Lacordaire, and Montalembert depart for Rome.

Lacordaire wrote this on 19 July 1830[1]. Ten days later, Charles X was no longer in power.

Who is not familiar with this sad story?

The Restoration created an inevitable conflict between those who had been diminished, divested of their power, and marginalized along with the Bourbons, and who wished to seize preeminence through them once again — and those whom the Revolution had elevated or enriched, and who had no interest in losing what they had gained.

Indeed, the match was not equal. This was evident as early as the month of March 1815.

Enlightened by such a brutal experience, the politics of Louis XVIII were constantly attempting to soften this antagonism. Charles X, on the contrary, did not take any of this into account. He had just done what his enemies wanted most, which was to appoint as prime minister a man of the court who was widely regarded as the personification of the *ancien régime,* the Prince de Polignac[2]. The chamber of deputies refused its assent. It was then dissolved and new elections were held[3]. It appeared to Charles X that the king was being forced to put down his sword. Rather than replace his minister, he preferred to put at risk his crown, the destinies of his dynasty, and the peace of France. But public sentiment rose up. Even the true warriors, for the most part, were averse to a coup d'état. Besides, Charles X did not have the personal wherewithal to sustain an armed struggle; he submitted.

As a result of his abdication and that of the Dauphin, constitutional law, in accordance with the *loi ancien,* called for the ascension to the throne of his grandson. Nevertheless, the throne was ceded to the Duc d' Orléans[4]. The politicians who pressed for this could think only of 1688[5]. They had just reopened the epoch of the Caesars.

Traditional laws having been sidestepped, how to establish a durable hereditary monarchy? An insurrection had caused the Duc d'Orléans to be made king; another insurrection could easily replace him with another Republic — only to be followed by an 18 Brumaire[6], too confident, in its turn, of public confirmation, which strongmen never lacked.

But these consequences, still far in the distance, did not seem to strike anyone at that time. Lacordaire himself did not seem aware of them, and he would become an eyewitness of the catastrophe. What, then, were his observations? He himself informs us:

"It was from the windows of the *Collège* Henri IV, that on 27 July 1830, I saw the first signs of the revolution that was to take place, and from which I heard the cannon blasts that greeted its arrival. On the morning of the 29th, after changing into secular clothes, I decided to visit an old uncle of mine who lived close to the Madeleine[7], and to see with my own eyes as I crossed Paris where things stood in the struggle between the people and power. I proceeded in the Faubourg Saint-Germain with the thought of crossing the Seine on the *Pont de la Concorde*; but the closer I came, the more the streets became deserted. Moving forward carefully along the embankment, I saw next to the House of Deputies the mounted sentinels of the royal army, and on the other side, around the Louvre, a thick smoke, which indicated to me that a final assault was being waged on the last refuge of royalty. I retraced my steps, and I was going to cross the Seine opposite the Hall of Justice, encountering everywhere on my way all the signs of a popular victory: open doors, innumerable people on the street, crowds pressing, and, in the midst of this incredible commotion, a sense of joy and confidence flowing through the crowd, all along the streets, strewn with the debris of a thousand battles. Returning around three or four o'clock in the afternoon, I crossed the *Jardin des Tuileries* and saw several bleeding bodies, lives sacrificed for their prince. The crowd had occupied the Tuileries, a sight I would revisit eighteen years later. Finally, I arrived home after having witnessed one of the most striking scenes on earth: the fall of a dynasty, the advent of another, a people standing on the ruins of a 1,000-year-old monarchy, a liberty that was victorious and confident that it would reign forever, all of the dreams of a nation at their highest pitch of intensity, and even the fire of battle in the midst of monuments erected to honor peace. I fell asleep certain that my fate had just undergone, in the hands of Providence, a complete transformation[8]."

The speed with which this political upheaval took place surprised Lacordaire, but not the revolution itself. For a long time, La Mennais, to whose side he had recently rallied, repeatedly stated that the revolution was at hand, and even Henri himself had early on sensed a wavering in his own faith in the endurance of the principles of 1814[9].

"Nothing is being built," he wrote in 1826. I am convinced of it! No one *wants* anything in accordance with the Charter. Now, no one *wishes* to build in accordance with the Charter: and no one *can* build anything in opposition to the Charter. What was the state of things on the arrival of Polignac? Lacordaire's visit to La Chênaie did the rest: it removed the final roots of royalism (that had always been based on logic, not on sentiment) that he still held onto from his association with the *Société d'Études*. Indeed, 29 July 1830 did not bring him any joy, but it did not cause heartbreak either. That day could not cause in him the deep and permanent wound that it caused in the souls of those who were legitimists by birth.

As for La Mennais, however anti-royalist he became during the ministry of Villèle, the elderly gentleman, the reactionary of 1815 trembled for a moment when on 8 August 1829, he saw one of his old political friends, Bourdonnaie, become minister and applaud the idea of an immediate and total coup d'état in the counter-revolutionary direction[11]. However, upset that *"everything* was not accomplished all at once and *everything* not done in *twenty-four hours,"* he lost hope in the Cabinet of Ministers as he had in the monarchy, and summoned up once again the full force of his misanthropy and contempt. See, for example, his response to Berryer: *Jam foetet* ["Already there is a stench," a reference to the death of Lazarus in John 11:39]. The supreme moment having arrived, he did not grant the brother of Louis XVI nor his daughter nor the final issue of Louis XIV, a single instant of sorrow, a single word of pity."

"The vanquished deserve their defeat, and this defeat is final[12]." Such were his words, the only words he spoke upon learning of the disaster of July 1830.

Charles X having gone into exile, what would happen next? What to do? These were the questions raised by recent events. An answer was needed, and it was needed immediately, in order not to be devoured by the Sphinx; anarchy waits for no one. At that time, could not France be compared to a ship battered by a storm? One faction of the crew has thrown the captain into the sea. Should one simply allow the ship to go down rather than to steady the course under the captain who emerges from the uprising?

La Mennais immediately took the opposite position[13], and on this point, one is hard put to find fault with him.

Because, finally, Charles X having departed, there still remained France; there still remained the Church.

"Every stand taken has its duties," he wrote. "But the duties in our current circumstances, I believe, are centered on one task: that of coming together to avert, if possible, the anarchy that threatens us, and so, to use openly the power that exists — as long as it provides us adequate protection even as it defends itself against Jacobism[14]."

"What will Jacobism do, if it is victorious? It will persecute religion, it will abolish all Christian education. It will violently attack individuals, properties, and all laws. And what will we end up calling for? Religious liberty, academic freedom, personal liberty, which is to say the free enjoyment of the rights without which one cannot begin to conceive of a society. And how can one even attempt to reclaim all these things without the freedom of the press? If that is destroyed, one can do nothing but bow one's head under the weight of all tyrannies[15]."

It was a mere step between these thoughts and the establishment of a newspaper. However, the initiative was not on the part of La Mennais, but on the part of an obscure young man, who was lacking decided convictions and sought in this endeavor principally an opportunity to latch on to something meaningful. His name was Harel du Tancrel. This young man opened up about it to Father Gerbet, who was most enthusiastic. As early as 9 August, he wrote about it to the Teacher, whose immediate assent was followed quickly by that of de Coux and Salinis and Rohrbacher.

All that was still required was to ensure the participation of Lacordaire.

Even after the Revolution of 1830, the latter was still intent on pursuing his plan to go to America. With this in mind, he had gone to Burgundy during the month of August to bid farewell to his family. It was in Dijon that he learned, via a letter from a friend, that La Mennais, supporting these recent developments wholeheartedly, was laying the groundwork for a newspaper, the goal of which was to reclaim for the Church its rightful share of the freedoms which the rest of the nation was to enjoy henceforth. On behalf of the Teacher, Gerbet beseeched Lacordaire not to leave France, but to join a few collaborators in a project both Catholic and national, from which was expected to ensue the emancipation of religion, the reconciliation of minds, and, as a consequence, the renewal of society[16].

"This news," continued Lacordaire, "caused me trepidation. From my point of view, it justified the mysterious rapprochement that had occurred between La Mennais and me. La Mennais was no longer the one who espoused absolutist doctrines that were generally rejected in the public square. But suddenly transformed, I saw in him the public defender of ideas that had always been dear to me, and for which I had previously thought it impossible that God would send such substantial help and such an exalted demonstration.

"Please note that this was not a question of a purely human and patriotic work, but of a religious work. In my youth, the liberal question appeared to me only from the point of view of the nation and of humanity. Like most of my contemporaries, I wished for the definitive victory of the principles of 1789 through the fulfilment from carrying out and the strengthening of the Charter of 1814. To us, everything seemed to be working in our favor. To our way of thinking, the Church was nothing more than an obstacle. It did not occur to us that the Church herself needed to invoke her liberty and to claim from the nation's common inheritance her share of the new rights. When I became a Christian, a new perspective dawned on me: My liberalism came to embrace together both France and the Church. The civil strife pained me all the more since, henceforth in defending one cause, I would be defending both causes, and those causes seemed to be irreconcilable enemies who would never listen to the one voice trying to bring them. Suddenly, there was La Mennais. One might have thought he was to become the O'Connell of France[17], and that he would obtain, after a noble struggle, the emancipation that had recently been the culmination of the Great Liberator's efforts and had crowned his head with glory."

However, as Lacordaire noted on his deathbed, O'Connell had a whole nation behind him; La Mennais had nothing more behind him than a small, holy band of soldiers, brought together slowly through the force of his genius. O'Connell had always remained the same: a child of Ireland, liberal and Christian. La Mennais began as an *absolutist*, praising King Ferdinand VII of Spain, and as an ultramontane reputed to be fanatic, and all of this enveloped in an abstruse philosophy that seemed to negate the value of reason. There was a great distance from this to the position he was to take in the new publication. "It was a misfortune. Integrity and conviction will always be among the most respected weapons [in controversy], the sign of a competent mind and a noble character. If La Mennais had been as early as 1818 what he became in 1830, he would not have gained, as he did in a single day — thanks to the royalist party — great renown; he would have proceeded gradually along his path of glory... He would thus have captured the abiding confidence of his contemporaries. And, even more so than Chateaubriand, he would have been the living symbol of true religion united to true liberty[18]."

Whatever can be said on this last point, La Mennais' past worked against him in 1830; it was an insurmountable obstacle, and for the writers of *L'Avenir,* it was a terrible curse. Nothing else played a greater role in leading them to excesses; indeed, in order for this newspaper to succeed in reconciling the liberals with the Church, it was important above all for the writers to be perceived as free of any hidden motive for a new Restoration. Thus, the newspaper's writers felt they could not give enough guarantees to those who persisted in seeing them as nothing more than disguised legitimists. With such preoccupations, and under pressure to produce articles on a daily basis, how could it not happen that these writers, especially the most junior among them, would never stray from the golden mean? They thought they must never for a moment retreat from holding the line [against this accusation].

On 20 August 1830, the prospectus of *L'Avenir* appeared[19]. This title was not chosen randomly: it constituted an entire profession of faith unto itself. It is sufficient to say that, according to the founder, the future belonged to democracy [i.e., government by the common people]. He called on the Church to ally itself openly with it, to reconcile it with religion through a common devotion to liberty.

The first issue came out on 16 October, inaugurated by an article of La Mennais entitled *"Considérations sur l'époque actuelle."*

This article laid out a program; disinterest as regards dynastic matters was laid bare.

The legitimists were revolted by this, as a defection all the more painful for those who least expected it. The liberals, on the contrary, except for the élite in the school of thought espoused by the *Globe,* refused to see in the article anything other than a disguise [for legitimist sympathies]. Neither group took at face value La Mennais' liberal statements at the beginning of 1829. Deceived as they were by the author's past writings, in favor of one side or the other, his latest work (*Des Progrès de la Révolution*) was not taken as a profession of faith, but merely as a tactic in the war against Messrs Feutner, de Vatimesnil, and Portalis.

It was in this that the character of la Mennais burst forth, shedding light on this contradictory life, of which the final half was consumed in cursing all that the first half had adored.

Unyielding in his will, la Mennais was ironically that way in his understanding about everything. For him the concept of the relative did not exist. Each of his opinions carried with it something of the rigidity, the inflexibility, of dogma. Excessive by nature, he never embraced a point of view halfway; without ceasing for a moment to be excessive, he often changed his basic notions. It was thus that he at first fanatically espoused the principle of authority, out of hatred for revolutionary anarchy. It was thus also that he became an ultramontane out of hatred for the schism caused by opposition to the Concordat. He even went so far as to establish as a tenet the right of popes to depose the king. But he then saw legitimists rise up against him, and very soon he loathed this. It was in this way, which is to say through a hatred different from the first, that he was led to fanaticism concerning the principle of liberty.

However, to rechannel one's passions is not to change one's basic nature. When he made an about-face, he did this with all his might, remaining inflexible as always. At the same time — and this is something one can believe only with difficulty, yet it was certainly the case — he had not even a trace of a memory of the opinion he had held the day before. In addition, he had a way of trampling others under foot, because the secret scourge of this soul — pride — betrayed itself incessantly, as was previously noted, through his enormous capacity for contempt. The royalists were his foster-brothers, comrades in arms day in and day out. The day he separated himself from them, he spoke of them only as a *brainless and absurd party,* "AS THEY HAVE ALWAYS BEEN[20]."

This execration of royalism could not but be extended to the Church, when the time came for the Church in its turn to disavow La Mennais. And that is how, born with a loving soul, the author of the *Essai* became incontestably the man of our time who evinced the most scorn and hatred.

From the very first day, he had set *L'Avenir* moving down a perilous slope.

In the aftermath of a revolution, two sentiments reign: the passion that had overturned a weakened government and wished to perpetuate the revolutionary turmoil; and the need for security, the instinct of preservation, which tends to try to stem the movements of nature that undermine society. Two opposing currents arise: one pushing ahead regardless of consequences [even to destruction]; the other resisting with all its strength. La Mennais declared himself to be opposed to resistance. According to him, the only way possible for France from then on, would be to a democratic republic, wherein the leader, moreover, could retain the title of king — a detail of little consequence. He believed it was necessary to abolish hereditary peerage, to establish universal suffrage, and to separate totally Church and state.

One can say this with confidence: at that time, there was not one in ten Frenchmen who desired these outcomes.

All of those living in the countryside, which is to say the overwhelming majority of the nation, were not familiar with public life, and did not wish to be involved in any way. Peace abroad, and tranquility at home, the two conditions of prosperity — almost equally essential to agricultural, industrial, and commercial work — these were what concerned villagers as far as politics was concerned.

Fed by its newspapers for fifteens years running, in a blind opposition to power, and, as a result, understanding little about the conditions necessary for overseeing a large country, a notable segment of the bourgeoisie dreamed of a government that did not govern, and, as we used to say then, "a popular throne surrounded by republican institutions." As an enemy of the aristocracy, the bourgeoisie detested naturally the hereditary peerage. However, I hasten to say that the bourgeoisie was far from unanimous on these issues. It was in complete agreement only in opposing all that could give some influence to the clergy. Saturated with the Voltairian sympathies of the press at that time, angered by the high degree of benevolence shown by the Restoration toward Catholics, they opposed any freedom that might benefit the Church.

And that was not all.

It was the bourgeoisie that had brought about the Revolution of 1830. But to accomplish this, it had to appeal to the populace of Paris, and consequently to passions stirred more deeply than by a simple opposition to Polignac. It was on these passions that the success of 1830 depended.

The revolution was occasioned by the conflict created by Charles X between the exercise of the royal prerogatives and those of the parliament. But the consequences far outstripped the original premises; how to keep the revolution fenced within the boundaries of the field on which it was victorious? Besides, the revolution had multiple causes, other than the expulsion of the senior branch of the Bourbons and the retrenchment of the nobility and the clergy, which occurred in its wake, but did not succeed in completely ushering them off the stage. Ambitions of all sorts and utopias of all kinds divided the middle classes; these ambitions and utopias were moving in all directions seeking satisfaction. The secret societies, organized against the Restoration, worked for the new establishment with the same vigor that had caused the other to collapse. Public associations formed with the same goal. In jealous competition, the rostrum and the press resounded with incendiary provocations. Incessantly stirred up by these provocations, workers from Paris and Lyons rumbled like waves which gather for the storm.

La Mennais perceived none of this. His thoughts inhabited an ideal world; as has been said of him, he had little belief in what he could not see. It seemed to him that all that needed to be done was to allow the right of association and universal suffrage, with which all is for the best in the best of all possible worlds[21]. As a result, he pushed for the fall of Guizot from his position as prime minister, as he would later combat Casimir Périer[22], who died in the breach so that France might be at the same time free and also governed. La Mennais maintained the strange illusion that the revolutionary movement, a movement in which *Catholicism*, he said, IS THE PRINCIPLE *and will be the governor,* was a replica of that which was brought into being and directed by the popes in the Middle Ages[23]. He had the mistaken belief that, the more laws disarm the government, the more powerless individual factions become. *L'Avenir* went so far as to demand the *license* of the press, so that, he said, Catholics might fully enjoy their freedom. Libel, as with perjury, was the province of divine law alone[24]. Was la Bourdonnaie very wrong in describing the politics of La Mennais as "speculative"?

L'Avenir created a sensation on several fronts. Five articles by La Mennais, two by Gerbet, seven by Lacordaire, gave to the first sixteen issues of this newspaper an incomparable luster and resonance. Indeed it was under these circumstances and under the impression left by these first issues that the young Charles de Montalembert wrote from Ireland to La Mennais to request the honor of joining the battle under his command. He rushed over, as he himself reported, with all the ardor of his twenty years, from the other side of the sea, where he had seen O'Connell leading a people whose religious emancipation had been achieved through free speech and a free press. He found a mere three priests and five lay people, gathered around the French O'Connell[25]. The faith of this son of crusaders was not shaken; he was of an age where one does not count the number of one's comrades-in-arms nor the number of one's enemies. Besides, one of those three priests was worth an entire army: Lacordaire.

"May it be given to me to describe how he appeared to me then, in all the radiance and charm of youth! He was twenty-eight years old . . . His slim height, his fine and regular features, his sculptured forehead, the regal way he carried himself even at this young age, his black and glittering eyes, a mysterious combination of dignity and elegance at the same time while modesty permeated his being: — all of this was but the encasement for a soul that seemed about ready to overflow. . . . The fire of his glance revealed caches of anger and tenderness simultaneously. . . . His voice, already restive and vibrant, often took on unbounded gentleness. Born to engage in combat and to love, he appeared to me to be both charming and fearsome, as the embodiment of virtue armed for the sake of truth. I saw in him one of the elect, predestined to that what youth holds in highest esteem: genius and glory[27]."

From the beginning, Henri Lacordaire and Charles de Montalembert were drawn to one another and developed one of those sovereign and excellent friendships that Montaigne spoke of: "where the souls are intermingled in a total bond that is seamless." "I love him as if he were an ordinary person" wrote Lacordaire. Given the prejudices of the times, he could not have said anything more meaningful.

They constituted the entire staff of *L'Avenir*. La Mennais was the general; Lacordaire and Montalembert were the aides-de-camp. But the staff was without foot soldiers. The acclaim of the general, the prodigious talent and productivity of these two young lieutenants, would soon have caused an army to rise up. But, to put it succinctly, the two of them by themselves were *L'Avenir*. La Mennais, still unwell, only wrote major articles, authoritative-articles, as we used to say. Gerbet, still unwell also, Rohrbacher, little suited to journalism, were heard from less and less. Lacordaire and Montalembert *created the edition* — just the two of them — each day. Lacordaire and Montalembert never abandoned the breach. It is appropriate to mention along with them de Coux, who spent his childhood enduring the trials of emigration, his youth in the free climate of public life in the United States, and who, having returned to France seven years earlier, brought to the offices of *L'Avenir* the qualities of maturity, the experiences of an adventurous life tempered by many life lessons, and ideas about political and social economy that were new at that time and completely unknown to the Catholic press. But he had nowhere close to the verve, the wide-ranging talents, the productivity, or the brilliance of the two young brothers-in-arms[27].

Lacordaire, Montalembert, de Coux (they are listed in order of their importance), comprised nothing less than *L'Avenir's* three men of action. One cannot help but marvel at what these three men were able to accomplish in the few months that this paper was in circulation. On 18 December 1830, they established the General Agency, a center for the defense of religious liberty, of network of mutual protection [like a mutual insurance association - Trans.] to counter all actions that would be taken against this freedom wherever they might occur in France. They undertook to redress these actions in the realm of public opinion, before the Chambers, before all the tribunals—from the Justice of the Peace to the Council of State. They divided responsibility for France: Lacordaire had the dioceses of the North and East; Montalembert, those of the South; and de Coux, those of Belgium. Moreover, Lacordaire was in touch with Switzerland and Italy; Montalembert with Germany and Ireland; de Coux with Belgium. They organized a general movement of petitions in favor of the freedom of instruction. And they did more. They took the attitude in principle that liberty is to be seized when those in power do not grant it. Accordingly, they personally opened a free school in Paris, at great risk and peril to themselves. At the same time, they made a strong impression in the Catholic press of the provinces, of which *Le Courrier Lorrain*, run by de Dumast, and *L'Union Bretonne* were on the front lines. They inspired local organizations — among others, *L'Association Lyonnaise* — to foster everywhere centers of Catholic enthusiasm and resistance to the arbitrary dictates of public officials, who almost everywhere in France were hostile to religious liberty. They countered the government itself in its nomination of bishops, after having forced it to back down from its initial choice for the episcopal see of Beauvais.

In this way, the ice was broken, and Catholics, who for such a long time had been unaccustomed to public life in France, began to heal little by little and conformed themselves to the activist spirit characteristic of free countries. Nothing contributed more to this result than a series of trials in which Lacordaire almost always played a primary role. At one point, he even considered donning once again his lawyer's robe; he felt he was authorized by canon law to do so, and by illustrious predecessors, notably the example of St. Yves de Tréguier[28], and, finally, by the abiding conventions of the French clergy. From another point of view, this could be seen a further application of the thesis maintained by *L'Avenir* about the total separation of Church and state. According to this thesis, the priest was nothing more than a citizen like any other: priestly consecration, in truth, established a bond between himself and God, and between himself and the Church; but the state had no right to concern itself with this bond. The administrative council for Parisian lawyers did not agree. It decided that Father Lacordaire could not be included in the legal profession's official roster.

This did not in any way hinder Lacordaire's ability to appear before the bar in matters which concerned him.

The first was a prosecution for slander which he directed against *Le Lycée,* a paper run by the *Université* that maligned the essay composed by the chaplains of Paris's royal *collèges* for Bishop de Quélen. At the opening of this trial, a question of public order presented itself: Which jurisdiction was authorized to hear the case? If the chaplains were simply citizens, the case could be tried in ordinary tribunals; if they were civil servants, a jury needed to hear the accusation. The lawyer to the king, Ségur-Daguesseau, today a senator, maintained that the chaplains had a public character, and one of the reasons that he gave was that they were the ministers of a *foreign ruler.* "No, Sir," answered Lacordaire. "That is not the case. We are the ministers of someone who is not a foreigner anywhere: God." Widespread applause followed. All the same, the tribunal of the Seine declared itself incompetent to hear the case. But the king's solicitor, Comte, appealed this decision on the highest grounds. He maintained that the only civil servants are those who represent the state to some degree, which clearly excludes from consideration the ministers of religion; that neither the oath taken by the chaplains nor the salary that they receive from the state, changes anything of the spiritual nature of their duties, no more than the salary allocated to a doctor in an institution run by the *Université* transforms the doctor into a civil servant. It did not escape Comte that this identification of the priest as a civil servant debased the character of the priest, that it represented an assault on the priest's independence and consequently on the dignity of his ministry. Nevertheless, the court of Paris did not accept this appeal; but, before rejecting it, it was obliged to hear a remarkable plea from Lacordaire, in which Comte's thesis was conclusively proven. Even if there was legal dissent, the truth nevertheless was forging its own path in people's minds.

A second trial had a thunderous impact: Lacordaire and La Mennais were brought before the Court of Assizes of the Seine, accused of having incited hatred for and disdain of the government. The trial concerned two articles in *L'Avenir:* one, by Lacordaire, addressed "to the bishops of France," took a position against the king's right to nominate bishops; the other, by La Mennais, was entitled *Oppression des Catholiques*. The prosecution's case was argued with skillful moderation by the first Advocate General, Berville, one of the most articulate men in the history of the bar in Paris. La Mennais was represented by a lawyer from Angers, Eugène Janvier, who, as a deist and a liberal — having proved his claim to both titles — created a sensation as he justified on the basis of history, philosophy, and the principles of liberty, all the theses of his client. What a novelty it was to hear developed with such brilliance before a court of justice doctrines unsullied by judicial controversy! In turn, Lacordaire stood up; it was seven-thirty in the evening. His extemporaneous speech is not available. Stenographers had not recorded it, and he refused at first to compile, and afterward, to commit to paper, the thoughts that inflamed him on the field of battle; he did not give in until six days later at the insistence of his friends. As a result, the recreation of his speech is missing the high-spiritedness of the live word and the enchanting, prophetic quality that characterized all of Lacordaire's improvised speeches. But his success with his audience had been complete, above all in the audience of public opinion. That fifteen-hour day was glorious on account of the sympathy of the crowd jammed together in the courtroom, the talent of the three combatants, and the ardent acclamations that welcomed the acquittal of the two defendants. The decision was not rendered until midnight. "When the crowd had dispersed," said Montalembert, "We returned alone, Lacordaire and I, walking in the darkness along the embankments. He was neither elated nor swept away by his victory. I saw that, for him, these small vanities of success were less than nothing—dust in the night[29]."

The third trial concerned the free school.

The Charter of 1830 promised, in its final article, that, with minimal delay public instruction and freedom of instruction would be authorized." Introduced there, in a somewhat idealistic thought, by the Protestant author of the Constitution, Bérard, this promise from the beginning had displeased the government officials in the new regime. Three ministers had succeeded each other; not one of them showed sympathy for this promised liberty. It was noted earlier that freedom of instruction was especially dear to Catholics — anxious to a degree that is difficult to describe — in order to safeguard the faith for their children. Far from taking this into consideration, after the Revolution of 1830, the *Université* tightened the reins of its monopoly. It was thus that the *Université* took back from the pastors of Lyons the property where they were giving free lessons in Latin to their altar boys. In denouncing this action on 3 April 1831, Lacordaire stated in *L'Avenir* that the question had to be decided between France [i.e., the French people] and the *Université*, [and not politicians], and that, as a result, before a month was over, he would open in the midst of Paris itself a school *without authorization,* in virtue of rights accorded by the Charter.

This was entirely his own idea; La Mennais took not the slightest interest in this event.

The school was ultimately opened on 9 May, in a location rented by Lacordaire. The plan was to teach religion, French, Latin, Greek, and mathematics. Lacordaire was the school's director, and Montalembert and de Coux were teachers there along with Lacordaire. The police official came to summon them to close the school. They protested and persisted. Sergeants from the city intervened, and Lacordaire submitted. Nevertheless, he was required to appear before the court along with his collaborators, accused of having overseen an unauthorized school.

The prosecution led to some incidents. The affair was brought by the administration to the Court of Petty Sessions. Lacordaire rejected the jurisdiction of the tribunal; he maintained that, if a crime existed, it was a political crime, and that, therefore, according to the terms of existing legislation, he could not be judged except by jurymen. He was outstanding in this phase of the legal proceedings. "One needed to hear his voice," said an observer, "to see his strained neck, his pale and trembling lips, his compact gestures. The most passionate applause interrupted him several times, and it is hard to describe the effect he created when, invoking, as did St. Paul, his rights as a citizen, he pronounced the Apostles' words: *Cæsarem appello,* which he translated boldly in this way: "I call on him [Caesar] to regard the rights granted by the Charter. – I call on the Charter."

Under these circumstances, the death of the Comte de Montalembert, father, meant that his son was invested as a peer (hereditary peerage was not yet abolished); the principle of the indivisibility of the prosecution resulted in the three being remanded to the Court of Peers.

The three of them appeared the bar before this court on 20 September. Persil, the spokesperson for the government, upheld the interdiction, as if a common lawyer, pleading a boundary case. Following his statement, and those of the lawyers for the defense, Montalembert took the floor. To him who was young, charming, recently orphaned, the French peers listened with paternal care. Even those who strongly disagreed with his argument "smiled at this vigorous eloquence, as an elder might enjoy the abundant and mischievous vivacity of the last descendant of his race[30]."

De Coux had the misfortune of not being able to make himself heard, and of allowing himself to be interrupted[31]. Persil responded. Lacordaire had saved the reply for himself. It was worthy of him.

His introduction was gripping. Let us visualize this young man of twenty-nine, a priest, standing before the bar of the Court of Peers, as he began his speech:

"Noble peers,

I view all of this and I marvel. I marvel at seeing myself as a defendant, while the Attorney-General is on the side of the government. I marvel at the fact that the *procureur-general* has dared to stand there as my accuser, he who is guilty of the same offense as I am, and who committed that offense only a little while ago in the same chamber in which he accuses me: here, before you. Of what does he accuse me? Of having exercised a right that is written into the Charter, that is not regulated by a single law! If he was permitted to do so, then I was permitted to do so, with the difference that he was asking for blood, while I wished to grant free instruction to the people's children. Both of us acted in the name of article 69 of the Charter. If the Attorney General is culpable, how can he accuse me?"

"I have other reasons to marvel, noble peers; because the Guards of Honor standing at your doors have broken extant laws along with me—and in the same way that I did. Long before the national army was organized according to the structure promised by the Charter, and when the army was still in the grip of what eventually destroyed it, it took shape, selected its own leaders, appeared as an armed force, not in one location in France, but throughout the country, and not under a proprietary commander. How am I culpable, if the army is innocent? How is it that, when I cast a glance around, I see certain abettors, and yet I and my friends are the only ones sitting on the defendant's bench? We could have asked for the heads of the ministers but by reason of a principle of liberty not regulated by law, yet written on the same page and in the same article of the Charter. When we gathered together some children from impoverished families to teach them the basics of religion and the humanities, the police came against us as disturbers of the peace. Our children were chased away, I was stripped of my residence, my door is still sealed. I have heard nothing in all that the Attorney-General has said that explains so much license granted in one area, and such strictness imposed in another — unless license is justice and strictness is not persecution. In that case, I understand both of them, and, after having experienced persecution, I dare, noble peers, to demand justice."

This brings to mind what Lacordaire wrote to a friend on 5 February 1823, when he had just finished arguing his first case: "I am convinced by this experience that even the Roman Senate would not be able to frighten me."

Persil entrenched himself behind the famous decree of 1811, which, not concerning itself with principles, imposed a penalty on those who chose to teach without an official approval from the *Université,* as if the Emperor had a right to establish penalties without consulting the legislative body. Following is Lacordaire's reply:

"Based on that, noble peers, I cannot marvel enough at the temerity with which the Attorney-General said to you: 'The decree of 1811 was executed, and therefore it has the force of law.' The decree was indeed carried out! But was it executed freely? Was it executed as a result of common consent? Was it executed in such a way as to constitute a liberty for France? Ah! Noble peers, what mockery! And it was with total temerity that the Attorney-General asked you to take note that the decree was executed under the Empire. Since he apparently wished to assume my role, I am resigned to repeating after him. It was under the Empire; it was during the time when France consented to nothing because nothing was offered to it for approval; it was during the time where the remains of the Republic, taken down from the scaffold, adored on its knees the Imperial riches; it was during the time when nothing existed in France except pomp and silence. But still, might we say at least that slavery had lasted a sufficiently long time that it had gained the power and majesty that comes with durability? Count the days, noble peers, and give thanks to Providence, which shortened them. Between 15 November 1811 and 1 April 1814, between the decree that placed the *Université* under the protection of an arbitrary penalty and the action that precipitated the downfall of Napoleon from the throne, two years, three months, and twenty-six days elapsed. Is this what is being used to mask the bondage of the veil that time casts over everything?

"The decree of 1811 had the force of law under the Empire. You were the one who said this, Sir; it is you who built my case, or at least provided its cornerstone, and who reminded the court, with a kind of pride, to take note that no one had been bold enough under the Empire to oppose the will of Napoleon. I rest my case, where you have yourself rested it, and I am careful to repeat the proof you used to establish that the decree of 1811 had the force of law under the Imperial scepter. The proof was, you said, that the decree was executed! However, anything can be executed by means of the sword; and, if no other condition is necessary for the will of a man to become law, then violence is the supreme legislator of mankind. A deed accomplished is a right, and the silence caused by fear is the voice of God. If other conditions are necessary, what are they? Were they fulfilled as regards the decree of 1811? The Attorney-General has told us nothing about these other conditions. He limited himself to this wondrous line, 'The decree was executed,' and he emphasized that this was under the Empire. Sure enough, under the Empire! Liberty and civil courage were in such abundance that the execution of the Imperial will carried the force of law, which is to say the stamp of national consent, or the consent of the nation's representatives—which is to say the stamp of justice! No. If the thesis of public service is true, if it were possible that in France a decree executed could become law simply by virtue of the fact that it is executed, we would need to flee our country and to request from the most low-ranking civilizations a scrap of that liberty that can never be lost completely — except among peoples who consider violence to be sacred and for whom the decree of the leader passes for law, as long as the slave has responded: 'I submit.' "

Allow me to cite Lacordaire's final words:

"If I had the time, I would have granted to the Attorney-General all that he wished, and, assuming that we were guilty of the breach of a decree and must be penalized, I would have extracted from our guilt the very proof of our innocence. Because, noble peers, these are blessed errors, and the breach of a law may, at times, fulfill a higher law. As for the first legal proceeding about the freedom of instruction, in that celebrated case in which Socrates succumbed, this was apparently a blasphemy against the gods, and consequently against the laws of his country. However, the posterity of the pagan peoples and the posterity of the centuries that have elapsed since the time of Christ's coming, tarnished his judges and accusers — these have absolved only the guilty one [Socrates] and the executioner. The guilty one, because he transgressed the laws of Athens in order to obey higher laws; the executioner, because he was in tears as he handed over the cup. As for me, Noble Peers, I would have proven to you, that, in trampling under foot this Imperial decree, I was using the laws of my country properly, serving its freedom well, and serving well also the cause of all future Christian peoples. But time has carried off my thoughts. I forgive it, because it leaves me with your justice. And this is enough. When Socrates, in that first and famous case concerning *freedom of instruction*, was about to take leave of his judges, he said to them: 'We shall part from each other, you to live, and I to die.' Noble judges, this is not the way we are leaving you. Whatever your decision, we will leave here to live, because liberty and religion are everlasting, and the simple feelings of an untainted heart that you have heard from our lips will not perish either[32]."

What gravity! What dignity! What vitality! What fire! What an unequal and triumphant struggle between a handful of Catholics, men of courage, and an ocean of prejudices, the passions of an era, based on France's secular behavior, embodied in the government of Louis-Philippe! Montalembert confirmed that the "entire chamber was spellbound by the speech and by the personality of this young orator. The appropriate boldness of his extemporaneous speech captured the attention even of those who sympathized with him the least[33]." The three defendants were condemned to the maximum penalty, a fine of 100 francs.

Lacordaire's departure for Rome prevented him from participating in person in the final legal action initiated by the *Association for the Defense of Religion*, an action initiated by the abbot of the Trappist Melleray Abbey, who sought reparations for the dispersion of his community on the basis of a decision by the prefect [i.e., the civil administrator] of the Loire-Inférieure[34]. The issue in question was important; it had to do with determining whether the civil protections against unlawful entry can be suspended in the case of religious only on the basis of their common life, in the absence of any criminal act[35]. This issue was argued before the court of Nantes. Janvier represented the Trappists. Billault, the now-deceased Minister of State, represented the Prefect. He was not worthy of his opponent. As might be expected, disarmed as he was by the law that prohibits judges from dealing with any kind of administrative actions, the court declared itself unauthorized to hear the case. But because of its subjective nature, the administration limped away from the battle.

I am focusing intentionally on these proceedings, because they were of decisive importance; they instilled in Catholics a momentum that was not stemmed until 1852, and from which resulted all that was attempted, and all that was accomplished, in the name of the freedom of the Church in France. Let me explain.

Certainly, in and of itself, Catholicism is not incompatible with the democratic spirit; one can see this in the United States. However, in France, since Henri IV, all the axioms, all the traditions of the clergy had been profoundly monarchical. The Gallicanism of the seventeenth century; that of the Third Estate in the Estates-General of 1614; that of Servin [36] and that of Omer Talon, were a reaction against the then tarnished memories of the League. Accordingly, Gallicanism had taken very far — too far — the religion of the second majesty, the bishops. Despite the noble example given by Bossuet and by a great number of doctors of the Sorbonne in 1663, despite the ultramontanism declared by Fénélon[37], the French episcopate accepted its manacles, with much less repugnance than previously. In the final analysis, this was because, since the crimes of the Revolution, the episcopacy had become not only monarchical but royalist. Regarding anything not formally censured by the Church, Catholics generally obeyed the government like sheep, whichever government it happened to be. During the Terror and ever after, all of them had submitted with no resistance. The Vendée[38] alone remembered the Maccabees; but it was crushed, it was destroyed, and it had not come back to life in 1830. In all of France, Catholics of the time remained passive and inert, as had been those of 1793 and 1797.

It was this age-old inertia among Catholics that *L'Avenir* succeeded in shaking up. They could not have been less prepared. For them, the schism of 1791 took the color out of 1789. The word *constitutional* was odious to them; was this not the proper name for schism, persecution, and anarchy? Moreover, this freedom that *L'Avenir* claimed for the Church of France had never been known by the Church of Louis XIV and never did the Church of Louis XIV demand it or regret not having done so. The *Université*, it is true, was a new thing. But it ended up being tolerated for twenty years, so how, at this point, throw off its yoke?

Such was the state of minds. Assuredly, to triumph over this, it was necessary to have the revolutionary upheavals of 1830. But it was also necessary to have the faith that moves mountains, as well as the ardor that brings with it heroic courage, served by superior eloquence. As was said by Montalembert, "The present generation could not imagine the strength and generosity of passion that inflamed hearts in those times. There were far fewer newspapers and far fewer readers than today. Postal and other communications were much slower and more difficult. There were neither railroads nor telegraph. On our trips to promote our cause, it took us three days and three nights to go from Paris to Lyons in those hideous coaches. But what life in souls! What passion in minds! What disinterest in worship of the flag and of its aims! What deep and fertile furrows were carved by an idea, by enthusiasm, by a stirring example, by an act of faith or courage! To understand what it was that caused this unsullied and disinterested enthusiasm to burst forth in the rectories of the young clergy and in certain groups of sincere and noble young people, one would have had to live in those times, to have read in their eyes, to have listened to their confidences, to have shaken their trembling hands, to have forged in the heat of battle bonds that only death could break. One must above all read the private letters of Lacordaire, he who on the day preceding the suppression of *L'Avenir,* wrote to a friend: 'As briefly as time will continue, it will take nothing away from the joys of this past year; the experience will always remain in my heart, as [the memory of] a virgin who has just died[39].' "

Those who felt this way must be forgiven, for they deeply loved the Church and they deeply loved France. But, in the final analysis, history owes them the truth, as history owes the truth to all people. Well, the truth is that the ideas expressed in *L'Avenir* often lacked a sense of balance in thought and in fairness toward people. It was not only impassioned; it was bombastic and even virulent. It was as unambiguous against Gallicanism as it was against the monopoly of the *Université*. But it was often wrong with regard to those who worked in the *Université* and those who were Gallicans. It was unjust toward Bossuet, toward the Restoration, even toward Louis-Philippe himself. Doubtless, Louis-Philippe disregarded the rights of Catholics. He aimed to hold closed forever the bronze doors [they could not be breached] that were forged to their detriment. He saw nothing in the nation other than the bourgeoisie, which had given him the crown, and he remained faithful to the prejudices and passions of the middle classes. "However, it would have been better," Lacordaire later recalled, "had our argument been ennobled by less abrasive language, and had our style embodied more of the Christian spirit than of the unbridled spirit of the times[40]." The ferocity of O'Connell's language could not be invoked in this case either as an example or as an excuse; O'Connell was not a priest, as were La Mennais and Lacordaire.

Furthermore, a sense of proportion was lacking even more than a sense of fairness. Certainly, under the weight of La Mennais' deserved unpopularity for his 1825 tract on the law of sacrilege [he objected to having the law cover Protestants and Jews, and not just the Catholic Church.- Trans.] *L'Avenir* could not justify enough the equality of religions before the law, which had been embedded in the customs of the French public even more than in its public law, and which could not be called into question at this moment in time without creating a major crisis for the Empire. Furthermore, given the religious situation in the country as well as the political circumstances, the freedom of the press was most definitely needed. Certainly it was important to proclaim this, and to proclaim it loudly. The sincerity of these statements would have been believed, because the need for Catholics to have this liberty was evident. Considering the nature of public sentiment, censure would be allowed, from then on only against the Catholics. But *L'Avenir* went further. It glorified liberty of conscience as it did liberty of the press; it declared them to be divinely ordained rights[41].

There is more. In the third issue of L'Avenir, La Mennais, deciding on his own authority an issue touching on the governance of the Church and on its supreme head, proclaimed that religion *should* now *be totally* separated from the state; that, as a result, the state should in no way be involved in the selection of bishops; that the Concordat of 1801 had ceased to be and could not be regenerated; and that, furthermore, no freedom was possible for the Church except under one condition, the suppression of the salaries that the state paid annually to the clergy (and La Mennais gravely requested that the bishops renounce this salary). *L'Avenir* maintained that the state should not consider the priest as a priest, but only as a citizen, with the consequence that, in countries with military conscription, the priest must submit like all other citizens; and that, if he openly breaks his vows by getting married, no one has the right to oppose him. This situation occurred also under the Terror, and the Church was deeply distressed by the experience. Now, it was being proposed that the Church lead the way to ruin and scandal. Absolutist natures are like that; they are oblivious to consequences; objections slide off them like a knife against armor plate.

It is not difficult to see that, in a country where the Catholic faith was still the faith of the vast majority of the people who had religion, this in effect degraded the faith, reducing it to the condition that it is in the United States, which is to say, to the status of a sect. Catholicism has nothing to lose by this in the bowels of a nation where they were from the beginning in the minority. But who cannot understand the point of view of those who live in countries where [Catholicism] has always been the national religion (without losing the universal aspect of the faith) — that they would find themselves diminished and debased by this? What's more, it was enormously naïve to imagine that an increase in liberty would be for Catholics a reward for this debasement. To be sure, the state does not have to name bishops or pay priests to find ways whereby it can oppress religion. Besides, to ask for this separation in the name of the Church was to ask that the Church suddenly go back to the catacombs; it meant placing the Church back in the predicament that its own enemies wished to inflict on it. It was, as Montalembert said so well, as if we were requesting today the abolition of temporal power out of love for the freedom of the Pope.

And so, it is easy to sense what effect similar ideas had on the French bishops. Accustomed for a long time to the traditions of the *ancien régime,* of those of the Empire, and of those of the Restoration to rely on civil authority, how would they have been able to reject suddenly all relations with this power to throw themselves into something new? How could they have been able to sacrifice the known for the unknown, certainty for uncertainty, a situation that was a given for a situation which they must actively create anew? Would they be able to rely — not just for a day, but for centuries — on the heroic devotion of the people, as in Ireland? Or on the neutrality of the government and on that of the political parties, as the bishops in the United States are able to do? The misfortunes of the Church in France began with the misfortunes of royalty; how could the fall of Charles X not remind the clergy of the fall of Louis XVI? And how could the earthquake that was 1830 not have represented for the priests — most of them royalists — what it represented for Catholic legitimists (which is to say, for the majority of French Catholics): the reopening of a chasm? Not only were they apprehensive about Louis-Philippe; but they dreaded far more, and with justification, the savage passions that threw the archbishopric of Paris into the Seine. And it was not on La Mennais and his theories that they relied to negate these passions. The revolutionary tone of *L'Avenir* certainly inspired more fear in them than confidence.

It is difficult to describe the level of opposition that was mounted against this newspaper in almost all the bishoprics and most of the seminaries. In several dioceses, reading *L'Avenir* was prohibited altogether by ecclesiastical authorities; young people who were leaning toward the new doctrines were kept at a distance from holy orders; entry into the seminary was even denied altogether to several of them. Professors of theology were stripped of their titles, some pastors were removed because they shared and propagated the proscribed new teachings.

The more the government solidified itself under the strong arm of Casimir Périer[22], the more the idea of the separation of Church and state lost ground among Catholics. On the other hand, all the more did the fluctuations in public opinion swell and threaten to bury *L'Avenir*. Repudiated in France, not only publicly, but without respite by the nunciature, denounced in Rome by many bishops, the newspaper began to lose its subscribers. Rome was persuaded to speak out against it, but only in the vaguest way, and without the possibility of discerning what was true and what was false in these rumors that were anonymously and persistently spread. "The funds," said Lacordaire, "ran out, courage wavered and influence was diminished through its exaggerated resort. After thirteen months of daily combat, it was necessary to begin considering a retreat. The movement begin by *L'Avenir* did not have an adequate base of support[42]. Besides, the newspaper was too unexpected and too fiery to sustain itself. A long-term success is always characterized by deep roots implanted in minds over time. Although O'Connell preceded us, Catholic France was not aware of him, ignored him in a sense, and we appeared to the clergy, to the government, to the parties, as a band of lost children, without forebears or hope for posterity. *L'Avenir* was a desert storm, not a rain that refreshes the air and nourishes the fields.

"The day after our decision," continued Lacordaire, "I went down early to La Mennais' quarters; I explained to him that we could not end our efforts in this way, but that we should travel to Rome to explain our intentions, to submit our ideas to the Holy See, and to give, in this bold step, proof of our sincerity and orthodoxy, which would always be, no matter what happens, a blessing for us and a weapon taken from the hands of our enemies."

"La Mennais should have answered me in this way: 'My dear child, give this no more thought. Rome is not in the habit of judging opinions that God has delivered into the hands of men to argue, and above all, opinions that touch upon the ever-shifting politics of varied times and places. Did you see O'Connell rendering himself to Rome to consult the pope? The pope, in the midst of the terrible strife in Ireland caused by the question of national and religious liberty, did he intervene to direct events or to stop them? No. Rome remained silent, and O'Connell continued to speak out for thirty years. We cannot do what he did, because we do not have behind us, as he did, the unanimous consent of a nation; but, in retreating from the struggle, our silence will have its own kind of strength and dignity. This is not the right moment for us; we should allow more time to pass. Our ideas will take root in the minds of others; they will take shape in a peaceful way, something which, at the moment, we are unable to accomplish, and, one day, maybe soon, whether after we are dead, or while we are still living, we will see our utterances rising from the ashes, schools opening freely, religious establishing themselves throughout our nation, provincial councils forming, and the antipathy of the country toward us transformed into that good will which God and men need at all times, and which is the true path to all the freedoms. It is not necessary to go to Rome to accomplish this; our very failure, in satisfying our enemies, will deprive them of a source of leverage; and the more profound it is, the more it will hasten the day where everything we have wished for will be realized.'

"Instead of this response, which would have been the wise response, la Mennais agreed without hesitation to my proposal. 'Yes,' he said, 'we must depart for Rome[40].'

"This decision was announced to the public in the final issue of *L'Avenir,* over the signatures of all the newspaper's writers. It was done with a certain pomp and circumstance; promises of submission were combined in a singular fashion with our final high-spirited pronouncements as journalists. And so, we set out on our travels, la Mennais, Montalembert, and I."

Endnotes

Numbers in bold print indicate endnotes added by translator.

1. Foisset is referring here to the quotation from Lacordaire at the end of the final paragraph of chapter III.—*Translator's Note.*
2. Jules Auguste Armand Marie, Prince de Polignac (1780–1847). Charles X named him foreign minister in August 1829 and prime minister in November 1829. De Polignac was opposed to the liberal tendencies of the Charter of 1814. Source: William J. Roberts, *France: A Reference Guide from the Renaissance to the Present* (New York: Facts on File Library of World History, 2004), p. 482. Accessed 12 November 2010, at
http://books.google.com/books?id=ogdZu2l2CYkC&pg=PA482&dq=Jules+Auguste+Armand+Marie,+Prince+de+Polignac&hl=en&ei=4mrdTJD4L8KclgflwvGNDQ&sa=X&oi=book_result&ct=result&resnum=1&ved=0CCoQ6AEwAA#v=onepage&q=Jules%20Auguste%20Armand%20Marie%2C%20Prince%20de%20Polignac&f=false.— [cdt]
3. Charles X issued the five ordinances of St. Cloud (25 July 1830). "They were—(1) the suspension of the liberty of the

225

press; (2) the dissolution of the new chamber of deputies; (3) a new system of election, so as to secure absolute power to the king; (4) the convocation of a new chamber; [and] (5) some ultra-royalist appointments to the council of state." There was a large outcry among French citizens against the ordinances, followed by the July Revolution and the removal of Charles X from the throne. Quotation from: *Histories of England, France, Germany, and Holland from the Encyclopædia Brittanica* (New York: Charles Scribner's Sons, 1883), p. 619. Accessed 5 February 2011 [cdt],
athttp://books.google.com/books?id=gxEMAAAAYAAJ&pg=PA619&dq=ordinances+of+st.+cloud+charles+X&hl=en&ei=I11NTdbrNYnagAeXg731Dw&sa=X&oi=book_result&ct=result&resnum=1&ved=0CDMQ6AEwAA#v=onepage&q=ordinances%20of%20st.%20cloud%20charles%20X&f=false.

4. The chamber of deputies elevated to the throne Louis Philippe I (1773–1850) of the House of Orléans. As a result of this action, Charles X was the last king of France from the House of Bourbon. Louis-Philippe's reign (1830–1848) was known as the July Monarchy.   [cdt]

5. In the Revolution of 1688, also known as the Glorious Revolution, James II of England was overthrown by William of Orange. Under the new king, who shared his rule with Queen Mary II, a new constitution was drawn up that allowed for a greater balance of power between the king and Parliament. [cdt]

6. 18 Brumaire refers to a date in the Republican calendar—9 November 1799—when Napoleon Bonaparte overthrew the French Directory and established the Consulate.

7. A Roman Catholic church in Paris (eighth *arrondissement*), originally built by Napoleon as a Temple of the Glory of his Grand Army. Replaced by the *Arc de Triomphe du Carrousel*, thus freeing the building for other uses, it was finally determined to become a Catholic church.

8. *Notice.*

9. Reference here is to the Charter of 1814.

10. 17 January 1826, to Foisset.—See also letter to Lorain, 18 January 1823.
11. Letters to Coriolis and to the Count de Senfft, 19 August 1829.
12. To Coriolis, 6 August 1830.
= See www.worksoflacordaire.com under: "Festivals of July".
13. To Coriolis, 6 August 1830.
14. The Jacobins got their name from the Jacobin Club in Paris (1789–1784), where supporters of the Revolution met. The term refers to radical republicans.— Prior to the Revolution, the building was a Priory of the Dominican Order, dedicated to Saint James [Saint-Jacques], whence the name of the club.
15. To Countess L. de Senfft, 5 September 1830.
16. *Notice.*
17. *Notice.* The name "Liberator" was bestowed on [Daniel] O'Connell; in Ireland, the two names became synonymous. — See the Internet at www.worksoflacordaire.com for Lacordaire's eulogy of O'Connell.
18. *Notice.* —François René de Chateaubriand (1768-1848). When the French Revolution became violent, he exiled himself in North America for one year. After a stormy life, he returned to Catholicism and wrote his famous apologia, the *Genius of Christianity.*
19. See in the newspaper, *Le Globe,* the *premier-Paris* of said day [20 August 1830].
20. He was not speaking to revolutionaries. He was speaking to the Countess de Senfft, for a long time one of his closest confidantes when he vehemently supported the monarchy. (Letter of 13 September 1830.—*Corresp.,* II, p. 177.)
21. "All is for the best in the best of all possible worlds": Quotation from Voltaire's *Candide.*
22. Périer: Casimir Pierre Périer (1777-1832): banker and politician during the Restoration. Head of the Conservative Party. Later, as Prime Minister of France he was somewhat ruthless in his administration.
23. *L'Avenir,* 27 January 1831.

24. Article by [Charles] de Coux, *"Des associations patriotiques,"* 21 March 1831.—The word "alone" was not actually used, but it was in the author's thoughts. This is clear from the text.

25. The three priests were Gerbet, Lacordaire, and de Salinis; the five lay people were Bartels, previously banished from Belgium; de Coux; Daguerrre; Harel du Tancrel; and Waille. Monsieur d'Ault du Mesnil did not join them until later. This constituted the entire editorial staff of *L'Avenir.*

26. *Le P. Lacordaire,* by the Comte de Montalembert;

- In-18 [in-decimo-octavo]: See endnote 46 in Chapter I regarding in-4 [in-quarto]. The latter makes for a book of large pages, about 9 x 12 inches in size, while in-18 makes for a smaller format.

27. And de Coux seemed also not to be what one could call a heavyweight. Having become a professor of *économie politique* in Louvain, he gave up this position in 1845 to become a writer for *L'Univers* with Veuillot, then left *L'Univers* for *L'Ère Nouvelle* in 1848, and ended up dying surrounded by the editors- writers of *L'Univers* (after their turn toward an anti-parliamentary point of view at the end of 1851).

28. St. Yves of Tréguier (1253-1303): became known as the lawyer for the poor. There is a Breton pilgrimage in his honor.

29. *Le P. Lacordaire,* by Montalembert, p. 31.

30. The Prince de Broglie, *Discours de réception à l'Académie.*

31. Wishing to express the idea that the kingship of Louis-Philippe was only conditional, since it was contingent upon his fidelity to the Charter, de Coux characterized him as only the *provisional* king of France.

32. *Moniteur,* 20 September 1831.

33. *Le Père Lacordaire*, by the Montalembert, p. 45.

34. Loire Inférieure: Department on the West Coast of France.

35. There were at Melleray Irish religious, who, not having residential rights in France, could not invoke our country's basic legal rights. But also residing there were French religious.

No law could deny them their civil rights, which included the proscription against unlawful entry.

36. Servin: unable to identify.

Omer Talon (1595-1652): a judge. Defended the right of Parliament against the crown.

Seconde majesté : unable to clarify. [Perhaps the bishops?]

37. François Fénelon, bishop and author (1651–1715).

38. La Vendée: a region in west-central France strongly supportive of the King and the Church.

39. Letter to Montalembert, 29 October 1831.

40. *Notice.*

41. It declared that they were *irrefutable consequences* of the free will that God granted to man (article of 12 June 1831).

42. 80,000 francs worth of investment and subscriptions had helped to found the newspaper; the number of subscriptions never exceeded 1,200 (half of the subscribers were priests, and half lay people). A special fund of 20,000 francs had allowed for the creation of the *Agence* [*pour la liberté religieuse*].

43. *Notice,* chapter II.—The thought of resorting to Rome was not a new one to Lacordaire. It was he who said in *L'Avenir* on 25 November 1830: "Even if we have to travel barefoot, we will bring our protest to the city of the apostles, walking in the faith of S. Peter, and we will see who will dare stop these pilgrims of God and of liberty."

La Mennais also had this idea before. As far back as 27 February 1831, he had approached Cardinal Weld, his close friend, asking to be given the opportunity to submit to the recently elected Gregory XVI a statement summarizing the tenets of *L'Avenir*. It was not until the end of October that La Mennais learned that this document had never reached the cardinal. (Letter from Lacordaire to Montalembert, 29 October 1831.)

Chapter V

THE ENCYCLICAL OF 1832

Rome in 1832; the diplomatic corps; Cardinal de Rohan; Cardinal Lambruschini; the Jesuits, Father Rozaven; Cardinals Zurla, Pacca, Bernetti, de Gregorio; Dr. Wiseman; some representatives of modernist ideas — Cold reception of La Mennais; his report to the Pope — Letter of Cardinal Pacca, the effect it produced on Lacordaire — He returns alone to France — Cholera in 1832 — The break between Lacordaire and La Mennais becomes more and more serious; with the latter announcing his upcoming return, Lacordaire, to avoid meeting him, leaves for Germany — Meeting in Munich — Encyclical of 1832; apparent submission of La Mennais; Lacordaire follows him to La Chênaie — Violent reaction and interior revolt of La Mennais against the Encyclical; Lacordaire's conclusive break.

On 30 December 1831, the three representatives of *L'Avenir* arrived in Rome.

To believe Lla Mennais, diplomatic messages from Austria, Prussia, and Russia, reached Rome ahead of them. In them, the Pope was pressured to make a pronouncement against those reckless revolutionaries, those seducers of the people, whom they incited to revolt in the name of religion. The French government was acting in the same way, upheld by the legitimist party, at whose head stood Cardinal de Rohan, Cardinal Lambruschini, and the Jesuits.

This is perhaps giving *L'Avenir* too much importance in imagining that it had so alarmed the three powers that they partitioned Poland among themselves. Surely the representatives of the three governments in Rome had no sympathy for *the pilgrims of God and of liberty*, and probably did not hide that fact. Did they go any farther? Were there any diplomatic notes in the tone presumed by La Mennais? I can neither affirm nor deny.

I doubt strongly that Casimir Périer, at the time the Prime Minister of Louis-Philippe, had considered to exercise any kind of pressure against the Holy See to obtain the condemnation of the teachings of *L'Avenir*. It is more likely that these disturbed him very little, disavowed as they were, and subsequently very openly by all the bishops of France. Be that as it may, I willingly admit that M. de Saint-Aulaire, our ambassador to the Pope, did not show himself to be a strong supporter of la Mennais, without, however, detracting from the extreme caution of his character.

As for the hostility of the legitimists, it was extreme. It is true that Cardinal de Rohan, having taken refuge in Rome after the days of July, following upon the violence attempted against him by the insurgents of Paris, was the likely agent of that hostility. But, from that quarter, La Mennais had little to worry about. On the one hand, this prince of the Church had formerly sought out Lacordaire and greatly admired Montalembert; he had received them most graciously, and, overall, his behavior was that of a perfect gentleman. On the other hand there were very few repercussions from the pontifical resolutions. Late as he was in entering the Church, La Mennais lacked the authority arising from ecclesiastical knowledge. Genuine piety, a lofty position, a name often honored by the hierarchy, assured him of great courtesy in Rome; but this courtesy was never influence.

To the contrary, Cardinal Lambruschini, from then on, enjoyed a large share in the confidence of Gregory XVI, for whom he would later be Secretary of State. A native of Genoa, but a member of the Institutes of Barnabites and called to Rome by his superiors, he had gained a rather notable reputation as theologian when Pius VII appointed him as Archbishop of Genoa. There, according to La Mennais himself, his application to the duties of his post, his life private, regular, and dignified won for him the respect of everyone. His nomination to the nunciature of Paris by Leo XII filled the author of the *Essay* with stimulating expectations; these did not last long. [Cardinal] Lambruschini listened to La Mennais; but he made his own decisions about men and matters and refused to believe that Charles X and his Ministers were enemies of the Church[1]. In 1830, he greatly deplored he Restoration and did not leave the founder of *L'Avenir* in the dark that, if the Nunciature valued the loyalty of this newspaper to the anti-Gallican beliefs, it was far from supporting the political principles of the paper[2]. More than that, he flatly refused to receive Messrs de Coux and Gerbet, who had come to request of him that he present to the Holy Father the expression of *L'Avenir*'s views. On finding him in Rome, vested in purple, and favored by the Supreme Pontiff, La Mennais had to expect to find him to be an adversary, and a formidable one at that.

It was the same with the Jesuits. Vigilant guardians of tradition in philosophy as well as in theology, they had, from the first day, kept distant from their teaching the doctrine of the *Essay* concerning certitude. Moreover, in 1832, the Assistant in France for the General happened to be Father de Rozaven, an outspoken antagonist of that teaching which he had just recently refuted *ex professo* [formally], pen in hand[3]. From then on, the opposition of the Jesuits to the *La Mennais School* never ceased for a day. The *Mémorial catholique* [a newspaper] complained about it strongly and the final writing of La Mennais (*Des Progrès de la Révolution*) [The Progress of the Revolution] had stunningly declared that the Institute of the Jesuits was not exempt from shortcomings, even serious ones, and was not sufficiently attuned to the mind of current thinkers, to the needs of the world. Accordingly, in Rome, La Mennais could not count on the benevolence of the Jesuits or even on their neutrality. Indeed, it was not solely in philosophy that the ideas of the supposed reformer frightened the Fathers, it was also in the field of social questions.

But the voice speaking even more loudly against him than the legitimists and the Jesuits was the horror of the revolutionary Hydra, the lively memory of the uprising in Bologna, that, in the spring of 1831, had almost stirred up all of Italy. That uprising was not an isolated accident; the soil was mined, all Europe felt itself atop a volcano. Even then, the secret societies had called for a meeting in the Roman States, first of all to assault the least armed of European kingdoms. To be sure, this kingdom was allowed to follow the instinct of self-preservation and the view that the grand purpose of *L'Avenir* — the separation of Church and State — could immediately become a weapon against the temporal sovereignty of the Pope. The final action of the editorial committee of the paper, the union proposed *to all those who still hoped for liberty* "to bring about over the rivalry of administrators THE FRATERNITY OF NATIONS," seemed to be a revolutionary act to the editor-in-chief. This was certainly more than enough so that, independently of the ill-will of diplomats, La Mennais would be received in Rome very coldly, just as he had expected[4]. What could be more meaningful than such a refusal?

Pacca, dean of the Sacred College, the last representative of the Rome of Pius VI and the unshakeable companion in the captivity of Pius VII, Lambruschini and Zurla become henceforth known to us. The Secretary of State Bernetti, brilliant student of Consalvi, and Cardinal de Gregorio, son of the King of Spain Charles III, were not men of ordinary ability. It was concerning Fr. de Rosaven that M. Dupanloup, bishop of Orléans, gave this encomium: "Since Bossuet, the Church of France has perhaps not had a more skillful theologian."

Freedom of thought, in the proper meaning of the word, was not lacking. In a current of more modern ideas, eminent members of the principal monastic orders met each other: Cardinal Micara, General of the Capuchins; Fr. Orioli, Conventual Franciscan, later a cardinal himself; Fr. Mazetti, of the Carmelites; Fr. Ventura, General of the Theatines, since then well-known in France; Fr. Olivieri, Dominican, Dean of the Sacred Office, "a strong and encyclopedic mind joined to a simple and upright heart[5]."

All of catholic Europe was represented there. Thus, Rozaven was French, Gregorio Spanish, Zurla Venitian, Lambruschini Genoese, Ventura Sicilian. At the time, there was even an English prelate who had a long-standing relationship with M. de la Mennais, Cardinal Weld. Finally, in attendance was the head of the English College, who, one day, would be Cardinal Wiseman.

Not all of these men lived exclusively in the past, as some would like to believe. Many of them were engaged in observing the state of religious and irreligious studies throughout the world. M. de la Mennais recognized that Fr. Olivieri, who personified the Roman Inquisition, the ancient man, said he, because of his character, his incorruptible rectitude, his wise and modest freedom, did not cease, despite the numerous duties of his office, to follow in Europe and beyond the movement of the human spirit and the sequence of events that day to day alter the state of society[6].

Moreover, virtue was no more lacking than was knowledge. In March 1832, the same La Mennais wrote: "We could never praise too highly and, generally, we could never praise too much the steadiness of the Roman clergy. The cardinals are an example of this, as well as of a sincere piety. As for studies, they are concentrated almost exclusively in the mass of religious. In this group you will find men who join the highest virtues to a deep and varied theological knowledge. These genuinely preserve teachings and tradition. By their skillful and wise counsels, they direct the works of the congregations that prepare, to submit to the Supreme Pontiff, the decisions concerning all the matters of the Universal Church. Free, for the most part, from passions and prejudices, with a superior mind, humble and calm, they have in their impartial and simple talent, in the touching simplicity of their behavior, in their friendly kindness, something completely appropriate to bind with them and with the common center the scattered members of the eminent Christian family[7].

This was Rome when La Mennais arrived on 30 December 1831, preceded by the universal disapproval of the bishops of France. He arrived, not as a submissive child — it is Lacordaire who reports it — but as a man resolved to maintain as a political and a social view the most absolute independence, such as to resume *L'Avenir* under a new format if the questions that he had supported were judged by the Pope to be contrary to his own. This disposition was obvious in all his conversations; they appeared to Lacordaire to be so lacking in wisdom, in appropriateness, in truth, that a painful icyness soon saddened their trip from Paris to the Holy City and destroyed in Rome all the charm of their being housed together[8].

Gregory XVI was promptly informed of this frame of mind that M. de la Mennais did not keep secret. The Pope wished to give him immediately the gentlest warning, one that would leave few traces, one that could always be reversed: he delayed in receiving him. This silent caution was misunderstood. After a very few visits to Cardinal Pacca (for which La Mennais had a letter from Fr. de Mazenod, Vicar General and subsequently bishop of Marseille), but especially from long-time friends of 1824, who had remained faithful (from Cardinal Micara, Fr. Orioli, who had translated the *Défense de l'Essai*, Fr. Olivieri, Fr. Ventura), the founder of *L'Avenir* along with his two young collaborators attempted to convince each other that there was between them and their adversaries only a misunderstanding that would be easy to dispel. They immediately got busy ~~in~~ preparing a report addressed to the Pope, a report that would summarize their doctrinal views and would explain the mode of action they adopted in France to spare the Catholic religion from the consequences it feared from the Revolution of 1830. Lacordaire was entrusted with the composition of this document that bears the date 3 February 1832[9].

This writing treats successively the state of religion in France under the Restoration, the danger it faced after the fall of Charles X, the modes of conduct that could be followed to avoid such a peril, the system adopted against the Church by the government of Louis-Philippe, the separation of Church and State, the impossibility of a schism given the state of minds and matters, the newspaper *L'Avenir* and the Agency for Religious Liberty; finally, the opposition that the paper had encountered, the causes and the consequences of that opposition. and

This report was a "plea for the defense"; the most capable lawyer will always present the facts in a manner very favorable to his cause.

Despite some corrections, the Restoration appears in it as a government that oppresses the Church because the latter, frightened by the unpopularity that her previous partiality for the clergy had aroused, had not abrogated the Organic Articles, nor maintained the colleges she had allowed the Jesuits to open. Moreover, she was accused of having prepared and fostered the elements of a schism because Mssrs. Lainé and Corbière had published flyers in support of the declaration of 1682, and because M. Frayssinous, writer of a document in favor of that declaration, had hopes of founding in Paris a school of higher ecclesiastical studies, intended to replace the ancient Sorbonne.

Lacordaire emphasized, with very sad but undeniable truth, the frightening hate against religion that had arisen because of its open protection by the Restoration, whence the danger of the Revolution of 1830. Under the attack of this revolution, in the presence of victorious irreligion, sitting on the throne and mistress of the public counsels to the nation, should she therefore have persisted in her support of whatever power reigned, or would it have been better for her to argue for the separation of Church and State, so as to forestall the disparagement and the subjection of the hierarchy by the indignity of the choices of bishops, as well as by the de-Christianization of the new generations by the monopoly of instruction under the exclusive sway of the State?

The foundation of the newspaper *L'Avenir* and of the *Agence* [Agency] had been, according to the report, an act of legitimate defense against such a peril and against the violence and the irritations [frictions?] to which the clergy and the religious orders found themselves exposed. The paper and the Agency rightfully could bask in the pride that Religion owed them for this witness which greatly contributed to the lessening of the hate whose targets they were. And yet, an ever growing intense opposition accused the editors of *L'Avenir* as revolutionaries and heretics. The political passion (the legitimacy issue) and the theological passion (Gallicanism) by themselves could explain such accusations.

Two conclusions arose from this account: one that, without the action of independent Catholics of all political parties and free from of all influences of power, Religion would be deprived of a kind of defense that it absolutely needed in this current crisis; the other, that this action could not obtain lasting success unless it were supported by the Holy See. In consequence, the latter's silence would weaken the courage of those who were devoted to it and confuse a number of undecided individuals, at the same time as Gallicanism would be increasing its efforts to impose itself as an obligation of conscience on seminary youth, in virtue of the obedience due to ecclesiastical superiors. It could no less be feared that the silence of the Holy See would be taken as a condemnation, something that would have two results: the first that, immediately it would be impossible to offer any resistance against the oppressors of the Church and from then on, the damage would increase with incalculable speed; the second that a large part of the population which, in France and in the surrounding countries, had become the enemy of Catholicism because the people judged it to be incompatible with civil liberty, but who had begun to approach it since the publication of *L'Avenir*, would immediately distance themselves from Religion and this, with greater hate than ever.

To be sure, this plea was specious, and the good faith of the lawyer cannot be gainsaid. But rebuttals in abundance were made and La Mennais even addressed some to himself.

"These considerations," one must reply to the adversaries of his ideas, "do not surprise us to the same degree as they do you. Moreover, in conducting business, one does not rely on such general statements, on vague forecasts of a distant future, concealed from the reckoning of practical knowledge. One sees results as near, positive, assured. Now the immediate results of what you propose would, as you yourself have said, be likely persecutions, an almost total change in the administration of the Church, the loss of Her property, the privation of the support still being offered, to a certain degree, by the temporal powers, in pursuit of their own interests.

"Do you have sufficient knowledge of the clergy, its spirit, its dispositions, in the various countries of Europe, so that you are certain that it would suffer persecution without faltering, that its patience would await the end [of the persecution], that it would not surrender sooner or later any less to the cruelties than to the seductions that would undoubtedly be used to break its resistance? Have you calculated how many parishes would remain without pastors by the suppression of the budget for religion, followed by the obstacles to clerical education? Can you calculate the effect on the faithful who have become accustomed to live without Catholic teaching and worship?

"Suppose that the Church escapes persecution or that

she triumphs over it: the tangled complication of difficulties that a break in the relations with the State would bring, especially in those countries where the religious organization is tightly linked with the civil organization — would this not create problems? A new conduct not only to be created but to have accepted by individual churches, is this something very easy, in your view? Who knows how much resistance could be met and where that resistance could lead?

"You consider the loss of property as something insignificant; but let us look at the consequences in the Roman States only. From the Pope and the cardinals up to the lowliest magistrate of a village, everyone lives on public revenues. Ecclesiastical management is the circle wherein gradually all interests fall. Make the slightest move against this arrangement, where everything is linked, how many concerns would be offended, how many lives compromised[10]!"

The adversaries of La Mennais did not lose the opportunity to add: "You give great value to the advantages of freedom; but these advantages, so certain in your mind, are more than questionable in our eyes. Is it therefore evident that the freedom of the good would triumph, all by itself, over the freedom of evil? Are you forgetting original sin? Are you denying that man is born inclined to evil and that the promotion of vice finds in original covetousness some points of support that the promotion of the good will always lack? Moreover, is it enough to break with the State for the freedom of the good to be assured? No doubt, the independence of the Church is safe in the Anglo-American Republic, where freedom is the common right and where we [i.e., Catholics] are so few in number that the public authority does not do us the honor of fearing us. But what did the princes and the legislative assemblies in Europe do to the freedom of the Church, wherever the number of the faithful frightened the governments?"

The report of 3 February 1832 was presented to the

Sovereign Pontiff by Cardinal Pacca, dean of the Sacred College. Although [Pacca] was a hold-over from another age, he showed much interest in La Mennais. This is how the document ends:

"O Father! Deign to lower your eyes onto some of the least of your children who are accused of being rebels against your infallible and benign authority! Here they are in front of you; read into their souls; there is nothing there that they seek to hide. If one of their thoughts, A SINGLE ONE, strays from your thoughts, they disavow it, they renounce it. You are the measure of their beliefs; never, no, never would they know any others[11]."

It appears certain that Gregory XVI did read the report, and that he even read it again several days in succession[12]. Obviously, the Pope could not give his approbation of all the theses of *L'Avenir*; but he was reluctant to issue a public rebuke to such enthusiastic defenders of Religion and of the Holy See.

And yet, La Mennais' reckless language increased and worsened. A fear arose that perhaps a political party would be created in Rome. Consider the effect produced when words such as these were repeated: "The Pope is an upright religious who knows nothing about worldly matters and *has no idea of the situation of the Church.* — The functionaries are ambitious, greedy, selfish, as cowardly as a stiletto, blind and foolish as the eunuchs of the late Roman Empire. There you have the government of this country; there you have the men who run everything[13]."

A few weeks later, on Saturday 25 February, the secretary of Cardinal Pacca brought to the three representatives of *L'Avenir* a letter from his master. In essence, it said that the Holy Father, while admiring the righteousness of their intentions and their talents, was displeased that they had stirred up controversies, at the least dangerous; that their teachings would be studied; but since that examination could take a long time, the Pope asked them to leave Rome as soon as it suited them to regain their country, where in time he would have them informed of his decision[14].

The letter was given to Lacordaire. He immediately brought it to La Mennais, who was still in bed. The latter read it without emotion and declared that he would remain in Rome to await the decision promised. Devastated, Lacordaire ran to Montalembert's room; he found him inclined to follow the example of the Master.

Here we have to halt, to reflect on Lacordaire. He was alone in Rome, absolutely alone, with no other counselors than his guardian angel and his conscience. Or rather, he was not alone; he was in the presence of a superior man whom he had accepted as master, and whose glory and genius weighed heavy on him. He was thirty years old, La Mennais was fifty. Under these circumstances — about which we will probably not give another example — Lacordaire gave proof of uprightness of heart, of discernment of mind, of determination of will that were truly admirable. A great light shone in this truly priestly soul. As Montalembert said, the inseparable weaknesses of what is human that mingled with divine matters in the Church did not escape his attention at all, but appeared to him as overshadowed by the splendor of tradition and authority. Without hesitation, faith, the docility of soul of a Catholic priest, won out in him over the vapors of pride, over all the training of talent, over all the memories, and all the frenzy of the struggle. The decision to remain in Rome appeared disastrous to him; it was a clear break with the promises of the report of 3 February; this breach of a pledge, so hasty and so obvious, must have saddened the Holy Father and could likely move him to have recourse to harsh measures that earlier he had no need to consider. Besides, the letter of Cardinal Pacca treated everything with caution; it took into account services rendered and goals. While announcing a forthcoming pontifical decision, the letter allowed for the belief that one would rather not give a decision, but "to leave time to cover in its folds the editors *of L'Avenir*, their teachings, and their actions." Girded

with these very decisive considerations, Lacordaire insisted on
the return to France and the absolute end to all political action.
But La Mennais was not accustomed to objections from his
disciples; a disagreement seemed to him almost treason. For his
part, Montalembert revealed himself offended by such a lack
of deference toward the Master. La Mennais called attention to
the effects (terrible, according to him) produced on Catholics,
and even more on non-Catholics, because of what he called this
denial of justice. It was his duty, he added, to see that in the
eyes of everyone, the cause continued to appear unresolved, so
as to avoid dishonor to the Holy See as well as the dreadful
consequences that dishonor would have all over Europe and
beyond. Consequently, he showed himself resolved to prolong
his stay in Rome; in this, he was encouraged by Fr. Ventura
who was all the more enthusiastic in that he hoped very
passionately to erase from the mind of La Mennais the
remembrance of the [Holy See's] public protest against
L'Avenir. How could Lacordaire have won in a contest so
unequal and more painful than we could say? After several
days of desperate attempts to persuade his two collaborators,
he believed he owed it to himself not to accept collusion in
what he judged to be a great error. Besides, his decision had
been made: even before the communication from Cardinal
Pacca — as soon as 23 February, remarkably — he announced
to a friend his return to France immediately after he would have
been received by the Sovereign Pontiff[15].

The audience was held on 13 March. It was very
graciously granted, wrote La Mennais to his brother, after the
request that the "Pilgrims" had made directly to the Cardinal
Secretary of State (Bernetti). But to prevent too favorable
conjectures that the friends of the paper could have drawn from
his sign of benevolence, the Pope had placed the condition that
in no way would there come before him any allusion to the
reason that had brought to Rome the editors of *L'Avenir*.
Cardinal Rohan, chosen to witness the need for this agreed-
upon silence, introduced his three compatriots. Gregory XVI

242

received them with impeccable kindness. Two days later, Lacordaire by himself left for France "with very woeful forebodings and very heavy-hearted farewells."

This was a separation, not yet a rupture. Lacordaire found himself in one of those ambiguous situations — not suited for a character like his — in which it was difficult to reconcile one's usual demeanor with one's inmost feelings. In fact, La Mennais was wandering toward the abyss. Lacordaire could see this; he was surprised to hear from la Mennais' lips words such as these: "One of the most beautiful days of my life will be that on which I will leave this large gravesite wherein are found only bones and worms... I need air, movement, faith, love, everything for which we search in vain among these ancient ruins, on which crawl, as if vile reptiles in shadow and in silence, the basest human passions[16]." But these were private outpourings, whose secret at the time was sacred. Friendship allows for all kinds of concerns; not one could be admitted before others. Consequently, Lacordaire left Rome under the weight of unspeakable distress. The idea of carrying such a burden any longer overwhelmed him all the more since he could not imagine how to reject [La Mennais] with honor.

Before entering Paris, Lacordaire paused for a few days in Burgundy, where he opened himself to the one who writes this [i.e., Foisset] about his hope that in Paris, from now on, he would no longer have any contact with his former collaborators. Since he remained silent about the reasons for this, so as not to betray a secret that was not his to divulge, the friend whom he consulted told him he could not do this without entailing reproaches for the inconstancy of his opinions and the instability of his character, in the absence of any excuse. Then, Lacordaire spoke of burying himself deep into the countryside. Then, said he, it will be obvious that I am a man without ambition. The worry he so greatly suffered gave some firmness to the dreams of his imagination. They were indeed dreams; his calling was surely not there.

It was with these problems in mind that he left Dijon

for Paris. But, when he saw again the house he had inhabited with La Mennais, at 98 Vaugirard Street, tears flooded his eyes. He tried to forget everything so as not to remember the struggles they had in common there in a burst of generosity for the Church along with the tribulations they received as reward. It seemed as if his duty was not to abandon La Mennais on the day of his trial, as long as there remained some hope of holding him, as well as Montalembert, back from the edge of the abyss.

Then he entered that house but found it almost devoid of inhabitants. For the first time, cholera had alighted in Paris; already the victims numbered in the thousands. Some men fell down in the streets never to get up. Coffins were at the doors, black banners in churches, fear everywhere. And, can you believe it? Such was still the passion against priests that Public Administration, even though short of hands to treat the sick, rejected the offers of help from the Archbishop of Paris. Nonetheless, wearing lay clothes, clerics could secretly enter hospitals. Lacordaire hastened to join the chaplain at the Necker Hospital; he went there every morning. Meanwhile, on learning that, at the Storage Grainery near the Bastille, a temporary hospital had been set up, which lacked chaplain, Sisters of Charity, priests from the parish, he went there every day, at the cost of *unbelievable insults* (these were his words), along with two other clerics. It was a heartrending scene. Lacordaire mingled with the students who surrounded the physician during his visit. From there, he took the opportunity to speak with the sick, trying to slip into the conversation some words about God, to determine if they were Christians. Here and there, one or two made confessions. Others were dying, without hearing and without speech; Fr. Lacordaire placed his hand on their forehead and said the words of absolution, confident of divine mercy. "It is rare," he wrote, "that I leave without having some satisfaction for having come. Yesterday, a woman had just been brought in; at her bedside, a military man, her husband. I approached, and since I was dressed in lay clothes, the soldier, in a whisper, asked if there was a priest available. — Indeed, I am one [I said]. — It is satisfying to be at hand to save a soul and to please a man[17]."

Despite the terrible diversion of the cholera, Lacordaire's situation was untenable. He had never been a follower of La Mennais except in politics; basically, he held on to the school by only one area, his ardent tenderness for Montalembert, the latter himself impassioned for the Master. And yet, suffering to the end the consequences of a first error, the consequences of his misunderstanding at La Chênaie in the month of May 1830, he maintained the attitude of a disciple and the appearance of a follower. His invincible sincerity struggled as best it could in that place. Pestered by l'*Ami de la Religion* [Friend of Religion - a newspaper], which pictured him as working to make a separate peace with Rome while disavowing his friends, at one moment he was on the verge of "giving everything that happened some inevitable publicity[18]." But La Mennais was quick to impose on his lips a domineering seal[19]. Thus restrained, Lacordaire sought refuge as best he could in his solitary and silent studies; he collected material for a work on the relationships of civil law with the Catholic Church in various eras of modern history; he was preparing himself for a time when the Church would again be oppressed and when like-minded individuals "could reappear to the cheers of the large majority of Catholics and of the clergy, with the authority of *men who knew how to remain silent*. Silence," he added, "is, after speech, the second power of the world[20]."

La Mennais, however, was at the opposite pole. On the very day he received the letter from Cardinal Pacca, barely a few hours later, he had sent to his first lieutenant, Fr. Gerbet, his new plan for the campaign.

This plan is summarized in these words:

To support the *Agence* as long as possible along with everything connected to it (the public lectures begun by Messrs. de Coux and Gerbet);

To preserve carefully and to assemble the elements of

the noble union some men, Catholic or not, who seek freedom;

To bring about their association, in France and elsewhere, as soon as funds were available;

To attempt to lift up *L'Avenir* by a similar association, whose journal it would be.

On 14 March, the day after the audience with the Pope, La Mennais wrote again: "Do not neglect anything to support and *to extend* the Agency, while we wait until we are able to take a stand on the subject of *L'Avenir*.

On 29 April, he sent word: "The unanimous advice of the people who are linked with us and to the sublime cause that we have attempted to defend is that, with as little hesitation as possible, we should begin *L'Avenir* again. It is to this side, and only to this side, that we need to turn our sights and our efforts. For nothing in the world should we dream of leaving France. It is only there that we can act. It is the center of the movement and of opinion[21]."

Challenged on this point, just as the other former collaborators of *L'Avenir*, Lacordaire made this response:

"Objectively, the execution of this plan is impossible.
— Morally, it would be the most disastrous enterprise we could attempt.

"Objectively, the execution is impossible because we will obtain no money from the Catholics nor from the side of the liberals. For their part, Catholics will see this real and actual alliance with a purely political party as a lack of fidelity to our obligations towards the Holy See and as a descent toward rabble-rousing. As for the liberals, in this alliance with men without a mission from the Pope, the bishops, and the clergy, they will not find a clear enough advantage to sacrifice their money.

"The execution is also materially impossible because even the men that La Mennais chose will not accept the alliance; should they accept it, they are precisely men who lack political influence and who would lose the barely discernible degree of it that they might have, on the day when they would have taken part in an enterprise of which we were members. — Impossible, finally, because they would sign this treaty only on condition that they have a voice at least equal to ours in the common action, and that this equality, being necessarily granted, it would be impossible to agree with each other on the first article to decide on the first question presented.

"The moral viewpoint is something else altogether.

"In this, we free our adversaries from the odious position wherein our submission has placed them; accordingly, we verify all their prophecies. La Mennais becomes a man who has attacked the bishops by depending on the Holy See, and, seeing the Holy See withdrawing its protection from him, will be giving a lesson to the bishops and to the Holy See by relying on an agent foreign to the Church. While in Belgium and Ireland, it was the ENTIRE clergy that allied itself to a political party, for a common cause — in this case, it would be a few men, separating themselves from the clergy to ally themselves with other men connected by all their predecessors to an impious liberalism that will become more so than ever on the occasion of a restoration. — From that day on, La Mennais will be seen as lost in the opinion of the clergy, and *his best friends will speak of it only while groaning.*

"Charles, listen carefully to what I am going to tell you: when La Mennais established *L'Avenir*, he lost a significant part of his former friends, the most enthusiastic of his collaborators; if he undertakes this new plan, remember that an even greater number of friends and collaborators will abandon him. With all of them misled by the liberals into an action with no chance of success, there is no word in the language sad enough to say what will happen[22]."

This is what Lacordaire was writing during the four months before the Encyclical, two years before the publication of *Words of a Believer*. Those who claimed that he was incompetent in practical matters would do well to consider this letter of 22 April 1832.

Accustomed to being listened to like an oracle and

obeyed like a king, La Mennais took offense at the objections from his Parisian friends — attributing them to the presence of Lacordaire. "There is one final step to take," he cried, "and we do not want to think about it: it is the universal union announced in the last issue of *L'Avenir*. But this is precisely the most unimportant matter in Lacordaire's mind, he who has an unusual leaning for the happy medium, for men, and for things²³."

Worn out by all that petty wrangling, Lacordaire tried to escape from the stay in Paris. He had attempted to seek refuge in Belgium, which he quickly left to avoid the pressures to get him to write for *L'Union*, a la Mennais broadsheet established in Brussels by Fr. Gerbet. He hastened to hide himself with a friend in a country parish near Laval. But the presence of the Duchess de Berry in the West had set fire to the entire area. The district of Laval was prepared for a siege; viewed as a suspect, Lacordaire had to return to Paris.

On his return, he learned that the resurgence of *L'Avenir* had been decided on. All the collaborators of the newspaper finally gave in to the influence of the Master. The latter had just met them in Brussels to resolve together the details for the execution of the new campaign. He would finally leave Rome, his soul embittered, after having stated that, with no response from the Holy See, and with no other guide than his personal convictions, he would return to France to restart *L'Avenir*²⁴.

Impartial History will have to say that, during his entire stay in Rome, he never ceased to be convinced of his illusions, not only by Fr. Ventura, but also by Fr. Olivieri and other theologians among the most distinguished in the holy city. It was unceasingly repeated that his teachings were irreproachable, that they would never be condemned. He received expressions of regret that he had to interrupt the publication of *L'Avenir*. Pressure was applied to have him take up again his work as journalist, without worrying about opposition from the bishops. In a final conference with

Cardinal Micara, at which Montalembert assisted, his Eminence had expressed to them in proper terms: "You are in order and perfectly free to redo what you have done, to say again what you have already said. If you strayed, the Holy See would certainly have told you so. It remained silent; what else could you ask of it? A formal approbation? It never gives any. Go, then, and begin again to defend the Church, which, more than ever, needs to be defended. Following the example of the Fathers, when they found themselves in similar circumstances, you have spoken with vigor: speak with even more energy. That is what I would do, in your place[25]."

Having arrived in Florence, La Mennais, accompanied by Montalembert, presented himself to the Internuntio. There, abruptly, with no introduction, he gave notice, rather than informing, of his intention to resume publication of his paper. "Since no one wishes to find me guilty, I consider myself acquitted," declared he. This scene took place from 16 to 20 July 1832.

In the eyes of Lacordaire, this was a third error, a more serious fault than the two previous ones. Immediately, he foresaw the consequences, despite all the assurances given to La Mennais by his friends in Rome and that Lacordaire had not overlooked at all.

In fact, from that moment on, condemnation became inevitable. Having been thus defied, the Sovereign Pontiff could hardly remain silent when the voice of M. de la Mennais was literally all-powerful not only over the most active faction of the French clergy but also on the entire Belgian Catholic party and the Polish migration. One word from him would shake up that portion of Catholicity like the wind stirs up the leaves of the aspen. Gregory XVI resolved to speak. It is a custom that goes back to the early centuries of the Church that, at the beginning of his pontificate, the successor of St. Peter addresses an encyclical letter to all the bishops. The troubles of the Roman States at Gregory XVI's election had not, up to that time, allowed him to conform to that usage. He satisfied it on the solemn feast of the Holy Virgin, 15 August 1832, taking the opportunity to explain himself concerning the political teachings of *L'Avenir*. But since he bore in mind the services rendered by La Mennais, while he condemned some elements of his teachings that were contrary to holy theology, he used the most general terms and did not wish to have the author identified even in the most indirect way. The editing of the Encyclical was entrusted to the Bishop Polidori, subsequently Cardinal.

Lacordaire was unaware of the imminence of this act; but he did not need a new warning to remain strong in his decision not to enter the political arena, on orders from La Mennais. To avoid the alternative of a public break with his former companions in arms, or to follow them, against the cry of his conscience, into the ruin being prepared, he made the choice of going to Germany with the idea of passing one or two years in privacy. The exile was voluntary, but it was an exile. This was a courageous resolution because he was penniless; how to provide for his subsistence in a country whose language he could not speak? He placed his trust in Providence and chose to stay in Munich because it was a Catholic city and life there was less expensive than elsewhere.

At the same time, La Mennais and Montalembert were wending their way toward France, and precisely through the Tyrol and Bavaria. Informed of Henri's intentions by one of his letters, they could not bear the thought of the embarrassment wherein Lacordaire's disagreement with them, made public by his presence in Munich as separated from them, would, in that city, make them face the illustrious Gôrres, the philosopher Schelling, de Baeder, and numerous friends, among whom the young professor Dôllinger, today one of the most celebrated men in contemporary Germany. They were the first to arrive in the capital of Bavaria. Lacordaire had barely, in turn, registered in a hotel when he saw Montalembert enter. It was the custom of German newspapers to announce every day in their pages the name and address of strangers who arrived the previous day. While perusing these papers, Montalembert learned of the arrival and the residence of his friend and hurried to try to ward off the embarrassment that I just mentioned. When one has read the letters written by Lacordaire to Montalembert, since Lacordaire's departure from Rome, we can imagine the enthusiasm with which they threw themselves into each other's arms in Munich. Lacordaire allowed himself to be dragged to La Mennais' quarters. For two hours, Lacordaire attempted to show the latter [i.e., La Mennais] the blow he was about to inflict altogether on his reason, his faith, his honor, by trying to resume the publication of L'Avenir. In the end, either because the arguments of Lacordaire convinced him, or rather that, at any price, he wanted to avoid the danger and the scandal of an open break, La Mennais told Henri: "Yes, that is correct; you have clearly understood[26]."

Thus was peace declared. The following day, 30 August, under these conditions, Lacordaire had no objections to accompanying La Mennais to a banquet that the most distinguished writers and artists of Munich gave for him at the gates of the city. Toasts were made to the unity of Catholics in France and in Germany. Towards the end of the meal, La Mennais was asked to leave for a moment, [at which time] a messenger from the Apostolic Nuncio presented him with a folded document bearing the seal of the nunciature. This was the Encyclical of Pope Gregory XVI dated 15 August 1832. A quick reading of the accompanying letter from Cardinal Pacca revealed to the founder of L'Avenir that there were unfavorable questions about some teachings of that newspaper. Immediately, his mind was made up, and without checking precisely the tenor of the pontifical letter, on leaving, he softly told his two collaborators: "I have just received an Encyclical from the Pope against us; we should not delay in offering submission[27]."

After returning home, he immediately prepared the following declaration:

"The undersigned, editors of *L'Avenir*, members of the Council of the Agency for religious defense,

"Are convinced that, following upon the encyclical letter of the Sovereign Pontiff Gegory XVI, dated 15 August 1832, they could no longer pursue their efforts without placing themselves in opposition to the formal decision of him to whom God has given the charge of governing His Church.

"Believe that, as Catholics, it is their duty to declare, respectfully submitted to the supreme authority of the Vicar of Jesus Christ, that they leave the contest in which they have loyally engaged for two years. They strongly enjoin their friends to give a similar example of Christian submission.

"Consequently,

"1° *L'Avenir*, temporarily suspended since 15 November 1831, will no longer appear;

"2° The General Agency for the defense of religious freedom is dissolved as of today. All the activities begun will be ended, and the accounts liquidated with the shortest delay possible [as soon as possible]."

If we consider the speed with which La Mennais presented this writing to his two collaborators and the great skill with which all the words were chosen so as to give the appearance of submission — all the while maintaining his independence — this leads us to believe that the preceding declaration was less spontaneous than Lacordaire supposed. It is difficult to imagine that the hypothesis of a possible condemnation never came to La Mennais' mind. I would gladly suspect the opposite, namely, that he did entertain that hypothesis, and that in this supposition, he had debated with himself ahead of time and composed in his mind the formula we have just read. This formula, basically, implied no rejection of the opinions held by *L'Avenir*, but only the discontinuation of the paper and of the Agency, that is to say, a purely exterior stoppage which La Mennais did not qualify. This was his exact meaning, this was the mental restriction behind the declaration we have just read. For a long time, La Mennais tried to see in the Encyclical merely an act of government and not a doctrinal decision. Charged with governing the Church, Gregory XVI, in his view, considered only inopportune the lifting of the defense by the editors of *L'Avenir*; the latter yielded and withdrew from combat, but nothing more. And yet it cost La Mennais a lot to appear to renounce indefinitely a full display of his political ideas. In fact, a few days after the banquet in Munich, he returned to France with Lacordaire. Montalembert had left them in Strasbourg. The two other pilgrims of God and of freedom alone climbed a hill near Saverne. Suddenly, La Mennais exclaimed abruptly: "Lacordaire, what if we added to our declaration the words *for now*? We would say: '*for now*, they leave the contest' ". Lacordaire had no trouble showing him that with such a correction, the declaration, in itself so insignificant, had no meaning whatsoever, and that it would be better to remain completely silent. La Mennais did not insist; but he had just betrayed the foundation of his thought[28].

On 11 September 1832, the *Tribune catholique*, a modest paper created by M. Bailly at the beginning of the year in the hope of gaining the heritage of *L'Avenir*, published the declaration above, with the signatures of Messrs de la Mennais, Gerbet, de Coux, de Montalembert, and Lacordaire.

The personal feelings of the signatories were far from being identical. Sainte-Beuve recounts that, having been in Paris to visit them in that same month of September 1832, he first of all noticed La Mennais, in a room on the ground floor, reporting on what had happened and on the Pope, in an no-holding-back manner that surprised his hearer and was totally at odds with his apparent submission. On the contrary, when he walked up to the next flight where Lacordaire lodged, Sainte-Beuve was struck with the contrast. Henri talked of the situation with extreme reserve and submission regarding his miscalculations. "I was less surpised," said Sainte-Beuve, "when shortly thereafter, I learned of the break that had occurred at La Chênaie[29]."

Sainte-Beuve's remembrances are accurate. La

Mennais' act of submission was dated 10 September. We can detect in his General Correspondence the tone in which he spoke of the Encyclical at that date.

This was not the moment to abandon La Mennais to himself; on the contrary, it was time to try the impossible in an effort to moderate the storm that rumbled in his heart. To this end, Lacordaire and Gerbet accompanied him to La Chênaie, at the end of September. The example of Fénelon, that naturally came to everyone's mind, could offer consolation to the author of the *Essay* by proving to him that theological errors, even unshaken, are not incompatible with an unblemished reputation in knowledge and virtue. "If La Mennais," wrote Lacordaire, "had been faithful to his praiseworthy movement in Munich, he would have become greater in contemporary generations by the sole effect of his silence, and he would not have needed ten years to regain the splendor of his renown. But, if the sky of Armorica [Brittany] had not changed, it was not the same in the heart of the Master. Fearful clouds sailed back and forth on this forehead deprived of peace; random and menacing words came from his mouth that had expressed the healing of the Gospel. Now and then, it felt to me as if I was seeing Saul; yet not one of us had the harp of David to remove those sudden outbursts of a wretched spirit. The fear of more sinister expectations increased from day to day in my disheartened spirit."

We are aware today whether there was some exaggeration in that language. The correspondence of La Mennais, published in part, reveals words such as these:

"Gregory XVI and Nicolas, those two understand each other; the Decrees agree with the Briefs, the Briefs with the Decrees. We have to admit, this is pleasing and justifiable comedy, following all the rules of Aristotle and of Laharpe. Only the Poles would request that we call it rather tragedy... *Quos vult perdere, Jupiter dementat* [Those whom he would condemn, Jupiter drives mad.]. Emperors, czars, absolute kings, constitutional kings, *and the others whom I leave unnamed,* see how all of them appear to be in a hurry to leave, so attentive are they not to overlook a single one of the follies that can assure and hasten their departure. Oh! The attractive parade! Move over a bit so that I can see it go by. Farewell, good people! Leave! Since that pleases you, it pleases me also. *Andate dunque, andate, e buon viaggio* [Go, then, go, and pleasant trip.]." (9 October 1832, to Coriolis.)

"Catholicism had been my life because it is that of humanity. I wanted to defend it, I wanted to lift it up from the abyss where it submerges itself every day. Nothing was easier to do. The bishops found that this did not suit them. There was still Rome. I went there and saw the most infamous cesspool that had ever soiled the eyes of man. The giant sewer of the Tarquins would be too narrow to allow the flow of so much filth. There, no other god but self-interest: nations could be sold, all humanity could be sold; the Three Persons of the Holy Trinity could be sold, one after the other, or all together, for a plot of land or for a few dollars. I saw all that, and I told myself: This evil is beyond the power of man — and I turned away my eyes in disgust and fear. What are being prepared are not changes that end in accommodations, but a complete overthrowing of the world, a complete and universal transformation of society. Farewell to the past, farewell forever; nothing of it will remain. The day of justice has arrived; a terrible day when justice will be meted out to everyone according to his deeds; but a day of glory for God, who will take up again the reins of the world, a world of hope for the human race, which, under the rule of the only genuine King, will inaugurate new and more attractive destinies." (To Madame de Senfft, 1 November 1832.)

Among almost everyone who learns and thinks, Christianity has been openly rejected; one is a Christian in name only. Genuine Christians are about the only few who were left during the first six centuries, the pagans having been dispersed in the countryside. (*Pagani*)."

"Moreover, Christians and non-Christians alike were

equally horrified by the abominable political systems that, everywhere, crushed people and from day to day created unparalleled misery, a moral and physical servitude against which both reason and conscience rebel, as well as all the deepest and most intense feelings of the human heart. And just as everywhere the Church adopts and defends these systems, by this very fact, she declares herself allied with those who established them for their gain, it follows that she alienates from herself, and consequently tends to separate from Christianity, populations that still believe, so that, unless something changes, we can foresee nothing other than a universal defection." (To Fr. Ventura, 30 November.)

"You are quite correct in saying that everything is going away. But is that which is going away all that much to be deplored? It is mud that pours into a drain, nothing else. Let us look from a distance and hold our noses." (To Madame de Senfft, 15 December.)

Now let us picture Lacordaire ceaselessly in the presence of these fixed ideas of the Master, unable to relieve him of them or even to distract him from them, separated from him by chasms and yet continuing to eat his bread without there being between them sympathy of character or commonality of viewpoints. Cornered in a terrifying blind alley and imagining no resolution except in complete confusion, as quick as it is universal, La Mennais believed in a general war and in the upcoming triumph of the republican party; he forced himself to see a great benefit, could see it in fact, and held on to these hopes with all the strength of his soul. Lacordaire placed no credence in all of that. He did not at all believe in war; he considered the republicans as "fools without ideas, afraid of nothing, either of the remembrance of Marat or of something worse, if such there were[30]." He complained with tears the huge current ill-conduct of him who had said: "I will make them see what a priest is!" He did not like or admire the Prince who personified the bourgeois royalty. But he tried hard to be just concerning the Orléans family members as for all the world.

Besides, he had the good sense to foresee that God would grant some time of governance to the middle powers. He preferred what was there, however long Providence would allow it, for this reason that at least the government would not react in horror regarding freedom, as would the republic[31]. He is *acting like Philippe*, cried La Mennais; and he was as shocked by this impartiality as by disloyalty.

On 11 December 1832 — I speak from the words of an eyewitness — there was an issue at dinner about the siege of Antwerp, where the young Duke of Orleans had just gained distinction. Newspapers attested to it. M. de la Mennais, incredulous from the start, explained the situation with a mockery that bordered on insult. Lacordaire attempted to bring him back to balance: the Master imposed silence on him with a poorly restrained arrogance. This was the drop of water that caused the bowl to overflow. Lacordaire became silent but his patience was at an end. An hour later, while La Mennais was taking his customary after-dinner stroll, Henri, by himself and on foot, left La Chênaie never to return, leaving as the only explanation the letter we will now read[32].

"La Chênaie, 11 December 1832.

"I will be leaving La Chênaie tonight. I am leaving for a motive of honor, convinced that from now on my life would be of little use to you because of the differences between our thoughts about the Church and society. This difference only increases from day to day, in spite of my sincere efforts to follow the development of your opinions.

"I do believe that during my lifetime and well beyond it, no republic can ever be established either in France or in any other place in Europe. Nor could I be capable of taking part in a system which would have as its basis an opposite viewpoint.

"Without renouncing my liberal views, I understand and I believe that the Church has had very cogent reasons, given the broad corruption of the factions, not to move as quickly as we would have liked. I respect her ideas as well as my own. Perhaps your opinions are more accurate, more profound, and in considering your natural superiority over me, I ought to be convinced of that. But rationality is not the whole man, and since I was unable to uproot from my being the ideas that separate us, it is fitting that I put an end to a life in common — which is totally to my advantage although at your expense[33].

"My conscience, no less than my honor, obliges me to take this step, because, after all, I have to make my life a worthy offering to God. Being unable to follow you, what would I do here except tire you, discourage you, hinder your projects, and destroy myself in the process.

"Only in heaven will you know how much I have suffered in the past year from the sole fear that I would cause you pain. In all my hesitations, my perplexities, my reactions, I looked only to you. However difficult my existence might someday be, no heartache will ever equal the one which I experience on this occasion. I leave you today at peace with the Church, higher in public estimation than you have ever been, so superior to your enemies that they are as nothing. Consequently, I could not have chosen a better occasion to cause you some grief, which, believe me, will spare you much greater ones.

"I do not yet know what will become of me, whether I will travel to the United States or whether I will remain in France and, if I do, in what role. Wherever I will be, you will have proofs of the respect and the attachment which I will always hold towards you, whose expression I pray you will accept, as it comes from a wounded heart."

ENDNOTES

1. See the *Correspondance générale* of La Mennais, from 14 February 1827 on.
2. *Op. cit.*, Book II, page 222.

3. The work of Fr. de Rozaven bears the title: *Examen d'un ouvrage intitulé: Les Doctrines philosophiques sur la certitude* [Study of a work entitled: the Philosophical Teachings about Certitude]. This appeared in 1831. The work he was refuting was that of Gerbet.
4. "The opposition against us has found support in Rome. Rome has allied itself with the most dangerous enemies of its own teachings and of its defenders. It encouraged, it even aroused our adversaries who are also its own." (To Mme de Senfft; Paris, 8 Nov. 1831.)
5. La Mennais, *Affaires de Rome* [Matters of Rome], p. 99.
6. *Ibid., loc. cit.*
7. *Des Maux de l'Église* [The Evils of the Church], p.214-215. Still unfinished, this work was composed among the Theatines both in *Sant-Andrea della Valle* and in Frascati, in the spring of 1832. In 1836, it was published by its author [as an appendix to] the work entitled *Affaires de Rome*.
8. Lacordaire to Montalembert, 4 January 1834. – There is some hint of this topic in the oldest letters of one to the other, 9 April 1832, and especially 19 August 1833. In the latter, we read: "Once on the way to Rome, my disagreement with La Mennais was COMPLETE. It was with terrible anguish that I sought to break all ties with him. It took me an entire year, all of 1832, to settle the matter."
9. For the complete text of this report, see Report presented to the Supreme Pontiff Gregory XVI at www.worksoflacordaire.net. - Trans.
10. La Mennais, *ibidem*, pp. 28-30.
11. See note 9. - Trans.
12. Lacordaire to Montalembert, 4 January 1834.
13. Letter to Gerbet, Rome, 28 January 1832.
14. There is every reason to believe that La Mennais destroyed the letter in question. He barely mentions it (*Affaires de Rome*, p. 88). The summary of that important letter I offer here is borrowed from Montalembert's travel notebooks, who recorded it on the very day in the words just quoted. Besides,

this summary is identical with the one La Mennais transmitted that same day to Gerbet. (*Œuvres inédites de La Mennais*, published by A. Blaize, vol. II, p. 99). In addition, it is equally in accord with the last memories of Fr. Lacordaire (NOTICE, ch. III). But on his deathbed, the latter remembered the facts incorrectly and placed the letter of Cardinal Pacca a few weeks AFTER the audience with the Pope. He should have said: It was several weeks BEFORE.

15. Letter to Lorain, 23 February 1832.
16. Letter dated Rome, 10 February 1832, to the Countess Senfft (*Correspondence*, II, 231).
17. To Montalembert, 22 April 1832.
18. Letter to Montalembert, 9 April and 4 May 1832.
19. La Mennais to Lacordaire, 23 April 1832 (unpublished letter).
20. To Montalembert, 22 April 1832.
21. *Œuvres inédites*, published by A. Blaize, t. II, at the dates indicated.
22. To Montalembert, 22 April 1832.
23. Letter of 10 May 1832. — *Œuvres inédites* (Unpublished works).
24. *Affaires de Rome*, p. 109.
25. Lettre of La Mennais to his brother, dated 1 July 1832. — *Œuvres inédites*, t. II, p. 116. — All the letters written from Rome in 1832, by La Mennais or Montalembert, are filled with details in the same vein.
26. Notice, ch. III.
27. *Ibid.*
28. I reproduce the conversation as it was related to me by Lacordaire. He was the only witness. Nettement is mistaken in reporting a bit differently (*Histoire de la litérature apres 1830* [History of literature after 1830, t. 1er, p. 340]) that Montalembert was a third party. For all that, the sequel will show that, if La Mennais did not insist on that day, he had not at all abandoned the burning underlying thought of taking up the contest again as soon as possible. Indeed, it is that

underlying thought that will complete his ruin.
29. *Nouveaux Lundis*, t. IV, p. 450.
30. Letter to Montalembert, 2 November 1832.
31. Letter to Montalembert, 23 July 1832.
32. See The Testament of Fr. Lacordaire, Chapter 3, at www.worksoflacordaire.com.
33. At La Chênaie, Lacordaire lived at the expense of La Mennais. Honor prevented him from prolonging this situation when it became evident to him that, in conscience, he could no longer do battle under [the latter's] banner.

Chapter VI

THE FALL OF M. DE LA MENNAIS

Lacordaire's return to Paris — Bishop de Quélen, Montalembert, Mme Swetchine — Brief from the Pope to the Archbishop of Toulouse — La Mennais asks Rome for a formulary — Brief to the Bishop of Rennes: false evasions from La Mennais — He signs an act of submissions without conditions — Lacordaire's renewed public acceptance of the Encyclical — *Words of a Believer* — *Reflections on the Philosophical System of Fr. La Mennais* — Encyclical of 7 July 1834 — Submission of Montalembert — *Affairs of Rome* — Conclusion

In order to understand more clearly the second to last paragraph we have just read, we need to know that, in fact, at the moment Lacordaire was writing (11 December 1832), the outward situation of La Mennais was excellent. His declaration of 10 September was taken in Rome as an expression of unconditional submission. One of his friends, Fr. Orioli, was entrusted with informing him immediately of the satisfaction of the Holy Father, and, on 27 October, Cardinal Pacca transmitted to La Chênaie an even more official assurance. But even more was done. Garibaldi, in his role as listener, at the moment was administering the nunciature of France, and had told De Coux: "I have been charged by the Supreme Pontiff to tell you of the great joy he experienced regarding the declaration of 10 September. The Holy Father was completely satisfied; if La Mennais thought it appropriate to write to him, he would receive an answer that would offer him altogether honor and satisfaction." But the recluse of La Chenaie excused himself from following upon this opening[1]. He feared (and this fear throws light on the situation) that "the Pope's answer was phrased in terms that implied on his part *a submission* wider than what was in his heart[2]." Nonetheless, the fact remains that on that date (11 December 1832), Lacordaire had been authorized to write to him: "Today, I leave you in peace on the part of the Church."

Much has been said, and it is still being repeated, that if La Mennais apostatized, it was because Rome did not treat him with the care due to his previous services. Nothing could be further from the truth. We have already noted that it is precisely because Gregory XVI had not forgotten either the talents or the services of La Mennais, that the name of the author of the *Essay on Indifference* is nowhere mentioned in the Encyclical, and that no reference is made about the newspaper *L'Avenir*. It is for this reason also that no retraction had been demanded. It was with these same benevolent dispositions that Rome hurriedly accepted — not hoping for anything more explicit — the collective declaration of 10 September, and that the Nunciature of France had intended to take the measures we have seen. Where is the severity? Is there in all this the shadow of annoyance or of obligation? — We return to our story.

I said that Lacordaire had left La Chenaie alone, on foot, while La Mennais was taking a stroll. "At a certain turn along the way," it is Lacordaire who speaks, "I caught sight of him through the bushes along with his young disciples. I paused for one last look at this unhappy great man. I continued on my flight, *without knowing what would become of me* and what merit I would have in the sight of God for what I was doing. Had I committed only faults? This public life, those passionate struggles, this voyage to Rome, those friendships so strong in the evening and broken today, finally the convictions of my entire life as a young man and as a priest — were they nothing but a mad dream? Would it not have been better that I hide myself as an assistant in the most insignificant of parishes, and, from there, that I call on God 'by duties simply fulfilled in favor of abandoned souls?' There are moments when doubts overcome us, when what he had thought to be fruitful now appears as sterile, when what we judged important is only a shadow without substance. Such was the state I was in; everything around me was crumbling and I had to collect the remnants of a certain natural energy to save me from hopelessness[3]." We have not sufficiently placed ourselves in the shoes of someone who had experienced a crisis like that one; we did not take sufficient account of the confusion, the anguish, and the heroic fidelity to the Church.

Another doubt arose in full force: what would the world say about such an abrupt break, quite unexpected and so to explain? But especially, what would Montalembert think of this, he whose friendship provided the single delight in Lacordaire's life? On the very day (11 December), the latter wrote to him from Dinan. He made no accusations against the one who was leaving him; he thought only of the misfortune of not being able to control his senses like La Mennais did, the misfortune of a personal and increasing disagreement "concerning many things that contained in their consequences all of present life *and all of future life*." For his part, the Master also was writing. He complained of that strange manner of running away, "as one flees from a besieged place." For all that, he expressed no resentment; he merely stated the fact that it had become forever impossible for the fugitive and him to have an association in activities for a common goal. La Mennais reproached Lacordaire only for his bent to act in a Philippian manner; "besides," he added, "this was something extraordinary and painful because of a complete lack of confidence and sympathy; in a solitary life, with no exchange of thoughts with anyone, the only thing common was the table." The last words leave no doubt about the inmost disagreement between the two men in this last stage of their life in common and about the intolerably unreal situation that arose for Lacordaire.

Having arrived in Paris, the latter wrote once more to La Chenaie. To La Mennais, his letter appeared to be "formal, stiff, dry, cold as a winter night when the north wind passes." It received no answer.

This is how the connection of barely three months ended. The prominence that *L'Avenir* gave to it weighed heavily on Lacordaire's entire life; even today, and for many reasons, this presses heavily on his memory in superficial minds. First of all, we can judge whether the reproach of ingratitude finds a place in this. Father Lacordaire had been a guest of Fr. La Mennais; on this basis, there were between the some sacred memories; Henri was not the man to forget hi ever. "As much as anyone else," he wrote, "I have deep feelings of the respect one owes to memories; should La Mennais become the most deadly heretic who ever lived, between his enemies and me there would remain a wide gap. No one would read what I would be obliged to write without noticing the pain of my position and the duration of my respect[4]." In the end, that was all he owed him. Let us not tire of repeating: he had no obligation toward him for any of his ideas. In fact, long before La Mennais had pronounced one word about freedom (especially when he anathematized it with all the passion of his soul), the love of political freedom was all Lacordaire's life. Therefore he owed nothing to the founder of *L'Avenir,* save certain exaggerations in the teachings and the contagious but happily fleeting examples of certain excesses in language. When Lacordaire went to La Chênaie, he was twenty-eight years old; he was an associate, a powerful helper, but not a disciple. He was never a disciple. From the first day, the air of idolatry that one could breathe at the feet of *Monsieur Féli* displeased the simple and frank nature of Lacordaire. After the break, La Mennais himself acknowledged "that Lacordaire had a kind of revulsion for this location, one that he was never able to overcome. It was not his fault," said he, "that I was unable to offer him more undersanding[5]." For his part, even during his time at *L'Avenir*, Lacordaire exclaimed: "Alas, my God! There is nothing I can do to please him[6]!" In fact, these two men did not agree on anything: one was domination, the other, independence. Unlike Gerbet, it was impossible for Lacordaire to be a soft wax imprinted with the seal of the Master.

But I am especially anxious to highlight this point,

that there was nothing in common, absolutely nothing, between Lacordaire and La Mennais before 1830; and that, after 1830, they were of one mind only concerning politics, nothing more than politics, and that for only thirteen months, just the life-span of *L'Avenir*. Yes, only thirteen months; because, once on the way to Rome, the disagreement was almost complete on politics as on everything else, and Lacordaire, who did not know how to flatter, sought only, with painful anguish, to rid himself of the yoke.[7] The result, on La Mennais' part, was an ever-increasing chill and an offensive lack of respect; on this point, Lacordaire was not afraid, several months later, to report this to Montalembert, who remembered it quite well[8]. The useless counsels given in Rome by Henri, the stubborn opposition he expressed in Paris to the revival of *L'Avenir*, his departure for Munich at the end of August, were not conducive to reducing the pressure of the situation. The rest of the story is well-known. After the Encyclical, they did not even agree on the significance of the act. The chill, the uneasiness had been increasing day after day, up to the point when Lacordaire took a decisive step.

We can see now that, by being the first to separate himself from La Mennais, a very long while before the others (something that has been too long forgotten), Lacordaire was not justified in thinking about what he was writing to the most cherished of his friends: "I will forever be proud of that period in my life because of the purity of my intentions, because of *my vision about the future*, and the resistance with which I opposed, unfortunately alone, a man who had gotten himself lost, because all his friends had been fascinated by his glory and adored him on bended knee... Even in this world, the future will perhaps announce which one of us was the more skilled because he was the more Christian[9]."

Whatever the case, Lacordaire's life was entering into

an entirely new and unusually sensitive phase. His first visit, on finding himself in Paris, had been to Montalembert; his second, to his mother, the third to his bishop, de Quélen, who had barely seen him for two years. La Mennais saw this bishop as a personal enemy; When Lacordaire returned from Rome, the Master imposed on him (I have written proof of this) the greatest caution towards the archbishop. And yet, even though he was a royalist and half-Gallican (to the degree that Saint-Sulpice also was), and besides, even though distant by nature from any philosophical or political novelty, de Quélen showed greatness and wisdom in blaming *L'Avenir* only with caution. We have already seen that he had a fondness for Lacordaire. He welcomed him with open arms, "as if I had been a child who had pursued some perilous adventure and returned wounded to the paternal dwelling." — "You have need of a renewal; I will see that you get one." — Almost immediately, he brought him back to his first refuge at the Visitation Convent. This represented asylum and nourishment, but nothing more. Just as at the beginning of his clerical career, Henri found himself alone with his mother, penniless, studying Plato and St. Augustine, pleased with the peace that was given him, but not quite the same peace he once had.

"While there," said he, "I brought back with me various memories, a reputation in which, it seemed to me, I had lost my priestly innocence much more than I had acquired renown — an appearance of treason towards an illustrious and unhappy man, and finally, a thousand worries, a thousand contradictions in the heart, no old-time friend nor any new one. The old ones were already too long ago in my youth, new ones were distant because of my isolation. However, thanks be to God, peace gained the upper hand. Signs of sympathy came to find me and to inform me that some affection and good wishes had followed me to my retreat[10]."

It was at this moment, in fact, that God was waiting for him, to send him Mme Swetchine. Let him speak.

"One day (this was in January 1833), Montalembert, who had grown cold toward me after the break at La Chenaie, but who nonetheless retained some remnant of friendship that the course of years would strengthen and reveal as gentle as unshakeable, Montalembert, I say, suggested that I visit a certain lady in the district of Saint-Germain who wanted to see me.

"The Saint-Germain district was unknown to me. With no illustrious birth and no fortune, I had never entered the drawing-rooms of any aristocracy and I had never even entertained the thought of trying to do so. Satisfied with little, sober in everything, lacking in envy, I had hardly noticed that there was above me an entire society, a stranger to me, one that did not exist for me any more than I existed for its benefit. The proposal of Montalembert came as a completely unexpected surprise. I decided to follow it.

"The person whom he presented to me was not a Frenchwoman. Born in Russia in the Greek faith, she had come to seek in France that first good of souls: interior and exterior freedom of conscience. Bound by all that was most illustrious in her former country and in the new one, she was well aware of the matters of the world and those of the Church; moreover, she had superb discernment that rounded out in her mind the understanding she had retained of those magnificent relations. Mme Swetchine received me with a graciousness that was not ordinary, and I quickly accustomed myself to share with her my anxieties, my worries, my projects. She *embraced them as if I were her son,* and her door was open to me even at an hour when it was exceptional for her to receive her close friends. What perception moved her to grant me her time and her counsels? No doubt it was by some kind of compassion; but, unless I am mistaken, she was bolstered by the thought of a mission to be accomplished for the benefit of my soul. She saw me surrounded by stumbling-blocks, led up to that point by private inspirations, with no experience of the world, with no other compass than the innocence of my views. Moreover, in making herself my caretaker, she believed she was following the will of God. From that day on, in fact, I made no decisions without ~~discussion~~ *discussing* them with her; no doubt I owe it to her that I have encountered many craters without toppling down into them[11]."

And so, by simply comparing the dates, it is evident that Mme Swetchine had absolutely nothing to do with Lacordaire's break from La Mennais (11 December 1832). At that time, Lacordaire had never met that lady, had never written to her; *for him*, she did not exist.

Nor did she ever do anything to keep Lacordaire in the bosom of the Church. The Encyclical of 1832 had not for an instant shaken Henri's faith. In Rome, as early as February of that year, even before the letter from Cardinal Pacca, we have seen that Lacordaire had already decided to leave La Mennais, to return alone to France. From then on, not for one day did he abandon the personal dissent that raised a wall between the thoughts of the founder of *L'Avenir* and his own. After all, the Encyclical only justified this dissent. In the time period that concerns us, all of Henri's most confidential letters were filled with the deepest compliance to the act of Gregory XVI. In June 1833, when Lacordaire was presented to Mme Swetchine, not only had he definitively broken the link between La Chenaie and himself but he had taken up again the peaceful exercise of clerical ministry in Paris, in perfect harmony with his bishop. If later Lacordaire wrote to Mme Swetchine with a bit of oratorical hyperbole: "You appeared to me as a messenger of the Lord to a soul floating between earth and heaven", this was not at all a hint of interior crisis, of a spiritual contest between faith and doubt; it was simply a moving remembrance of the external situation that Lacordaire has just described, the situation of a priest who has lost, as he himself expressed so well, his priestly virginity, a priest suspected of heterodoxy by some, repudiated by others as a traitor, in doubt about himself, his friends, his counsels, with almost no human support (since de Quélen only half supported him against the enormous mistrust he himself still faced). Mme Swetchine was the only one who understood the situation. Generous, like all persons of a superior nature, and besides, loving souls with supernatural and fully Christian affection, how would she not have been moved to a lively commiseration for Lacordaire, for a priest who offered such great hope, still very young and yet in such great danger? She wanted to meet him. But she wanted more: to break that sea of ice that had formed around him and that made him useless. This was to be her task.

"Mme Swetchine," said de Falloux, "mastered par excellence that difficult art of reading easily into the heart of others. She was able to grasp admirably the strength and the weakness of a person, the damage and the remedy of a situation. She penetrated into the essence of questions, she removed veils, she investigated the slightest details, because she brought into everything the ardent care of a sincere affection; because her perception was always alert, her attention was always maintained, backing up and infusing her uncommon intelligence." She was deprived of the happiness of motherhood; but, endowed with the most maternal heart ever, she poured ceaselessly into all those for whom she could be helpful her treasures of inexhaustible and boundless goodness. She was fifty-one years old when she met Lacordaire. She quickly discovered in him a proud soul, but one more upright and more simple than we have words for, and soon she loved him as a son[12]. It was she who completed the purification of that soul, so troubled for three years by the most violent and most contrary winds. It was she who decided the action of 13 December 1833 that placed a seal on Lacordaire's reconciliation with his archbishop and with the Church.

Why did this action of 13 December appear so necessary to Mme Swetchine? To answer that, one has to have witnessed the interior storms and especially the public vacillations because of the thoughts of La Mennais during the year 1833.

Here, we need to bring back to mind those interior storms and the regrettable uncertainty that followed, without forgetting for a moment that, in the opinion of the public, Lacordaire inevitably suffered its consequences — the break having been overlooked on the outside and La Mennais and he having remained in fellowship together.

"I am full of words; a spirit within me constrains me... I will speak and I will breathe a little[13]." This was, at that terrible time, the private state of mind of La Mennais, such as it burst out in all his subsequent correspondence.

Not for a single day did he abandon his opinions, not even the idea of spreading them by the voice of the press. The restriction that he had proposed to Lacordaire, at Saverna, had remained alive and active in the depths of his thought, as a mental reservation. And as for this mental reservation, how did La Mennais intend to reconcile it with his declaration of 10 September 1832? By taking leave, without fuss, of his previous life to inaugurate what he called a new phase, wherein, setting aside completely his character as priest, he would attempt to place his future action entirely outside the Church's sphere. As if it were possible for him to divide himself! As if the priest, the citizen, the writer, were not in him inseparable! But who is not aware that passion is always this shrewd with itself?

Besides, where did his Catholicism stand at that time?

We will see, after his definitive separation from La Mennais on 13 December 1832, that Lacordaire had acted rashly like a man who for no reason at all breaks the bonds he has contracted.

As early as 21 January 1833, La Mennais wrote to Montalembert:

"*It is good to resume our conversation*, to prepare the position that will henceforth be ours, AS SOON AS we have become sufficiently disentangled from the one who has given us so many vexations. Instead of making us champions of Catholicism, let us leave it in the hands of the hierarchy, and present ourselves simply as men of freedom and of Humanity."

And what did he think thereafter of the Church?

"The former hierarchies, both political and *ecclesiastical* leave together; *they are now only two specters who embrace in a tomb*. God, by means unknown to us, will no doubt regenerate his Church; she is immortal, because SHE IS NOTHING ELSE BUT the *very society of the human race*, under the law of Redemption brought about by Jesus Christ. But under what form will she appear after the purifying fire will have consumed the dry envelope that today covers her from all eyes? I do not know. Not much more was known when the Synagogue died, or, to speak more accurately, when it underwent the predicted transformation[14]."

Is that obvious?

Thus, the teaching Church, under Gregory XVI, was the Synagogue under Caïphas. La Mennais no longer believed in the Church, in the Hierarchy, as he called her, since he declared her blinded like the dying Synagogue, an enemy of Jesus Christ like the Sanhedrin. Understand rather: "Jesus Christ is today the great enemy, and *there* (in Rome) as elsewhere, and *more than elsewhere*[15]."

Thenceforth, La Mennais believed only in Humanity. For him, the Church, the true Church IS ONLY *the very society of the human race*. Let us stop the evasion, La Mennais is no longer a Catholic. He was aware of it and wrote to Montalembert: "I would like to bring a change to our language on one point and substitute the word *Christianity* for that of *Catholicism*, the better to show that we no longer wish to have anything to do with the Hierarchy[16]."

An incident that should have stopped La Mennais in his tracks along this fatal slope, on the contrary succeeded in plunging him into the abyss.

On 22 April 1832, long before the founder of *L'Avenir* had left Rome, d'Astros, archbishop of Toulouse, in union with many bishops of France, had referred to Rome fifty-six propositions culled from the writings of La Mennais.

This effort was judged severely in Rome; it appeared undignified in view of the long-established authority that French theologians had enjoyed in the Church. However, in respect for the episcopal character and especially for d'Astros, who had suffered for the Church during the captivity of Pius VII, Rome was in no hurry to express itself.

It was only on 28 February 1833 that the criticism of the bishops was set aside, by unanimous vote, as was assured by the congregation charged with examining it. It seems that the gall with which La Mennais spoke about Rome during the previous fifteen months should have been mitigated somewhat. That was not to be. It was with the most contemptuous indifference that he informed his friends of this news. "Since I have seen up close the springs that make everything move," he wrote, "such matters interest me almost as much as what is happening in China in the great College of Mandarins[17]."

It was even worse after the archbishop of Toulouse had published, in July, the Brief that Gregory XVI had sent to him on 8 May, in answer to the episcopal request of the preceding year. The Pope avoided explaining himself on the little success of the request of the bishops; he limited himself to praising, in very general terms, their zeal and their respect for the Holy See, referring moreover to the Encyclical. Calling to mind the declaration of La Mennais of 10 September, this is how he explained himself:

"At first, this declaration inspired confidence that the authors and the followers of the projects that were especially the object of our complaints, had complied with our judgment, with sincerity, fully, absolutely, with no ambiguity — that subsequently they would offer more convincing evidence, with the expressions of faith they had often repeated and in most resolute terms, that they were enthusiastically in favor of the Vicar of Jesus Christ. This very charming hope had uplifted our soul; but what is still being spread around today in public again plunges us into sorrow[18]."

Indeed, the publicity given to the Brief by the archbishop of Toulouse was not, on his part, an act of benevolence. It would seem that it was up to the Sovereign Pontiff himself to decide whether to keep this document secret or to make it public. Whatever the case, did La Mennais have every right to cry out, as he did, against the libel and the injustice? Was it true that in Rome, Naples, Florence, Toulouse, he had written what we have just reported, or other things absolutely similar? Should he have been surprised, then, that these written feelings would have some repercussions on the outside, that copies of his letters arrived in Rome one after the other through the efforts of his adversaries and that Rome be roused by them? As early as February 1833, these indiscretions troubled even Montalembert, who himself, in the hasty outbursts of his nature, and in the excitability of his twenty-three years, offered on his part many vulnerable points to the blows of the enemy.

This was the time (May 1833) when he published *The Book of Polish Pilgrims*, by the poet Mickiewicz. In the Preface to his translation, he placed a juvenile foreword filled with admiration for the master, that in Rome was judged differently. It was also the time when he founded the newspaper *le Polonais* [The Pole], about which the hermit at La Chenaie expected *boundless results*. "There," he wrote, "the question of freedom in all its aspects and in all its applications would be covered; it will be wonderful, it would be the future of the world[19]." Finally, it was the time when La Mennais wrote to Mexico that, to put a stop to *L'Avenir*, "the absolute sovereigns had banded together with Rome and with the Episcopacy, unfortunately imbued as it was with the thought that Religion would perish without the material support of the earth's powers, and who, in theory besides, were the *enemies of freedom*[20]." Was Cardinal Bernetti, Secretary of State for the Pope, that far wrong in stating: "These gentlemen pretend they are silent, but we know they are agitating; it is the silence of the Jansenists[21]." In the presence of all these facts, could Gregory XVI have complained in milder terms than those we read a while ago?

For all that, La Mennais claims to be have been libeled, and defends himself with his usual bitterness. He considered as worthless his letters, today public, of which many, as I have said, even then leaked out, and moreover appeared in certain newspapers. Much more, at that very moment (July 1833), spurred by the excitement of Mickiewicz's book, he had just completed writing *Paroles d'un Croyant* [Words of a Believer], which only appeared, it is true, the following year. Yet he maintained the strange illusion that this was simply a political work, sheltered from all religious censure. "My teachings," he wrote, "remain intact. More and more it is evident that the Pope fears and *disavows completely* my political views. *As regards the relationship between the government and the Church,* he is judge, I am not; it is up to him to command and for me to obey; it is my duty, and thanks be to God, I hope never to fail. But outside of the Church, in the purely *temporal* order, I acknowledge no authority that has the right to impose an opinion on me and to dictate my behavior. I say it aloud, in this sphere — which does not belong to spiritual power — never, as regards *thinking* and acting, will I take counsel other than from my conscience and my reason[22]."

All this was part of an unfortunately very superficial theology. No doubt, there exists a spiritual power and a temporal one: what Catholic would deny this? But where does the spiritual realm end? Where does the *purely* temporal one begin? Surely, as La Mennais himself recognized, the temporal order, *insofar as it touches*, under multiple aspects, the *Divine Law*, is subordinated to the Church, guardian and tireless interpreter of that law[23]. Who, then, will be the one to trace the line of demarcation? Will a simple believer tell the Pope: Here ends the spiritual realm; you may come to this point but no further?

But events rushed forward. A violent storm had come up in Rennes at the reading of the Brief of 8 May. The bishop, de Lesquen, in whose diocese was found Saint-Malo, where the La Mennais brothers were born, threatened, it was said, to suspend all religious establishments submitted to the influence of the two brothers. The institute founded by Fr. Jean to provide primary instruction to the children of the people filled all of Brittany and gave outstanding services to Religion. The imagination of Fr. Féli exaggerated the danger that he spread about the institute. In fact, on 28 July, he regarded it as "a very grave fault to make *any* new declaration[24]." And on 4 August, he committed that fault, not finding, as he said, any other way "to save from immediate destruction the schools wherein thirty thousand students received a Christian education[25]." This was an unfounded fear but it seems to have been honest.

Whatever the case, M. Féli wrote to the Pope and asked the bishop of Rennes to transmit his letter to the Holy Father. In that document, dated 4 August, La Mennais protested that, the more he questioned his conscience, the less could he find something to serve as basis for a reproach. Has not *L'Avenir* ceased publication? Has the Agency not been dissolved? Since then, no one among us, cried out La Mennais, has *even dreamed* of undertaking anything similar. (On this point, his memory failed him since he never stopped holding the thought of starting a newspaper[26]; moreover, we have seen the advantage he hoped to enjoy from the *Polonais*.) This is how La Mennais ended the letter:

"I declare,

"1° That, for many reasons but especially because it belongs only to the Head of the Church, to judge what is good and useful, I resolved to remain, in the future, in my writings and my actions totally dissociated from matters touching her.

"2°That no one, thanks be to God, is more submissive than I am, *in the bottom of my heart and with no reservations*, to all the decisions that have come or will come from the Holy See dealing with faith and morals, as well as the laws of discipline declared by its sovereign authority.

"That, if the expression of my feelings is not clear to Your Holiness, may you yourself deign to let me know what terms I need to use to satisfy you fully[27]."

Lacordaire judged the letter of 4 August with his usual shrewdness, and found it neither frank nor Christian.

"La Mennais," he told Montalembert, at that time in Germany, "begins by expressing his surprise at the Brief to the archbishop of Toulouse and his own complete ignorance of the reasons behind it. Now, he knows full well what he is being upbraided for, namely: of keeping under control the group of *L'Avenir*, of encouraging it by letter and menacing expectations, of keeping this group distant from bishops and from the Holy See; of broadcasting on the moral and political situation of Rome some lectures calculated to foment the disaffection of Catholics and the contempt of unbelievers. *Were these matters ignored, would he himself not be aware of them? Does he not have an intimate awareness of what he is doing, of what he desires, of what he is expecting?* ... In a word, I believe he lacks the honesty to tell the Pope that no one knows what he is complaining about.

"La Mennais then declares that, for all kinds of reasons, etc., 'he resolved to stay away from matters that touch the Church.' I call attention to the fact that there is nothing more anti-Catholic than this phrase, whether we consider its open meaning or its hidden one. — The *open meaning* states that there are circumstances in which a Christian ought to remain away from matters that touch the Church, and one of those is that the direction of the Church belongs to the Holy See. If that were true, the Church would be very unhappy. Never should her children (all the more her priests), under any pretext, be strangers to what touches her; everybody needs be involved, according to their status and their ability, as La Mennais had always done until now; but all must start by being submissive to the direction of the Holy See and not by trying to direct it themselves. — The *hidden meaning* refers to the thought that La Mennais wished to deal only with philosophy and politics, two areas that he believed to be independent, with the result that, both as citizen and as philosopher, he would avoid the influence and the censure of the Church, which is the repudiation of Religion. — From this point, he protests his submission to everything that the Holy See will decide related to faith, to morals, and to general discipline. Very good — but are philosophy and politics included? That is the question. In my view, there are too many back doors... No talent, no services can compensate for the harm done to the Church by any kind of separation, any action outside of her structure. I would rather throw myself into the sea with a millstone around my neck than to imagine a host of hopes, ideas, of good works, even, aside from the Church[28]."

The judgment in Rome will be no different.

On 5 October, the Pope sent a Brief to the bishop of Rennes in which, afer having recalled the letter La Mennais published in the *Journal of the Hague* of 22 February, in which he stated his upholding of all the principles he had held previously, after his having lamented the preface to *Livre des pèlerins polonais* [The Book of Polish Pilgrims], that he well knew about, and after having made allusions to other facts that indicate the persistence with which concerted effort was made for what had been projected and undertaken at the time of L'Avenir, Gregory XVI cited the protest of remaining totally apart, from then on, from questions that interested the Church. Then, taking the opportunity from La Mennais' last declaration, which asked the Supreme Pontiff to deign indicate what wording he needed to use in order to satisfy the Holy See fully, the Pope demanded that he promise to follow solely and absolutely the teaching expressed in the Encyclical of 1832, and neither to write nor to approve of anything that *did not conform to it.*

As we shall see, this was to require of La Mennais what, in his frame of mind, he did not wish to promise, and especially did not wish to follow.

Since his letter of 4 August to the Pope, he plunged

ever deeper into his excessive rebuke of the Church.

Not only was the human race, as in the days of Jesus Christ, divided into a corrupt gentry and a blinded Synagogue, but he saw in Rome the Babylon of the Apocalypse, the ill-famed prostitute who committed fornication with the kings of the earth and who corrupted the world by her lewdness[29].

Besides, he was not lacking in projects. "Completely apart from the clergy," he wrote, we will not longer have to worry about persecutions; we will be able to do good, *and all kinds of good, with total independence*]." Moreover, he considered establishing a Revue while waiting to found in Paris an institute of service to Polish youth, and to other things as well[30]. He resisted his German friends who, through the publication of Montalembert, pressured him that he not act outside the Church[31]. He was working enthusiastically on his *Esquisse d'une Philosophie* [Sketch of a Philosophical System], fully decided to pass the entire winter at La Chenaie and perhaps the following summer, so as not to be disturbed in his meditations[32].

It was in the middle of these thoughts that the notification of the Brief of 5 October found him.

This notification was to tear away all veils.

Thus forced into his barricades, La Mennais abruptly fled to Paris, where he arrived on 1 November, after having written a brief letter to the bishop of Rennes during the few hours left before his departure. At the time, his health was very poor, which, along with other reasons, forced him postpone dealing with the repercussions of this matter until after his trip — an issue serious enough, besides, for him to act only after reflection[33].

We need to say it: this letter was very unworthy of him. It was not true, in fact, that the notification from Rennes surprised him as he left for Paris; rather, this notification was the only cause for his hasty departure[34]. But all these reflections must have already been made: was he not the one who asked the Pope, on 4 August, to *dictate* to him the terms by which he was to submit to the Encyclical? The Pope indicated to him these terms: if La Mennais had been sincere on 4 August, he had no reason to discuss them, he had only to place his signature. Evidently, the way things were, La Mennais could not draw back without exhibiting the most flagrant contradiction.

And yet, that is what he tried to do, on 5 November, by addressing the following letter to the Pope:

"Most Holy Father,

"It will always take only one word from Your Holiness for me, not only to obey him in everything that Religion demands, but also to please him in all that conscience allows.

"Consequently, the Encyclical Letter of Your Holiness, dated 15 August 1832, containing items of diverse natures, *some on doctrine, others on governance*, I declare:

"1° Insofar as it proclaims, following the expression of Innocent I, the *apostolic tradition*, that was simply divine revelation itself perpetually and infallibly proclaimed by the Church, requests of its children a perfect and whole-hearted faith, I adhere solely and absolutely, realizing myself, as every Catholic, obligated to write or approve nothing *contrary* to her.

"2° Insofar as it determines and regulates diverse points of governance and ecclesiastical discipline, I am equally submitted to it without reservations.

"And yet, in the current state of minds, particularly in France, so that fiery and malevolent persons may not give to the declaration that I place at the feet of Your Holiness false interpretations — that, among other consequences I wish and need to prevent, would cast suspicion on my sincerity — my conscience compels me to declare at the same time that, according to my firm belief, if in the religious order the Christian knows only that he has to listen and to obey, he remains, as regards the spiritual power, completely free in his opinions, his speech, and his actions in the *purely* temporal order."

We are already aware of this distinction: the addendum to the declaration of 5 November had not been any less ambiguous. La Mennais upheld the Encyclical but only *insofar as* it proclaimed apostolic tradition; this left room for the right to discuss at which point this or that passage of the document was justified by tradition or not. He promised not to write anything contrary to the Encyclical, but did not promise to refrain from writing anything that was not in agreement with it. In other words, he pledged not to oppose the teaching of the Encyclical but he did not pledge to uphold it. He is irksome, he is insufferable, I sense it, in bringing up again these contrived will-o'-the-wisps. Indeed he had to do this so that his reader would grasp the weight of his argument and understand its consequences.

Concerning this serious matter, La Mennais had many conversations with de Quélen. In 1829, this Prelate had published a pastoral letter against one of the writings of the author of the *Essay*: *The Advances of the Revolution*. La Mennais had taken up the gauntlet with boundless contempt in two bloody pamphlets. Nonetheless, in November 1833, de Quélen was more than gracious and tactful about the matter in his proceedings against him, to the degree that he won over the trust of the cynic of La Chenaie — something surely not so easy to do.[35] Carried away by his passions as a refugee, the bishop of Rennes, a former soldier in the army of Condé[36], incompetent canonist, had provisionally suspended Fr. F. de la Mennais, without taking care to have him make a definitive statement concerning the Brief. The procedure was disproportionate. Struck down without having been heard, the Breton priest took this opportunity to publicize in newspapers his letters to the Pope, notably that of 5 November. Nonetheless, the archbishop of Paris succeeded in having him understand that the final declaration in that letter needed mitigating explanations; and this is what moved a Mennais to compile his report to the Pope on 6 December 1833[37].

But before that report was able to reach the Sovereign Pontiff, La Mennais received a final letter from Cardinal Pacca, dated 29 November. This Eminence insisted on a submission without reservation[38]. The letter was delivered to La Mennais on 10 December. The following day, through the mediation of de Quélen, he addressed to the Dean of the Sacred College this letter:

"I the undersigned, declare, in the very terms of the formula used in the Brief of the Sovereign Pontiff Gregory XVI of 5 October 1833, that I will follow exclusively and absolutely the teachings expressed in the Encyclical of the said Pope, and bind myself neither to write nor to approve anything save what is in conformity with that teaching.

"Paris, 11 December 1833[39]."

Cries of universal joy accompanied an act of submission so fully explicit. In Rome, this joy was all the more lively in that the steps we have just seen were less expected. On 28 December, Gregory XVI hurriedly sent to La Mennais his most paternal congratulations[40]. Garibaldi, chargé-d'affaires of the Holy See in Paris, went to see him. Entreaties were made to the illustrious writer to attract him to Rome, where, it was said, he would be offered a position to his liking; the Archbishop of Paris reinforced those entreaties.

Alas! Sheer illusions! In fact the man whom we

thought was living was dead. He had renounced the faith of his baptism and the religion of his mother. He had renounced the Church (the country of souls), *everything without exception* (in his own words), *all that had filled his previous life*[41]. All that was over with for ever.

By a remarkable coincidence, darkness had fallen on his conscience at the same time as it did elsewhere. In losing his faith, he had lost the meaning of the most common truthfulness. Would we believe it if we had not read the avowal written in his hand? At the very moment when he was recording impulsively in such clear terms his declaration of 11 December, even at that same moment, he was writing to Cardinal Pacca: "I was pained to see that the His Holiness had considered certain expressions of my declaration of 5 November as restrictive clauses to my submission to the Encyclical, NEVER *did I have that thought.*" As I was saying, at that moment, within himself, he held the Encyclical as something excessive and what he wrote to Rome as words in the air that did not bind him *either for the present or for the future*[42].

This compliance," he wrote, "must have strongly clashed with my conscience because it implied, to my mind, the recognition of the personal infallibility of the Pope, something that he had said and in whatever mandate it was, namely, the veritable deification of that same Pope. And yet, if I refused this required compliance — this incompatible compliance, at least in my eyes — *with some fundamental principles of Catholicism*, no doubt a violent storm would rise before me and that I would be labeled to the world as a rebel and a schismatic. The thoughts suggested by this unusual stand led to major doubts on many points of Catholicism, doubts that, far from weakening, only grew stronger from then on. Now, *putting aside the question of truth* that worried me up to that time, I saw in this distressing matter a question of peace at all costs, and I resolved to sign not only what was asked of me but also without exception whatever anyone wished, *even to declaring that the Pope was God*, the great God of heaven and earth, *and that HE ALONE should be worshiped*. But, at the same time, I decided to end all clerical functions, and that I did[43]."

Profound wretchedness for the human genius! You have here a superior mind that, because one day it felt that the Pope was mistaken, all at once chose to believe that the religion was false. To him, who had written a book against the illusions of individual evidence, there never came a moment of doubt in his thoughts concerning his common sense. It never came to mind to suspect that perhaps he, Fr. de la Mennais, was the mistaken one when he pronounced so domineeringly that the Pope trampled on his term *some FUNDAMENTAL principles of Catholicism*. And yet, with no reason other than the supposed evidence of the fact, thereupon he persuades himself suddenly that what he believed all his life was no longer worthy of his belief. Then, since in his eyes Religion had ceased to be genuine, he concludes... what? That, without any scruple whatsoever, he can sign all the professions of faith presented to him! He called that "peace at all costs." Peace at the price of loyalty! And what kind of peace! Thus, he prefers to lie solemnly rather than be "labeled to the world a rebel and a schismatic." Who will understand him? In the end, what do these qualifications matter for one who mocks the Church, for one who has stopped believing in Catholicism? Besides, does La Mennais not see that, with perseverance in an impossible hypocrisy, he will not escape, one day or another, the designations he fears? At the moment when he wrote in his own hand his declaration of 11 December, thereby removing the restrictions he had made on the previous 5 November, did he not bring to Paris the *Words of a Believer*? Did he not dream of publishing them someday? Does he not perceive that with this publication he would incur the double charge of rebellion and schism? Does he not see that his unlimited adherence of 11 December to the pontifical decree would have labeled him, moreover, with the characteristic that weighs most heavily on a man of honor? Is this enough of contradictions? Is this enough of consequences? When a man of honor such as La Mennais reaches this point of logical blindness, are we not allowed to see this as a chastisement from above?

Be that as it may, let us return for a moment to a few previous days. Let us refer to the impression produced by the Brief of Gregory XVI to the bishop of Rennes, by the flight to Paris of La Mennais immediately after he learned of that Brief, by the publication of his tortuous correspondence with the Holy See. Great doubt arose everywhere against the sincerity of the signers of the 10 September 1832 declaration. This doubt reached and enveloped Lacordaire. He had publicly left La Chênaie but under what circumstances, for what reasons? All that we know so well today about his disagreement with La Mennais, by the end of 1831, even before they had arrived in Rome, was at the time completely unknown to all the world.

Mme Swetchine judged that the general ignorance of the actual state of matters should not go on any longer. In her eyes, the time for Lacordaire to speak had arrived; it had become urgent that his situation be perfectly clear and that the truth become known. The insufficiency of the declaration of 10 September 1832 was subsequently obvious; but Lacordaire nonetheless did not hesitate to publish an updated declaration of his outlook. His return to the good graces of his bishop seemed to be the answer to everything. Mme Swetchine gave her soul and all her spirit to triumph over the repugnance of her action; she succeeded. It is true that in the meantime there occurred the measure of 11 December undertaken by La Mennais (his final latter to Cardinal Pacca and the act of submission without reservations joined to it). This step clearly simplified matters. By following the same path, Henri no longer left himself open to *the appearances of a betrayal.*

On the evening of 12 December, the archbishop had Lacordaire summoned. His face radiant with happiness, de Quélen showed him the letters of La Mennais and of Gerbet, adding that a similar declaration on his part *would put an end to the matter*, and would insure the satisfaction of the Sovereign Pontiff[44]. On the following day, Lacordaire wrote him as follows:

Paris, 13 December 1833

"*Monseigneur* [My Lord],

"Since the one month that the Brief of the Supreme Pontiff to the Lord Bishop of Rennes, dated 5 October last, 5 October last, has been known in France, I have not believed it necessary to prove my complete and filial submission to the Encyclical Letter of His Holiness. Besides the declaration that I had signed on this point on 10 September of the preceding year, shortly thereafter, I had presented myself, as you know, my Lord, to place myself into your hands and to take up again ecclesiastical duties in your diocese so that my actions give to my sincerity a stronger witness than all the suspicions. As God is my witness, *that is not the only thing I did*, for two years, *in favor of peace in the Church and the tranquility of my conscience*. No one has suffered more than I in his mind and in his cherished feelings to reach this goal. I broke bonds I had considered sacred; I added to the sorrows of a man who, despite his talent and his fame, had little consolation left here below save for the loyalty of friendship. I placed the Church above everything else in my heart, and I thought that I had placed the word she received from me above all wrong.

"But, after mature reflection, knowing that part of those matters was known only to God and to myself, that the rest was known by only a small number of persons — persuaded that too much could never be done for the Church, to whom we owe life and truth, nor for peace, glory, exaltation and love of the Holy See, I had resolved to give it a new sign of my love and of my faith.

"Consequently, and in conformity with the Brief of His Holiness dated 5 October last, I bound myself to follow solely and absolutely the teachings presented in his Encyclical Letter of 15 August 1832, and to write or approve nothing that did not conform to these teachings. I was pleased to have had this opportunity to place at the feet of the Holy Father the acknowledgment of my deep respect and the everlasting remembrance I hold for his welcome full of goodness: pleased also, to transmit to him, through you, this filial act, through you whom for nine years I found such a generous heart, unaltered by difficulties, except that it has become as noble as it was generous[45]."

While Lacordaire opened his heart in this way, many other thoughts, as we have seen, bubbled up in the soul of La Mennais. His position, as he realized, was more insincere than words could tell. Catholics weighed him down with congratulations that he did not know how to decline and that overpowered more and more his natural loyalty. He tried hard to quiet his pangs as an honest man, by informing the Archbishop that he had curtailed all ecclesiastical functions, and in telling the chargé-d'affaires of the Holy See that what he had done was in the interest of peace. Moreover, he had irrevocably decided that, from then on, he would in no way get involved in matters pertaining to the Church and Religion, but resolved to fulfill, following conscience and reason, the obligations to his country in all the circumstances that an action on his part would be useful to it[46]. His words were misunderstood; Catholics, of course, judged them less important that those of the declaration of 11 December, which seemed to exclude absolutely any mental restriction.

De Quélen continued to shower him with the warmest signs of his affection. At that moment, he was also busy trying to satisfy the requests of Ozanam and the youth in Catholic schools by setting up the conferences of Notre-Dame of Paris, and presenting them La Mennais. He told them: "There, gentlemen, is the man for you if the weakness of his voice would allow him to be heard. The doors would have to be opened wide to accommodate the crowds and the cathedral would not be vast enough to hold all those who surrounded the pulpit." — "Alas, my Lord," La Mennais responded in sorrow, "as for me, my career is over[47]."

When the congratulatory Brief of Gregory XVI was received in Paris, de Quélen strongly urged La Mennais to write a letter of gratitude to the Holy Father. Propriety obviously required it. La Mennais replied that silence appeared to him as being more respectful; besides, by writing, he could hardly avoid, from what the Archbishop knew of his feelings, one or the other of these objections: either to displease Rome, if he held fast to vague generalities, or to bind himself beyond what conscience allowed, if he expressed himself in a way that would completely satisfy the Holy See[48].

The truth is that, at the moment this meeting was being held, the manuscript of *Paroles* [Words] was probably already in the hands of Sainte-Beuve, whom La Mennais had charged with its publication. At least, as early as 23 March 1834, the author announced to Montalembert that publication would occur in about twenty days[49].

Here now is the story of Sainte-Beuve.

"At the very end of March or the beginning of April

1834, La Mennais wrote me a note in which he expressed his desire to see me about a pressing matter. I hastened to his residence. On my arrival, I saw a carriage, and in crossing the courtyard, I met the Archbishop of Paris, de Quélen. Entering in my turn the room which the Prelate was leaving, I noticed that La Mennais was very agitated. 'My dear friend,' said he, 'it is time for *all of this* to end. Here', he added, while opening the drawer of a small wooden table near where we were seated, 'here is a modest document that I would like you to have appear as soon as possible. I leave in two days, arrange that in advance with a publisher, quickly, very quickly I pray you. I do not want my name to appear.' On the following day, his thought had changed; he agreed to have his name placed on the book[50]."

For all that, what is the importance of knowing whether the manuscript of *Paroles* was transmitted to Sainte-Beuve on 22 or 28 March? The drop of water that caused the overflow of the vase was certainly a visit by the Archbishop of Paris. Realizing more and more the utter falsity of his situation from the very signs of respect given by the Catholics who encircled him since his previous declaration, La Mennais wanted to focus the eyes of everyone sharply on the position he intended to take in the future. The *Paroles d'un Croyant* [Words of a Believer], just as Sainte-Beuve said, was the canon shot used at sea to clear the fog.

The blowup was immense. People in workshops, the youth in schools were intoxicated to ecstasy by this heady wine. It was especially by this work that La Mennais, following an enduring word, fell among the intellectual evil-doers of his time[51]. Among Catholics, the scandal was widespread: the Apostle had taught them that power came from God; a priest of Jesus Christ stood up to teach that power is the offspring of Hell. Besides, the very form of the work was an additional scandal. It was a blend of biblical style, "an apocalypse streaked with prayers and blasphemies[52]." The basis of the book was no less trite; all kings are monsters; priests are their fanatical supporters. But La Mennais made over these common rebellious places the sign of the cross. Molé used to say: "It is a club under a bell tower." Royer-Collard had said with the same meaning: *It is a ninety-three year-old man making his Easter duty.*

The *Paroles* appeared at the end of April 1834. On 2 May, one could read in *l'Univers religieux* an article "on the state of the Church in France." This article was signed by Lacordaire. He could have omitted his signature because who else would have been able to write it? The author returned to thirty-four years earlier when the Church in France presented to angels and to men only vast ruins; he recounted, as we have seen in the *Introduction*, with that brilliance of style that only he possessed, the doctrinal powerlessness of the eighteenth century personified by the French Revolution, and subsequently by the Concordat and the Coronation. He was able to show that in 1830, in the absence of any religious teaching that they could offer the people, the winners had no choice but to allow France to enjoy quietly the true Religion that the eighteenth century was so sure it had eliminated. He stated that, "rising from these ashes young and virginal, the Church of France had to conquer only one evil worn down by the victory." Unfortunately, minds were profoundly divided by questions of the greatest importance, in particular, on teaching philosophy. Quite rightly, Lacordaire blamed this division on La Mennais and his system on certitude as well as on the school he founded. He took the opportunity to make this solemn declaration: "Yesterday, the school of which we speak was still in existence; enfeebled and divided by a word from the Apostolic See, it seeks nonetheless to retain its head and its disciples. Today, we can announce that *the school, which we had left a long time ago*, NO LONGER EXISTS; that all cooperation in activities is now broken among its former members, and each one, *faithful to whatever respect concerning the past his heart will demand*, knows no other guide than the Church, no other need except unity, no other ambition than to press around the Holy See, and around those bishops that Her forgiveness and divine mercy have given to France."

All was well up to that point. Since the compliance without reservations of La Mennais to the Encyclical did not prevent him from publishing *Paroles d'un Croyant,* because he saw nothing irreconcilable between these two actions, it was Lacordaire's right, perhaps his duty, to disavow this book publicly in spite of the triumphant cheers it was receiving. Nor can we deny that, as we have seen, he did this in language filled with generosity and irreproachable moderation[53].

And yet, once relieved by this avowal from all solidarity with the *Paroles*, it was appropriate, I do believe, that he go no further. A refutation of the La Mennais' philosophical system, however justified and cautious, was not fitting for Lacordaire to undertake. He should have left that to others. His close relationship with La Mennais, however brief its duration, should have silenced his mouth on this subject.

He himself felt this when, on 17 April of that same year, he wrote to Montalembert: "*I have prepared, to appear in a few years, — when I will be able to do so conveniently —* a work half finished concerning the philosophy of La Mennais, studied from what I believe to be a completely novel viewpoint. I struggle against this philosophy and that is why some years must elapse before I have the right to express my thought."

This was the advice from de Quélen when, shortly

after his departure from La Chênaie, impatient from then on to mark his break with La Mennais authentically, Lacordaire opened his heart to his bishop regarding his intention to criticize the second volume of the *Essai*[54]. Perhaps in this matter, the Prelate was simply giving in to his constant fear of every rumor and of all vacillations in the minds of people.

But the emotions aroused by the *Paroles d'un Croyant* managed to tarnish in Lacordaire's mind a fitting judgment of the propriety of his own personal situation. Something that I would never be too surprised about, this emotion took over the invariably calm soul of Mme Swetchine, to the point of troubling the usual certainty of her own judgment. She too believed the occasion to be favorable and counseled the publication of *Considérations sur le système philosophique de M. de la Mennais* [See

www.worksoflacordaire.com on the Internet under: Reflections on the philosophical system of Father de la Mennais.] This work appeared on 29 May 1834. Evidently Lacordaire was in a hurry to accentuate more and more his separation. By criticizing the basic logic of La Mennais' teaching, the main idea of the system, the foundation stone of the building, he was burning his ships; while respecting the person of his former general, he was making his break openly and absolutely irrevocable (and this is what he wanted to do). This is what drove him along.

"Those who judge me severely," he wrote to a friend, "do not know everything that is confined in the depths of my heart; how many months (and more than months) *I saw ahead of time all that was being prepared, without being able to make La Mennais or even one of his friends understand*; how deeply I was offended by a man whom I had so cordially served; with what unkindness he pushed me away when he felt the beginnings of resistance; how little, basically, I owed him (not even one thought!). And yet with what slow and painful steps did I separate myself from him! On 22 November 1831, the day we left for Rome, up to 20 May 1834, day on which I published my *Considérations* [Reflections], I have not stopped struggling, remaining silent, restraining myself, eating my tears. All that because a man sought to lose himself for nothing, for no reason, for no shadow of a reason, to plunge (with all his followers) into a bottomless pit, desperate, without considering that it depended entirely on him to gain more glory and authority than ever. When I was going to Munich, with a hundred borrowed *écus* [crowns, i.e., coins], it was not to rejoin him but to avoid seeing him in Paris, to separate myself by flight so as not to be forced to say a word against him, or even to remain silent. When I returned to La Chênaie in September 1832, it was not because of my faith in him, but to remain as a friend to him in his disgrace. When I left, it was because every day he was betraying his given word. With my future destroyed, and *destroyed by him*, I arrived in Paris in full winter wearing summer clothing, with no more than five francs in my pocket[55]." This is what Lacordaire could have replied to his critics.

Besides, he was blameless. The root of evil, the logical root of La Mennais' errors was exactly where Lacordaire saw it: in his system of philosophy, in that strange idea of the infallibility of the human race, posited as the unique source of certainty, as the only legitimate claim to authority. It was, as has been remarked[56], the sovereignty of numbers, applied not only to politics but also to Religion and to the entire domain of ideas. If the human race were infallible, the Church would obviously lose all authority on the day when she ceased to be the echo of the human race. Was Lacordaire not speaking with crushing truth when he called the human race a church without priests, without pope, without Bible, an authority without spokesman, an empty temple if not one of ruins? Who will decide, he asked, whether this teaching is of universal oral tradition, while this other one is not? Who will collect the scattered proofs? Who will interrogate all times and all places? Who will listen, who will convey their answers? Evidently this will involve each man's reason, each man's private meaning. "Each one of us, wandering in this circle without limits, makes himself the center of humanity, proclaims his own thoughts as universal, and if indeed he wishes to verify their universality, he drags himself alone in difficult research; he shouts, and his voice, striking the indeterminate spaces which surround him, provide him with only an echo of his proper intellect .... Should other voices answer him, he considers the distant and harmonious chorus of those minds as the universal word....Every man remains free, by a Protestant interpretation, to turn the human race against the Church, to invoke against the authority of the Church the infallible authority of the human race." This is what Lacordaire rightly called the most extensive Protestantism yet to appear[57]. And with what exceptional acumen he added: "I have warned the Church that war was being prepared and has already begun against Her, in the name of *humanity*[58]."

    That was indeed the situation, yet no one was aware of it at the time. Had it been noticed, Lacordaire would not have been allowed to the right to say so because of the dismaying relations he had entertained, so very recently, with La Mennais. There came a man who would be little known in the future but who would have left behind him a long beam of light had he been better organized, a man who squandered on every road the treasures of a vast erudition in the service of an outstanding mind, Baron d'Eckstein[59], who made himself the interpreter of public feelings. He chided Lacordaire for beating his wet-nurse and for applying the discipline [a whip for personal flagellation - Trans.] to the back of his master, at a time when everyone was casting stones on the latter [i.e., La Mennais]. Moreover, he accused Lacordaire being too young, frivolous, that he sacrificed reason to Religion; he did concede that Henri did not *belong to the sacristy*, one of those injurious terms that opponents invent so easily to render their antagonists detestable, but that honest opponents never use.

Lacordaire's rejoinder was fitting. "You are completely unaware," he told the baron, "of the nature of my relationship with La Mennais. In fact, he was neither my father nor my master. Of the ten years that have just passed, there were six during which I resisted the repeated requests made to me in his name to bind myself to him. There was one year in which I served him devotedly; there was another in which I struggled painfully against the need to separate myself from him; the rest happened during that separation....There it is, Sir, my entire history, since you force me to relate it. My wet-nurse, in the spiritual order, was the Church; my father, Jesus Christ. I preferred them over men because a Christian does not involve himself save in the loyalty he owes them. ... I had no intention of establishing a school in place of his, but to attend the universal school. One is never too young for that, Sir.... My book was an appeal, not an injury. Had my book been an assault, it would not have been one of the strong against the weak, but the defense of the weak against the strong. You are too clear-sighted, Sir, not to have judged the situation as it really is. Never was La Mennais as influential as he is today.... The fundamental thought of my book is not 'the complete renunciation of human reason,' but absolutely the opposite. Moreover, I will take pains to show you after you yourself will have taken the time to ground your assertion....God knows whether I was mistaken in seeing interests of great importance where you saw only *a quarrel of the sacristy*.... And yes, as regards the question of sacristy, I wish to set aside the praise that is pleases you to address to me in acknowledgment. You believe that I belong to the *clergy* and not to the *sacristy*. You are mistaken, Sir; I do belong to the sacristy: I hold fast to all the names that malice or frivolity successively create against the Church .... Besides, time will declare which one of us, in this matter, was the thoughtless and inconsiderate man[60]."

D'Eckstein tried to reply, but he was not successful. Even before his rejoinder could reach Lacordaire (at the time in Germany), the Encyclical of 7 July 1834 had ended the contest. It condemned the *Words of a Believer* as anarchic and subversive to Catholic teaching concerning the submission due to the Ruling Powers, as turning from their true meaning the words of God and fabricating for people a new gospel. The Encyclical also condemned La Mennais' system of philosophy as ineffectual, trifling, inconsistent, lacking the approbation of the Church, incapable of upholding truth. This was a startling authorization of the thesis just proposed by Lacordaire. The La Mennais school, already struck down for its politics but up to then standing as a school of philosophy, found itself henceforth ruined from top to bottom.

Most of its disciples had left: Lacordaire, as we have seen by 1832; Fathers Combalot and Guéranger, in August 1833; Messrs Gerbet, de Salinis, and de Coux, on the eve of the publication of *Paroles*. What was happening to Montalembert?

With Lacordaire, he had been the most liberal of school members. Born of an English woman, reared in England on the knees of his maternal grandmother, he had even in childhood breathed the air of a free country and a love of freedom for itself. Having returned to France with his father, who brought back from England the same political principles, he met the opposite current in the Saint-Germain [a quarter of Paris], and fought against it with all the energy of his being. At age twelve, he made his younger brother swear to remain faithful to the Charter. He had brought his opinions to Sweden, where his father represented France as ambassador; to Ireland, where Charles de Montalembert was introduced to O'Connell the day after the political emancipation of Catholics. With the inspiration of these same opinions, he joined *L'Avenir* at age twenty.

Fascinated by La Mennais who treated him fondly and spoke to him in familiar terms as with a son, he adopted enthusiastically and without discussing them all the views concerning the union between Religion and liberty. In spite of Lacordaire, he had persevered in that misleading way, confirmed in his illusions, alas!, by Cardinal Micara, Fathers Ventura and Olivieri as well as the other Roman friends of La Mennais. The premonition is there that after the break with the Master by Lacordaire, Montalembert was more divided and his mind more battle-worn than ever. On the one hand, he made it a point of honor to defend La Mennais against Lacordaire; in his letters to the latter, he contested the ground inch by inch with almost nothing betraying the interior disturbances that his friend's exceptional advice caused him. On the other hand, he made it his duty to repeat, word for word, to La Mennais, but as if coming from himself, all the arguments of Lacordaire. The answers from La Chenaie, that I have before my eyes, are unimpeachable evidence of it. Montalembert did not rebel against the Encyclical; as he himself said, he was only wavering and troubled. Besides, he knew full well that, the day when he would have made a gesture of full and complete adherence to the teachings of the pontifical act, he would lose all influence over the recluse of La Chenaie; he shuddered at the thought of smothering the wick that was still smoking. On the contrary, as long as he had not made his absolute submission, his filial enthusiasm for the Master, the startling scorn of the young Peer concerning the politics of the day, his passion for the cause of Poland, assuredly granted him a certain grip on the mind of La Mennais. It was because of this that he had obtained from him, in July 1833, not only the aborting of the publication of *Paroles d'un Croyant*, but also the promise of complete inaction[61]. Montalembert never got tired of preaching to La Mennais, withdrawal, silence, submission, renunciation of any action outside the Church, to the point that the rebel wrote to him: "It is for someone like you that the pope is God[62]."

In the end, he persisted simultaneously in not accepting the formula of unlimited submission to the Encyclical signed by La Mennais on 11 December 1833; and this persistence was distressing to Lacordaire. Never was a soul so loved with the fondness Henri had for the soul of Montalembert. This fondness along with the situation impelled him to write a series of letters so eloquent that I believe there is no second example in the language of men.

With a sincerity that will honor him forever, Montalembert himself reported this moment in the life of his friend. Let him speak:

"Among the souls 'sincerely misled' and profoundly troubled by the sway of the deadly genius of La Mennais, there was one that Lacordaire cherished more than all the others and who persisted, after all the others, in a disinterested loyalty, less perhaps to the person of the fallen apostle than to the lofty idea that seems to have been buried with his fall. From the midst of those struggles along with his personal contradictions, it was on this soul that he expended the supreme enthusiasm of his zeal, the most uncontaminated and strongest passion of his heart. It was for this soul, unknown to the world that he spent the richest treasures of his eloquence: *Vadit ad illam quae perierat, donec inveniat eam* [He looked for the lost soul until he found it.]. How I long to make everything known and to cite the numerous letters, which for almost three full years, engaged in that ungrateful task! Perhaps one day, when all the witnesses and all the participants in this struggle will have disappeared along with him, these letters will fall into hands that will be able to write in the history of that glorious life one page that will not be the least in arousing emotions. I have just read them over again, after so many years, with an emotion that no words can express. I do not know whether his genius and his kindness have ever cast so much light on that hidden and determined struggle for the salvation of a beloved soul. With the forlorn hope of protecting myself from the sorrows and the storms of a very grievous encounter, I sought refuge in Germany, where I had been pursued by appeals from La Mennais. While considering himself, as a priest, obliged to sign forms, this unfortunate responded to my fears, to my filial protests, by congratulating me for the independence I had as a layman; he encouraged me to maintain it at any cost. "This word," he wrote, "that formerly moved the world, today will not move a school of little boys[63]." The same couriers who delivered these poisoned letters to me also brought others even more numerous wherein the genuine priest, the true friend reinstated the rights of truth by showing me the always accessible heights of light and of peace. He came in person to find me and to preach to me near the tomb of St. Elizabeth. Before as after this short trip, he returned unceasingly to the duty with boundless energy, with unyielding perseverance. Lost, misunderstood, pushed aside, nonetheless he did not cease to squander warnings, always fruitless, predictions always verified; but with what judgment, what spiritual and touching eloquence, what delightful mixture of severity and humble fondness, what beneficial choices of pitiless frankness and irresistible kindness! No, the most tender of care-takers could not have done more or better. After having established truth in its stern and sacred majesty, he adorned it with all the flowers of his poetry; moreover, using entreaties and reasoning, one after the other, he mixed in with unassailable arguments a cry of an incomparable heart in his fraternal and tireless devotion. Judge for yourself from this page taken from among many others in the same vein:

The Church does not tell you: *Look!* She does not have this power. She tells you: *Believe!* She tells you, a twenty-three year old bound as you are to certain thoughts, what she told you at your first communion: Receive God, hidden and incomprehensible; bow your mind before that of the Lord, and before the Church, His spokesperson. Well, why was the Church given to us if not to bring us back to the truth when we have substituted error for it? You are surprised by what the Holy Father requires of La Mennais. ...Indeed, it is more difficult to submit when one has spoken out before men than when everything takes place between the heart and God. This is the trial reserved especially for great talents. The significant men of the Church had to break their life in two, and on a lower level, all conversion consists in this ... — Listen to this too despised voice, because who will warn you if I do not? Who will love you enough to treat you without condescension? Who will cauterize your wounds, if not the one who kisses them with such love, and who would like to draw out the poison from them, at the peril of his own life?

"I was not a rebel, as one might believe from those earnest rebukes. I was simply wavering and troubled. While I stubbornly resisted the pressing entreaties of Lacordaire, I reminded La Mennais of the loyalty of my enthusiasm, I, the most obstinate of all the followers he had attracted, to obtain from him both patience and silence. But I envied my friend for his having followed another road, more public and more decisive. I reproached him recklessly for the apparent forgetfulness of his liberal aspirations whose sweep had excited both of us. When I finally gave in, it was only slowly, as if regretfully, and not without having distressed that generous heart. The struggle had lasted too long. I speak of it with shame, with remorse, because at the time I did not give him all his due. Now, I atone for this fault by admitting it, and I make of this admission a tribute to a noble soul which has now found the judge it had appealed to with such legitimate trust. It was after this, and it was in this way, that I was able to cast into the innermost folds of that soul a glance, at first distracted, irritated, but subsequently and even today, bathed in the tears of an undying gratitude. It is from this soul that I learned to understand and to hold in reverence the only power before which we grow by bending down. Captive of error and of pride, I was ransomed by him who appeared to me as the ideal priest, just as he himself defined the man: 'As strong as a diamond and more tender than a mother[64].' "

The grace of God has its moments whose secrets escape men. Lacordaire despaired of persuading his friend; he had discontinued all his entreaties for two months when, for his part, Montalembert despairing of La Mennais, in an unexpected move on 8 December 1834, submitted in Pisa his submission to the two Encyclicals, and handed this document to Cardinal Pacca. Lacordaire was enraptured by it, while La Mennais uttered a moan, a poignant outcry of surprise and of pain.

Twenty-two months later (October 1836), La Mennais published the book of his apostasy, *Affaires de Rome*, and everything was over. What we have just read is a comprehensive refutation of that book, through the very letters of the author. It has been said that the apostasy of La Mennais is the suicide of perhaps the most brilliant soul to be found in history[65]. But he is also the one and only example of a man who, having within himself all the makings of the most challenging heretic, was unable to separate from the center of unity even the least of his followers[66]. Others have chosen to see in La Mennais a prophet out of his element, but a prophet nonetheless; the future, they thought, would not deny it[67]. I dispute that. Only one thing did La Mennais greatly lack: foresight. During thirty years, he predicted as imminent a cataclysm that never occurred. He uttered twenty other prophecies that we cannot read without shrugging our shoulders. Even though the Christian world, like the Roman world, is likely to fall into ruin some day in a universal democracy, how, in the judgment of posterity, would La Mennais surpass, as a thinker, the common level of the socialists of our time? He is superior to them only by his style. However great a writer he was, as a democrat, alas!, he will always remain no more than an eloquent reporter of the commonplace[68].

ENDNOTES

1. *Correspondence*, t. II, 245.
2. La Mennais to his brother, 10 October 1832. (*Œuvres inédites*, II, 125.)
3. *NOTICE*.
4. 19 August 1832, to Montalembert.
5. La Mennais to Montalembert, 12 February 1833.
6. Lacordaire to Montalembert, 29 October August 1831.
7. Lacordaire to Montalembert, 19 August 1833.
8. Letter of 9 April 1833.
9. To Montalembert, 15 May 1833.

10. *NOTICE*, Ch. III.

11. *Ibid.*

12. "Do you wish to see the mother of the preacher?", it was said one day in 1846 to someone who was attending one Lacordaire's conferences at Notre-Dame. — She died ten years ago. — But not at all: look, there she is, look at her! And Mme Swetchine was singled out; her visible satisfaction had provided the opportunity for this touching impression.

13. *Plenus sum sermonibus et coarctat me spiritus uteri mei... Loquar et respirabo paululum.* (Job, 23:18-20).

14. To Mme de Senfft, 25 January 1833.

15. To Mme de Senfft, 26 March 1833.

16. 2 May 1833.

17. To Mlle de Lucinière, 2 May 1833.

18. *Quae quidem declaratio eam illico nobis spem indidit sincere ipsos (auctores fautoresque consiliorum de quibus præcipue querebamur), plene, absolute, omnique depulsa ambiguitate, judicio nostro paruisse, idque luculentioribus quoque monumentis fore in posterum testaturos, ea fide qua se erga Christi Vicarium incensos toties disertissime professi sunt. Huc sane perjucunda spes animum nostrum, in summa temporum difficultate pro rei sacræ incolumitate sollicitum, erexerat; at dolorem adhuc injiciunt, quæ etiam nunc perferuntur in vulgus.*

19. To Montalembert, 1 May 1833.

20. *Correspondence*, II, 270.

21. Words cited in a Lacordaire letter to Montalembert, 13 July 1833.

22. To Mme de Senfft, 1 August 1833.

23. Report to the Pope, 6 December 1833. – *Correspondence*, t. II, p. 334.

24. Letter to Montalembert, on that date.

25. Letter to Mme de Senfft, of 31 December 1833. — Letter of

4 August to Montalembert.

26. To Montalembert, 26 January and 19 May 1833.

27. *Correspondence*, t. II, 304-305.

28. Letter of 6 October 1833.

29. To the Countess de Senfft, 27 September 1833; Correspondence, t. II, p.316-317. — La Mennais limited himself to refer Mme de Senfft to chapters XVIII, XIX, and XX of St. John. But Forgues was careful to add a short extract of those chapters, clearly revealing the thought of the letter's author.

La Mennais insisted on this point (to Montalembert, 10 October 1833).

30. To Montalembert, 10 September 1833.

31. To the same, 25 and 28 September, 19 October 1833.

32. Letter to Montalembert, 21 September 1833.

33. *Affaires de Rome*, p. 140.

34. This is what allows us to question the drawing closer the letters of 21 September and of 5 November to Montalembert. – See Letter to Coriolis, 9 November 1833 (*Correspondence*, t. II, p. 324).

35. Letter to Montalembert, 2 February 1834.

36. Condé: Louis II, prince of Condé (1621-1686). Distinguished in several battles. Very impetuous individual, with a keen eye.

37. *Affaires de Rome*, p. 147 sq. — Corres. t. II, 331, seq.

38. See the letter of Cardinal Pacca, *Affaires de Rome*, p. 145 seq.

39. This final declaration of La Mennais was in Latin. Here is the text:

Ego infrasciptrus, in ipsa verborum forma quae in Brevi summi Pontificis Gregorii XVI, dato die 5 octobr. an. 1833, continetur, – doctrinam Encyclicis ejusdem Pontificis litteris traditam me unice et absolute sequi confirmo, nihilque

ab illa alienum me aut scripturum esse aut probaturum.
Lutetiae Parisiorum, die 11 decembr. an.1833.
P. La Mennais

40. See that Brief in Appendix XII, page 537.
41. Letter to Montalembert, 13 December 1833.
42. Letter to Montalembert, 10 February 1834.
43. To Montalembert, 1 January 1834.
44. Letter to Montalembert, 14 December 1833.
45. See Appendix XIII, page 539.
46. Letter to Montalembert, 1834.
47. Comment by Mme Ozanam, as her husband remembered it. — This took place on 13 January 1834.
48. This is the way La Mennais spoke of the meeting, to which he assigned the date 28 March. (*Affaires de Rome*, p. 167.)
49. I have before my eyes the letter I call to witness.
50. *Nouveaux Lundis*, t. Ier, p. 97.
51. The word is from Guizot, *Mémoires*, t. III, p. 82.
52. Nettement.
53. We can see how Nettement's memory failed him when he wrote that Lacordaire had marked his separation by *an impetuous reply, too impetuous perhaps*, to his former master. (*Histoire de la littérature sous le gouvernment de juillet*, t. 1er, p. 350.)
54. On 26 November 1832, two weeks after having definitively left La Chênaie, Lacordaire wrote to Montalembert: "It is concerning the philosophical teachings of La Mennais, as I see it clearly, that the public quarrel between the episcopacy and him will resume; I fear that this will greatly complicate matters. One day I will have to present my views about this philosophy." The disapprobation is already manifest.
55. Letter to Foisset, 12 February 1838.
56. By Nettement and later, by Guizot.
57. *Considérations sur le système philosophique.* – See

Internet www.worksoflacordaire.com, Reflections, Chap. 11.
58. *Considerations...* – Conclusion.
59. See Internet www.worksoflacordaire.com, *To Baron d'Eckstein*.
60. *Univers religieux,* 22 June 1834. See also **59** above.
61. Letter of Montalembert to Lacordaire, 6 December 1833.
62. Letter of 1 January 1834.
63. Letter of 5 August 1834.
64. *Le P. Lacordaire,* par le comte de Montalembert, pp. 76-80.
65. Nettement, *Histoire de la litérature sous le gouvernement de juillet.*
66. *Le P. Lacordaire,* par le comte de Montalembert, p.76.
67. Sainte-Beuve, *Nouveaux Lundis,* t. I, p. 40.
68. For Lacordaire's definitive judgment on La Mennais, see letter to Mme Swetchine, 31 March 1854. — NOTICE, chaps. III and XI. — See especially Appendix 14, page 545.

Chapter VII

Conferences at Stanislaus College

The personal life of Lacordaire in 1833 — First attempts at preaching: he discovers his true oratorical calling — Paris at the end of 1833. Followers of Saint-Simon. Moral reaction: the Society of St. Vincent de Paul; the need for a renewal of the Catholic pulpit;

steps taken by young students to Msgr. de Quélen — Father Buquet asks Lacordaire to give some conferences at the Stanislaus College — The Archbishop inaugurates conferences at Notre-Dame of Paris — Lacordaire's success, the opposition he faced; the pulpit of Stanislaus College is closed to him.

Until the star of La Chenaie completely disappeared from our horizon, it dominated everything with its brilliance. Lacordaire himself did not hold our attention except while he moved in that powerful orbit. The time has come now for us to deal exclusively with him "who placed the Church in the forefront of his activity as in his heart," to him, who — the first and for a long time the only one — saw clearly in the present and in the future of La Mennais, to him who, as early as the month of April 1832, wrote these prophetic words: "Our language has no words heart-rending enough to say what will become of him."

While the author of *l'Essai sur l'indifférence* was falling rapidly from group to group, to the bottom of the abyss about which he echoed the words of the Wise man: *Impius, cum in profundum venerit, CONTEMNIT*[1], — what was the *private* life of Lacordaire like, he who had barely escaped from La Chenaie?

We find him, as in 1828, in his narrow and curved street in the Latin quarter[2], at the foot of Mount St. Genevieve. There, he studied deeply St. Augustine, whom he called the St. Thomas [Aquinas] of the early centuries of the Church[3]. awakened and regained his serenity day by day, just as Montalembert wrote, in prayer, work, solitude, in a very priestly life, serious, simple, poor, ignored, truly hidden in God. He held fast to all of this and rebuffed any entreaty. Thus it was that, twice (December 1833 and December 1835), he turned down the direction of the newspaper *l'Univers*. "I did not want," he wrote, "to enter the career of journalism. I did my time in that service, albeit brief, and I received a sufficient number of wounds to be deemed disabled."

On that occasion, there was talk about Lacordaire's taste for solitude, and that was true, but one must understand what it means. Solitude, with which he was always taken, was not isolation, it was only a withdrawn and calm life. The cell of a hermit would have weighed heavy on this soul that had such a need to reach others. We are aware of his letter of 10 November 1823 to a young member of the Paris Bar, to an every-day friendship, to that gentle benevolence that every man needs to receive and to grant[5]." Since that every-day friendship was not granted, Lacordaire sought the gentleness of affection in a life shared with another, with a young man from the *Société d'Études* of Dijon, like him, a lawyer in training in Paris[6]. After he entered the seminary, and for the same reason, he took as roommate the younger brother of the latter[7]. In 1833, at the Convent of the Visitation, he associated himself even more closely with M. Chéruel[8], from whom he soon kept no secrets. It is one of the remarkable traits, albeit one of the least known, in the biography of Henri Lacordaire that even before becoming a monk, he could never live without another. This soul, more affectionate than we ever knew, and revealed to us today in his personal letters, was repressed by circumstances at college. It was very early there that he contracted the habit of withdrawing into itself. A dangerous habit, to be sure, because unless God introduces His hand, it turns man to bitterness, the natural effect of everything that withdraws into itself. But Lacordaire only gained a greater need to give of himself, to

309

open his heart on occasion. The contradiction was plausible even though it was rarely understood.

A letter he wrote at this point in his life that we have come to, at age 32, shows the exposed interior of his soul during the ten stormy years that followed his conversion.

"In the ten years since my entire life suddenly changed by my dedication to the clerical state, I have not had a moment of stability and interior rest *except in the unshakable awareness of my vocation.* Other than that, my spirit is full of disturbances, alterations, errors, doubts; I was laboriously giving myself birth into Christianity, bereft of counselor, of guide, not even having a confessor with influence on my soul and who could do more than simply grant me absolution for my sins. In seminary, not one among the spiritual directors, by his mind, inspired in me that confidence which holds in check. Honest and virtuous men as they were, I appeared to them as an untamed horse, and to me, they appeared incapable of placing a halter on my neck. Those of my classmates whom I cherished for their behavior and their heart were the young ones, younger than I was, with whom I chatted freely; but they respected my influence too much to be for me anything other than gentle and lovable comforters. Outside of the seminary, I had no one, except for a confessor who had seen me shortly after my entrance, Boudot[9], and another Vicar General, Borderies, whom I knew even less, and who was repelled by my manner which indicated that I was not looking for a protector. Gerbet, a humble man, reserved, did not attract me for himself and for his school, despite his attention; I found him suspect or unsympathetic because of his intense self-confidence. This situation from emotional isolation, *joined to my retiring and ingrained habits of mind*, had two results: a fearful interior struggle and a great dread of making myself known. The more fearful the struggle grew, the more disclosure became offensive to me. More often did I burst out in the manner of volcanoes. Nonetheless, a real gentleness flowed over my storms. The invincible feelings about my calling gave me the courage to move forward. And yet, how many ideas along the way! How many questions, now resolved in this meaning, now in another! I was on the edge of becoming a Jesuit, on the edge of settling in Poland, on the edge of moving to America. (Do I really know all of what I was thinking, of all that I wanted?) There is within me something energetic and unexpected. And yet, there is also a basis of reserved, steady reason that finally brought me to port with the grace of God. If I had found, ten years ago, a man to cherish me, who wanted to be my guide, gracious me! God knows how I would have accepted with joy! From how many troubles he would have spared me! But I did not find one. Perhaps it was necessary that I be tamed. God sent me on my path a hand of iron, a hand much stronger than mine, one that nearly broke me apart. Perhaps that was the only remedy I could take: God, who knows everything, knows it. This is my history, the history of my reserve[10]."

We can now understand better the sincerity of these words: "With joy, I feel the solitude spread around me; it is my element, my life...[11] One can do nothing without solitude; this is my great maxim. Even when it is not giving of itself, the heart loses in opening itself too often in the presence of strangers; it is like a flower carried outside[12]... man builds himself up within himself and not outside[13]."

Nonetheless, added Montalembert, a certain inkling about the future reserved for him made an appearance now and then in his soul, like a lightning bolt in the night. And so, while living alone and studying, he had the idea of writing a book and simultaneously he was preparing himself for preaching; two activities, he would say, without which his life would be incomplete. The book that he dreamed of presented itself to his thought under a rather juvenile title: "The Church and the World in the Nineteenth Century." But he was in no hurry; he did not expect the work to be ready and published before ten years, either because he did not consider himself mature enough, because he needed all that time to erase many prejudices, or, finally, because he would have to speak in it of matters in which he had taken a more or less direct part and that it was not appropriate for him to speak too early[14].

Here again we find a trait very characteristic of Lacordaire's personality: as passionate as he was, he knew how to be patient. "A man," he wrote, "always has his moment; it is enough for him to wait for it and not do anything against Providence[15]."

His moment would come.

On leaving La Chênaie, these were his first words: "I do not yet know very well what I will do with my time; perhaps I will involve myself in working for Catholic youth and in preparing conferences *for them*[16]."

Very likely, in his thoughts, it was simply a question of secular conferences, of the type begun in Paris by Gerbet on philosophy and De Coux on political economy.

Soon, however, he wanted to try to see if had been born for preaching and what kind of preaching would fit him. "In a college, I have preached successfully," he wrote to a friend, "but in a parish, in such a way that it was greatly displeased at me[17]."

The college was Stanislaus College, an institute founded under the Empire by a man of great pedagogical ability, Father Liautard, to assemble there and to educate the elite of the Catholic youth of France.

The parish was St. Roch, the same church which Montalembert wrote, nineteen years later, would hear the last thundering accents of his voice in Paris. Lacordaire had written his sermon. He failed completely. Everyone left telling himself: *He will never be a preacher.*

He himself believed it. "It is evident to me that I have neither physical stamina nor flexibility of mind, nor sufficient understanding of the world in which I had always lived and will always live as a recluse, in the end, with not enough of what it takes to be a preacher in the full meaning of the term[18]. This is the second time I experience how my thinking is so little congenial to an ordinary assembly of the faithful. Besides, my voice is not forceful enough for a church and I would ruin my lungs in very little time[19]."

But, at the same time, he had a clear inkling of his true calling as priest and as preacher. "Youth is more my concern; every time I had occasion to speak to them in the chapel of the college, I did some good[20.] Some day I may be called to a work for youth, devoted entirely to youth[21]. If I can use my speech in favor of the Church, it will be solely as regards apologetics, namely, in that form wherein are assembled the beauties, the grandeurs, religious and polemic history, to advance Christianity in minds and to implant the faith there[22]." What better early definition of the very special apostolate to which he was called from above!

Moreover, harvest-time was approaching.

The movement of ideas that peace and the Charter of 1814 had created, spread quickly and could already be seen in Catholic youth. The *Correspondant* [a newspaper] that we will see later grew out of this movement; in that same year (1833), it would produce an admirable organization, the Society of St.-Vincent-de-Paul. Concerning this relationship, no misunderstanding is possible. The struggle over teachings naturally provoked on one side and the other opposite endeavors: the *Correspondant*, Catholic as always and more legitimist at its origins, was the counterpart of the *Globe* of the

Restoration, which was deist and revolutionary. For its part, the Society of St.-Vincent-de-Paul, as we will show, was in turn the direct response to a challenge by the Saint-Simon viewpoint. Besides, I have no more to tell to anyone about the intellectual fervor that was then moving Catholic youth; the letters of Ozanam at that time are evidence as incomparable as it is unimpeachable.

But what we did not know before the publication of those letters is that, from the early days of June 1833, Ozanam, moved by an overwhelming desire to have an important Catholic teaching to counterbalance the bad effects of the lessons of Jouffroy and the other courses of the rationalist Sorbonne, appeared before de Quélen. He was accompanied by the young de Montazet, grand-nephew of the Archbishop of Lyons by this name; he carried with him a petition filled with one hundred signatures. The prelate received them graciously, offered them some hope, and dismissed them with effusive embraces.

The impulse having been given, Ozanam's thought made its way. It fired up the Society of St.-Vincent-de-Paul, which had just been established (May 1833). An honorable man, sincere, a stranger to every spirit of prejudice, *l'abbé* Buquet[23], at the time Dean of studies at the Stanislaus College, embraced this idea. Filled with the memory of the effect produced by one or two sermons of Lacordaire on the students of his establishment, he proposed to him to give them a series of religious conferences. Lacordaire accepted without hesitation. It was to be a very limited task, but, after all, it was no longer isolation but action. This was a first step to the outside, to fresh air; the barrier was lifted. At Stanislaus, Lacordaire, by the very fact that he was speaking to young men, felt himself at home, master of his territory, getting used to the spoken word, *which was as yet only an intuition in him*[24].

The first of these conferences was held on Sunday 19 January 1834: in attendance were only the students and a few friends of the establishment; there were only one hundred unoccupied seats. The following Sunday, the hearers from the outside were much more numerous. At the third conference, most of the students had to be turned away to make room for a multitude of unexpected guests. Lacordaire wrote to Montalembert, at the time in Germany: "My conferences are going well, like a seed in development." In March, there were six hundred attendees. In April, the chapel had to be extended to allow for a balcony. The sincere tone of the speaker, said M. Nettement, the daring and inspired words, the novelty of this type of eloquence, became an attraction for the most varied of listeners. The most eminent men from political groups, the bar, and letters, soon flocked to his conferences. In that small chapel for children, one day saw the presence of Messrs de Chateaubriand, Berryer, Lamartine, Odilon-Barrot, Victor Hugo. The story was told that Berryer, having arrived too late, was obliged to ask for a ladder so he could enter the chapel through a window. In the midst of our skeptical age, everyone wanted to hear Catholicism affirm itself by the mouth of this contemporary child, who, in the current language of his audience, found a way to minds and hearts simply by allowing free expression to his feelings and his thoughts[25].

At Stanislaus, Lacordaire was always an extemporaneous speaker. He learned that he had no other way to reach souls except this one and decided that, from then on, he would no longer speak from a written text[26].

There was nothing really new in his early conferences. God, creation, the origin of evil, original sin, the promise of reparation, the human race, the Jewish people, the prophecies, the Incarnation: this was the outline. How many times had the Christian pulpit approached these topics, as ancient as

Christianity?

What did one seek in the narrow chapel of Stanislaus College? One looked for the living word which was the *man himself*; a spontaneous word, unexpected, thrilling, flowing from one soul to another soul; a word full of wonder, of witticisms, of flights of fancy, impassioned, sparkling, stirring beyond any idea; a voice sometimes belabored and heart-breaking, that set into vibration to an unspeakable degree the strings of human nature.

This was a great novelty in the pulpit, such as Bourdaloue[27] and Massillon[28] had done previously.

After them, in fact, the priestly word was a simple echo of tradition, committed to writing, an echo more or less powerful, more or less weakened, but almost entirely impersonal so much had it been fully subjected to the classic and approved rhythm. The word remained serious and noble, but with the seriousness of a nobility of agreement; no doubt this did not entirely extinguish individual originality, but it did restrain it undeniably to rather narrow limits. The man disappeared too much behind the priest. The preacher was still allowed to show emotion, but a very discreet emotion, regulated almost to fussiness. Consequently, with the pulpit seen in this way, art ended up supplanting nature and bombast appropriated more and more the place of eloquence. And so we had wise, accurate sermons in a convoluted style, of modest warmth, perfectly irreproachable, but no less perfectly ineffective. They satisfied pious souls, more or less, but they were unable to attract the sheep that strayed from the fold. Preachers of missions were the only ones who, by their more passionate and more familiar instructions, by less uniform sermons, not products of conventional molds, were still able to produce genuine conversions. But even if the missionaries obtained some success in the provinces, they had no grip on

Paris; the band of cultured men would have spurned their reasoning as trite and old-fashioned.

There was nothing like that at the conferences of Stanislaus College. These were nothing like what had been heard before. All conventional form had disappeared; no introductory quotation to the sacred talk, no divisions, almost no citations from the Fathers and the Doctors. The ancient mold of preaching flew into pieces; one really felt within the full nineteenth century. Never was a sacred orator so much a man of his time; in Lacordaire, the defects as well as the qualities were exclusively of our period. To be sure, the preacher would have dreaded to innovate in doctrine. I will say more: his studies at Saint-Sulpice, his recent lectures at Saint-Augustin, and more to the point, I don't know what natural instinct about orthodoxy (that had saved him in Rome and that he never abandoned) protected him more than was believed against involuntary errors of the mind. Finally, extemporaneous talk has its dangers; more inclined to the clever by the bend of his mind, Lacordaire, I recognize, never let himself give truth the appearance of ambiguity. Sometimes, perhaps — as he himself has said — he seemed to skirt closely the boldness of thought by that of language.

Opposition was not long in coming, but it lacked comprehension, fairness, and moderation. Is proof needed? Lacordaire had spoken before priests, all of them less disposed in favor of new ideas: for example, before M. L'abbé Augé, superior of Stanislaus, former professor at the Sorbonne and Vicar General of Paris. None of them had ever noticed in his conferences the slightest lack of orthodoxy. If some words might have been expressed in too contemporary a form, they passed as if covered and swallowed up by the others. Nonetheless, the spirit of routine was shocked. Prejudiced minds cried aloud, plotted together, pressed charges with the

Archbishop, the Vatican, the police. Alone, busy, confident in God and in the future, Lacordaire remained calm and above the pestering against him; only one day did he reveal his agitation[29]. Nonetheless, this ordeal was not of a nature to diminish the troublesome consequences that the reactions organized against *l'Avenir* had previously left him concerning the place of the legitimists [i.e., the royalist partisans]. Those results registered more and more in his memory.

And yet, the Archbishop, however faithful he remained to the lost cause — the Archbishop, by his nature, so little favorable to the kind of preaching Lacordaire had undertaken — the Archbishop, at first, supported him. That will be the everlasting honor of his memory. Rome, for its part, replied that as long as the Ordinary did not deal severely with the matter, there was nothing for it to do. It seems that the police were less trusting[30]. One day, de Quélen called for Lacordaire and showed him an official letter he had received about him. The contents painted the embarrassment of his situation as it affected the new government — which the bishop had to protect all the more because he dealt with it every day — that this government had a harder time in forgiving him for not having appeared at the Tuileries. Without giving Lacordaire any orders, the bishop had him abruptly stop his conferences. The former wrote to the bishop, to announce his decision, in a cautious but firm letter[31], and left his hearers on 13 April 1834, the second Sunday after Easter.

Thus, the conferences at Stanislaus had extended over three months. It was only one test, but a decisive one.

We will get to understand it.

Six days before Lacordaire opened his conferences in the chapel of Stanislaus College without a preconceived design and as a result of an appeal he had not sought, Ozanam and two of his friends[32] presented to the Archbishop a new petition from young scholars, signed this time with two hundred signatures. This was on 13 January 1834[33]. The three students, with respectful frankness, detailed to de Quélen their desire for instruction that was outside the *ordinary tone of sermons*, in which the questions that occupied their minds would be discussed and answered, in which Religion would be studied in its relations with society, in which, at least indirectly, responses would be given to the principal rationalist publications of France and Germany. Then they went further: with the confidence of youth, they provided two names, that of Lacordaire, known to them through *l'Avenir* and that of M. Bautain,[34] contemporary of Jouffroy[35] at the Normal School. M. Bautain was for a long time the preferred disciple of M. Cousin[36], then became a brilliant professor of philosophy at Strasbourg and in the end was brought back to the study of the Catholic faith and became a priest of Jesus Christ. But the Archbishop's choices had been settled. Not wanting to explain any further, he told the young men that he was going to try an experiment that he hoped would please them.

The following day, *l'Univers* printed a report of that visit. Grieved by this indiscretion, Ozanam and M. Lallier went immediately to the Archbishop. He embraced their heads in his arms, kissed them paternally, then led them to the door of a room where he said they would find the preachers to whom he had entrusted the teaching they had requested. He encouraged the students to hear each other and to express what they desired while he himself went to breakfast[37].

What these young students sought was not the kind of preaching honored at the residence. Even less was it the plan of apologetics devised by De Quélen. There was absolutely no agreement on the topics to be treated; before long, the discussion became so lively that no one listened to the other.

So as to have no reason to reproach themselves, the students made a supreme effort: in the extreme frankness of their enthusiasm and of their age, they addressed to the Archbishop a note written by Ozanam[38], a series of topics that Catholic youth would like to hear treated in the pulpit of Notre-Dame. But the decision of De Quélen had been taken.

This involved a misunderstanding that lingered and that requires an explanation.

A student of Emery[39], de Quélen, more than anyone else, had in mind the example of apostolic teaching of Religion given at Saint-Sulpice by Frayssinous at the beginning of the century. He was well aware how the success justified the aptness of that experiment. On 14 May 1807, Portalis wrote to the Emperor: "The number of Frayssinous's listeners is huge. At each conference, there are a thousand young men from different schools. Beside this youth, can be seen wise men, cultured men, public servants, professors, and men of all classes, somewhat distinguished by their education and their knowledge." This example weighed heavily on the resolution of the Prelate; but, the decision to reopen the apologetic conferences, also determined the original direction they had. Formed under the Empire at the school of the last representatives of the Church of France in the eighteenth century, faithful heir to the inhibition of their mind, de Quélen could see no one over the horizon other than Frayssinous; he sought only to follow scrupulously the respected traces. It was the misfortune of the time when a society suddenly disappeared into a chasm, that *the remnants of another age*, as Chateaubriand labeled them, were fundamentally unable to understand the new times. de Quélen was not yet an old man (he was then fifty-six); by his family traditions, by his education as a gentleman and as priest, by the character of his mind, by all his relationships, he was, in the full meaning of the word, a man of the past. Accordingly, he was unable to notice that for all those who were young, an entirely new kind of evangelization was called for.

"Bright and intelligent of mind, an accurate writer, an orator by the majesty of his bearing and his features, Frayssinous," Lacordaire declared aptly, "had opened a new route which he followed honorably; but he had limited himself to the porch of the church, and had not penetrated into the depths of Christian dogma. *Besides, another century separates us from his.* Frayssinous had spoken under a despotism that was unable to bear for very long his refined judgment. We had a lot to talk about under liberty. By his age and his traditions, he was a venerable portrait of the former French clergy. By our clergy, we were the image of a lively generation, emotional, and asking of the Church that freshness of forms and ideas which was never incompatible with her unchanging antiquity[40]."

Everything had been renewed: not only politics, but philosophy, history, literature. In the place of Condillac and Cabanis, Cousin and his disciples prevailed. In place of *l'abbé* Millot and d'Anquetil, we had Augustin Thierry and Guizot. La Harpe and Delille were in the distance; Chateaubriand eclipsed everything with all his rays of the setting sun. Moreover, it was the time when the author of *l'Essai sur l'indifférence* was about to publish the *Paroles d'un Croyant*. Well! It was in this state of mind that de Quélen announced the new project as a lenten practice in two points: on repentance and on faith, exactly as he could have written it for the Cardinal of Périgord in 1817. No emotion, no feelings, nothing current, nothing that answered the impatient enthusiasm of young souls. The Archbishop never even mentioned the word *Conferences*: "he announced a lenten series concerning the fundamental truths of Religion." Between Ozanam and himself there was the distance between 1804 and

1834. Besides, in order to open this series more solemnly, the Prelate had decided to appear himself in the pulpit of Notre-Dame, on the first Sunday of Lent. He was to be followed successively by seven preachers[41], who would speak under his supervision on subjects he had assigned to them. The illusion he created for himself was concluded.

The cooperation of Lacordaire had not been requested. Only approached on this point, but in an indirect manner, he had declined any participation in conferences understood in this way, "not willing to plunge into the labyrinth in which he felt it would be very difficult to agree and to be heard[42]."

As he had proposed, the Archbishop opened in person the conferences of Notre-Dame with a rather numerous audience of males on 16 February 1834. He was speaking well and loudly in an episcopal manner, especially toward the end[43]. On that very day, Lacordaire was delivering his fifth conference at Stanislaus. "It was on two points at once that the rift opened up. No one had previously imagined this contest between two minds, between two endeavors. It was not long before the question was asked: who would win mastery and the harvest[44]?"

The question was not asked for very long. Despite the undeniable talent of the preachers of Notre-Dame, they lacked innovation. Their teaching never left the *ordinary tone of sermons*. At that time, De Quélen would never have approved their deviating from it for one instant. And so, it was always the ancient model. The talks were written and memorized, on familiar themes, without a single unexpected idea. How could they have won, given the sparkling and always novel informality of Lacordaire?

The young people did not hesitate in making their choice. Catholic youth set things in motion. Ozanam was the recognized chief, the cherished head, *princeps Juventutis* [prince of youth]; no one admired the conferences of Stanislaus more than he did. He had no difficulty in dragging along members of the Society of St.-Vincent-de-Paul, a genuine knighthood of study and charity, whose soul he was, and which he had established, even in the early days, as the most lively hearth of the Catholic flame.

The origins of the Society are well-known. From the uproar and the conflict of teachings that quarreled over France on the day after the revolution of 1830, there appeared a school of social reorganization that passed itself off as a new religion, the religion of the future. It had assumed the name of a utopian who had just died and whom it acknowledged as its patriarch: it was called the religion of Saint-Simon. The early instructions of that school brought about considerable renown. One of its principal theses was to glorify Catholicism in its past, but to proclaim its impotence and replacement in the present. It was to refute by existing evidence the proclamation of impotence that the eight young Catholic students got together with the idea of establishing (what had not yet been seen in the Church): an association strictly of lay people, committed to visiting, helping, and evangelizing the poor; they placed this association under the patronage of the venerated name of St. Vincent de Paul. Truly, not one of them had foreseen that this grain of seed would become a large tree, the core of an extensive family, with France remaining as its center, but one that would spread throughout Europe and in a wide section of America.

I am not getting off the subject, because it was the youthful enthusiasm of original members of the Society of St. Vincent de Paul that began, in 1834, the success of the conferences of Stanislaus. The approbation of men such as Chateaubriand and M. Berryer, on granting it their seal, provided a genuine radiance to the brow of Lacordaire.

Nonetheless, the latter had withdrawn, pursued by the accusation of having preached doctrines imbued with a spirit of revolution and anarchy. This would, for a long time — as he himself said — be the weapon of his adversaries; even at this hour of my writing, it has not been broken up entirely in their hands. And yet, De Quélen had never reproached him; but when Lacordaire asked of him, in October 1834, the formal authorization to resume his conferences, the wavering character of the Prelate was sorely pressed. He was especially unhappy to refuse Lacordaire in that, in order not to leave Paris, the latter had declined an offer of a chair at the University of Louvain[45].

What followed next needs to be told extensively, because it paints a picture of the times and of the men. Not one development, not one detail that lacks interest and importance.

There was much pressure on Lacordaire to resume his conferences, and he himself hoped to do so. He was astonished by the rush brought about by his experience the previous winter. "It is necessary," said he, "that enthusiasm move the man as well as the priest; I am in awe as to how the contact of the mind with an audience enlarges the imagination and all the faculties." Accordingly, he thought of resuming his conferences from 15 November to 15 April, either at Stanislaus, or in a parish, such as Saint-Jacques, for example, or even at Saint-Séverin whose staff had made offers.

The first time he talked about this to the Archbishop, the Prelate expressed only the desire that he not speak during Lent, "not that I am jealous of your talent," he added, "but because I believe it is better to avoid rival comparisons." Lacordaire agreed immediately, with no effort at all. De Quélen then asked for some time to think.

As to what touched the Archbishop, the moment was hardly favorable; he had just received a kind of denunciation made to the entire Church by De Trévern, bishop of Strasbourg, against the teaching by a priest of superior merit, but outside the beaten path, Bautain. This was a solemn cry of alarm against the spirit of novelty in the bosom of the Church.

Eight days later, Lacordaire returned; the Archbishop presented him with nothing but fears; he alleged the division of minds, the possibility of a troubling intervention by the Government. Lacordaire defended himself favorably. In proof of the orthodoxy of his conferences, he invoked the judgment of all the priests of Stanislaus College. Now, if orthodoxy is preserved, how important is the division of minds? What work, since the origins of Christianity, had not divided them? As for the objection about politics, Lacordaire offered to do nothing without having assured himself of the intentions of the Government regarding the location for his talks. Since he had already made his sacrifice, he remained very calm and spoke with a kind of detachment, even while presenting all his reasons. He tried to make the Archbishop understand the peril that Religion faced with these obstacles brought against the best works, on the pretext that the times were wretched, and that (here is what was distinctive) it was necessary *to avoid agitating minds*, always ready to dispute each other. De Quélen was embarrassed; he hurried to dismiss his visitor with these words: "I am not cutting you short, I cannot do that; go see, examine, consult." From this conversation, the young preacher left with the impression that the conferences at Stanislaus did evidently trouble the Archbishop, but that, with no definite harm to blame on the speaker, ecclesiastical authority left him free to pursue his task.

Nonetheless, he left quite determined not to mount the pulpit; besides, the two or three friends he consulted thought as he did. Soon, after thinking it over, his feelings changed. "If you had received an order," they told him, "clearly you would have to remain silent, and leave the responsibility for your silence to someone else. But you have no order, no one will given you an order, no one wants to give you an order. Now, as long as one is free, he must move forward. *If you stop this year, it will be forever; you impose a restraint on yourself that you will never remove.* By a providential happenstance, some Vicars-General had just been named: Messrs Carbon, Carrière, Afre, Jammes, all young men, who are able to go hear you, while last year, the Archbishop's council comprised only elderly men. Ask the Archbishop to send some of them officially; thereby, you place slander at the foot of the wall. Finally, there is a consideration taken from the supernatural order that settles all difficulties: you are aware of the good that you do at a moment when only you can operate in this way; you are, therefore, bound to do so, unless authority expressly forbids you to meddle[46]."

Lacordaire was greatly perplexed. Humanly speaking, he would have preferred his peace and quiet above everything else. No hint of pride was pushing him to appear before an audience; he felt within himself only great compassion for these young people eager for religious teaching. He could not persuade himself to abandon so many souls, to whom no one offered bread. At this point, he did not know who to ask for what was the will of God. He had never felt so strongly how great a loss for him was the absence of Mme Swetchine. She had left for St. Petersburg where she wanted to have dismissed the order calling her husband back to Russia. Should one be prudent only by being weak? Should one rely on Providence, only to be broken? This was the issue. The solution could not be postponed because to delay the resumption of the conferences would be to abandon them for this year and to destroy hope for the years to come. This would have led everyone to believe that the Archbishop had not left Lacordaire free to mount into the pulpit. Should he accept this compromising situation since the Archbishop did not impose it on him?

Two weeks had barely passed when a man of great virtue and immense talent, but extremely prejudiced against Lacordaire, Rauzan, former superior of the Missionaries of France, declared to *l'abbé* Buquet, prefect of studies at Stanislaus, that the conferences at that college would not be resumed, and that he knew this from the very mouth of the Archbishop. As can be seen, the predicament of de Quélen began to worsen, and Lacordaire's no less. de Quélen did not wish to take responsibility either for Lacordaire's words or for his silence. The latter, endlessly called upon by his previous listeners regarding the resumption of his conferences, affirmed (as he had the right to) that the Archbishop had not silenced him; and yet a priest of the highest authority affirmed, from his point of view and almost that of de Quélen, the very contrary.

This is what explains the letter to the Prelate from Lacordaire on 31 October 1834. Throughout the letter, one perceives the tone of an honorable and proud soul, wounded — appropriately, it must be said — by unjustifiable mistrust. To be sure, Lacordaire had gone far-out in certain articles of *l'Avenir*: that is unquestionable and not disputed. But after all, had he not, since then, given orthodoxy most striking proofs? Was it confirmed, yes or no, that he had left La Mennais by 15 March 1832? Was it confirmed, yes or no, that he had written his retraction on 13 December 1833? Was it confirmed, yes or no, that he had finished burning his ships by publishing his *Considerations sur le système philosophique de M. de la Mennais*? To hold all this as something that did not happen, what kind of justice is that? A submission that prompt, complete, and besides, with a sincerity so well proved by the behavior of Lacordaire, since his departure from La Chênaie:

does that not deserve to be encouraged, such as was the case of all dissidents when they manifested a genuine desire to return to the Church?

On this point, I am merely expressing the thought of a man whose authority cannot be denied or diminished. This is how Affre (I would name another if I could find one less suspect of the Lammenais doctrine, less free from temerity of mind, and from republican tendencies) explains matters in his journal:

"Shortly thereafter, before I had met *l'abbé* Lacordaire, he had given, in the chapel of Stanislaus College, a series of conferences that produced among the young persons the greatest of enthusiasm. Unfortunately, they produced the opposite effect on *some listeners*, restless, not without reason, of all that is extraordinary and bold in the root of ideas, of boldness or recklessness in certain expressions. If those who complained had been above all suspicion of rivalry, their furor against the young speaker would probably have been less fiery. But they were accused, no doubt wrongly, of seeking revenge for the little interest they had aroused by trying to silence a rival who had received a very warm welcome.

"I had recently read the document in which *l'abbé* Lacordaire had written a retraction that I found very frank. I was admiring his talent, and while not hiding his faults, I thought I found there traits that revealed *a great soul* along with the gifts of a privileged mind. Consequently, I believed I had to plead his cause without masking the drawbacks of extemporaneous speaking on the topics he treated. I thought that these drawbacks would lose a great part of their menace by reason of the sincere and candid character of *l'abbé* Lacordaire. Indeed, he *could not be farther from the spirit of sectarianism* and is well-disposed to listen to the advice of those who are interested in him. Consequently, I could hope that, if he made an inexact assertion, it would not have been by *voluntary* error, or even less by *obstinate* error and that it would never be matter for a debate, but would disappear with the spontaneity that had produced it.

"And so, I spoke in his favor to the Archbishop. I made a point of remarking how different the times were, that if we had to regret no longer having as before a Sorbonne, always ready to strike down an offensive proposition, *neither did we have persons disposed to abuse, by taking over those propositions that could escape Lacordaire's notice*; that we could fear, on the contrary, that this clergyman become, without wishing to, a pretext for Christian youth to complain about the top pastor [i.e., the bishop], to separate themselves from him, while the conduct of Lacordaire, for the past two years, gave hope for significant docility, namely, the disposition most opposed to the character of innovators[47].

These reflections of Affre remained without retort and it was the fault of de Quélen not to have gotten to the matter immediately.

As Lacordaire noted on 31 October, it was no longer the case, as it was in April 1834, of a provisional interruption in his teaching, but a question of learning if his teaching would continue or definitely be suppressed. It was impossible to prevent the public from phrasing the issue in this way. With that having been said, Lacordaire discussed and refuted with great superiority, it must be admitted, all the objections raised against his resumption of the conferences: the idiosyncracy of his language, the intention of undermining the sermons at Notre-Dame, the accusation of *republicanism*, the concerns attributed to the Government on this point, the charge of alienating minds. With these grievances dispelled, the preacher declared openly that, if he were free, he would resume the conferences because they constituted the only ministry for which he was well-suited, and, by renouncing it, he would be giving up all priestly activity. "I am an exceptional man," he wrote in all frankness, "I have only one gift, and I am not even using it; as a priest, I have been reduced to nothing." He added quite rightly that his whole reputation depended on the resumption of the conferences; people looked forward to them so as to learn whether the Church, through the mouth of her bishop, believed in his sincerity or not. "I ask of the Church," said he with dignity, "I ask of the Church, in the person of my bishop, that she grant me her trust, that she pay respect to my priesthood. If she chooses not to," he continued with pride mixed with some bitterness, "I will have to think things over. I have reached the age of thirty-two. If I had stayed in the world, I would, at this age, be in a position to command respect when I dealt about myself and about others. For having sacrificed my life to the Church, it is not just that I be the plaything of sordid intrigues, the toy of the malevolence of a party that does not forgive me for not devoting to it my being and my priestly consecration. My Lord, I ask you for justice; I claim the only benefit of the priest, the only honor of the priest: freedom to preach Jesus Christ, up to the time when it has been established that I lack orthodoxy, which is the highest of all things, the one thing, with the help of God, I will never lack, at least not on purpose[48]."

No doubt, there was something of the man, something of the layman in that language. And yet, even though he left himself open to criticism by the explosion of a sensitivity perhaps all too human, and even though he did himself some harm by the way he did it— after all and basically, Lacordaire was in the right. He was justifiably offended by what was happening to him. In the face of this, his attitude toward his superior, it must be said, was not like the insufficiently virile behavior of our times. But many an example can be found in the early years and in the Middle Ages of men whom the Church has nonetheless placed on her altars. If the Catholic Religion is a great school of respect, it is also a great school of sincerity and consequently, of legitimate freedom in language. Nonetheless, de Quélen was far from being accustomed to such animation of tone on the part of his priests. He was doubly annoyed. On the one hand, after hoping to settle the matter in a friendly and indirect manner, he found himself obliged to answer a clear yes or no. On the other hand, he could not accept such a glaring failure, in his eyes, of priestly modesty. He saw in Lacordaire's letter a challenge — that was his term — and nothing could have hurt more the idea he had of the reverence due to archiepiscopal dignity. In spite of this, he got hold of himself and gave no hint, I am obliged to say, of any expression that was not moderate and generous. In this, he found his natural advantages. " In my diocese," said he, "I believe I am not only the judge of doctrine but also of the manner in which to teach religion, of the choice of mode according to circumstances, of the direction to be given to priests whom I assign to teaching — without being obliged to explain in detail, at every request I receive, the decision that had seemed appropriate to make on the matter. Persuaded as I am, after long and serious thought, that there could be more than one drawback in the resumption of the conferences *unless you first submit them in writing for preliminary review and correction*, otherwise, without this condition, I could not assent to allow you to begin anew nor to decide on giving you a canonical mission. The clerics whom I had chosen for the conferences at the cathedral did not recoil before this stipulation, and God blessed them."

The example was plausible but basically not conclusive since it was well-known that, precisely because they were written and learned by heart, the prepared sermons of the last lenten series at the cathedral had greatly failed. On that point, the most basic propriety prevented Lacordaire from responding. He wrote to de Quélen that, deprived of the word that he had consecrated to the service of God, he would have to consider placing for the benefit of Religion the single freedom with which he was left and that he saw nothing better than to publish in writing what he had proposed to teach in full voice. "I regret, My Lord," he added, "that you have judged my work without having known it. After a few days of bitterness against you, I gained the upper hand. I will no longer speak to you about it. I had relied on two men: the first, I left because he betrayed the hopes of everyone; the second failed me. I now rely only on God."

Those were sharp words, no doubt too sharp. Should we be surprised at them? This was the cry of an unrecognized fidelity, the cry of a man buried alive as his only reward for what he had done for the Church. It would have been more noble, more Christian to have suffered in silence; who can deny that? But when legitimate authority has been mistaken, who would not wish to tell it so in such a tone that it would come to regret its action and repair the error?

As expected, de Quélen did not reply. Only, a few days later, *l'abbé* Dupanloup went to Dumont, professor of history in Paris, with whom Lacordaire had ties. Dupanloup told Dumont that the will of the Archbishop in no way intended to restrict Lacordaire to a preliminary writing of his conferences since he could have purely and simply recited what he had written. He only had to have a general plan of the talks and a particular plan for each one, so as to follow the connections of the thoughts of the preacher in the exposition of Christian doctrine.

Lacordaire hurriedly wrote to the Prelate that, if these were his intentions, he admitted to have sincerely misunderstood them, but that he would joyfully comply. "I refused," he added, "to write and recite my conferences because it is impossible for me to recite what I wrote without losing oratorical power altogether. Speaking and writing are two very separate faculties for me; one cannot be exercised unless apart from the other. Far from withdrawing from episcopal oversight, I did not want my conferences to be published before they had been seen by *l'abbé* Carrière or *l'abbé* Affre[49]. Lacordaire then bound himself to submit in writing and leave in the hands of the Archbishop every Thursday the plan for the following Sunday's conference. In the meantime, he placed before the eyes of de Quélen the series of topics he intended to cover.

One must believe that in the interval between Dupanloup's communication and 24 November 1834, hostile suggestions had been given and had overcome the momentary regret of the Archbishop. Indeed, on 2 December, the latter unfortunately replied that he had authorized no one to speak in his name, and that he believed it to be his duty to stick to his letter of 5 November, declaring that, from the first, Lacordaire had not misunderstood him at all.

Affre who had done all he could to have Lacordaire's proposals accepted, received from de Quélen the difficult task of softening as much as possible the nature of the stand, from his viewpoint, he had taken against Lacordaire. "What should I tell the Archbishop from you?" the Vicar General asked, after completing his mission. "You can tell the bishop," Lacordaire replied, "that, considering myself alone, I am pleased not to have to preach my conferences any longer; that there will be for me greater advantage, tranquility, and honor in writing them down. Nonetheless, I regret to preach no longer because of the youth, who needed it, and because of the Church of France herself, which will be blamed for the rumor that has already spread: that no one with any talent can avoid being persecuted. The Archbishop had in me a simple and honorable means of refuting those disagreeable impressions; he sacrificed me without knowing the reason. And yet, even though I find some weakness in his behavior, I am not bitter at him." Affre had hoped that Lacordaire would show some regret for having written hastily. The invincible sincerity of the latter refused to make such a declaration. Affre did not insist[50].

I really meant to report everything about that painful incident. *Ne quid falsi dicere Historia, ne quid veri non audeat*[51]. Once more, it would have been more faultless on Lacordaire's part not to complain, even to the Archbishop. But whatever fairness can be attributed to the prevailing circumstances, de Quélen, from all that we have seen, does not appear to us as without weakness; in this, he had yielded, less because of his personal prejudices, however deeply-rooted they were, than because of the unceasing pressure of his attendants. What is about to follow will offer indisputable proof. In what he had replied to Affre, Lacordaire had indeed spoken of all this as History would in the future. It is truly good of History to speak of such past events so as to make them more rare in the future, if possible.

Besides, apart from the deep but legitimate emotion (we dare not deny it) which breaks through in the letters of Lacordaire to his bishop — emotion that would have been more heroically Christian to suppress completely, no doubt — the behavior of the young preacher during this trial was altogether admirable.

In fact, Mme Swetchine was in St. Petersburg; Lacordaire was fully abandoned to himself. For all that, in the isolation and given the blow of such an injustice, except for what he wrote to the Archbishop, he never grumbled. I have before my eyes all his letters to Buquet during this entire crisis:

they are completely blameless. Other letters, written in most secret intimacy, offer similar witness to Lacordaire's feelings. No trace of any bitterness whatsoever. "Obedience is costly," he wrote to Montalembert, "but I have learned from experience that sooner or later it is rewarded and that God alone knows what we need[52]." Enlightenment comes to him who submits as light comes to the man who opens his eyes[53]." — And to Mme Swetchine on 8 December: "Today, I am more than calm and happy. I have abandoned myself completely to Providence, which, up to now, has never been lacking and which knows better than I what is good for me. From a spiritual viewpoint, this docility is very useful for me before God. Perhaps I had judged La Mennais too severely and God wanted to make me feel by my personal experience how much, when it affects us directly, resignation is a very difficult choice. From a human viewpoint, persecution is always of benefit to those who suffer it with dignity. Perhaps also I would not have been able to settle down through my oral conferences; perhaps I have always uttered phrases subject to unpleasant interpretations, instead, by writing, everyone will appreciate my teaching and I will be no less helpful to the Church."

In fact, Lacordaire had started writing his conferences the previous winter and had dealt with a book dealer for their publication. He did not feel any less deeply how difficult and precarious his situation was. As he wrote later[54], his fate hung by a thread. If the Archbishop had persisted in his refusal, the very person of Lacordaire would *ipso facto* have been placed on the *index* [the list of forbidden books - Trans.]. Nothing could have saved him from this brink. His protests achieved nothing, given that his sincerity was suspect. Never, therefore, had he been closer to the abyss, never closer to complete downfall. He had considered withdrawing to the house of Mme Swetchine, who had made hints to that end. But God had other designs for him.

ENDNOTES

1. "The impious man, when he has reached the deepest part of the abyss, scorns it." — This is the inscription of the *Essay*.
2. Rue Neuve-Saint-Étienne-du-Mont, n° 6.
3. Letter to Lorain, 1 July 1833.
4. To Lorain, 24 February 1834.
5. See letter in the work by Rev. Father Chocarne, t. 1, 39.
6. Hippolyte Régnier.
7. Joseph Régnier.
8. Since then, Vicar General to Gerbet, at Perpignan, today pastor of Saint-Honoré in Paris.
9. Vicar-General of Paris, born at Châtillon-sur-Seine.
10. To Foisset, 25 August 1834.
11. To Montalembert, 8 September 1833.
12. To Montalembert, 15 February 1834.
13. To Montalembert, 25 August 1835.
14. To Lorain, 16 February 1833.

In the first letter of Lacordaire to Mme Swetchine (13 December 1833), we read: "I will continue, as we have agreed, the chapters *uniquely* related *to philosophy*; moreover, I will place a note at the bottom of the booklet that you have, so that, if an accident should happen, one would not believe that I had continued this work under the same intentions as before."

I have no doubt that the booklet in question was the first section of the book *The Church of the Nineteenth Century*. Perhaps this was what became the preliminary chapter of the *Considérations sur le système,* with this difference that apparently the original draft — concerning the school at La

Chênaie and the trip to Rome — dealt with personal explanations Lacordaire had to remove when he learned, on 12 December 1833, that the night before, La Mennais had submitted unconditionally to the Encyclical.

15. To Montalembert, 30 June 1833.
16. To Lorain, 18 December 1832.
17. To Lorain, 6 May 1833.
18. To Montalembert, 30 June 1833.
19. To Lorain, 6 May 1833.
20. To Lorain, 6 May 1833.
21. To Montalembert, 30 June 1833.
22. To Montalembert, 19 August 1833.
23. Subsequently, Vicar General of the Archbishop of Paris, then bishop of Parium.
24. To Montalembert, 20 January 1834.
25. *History of literature under the government of July*.
26. Letter to Lorain, 2 May 1834.
27. Bourdaloue, Louis, SJ (1632-1704): one of the most eminent French preachers; strong in reasoning, severe as regards morals.
28. Massillon, Jean-Baptiste (1663-1742): great French orator; much emotion in his sermons. Later bishop of Clermont.
29. See the eloquent letter of Lacordaire to de Quélen, of 21 March 1834: Appendix XV, page 548.
30. I say *the police* and not *the government*. Guizot, then Minister of Public Instruction, with whom Lacordaire obtained a meeting a bit later, stated to him that never had the Government harbored suspicions concerning the conferences at Stanislaus, and that he himself saw them with great satisfaction. (Lacordaire to Mme Swetchine, 8 December 1834.)
31. 14 April 1834. See Appendix XVI, page 553.

The letter ends with these words: "No knowing my faults nor my enemies, nor what is expected of me, as a child of the Church, I remain silent; I trust in God who sees the bottom of hearts and upholds those who have no other support on earth than an honorable conscience."

32. Lallier, today President of the Tribunal of Sens, and Lamache, Professor in the Law School of Strasbourg.

33. And not *13 February*, as was erroneously printed. The *Univers* of 14 January, which I have before me, leaves no room for doubt on this point.

34. Bautain, Louis-Eugène-Marie (1796-1867): philosopher and theologian; later condemned for a taint of *fideism* [reason cannot arrive at first principles except through faith].

35. Jouffroy, Théodore (1796-1842): French spiritual philosopher; introduced Scot philosophy to France.

36. Cousin, Victor (1797-1867): philosopher (eclectic school) and politician. He tried to combine ideas from Descartes, the Scot School, and Kant into a spiritualism that was more brilliant than solid.

37. See the names in note 41, below.

38. The note inserted in the *Letters* of Ozanam wrongly asserts that the Report was given to the Bishop on his first visit to the students.

39. Emery, Jacques-André (1732-1811): French theologian, Superior of the Sulpicians.

40. NOTICE.

41. Messrs Dupanloup, Pététot, Jammes, Annat, Veyssière, d'Assance, and Thibault, who died as bishop of Montpellier.

42. To Montalembert, 20 January 1834.

43. To Montalembert, 17 February 1834.

44. NOTICE.

45. Letter to Montalembert, 17 April 1834.

46. To Mme Swetchine, 14 October 1834.

47. *Histoire de monseigneur Affre* [History of Bishop Affre], par *L'Abbé* Castan, pages 72 and 74.

48. 31 October 1834. See Appendix XVII, page 556, for the entire letter.
49. 24 November 1834.
50. Lacordaire to Mme Swetchine, 8 December 1834.
51. Cicero, *de Oratore*, II, 15. "History will not say anything false, and nothing true will it not dare to say." [Trans.]
52. 12 November 1834.
53. 24 December 1834.
54. To Mme Swetchine, 15 September 1835.

Chapter VIII

FIRST CONFERENCES AT NOTRE-DAME

De Quélen unexpectedly offers Lacordaire the pulpit of Notre-Dame of Paris — Difficulties of the situation; advantages proper to Lacordaire; frame of minds — Subject of the conferences of 1835 — Nature of these conferences — The preacher's type of eloquence — Summary of the conferences of 1835 — Results of these conferences — They are disputed — Attitude of the Archbishop; Lacordaire appointed honorary canon of Paris — Death of his mother — Conferences of 1836 — Lacordaire retires to Rome; reasons for this decision.

In the month of January 1835, Lacordaire was crossing the Luxembourg Gardens. "I met," said he, "a cleric whom I knew fairly well; he stopped me and told me: 'What are you doing? You need to go see the Archbishop and settle things with him.' A few feet from there, another priest, less known to me than the first one stopped me also: 'You are wrong in not going to see the Archbishop; I have reason to believe that he would be very willing to speak with you.' This double invitation surprised me and, aware that I am somewhat superstitious in matters of Providence, I walked slowly toward

St. Michael Convent where the Archbishop was living.

"It was not the door-keeper who opened, but a Choir Sister, who was favorable to me, *because*, she said, *the whole world is against you*. From what she told me, the bishop was receiving absolutely no one, 'but,' she added, 'I will inform him and perhaps he will receive you.' The response was favorable.

"I found the archbishop pacing in his room, with a sad and troubled mien. He gave me a half-hearted greeting, and I began walking at his side, without his saying a word. After a rather long period of silence, he stopped abruptly, looked at me with a searching eye and said: 'I have the intention of entrusting you with the pulpit of Notre-Dame, would you accept it?' This sudden overture, whose source escaped me completely, in no way enraptured me. I replied that time was very short for me to prepare, that the location was rather impressive and that, after having been successful before a small audience, it would be easy to fail before a gathering of four thousand souls. The outcome was that I asked for twenty-four hours to think it over. After having prayed to God and consulted Mme Swetchine, I answered in the affirmative[1].

"What had happened? For several weeks, *l'abbé* Liautard, former superior at Stanislaus College, and at the time pastor at Fontainebleau, had arranged several weeks previously to have circulated among the clergy of Paris a written document in which he strongly accused the Archbishop's administration[2]. This bulletin was presented to the Archbishop on the very day of the scene I have just related; he had just finished reading it at the hour when Providence sent me to him. To be sure, in that incriminating piece, the conferences of Stanislaus were mentioned; moreover, in it the Archbishop was accused of lack of intelligence and of weakness in his conduct towards me. I have no idea whether he had previously thought of opening the pulpit of Notre-Dame to me; but when he saw me arrive at the very moment when he was greatly affected by the judgment of his administration by an intellectual, it is quite possible that this coincidence — almost marvelous, so unexpected was it — struck him like a warning from God; a lightning bolt crossed his mind and showed him that, in my promotion to the cathedral pulpit for the conferences, lay a brilliant response to his personal enemies.

"When he made known his decision on my account to his entourage, he was surprised at the little opposition he encountered. This was so, because my adversaries with whom he was surrounded, hoped that this triumph would be the occasion of my fall, persuaded as they were that I had neither the theological resources nor the oratorical abilities to sustain me in a task that needed both to a high degree[3]. They did not know that for fifteen years I had never stopped giving myself over to serious philosophical and theological studies and that, also for fifteen years, I had exercised the ministry of the word in the most varied places."

The condition of having first to write down the full conferences was no longer required, but the Preacher had to submit an outline to one of the Vicars General of the diocese, among whom the Archbishop allowed him to choose. The speaker chose Affre.

For Lacordaire, as for the Archbishop, the test was no less frightening.

As the Prince Albert de Broglie said, this was 1835, that is to say, during a lull of relative calm, during a moment of truce between revolutions. But we were barely recovering from the terrible war that, under the senior branch of the Bourbons, the spirit of political opposition had inflicted on the Church, in the name of freedom. During all of fifteen years, from one end of France to the other, everything had become a weapon against Christianity: the rostrum, the press, public instruction. Moreover, according to the remark by Lacordaire, in a calamity worthy of tears, no somewhat popular voice was raised in favor of Christ. It is not that, under the Restoration, the Catholic cause lacked orators and writers. But all of them had marched, banners unfurled, in the opposite direction than that which carried away the nation. The voice of Vicount Bonald, that of Count de Maistre, that of La Mennais before 1830, reached the crowds as menacing echoes of a past that had been rendered hateful to them. From this viewpoint, it is true, Chateaubriand shone as the exception, but he was alone. Besides, more occupied with politics than with religion, he filled his old age with impotent protests in favor of a lost cause, that he disavowed inadequately, all the while pretending to serve it. Near these capable minds without influence or power, the Church of France, as a last misfortune, had a host of those defenders who *exaggerated the theses, thinking to make them stronger,* and who, with the best of intentions of saving everything, were compromising even God himself, as if He could be compromised[5].

Consider the lot of the young generations placed between these two camps. They left their childhood only to despise or hate the Church, and as the summit of destruction, freedom — running ahead of them — veiled with its generous image the impiety that was devouring them[6].

This is where France stood in 1834.

In the midst of generations prepared in this way, what a miracle it would be for religious truth to regain popularity! Well it did! This miracle took place before our very eyes. Never, I feel it, never will those who did not live before and after 1835 will be able to imagine this passage from one period to another. "For us," wrote Lacordaire, "who belonged to one or the other period, who saw the contempt, and who saw the honor — our eyes water with involuntary tears on thinking about it — we kneel in thanksgiving before Him Who *is incredible in his gifts*[7]."

From a human viewpoint — we must not tire of repeating it — humanly speaking, nothing served truth better, nothing contributed more to its triumph than to have it be proclaimed by a genuine son of the nineteenth century, fully reared in the school of modern thought, strongly faithful to all generous ideas, to all the noble feelings of his country and of his times, having lived through the errors of the period without defiling himself, and attacking them head on without insults and without curses. Who can be surprised at this? To get a handle on men, is there not a need to know and understand them, to speak their language, to have some points of resemblance to them? Even the faults of Lacordaire in his political life seem to have been allowed only to give the orator of Notre-Dame a personal and powerful effect on a great number of souls misled by the contemporary liberalism. "God," as he himself said, " had prepared us for this task by allowing us to have lived rather many years in forgetfulness of his love, carried along those same paths which He destined us to retake, one day, in the opposite direction. As a result, to speak as we have done, we had need of only a little memory and of hearing, and in the depths of our being, to keep in touch with the spirit of a period we had all liked very much[8]."

From more than one viewpoint, the hour was favorable. The school of Saint-Simon had just gone up in smoke, but not before shaking up greatly deep topics as well as numerous minds. Cousin, who, for his part, not long ago did not arouse any great expectations, had just left his chair, filled with the hidden feelings of his doctrinal impotency. His school, worn out at birth, seems to have been preserved to demonstrate how philosophies terminate. The time seemed to have come for the Church to take the word, in her turn, and to announce to Athens the *unknown God*[9].

Never before, in the ages of faith, had the pulpit of Notre-Dame seen at its base so many feet of assembled men as the first time when Lacordaire was due to appear there. Six thousand hearers pressed each other in the confines of the long nave[10]. The women were driven back to the side naves.

No doubt this was no longer the audience of Bordaloue and of Bossuet, an audience that was Christian by birth and by education; Christian by family tradition and by all the habits of public and private life; an audience wrapped, almost imbued, even in its worldly elements, with a wholly Christian atmosphere. Lacordaire's was less an audience than a populace and of a strange mixture at that: the leftovers of the eighteenth century, students from the central schools of the *Directoire* or those of the imperial University brushed shoulders with the young men of Ozanam's and Montalembert's age. Those who had grown up under the regime of godless men, at a time when France no longer knew public worship; those of the generation that followed (reared for war and by war), in a word, the offspring of a de-Christianized France were undoubtedly in the majority — and that is what should never be forgotten.

"The day having arrived," Lacordaire takes up his story, "Notre-Dame was filled with a multitude such as it had never seen before. Liberal and *absolutist* youth, friends and enemies, and that crowd of curious persons which a major capital always keeps at the ready for any novelty, had come in tight waves into the venerable cathedral. I went up into the pulpit, not without emotion, but with steadiness, and I began my presentation, my eyes fixed on the Archbishop, who was for me, after God, but before the public, the most important person in that scene. He listened to me, head slightly bowed, perfectly impassive, like a man who is not simply a spectator or a judge, but who ran some personal risks in this solemn adventure. When I got settled in my topic and beheld my audience, my lungs expanded in the need to grasp such a vast assembly of men, there escaped from me one of those gasps which, when one is sincere and intense, never fails to touch. The Archbishop trembled visibly; a pallor which even I could see covered his face. He raised his head and gave me a stunned look. I realized that the battle had been won in his mind, as it was won in the audience. After returning home, he announced that he was going to name me an honorary canon of his cathedral. With difficulty did I restrain him and make him wait until the end of the series."

The cry to which Lacordaire refers, was preserved for us in the written copy. "Assembly, assembly, what are you asking of me? What do you want from me? The Truth?... Of course, because you do not have it within you! You seek it, then; you wish to receive it You came here to be instructed."

That cry, I think I hear it coming from the soul and the chest of Lacordaire. I can imagine the surprise — I almost said the fear — of de Quélen, that unbending representative, that restless guardian of tradition, so opposed to the unexpected anywhere, but nowhere, to be sure, so much as in the pulpit. I see his face blanch at that sudden outburst of voice, at that unexpected expression, at this taking hold of a part of the audience by the preacher. Yet, how promptly was he reassured when seeing this diverse audience shudder as one man at this jolt of electricity! As Lacordaire said, the battle was won all along the line; the new preaching had just won its letters of adoption beneath these time-honored arches. de Quélen was won over like everyone else; from then on, this successor of Maurice de Sully felt proud of the modern eloquence of the young fellow, countryman of St. Bernard.

Besides, what those six thousand men assembled in the venerable cathedral wanted, as Prince de Broglie said, Lacordaire knew better than they themselves did.

"All that France had been seeking for forty years of effort since 1789: free institutions, popular royalty, equality in law as in behavior, power tested in competition and won brilliantly by the most worthy — all these goods belonged to the French society. It had all the hopes for them but not yet the satisfaction. The happiness of gaining them was mixed with the pride of having conquered them. And yet, neither of these feelings satisfied France. In full freedom and complete rest, interests were worried and imaginations ill. Noble instincts, aspirations toward the infinite from which no soul can break away, did not know where to choose in the scattering of public beliefs.

"This is what brought to the foot of Lacordaire's pulpit most of the people who came to hear him and who raised their eyes to him in a vague hope of finding solace. This priest had emerged from the new century and was known to like it still. He had partaken of its illusions: would he understand the suffering? Would he be able to name its unknown sickness, to heal it?

"Lacordaire believed he could and was willing to try; This was the authority and the attraction of his *Notre-Dame Conferences*. In his eyes, the sickness had a name and an origin that he defined in two words: The old society, he used to say, perished because God had been expelled from it; the new one is suffering because God has not sufficiently entered into it[11]. To make God enter into the modern society, that was the remedy. Lacordaire did not have the pride to think that such a glory belonged to one man; but it was a work in which he thought it possible to contribute[12]." His mission was to "*prepare* souls to receive the faith[13]." Never did he claim any other.

Unfortunately, de Quélen had been late in making his decision. Seven weeks: a short time to choose the topic for the Conferences of Notre-Dame, to develop an outline and to arrange all its components. Lacordaire decided to treat of the Church. This fundamental thesis had often occupied his thoughts. He felt that this was the topic for which he was best prepared. We remember that when he left La Chênaie, he needed ten years to write his *l'Église et le Monde du dix-neuvième siècle* [The Church and the World in the Nineteenth Century]. Later, he wanted to consider successively the Church in the philosophical order, in the political order, in the moral order, in dogmatic order — moving him to write: "This is a task for an entire life[14]."

It has been said that this is not the logical order to follow in the controversy about Christianity; that first, one must prove the need for a revelation, then the historical certitude of the evangelical revelation, and only in third place, the divine institution of the Church by Jesus Christ. This objection does not bother me very much. To be sure, apologetics is perfectly free to change this ordering.

Did not St. Augustine himself say: "We see the Church; may the name of the Church lead us to believe in Jesus Christ, whom we do not yet see[15]."

Before anything else, an audience had to be assembled and made to listen. The nineteenth century, as we know, did not have any taste for abstractions; it asked for facts. Tested by political revolutions, it was occupied especially with political and social problems. To ask it for fifteen minutes of attention, as *l'abbé* Perreyve remarked, one had to say to it: Christianity is also a society, and a society, just like you, deals with the dignity, the freedom, the happiness of men. Christ is also a legislator; the Gospel is also a constitutional charter. Who does not see an opportunity in such a plan?

Besides, it was necessary, first of all, to shake up the anti-Christian prejudices, to bring about the awakening of minds. Lacordaire's work, as he himself said, being a *preparation*, and not an *evangelical demonstration*[16], who can blame him for having taken a program that offered greater flexibility to his freedom as orator?

These were not sermons but Conferences (namely, loose conversations), that suited the audience of 1835. Never were those splendid impromptu talks better characterized than by Lacordaire's successor at the French Academy. "Bold generalities, better suited to open great vistas than to befit rigorous demonstrations; the dogma expressed, not in its deepest mysteries, but in its relationship with the needs and the history of humanity, *depicted*, so to speak, *from the outside by its external frame* — and yet, here and there, full days reserved *so that attention could peer more into its depths*; comparisons sometimes strained, but *always gripping*; few quotations from Sacred Scripture but a clever and *unexpected* application, many references to memories of ordinary life and education, from those of classical antiquity to those of revolutionary and imperial France; — a constant greatness in his thoughts, preserved from pomposity by an expression whose character was not without some forethought; at long intervals, a familiar expression, a contemporary neologism which allows the hearer a moment of rest, novice in theology as he was, and even to give him the same kind of pleasure a traveler in a distant land experiences on hearing suddenly the language of his birthplace; sometimes, finally, outbursts of feelings, statements about his unfaithful youth, appeals from the heart, more sharp than tender, like the cry of the shepherd who calls back the sheep that has strayed. The result of this mixture was a preaching very abundant in contrasts, most unexpected in its witticisms, composed so as to charm the crowd, *the most impossible to predict and to imitate there ever was.*

"The effect was boundless. The holy word seemed to have left the Church and go out, as in the days of Christ, to find toll collectors in the noisy midst of their business or of their banquets! Christianity from which that generation thought it was so removed, reappeared beside it and within its reach. It found again Christianity's erased marks behind its customs, its monuments, its laws, even in its thoughts, and cried out, like the pilgrim in the Bible awaking from his sleep: Truly, God was here and I did not know it.

"On youth, especially, the impression was intense. What beguiled it was not only the innovation of a preaching *full of hope,* that did not condemn youth like others for trying to attempt the idle fancy of a return to a past little wept over. It was also the pleasure of finding, while listening to him, a harmony between all the noble feelings of which that confident age had need... There we were, divided, since childhood, from preoccupations and habits; these were brought to Church by a hereditary faith, those by a curious doubt; some having learned to read through the pageantry of the crusades, others through bulletins of the Republic and of the Empire; others, finally, (fewer in number but no less convinced) through the Charter and its first masterpieces of parliamentary eloquence. *L'abbé* Lacordaire had words for everyone of us and brought us back to a common center; at one moment, he gave us immediate hope, at another, the illusion of unanimity[17].

"This is enough to explain the success of the preaching. As for the preacher, how can he be described? How to relive what has been extinguished forever, those noble and fine traits that no portrait could reproduce, the dark and deep eyes, but especially that transfigured face, that inspired gesture, that look full of lightning bolts, that penetrating and very personally moved voice which at one time shot a word like an arrow of fire throughout the holy place, at another a voice from his innards, a tone of voice that troubled the orator himself, one that he did not know he had[18]. Ah, yes! as Montalembert said, that tone which he himself did not recognize nor did we. No one among us had ever heard anything like it, and among those who heard it, no one will ever forget it."

Father Lacordaire had sublime eloquence to the highest degree: the sudden emotion, heartfelt, accessible, exciting. Topping off the rapture of the audience was the receipt and the return of the spark; it was to assist at the spontaneity (if impossible to deny) of the preacher, to the unceasing gush, sudden and yet controlled, of his word as of his thought; it was to see "spring from a priestly breast, as from the rock struck by the divine rod, a bubbling stream, powerful like a torrent in the Alps." Who else will offer us these surprises, this boldness, these informalities, those adventurous spurts, whereby a talent, bold and sure of himself, made light of skirting the edge of the cliff without ever falling off it, then of soaring into the heavenly heights with a spring that only Bossuet had surpassed in the French pulpit? Lacordaire literally enraptured his hearers; he left them seized by an emotion that only one word can express, this word *ravished*, so vulgarly abused, but which, when applied here, reminds us of the miraculous ecstasies of St. Paul: *Quoniam raptus est in Paradisum*[19].

Like all spontaneous speakers, he did not always follow his thought to its conclusion. His outlines leave much to be desired; but the genius that conceived and distributed the Summa of St. Thomas was not something Lacordaire needed for his mission. He was not thorough; what good would it do to deny it? But then, who is ever thorough? God is Master of His gifts; He gives them and parcels them out as He pleases.

Must one accuse His Providence? The Church has more than one kind of worker; she has some of every character, formed by that Spirit which blows where it will, which gives without measure, but with *apportionment*, that makes "some apostles, others prophets, these evangelists, those pastors and teachers, finally, using everything holy for the ministry that builds up the body of Christ[20]."

Among the workers of the Church in the nineteenth century, Lacordaire's place, however incomplete it is said to be, is — without a doubt — not inferior to any other. As for ourselves, it is sufficient for us to know that God did this purposely to found all by Himself that great Catholic institution, the Conferences of Notre-Dame of Paris. I say *by Himself*. In fact, there were indeed other eminent successors to the cathedral pulpit; no one, not one of them could have *created* that audience which Lacordaire had spring from the ground in 1835, and which lives on even to this day. That glory, whatever anyone does, remains exclusively his.

Who remembers the last Christian orators of the Massilon school, de Boulogne, the preacher most extolled of the Church of France under the Empire, Father de Maccarthy, so admired, and rightly so, in the final years of the Restoration? Who has read them, what do we know about them, other than their name? One could compare their oratorical works with tragedies poured into the mold of Racine. They did contain well-composed phrases, delightful passages, well-balanced periodic sentences, but no effect that was not known and too-well known, nothing or almost nothing that was unforeseen, and consequently already stale; the conventional everywhere, spontaneity nowhere. All that, as has often been said, had seen its time, was worn out and powerless. Something else was needed for Catholic youth, of which Ozanam was the example; something completely different for that other youth, disinherited of faith, who filled the schools of that great capital of the modern world; something altogether different for that dissimilar and indifferent public that I painted a while ago. What all of them needed was certainly Lacordaire with his background and — dare I say it? — even with his defects, but also with the two truly incomparable gifts God had given him. It was Lacordaire and no one else. Only he could teach the road of the Church to so many men who had so completely forgotten it or had never known about it. This is what was needed before anything else: *Quomodo credent si non audiant*[21]?

And now, may I be allowed to retrace the major lines of these first conferences of Notre-Dame, those of 1835?

We remember that the unbelieving Lacordaire was first of all touched by the social and historical evidence of Christianity. We remember that in the first days of his conversion, he wrote to Lorain (15 March 1824): "I came to Catholic beliefs through my social beliefs. Today, nothing seems better demonstrated than this conclusion: Society is necessary, therefore the Christian religion is divine because it is the unique means to bring society to perfection, by taking man with all his weaknesses and the social order with all its circumstances." It is from this angle that he liked to have faith penetrate into minds, and the following is how he proceeded.

Man is a being who needs to be taught. This is also true of man as a child; it is also true of people, that is to say, of almost all the human race. But what is there that human teaching agrees on? Let us not leave that capital, the county seat, it is said, of human civilization; count the teachings which for eighty years have had their passage, and from there spread throughout Europe. And so, either truth is only a word or man is but a plaything of opinions that follow each other unceasingly, or else there has to be on earth a permanent divine authority which teaches man, that being who needs to be taught, and who is necessarily misled by the teaching of man. — By what sign will this authority be recognized? By this sign that no false authority possesses, that no one can counterfeit: the sign of universality. If there is one remarkable thing in this world it is that no human authority has been able to cross the borders of a certain class of men or of a certain nationality. Only the Catholic Church has established a universal authority, despite the unspeakable difficulty of the task. Thus, the Catholic Church has been established by God to teach men[22].

Now, no one has the right to teach unless he is certain of what he teaches, and no one has the right to require faith in what he teaches unless he is infallible. Moreover, the Catholic Church is altogether certain, historically, from her institution by God, and infallible in the transmission of that divine revelation with whose deposit she has been entrusted. — The moral authority of a teaching body rests on two conditions: knowledge and virtue. These two conditions are found in the Catholic Church and only in her do they reside. The Church has knowledge: it sprang in knowledge, in a century praised above others by its enlightenment, the century of Augustus. She preserved knowledge in the days of the barbarians; she remained faithful to that knowledge when false knowledge rose up against the faith. Neither in the pagan religions nor in Islam is there a place for knowledge. It is true that the Christian sects, by cutting themselves off from the Church carried along knowledge under their coat, but they are devoured by it. The scabbard was not strong enough and was worn down by the sword. The Church was the only one able to resist false lights. In the second place, the Church possesses virtue; her teaching itself is a virtue. Non-Christian religions, on the contrary, are sensual religions. As for the Christian sects, there is some good in their heart and it is not altogether in vain that they honor Jesus Christ. Neither the Russian Empire nor the entire

Protestant powers together were able to produce a Sister of Charity. Not one of the Christian sects has known virtue to a heroic degree, to the degree that produces saints. Where, then, is the teaching whose authority can be compared to that of the Church? — Nonetheless, it is not sufficient for the Church to be certain of its mission and of its divine institution; it is not sufficient that she have, for herself and for the others, an incomparable moral authority; she needs also to be infallible. Because, if she were to be wrong only once, the minds that it is her mission to teach, would remain as judges of the issue to learn if, in any given case, she had not erred. She would then cease to be effectively a teaching authority in the name of God. The Catholic Church is the only one who dared to pronounce herself infallible; in fact, it was to her, and to her alone, that it was said: *I am with you until the end of time*. But it is one thing to label oneself infallible; if one is really not infallible, nothing can prevent variations and contradictions in teaching that arise from different opinions. Infallibility is greatly obvious in the Catholic Church by an indestructible constancy in her beliefs and in her moral teaching, despite the differences of time, place, and people. This is a privilege reserved for the Church. And this privilege of the Church is most necessary for men since it is the unique means that can be imagined for the primitive union of man to truth, reestablished by Jesus Christ, to be maintained on the earth. If there is something unusual in this, it is not because the truth was given by God to the human race in a teaching that could not fall into error, but because the teaching could be misunderstood despite our need for it[23].

Here, an objection arises: If a teaching Church is necessary, why was it established so late? The answer is simple. The Church, it is true, under its definitive form, dates only from Jesus Christ; but taken in her essence and her total reality, she began with the human race, according to that strong expression of St. Epiphanius: "The beginning of everything is the Holy Catholic Church." In her essence, the Church is the society of minds with God by faith, hope, and charity. Now, as regards man, that society was founded as soon as man left the hands of God. From the beginning, the original Church had her priesthood, her sacrifices, her laws, her teaching. From the beginning, the human race believed in God as creator, legislator, and savior. It is the extreme boundary of light in this world, just as the final goal of goodness is the imitation of God manifested by creation and redemption. From the beginning, God taught men through conscience and tradition. Tradition is like a river; five times in forty centuries, God opened the source or widened its shores by Adam, Noah, Abraham, Moses, Jesus Christ. At each earthquake of tradition, it was impossible not to listen and not to hear. Accordingly, God has constantly seen to the teaching of the world, before Jesus Christ as well as after Him — not always to the same degree, but always sufficiently enough so that salvation was everywhere possible for men of good will. What are, then, the necessary conditions for salvation? There are three: to live the truth to the degree that we know it; to embrace a superior truth as soon as it is possible to know it; to die while loving God above all things. With those, our fate is in our hands. It is not that God is lacking to man, it is that man is lacking to God[24].

Accordingly, there was always on earth an authority that perpetuated divine revelation by a divinely established teaching. That authority is the Catholic Church.

All authority implies a hierarchy, that is to say, a group of men organized to act for the same goal, and a power that this hierarchy possesses and uses as it wishes. From this arises the apostolate, an institution exclusively proper to the Catholic religion; namely, the choice of a certain number of men sent throughout the world to teach it the truth. Pagans enclosed priestly knowledge within their temples; philosophers confined their teaching to the interior of the school. Jesus Christ was the first and the only to say: "Go, teach all nations, preach the good news to every human creature." There you have it for universality. But who will retain in one bundle, in one teaching those scattered apostles? No bundles without a binder, no durable universality without unity. From this there arises a central apostolate, a unique chief given by Jesus Christ to His apostles and to their successors, the bishops — one spiritual head for the entire universe. Indeed, that thought was more than new and bolder than that of the apostolate. Yes, this was something new, bold, impossible, but it did come to be. And yet the Church was not complete. To the apostles, there had to be numerous associates who could directly and habitually communicate with the ordinary faithful, offer for them the Holy Sacrifice, administer the sacraments, break for everyone, without respite, the bread of the word of God. From this came the presbyterate. Thus constituted, the Church has the unity of a monarchy, the expansive action of a democracy, and between the two, the temperament of a strong aristocracy (free from the spirit of caste, inherent in the aristocracy of blood). In this way, the Church joined the unity which coordinates, the action which extends, the moderation which keeps the unity from becoming absolute, and the action from making itself independent; a perfect economy that man never before had because in all human governments the three elements of power had always sought to destroy each other by reason of man's passions. This was the hierarchy that was founded to insure forever the destinies of truth. — But what power would this hierarchy wield? In the world, there are two powers: force, and persuasion. Which of the two was given to the Church? It was not force, it was persuasion. Persuasion is first based on reason. The Church, therefore, possesses the highest reason under the heavens: she ought to be and is the highest metaphysical power, the highest historical power, the highest moral power, the highest social power there is in the world. — The *highest metaphysical power*: for all problems of a supernatural order, Catholic theology has the most rational, the most sublime solutions before which could not hold fast the religious and philosophical teachings proposed in various times.

The highest historical power: we are the only ones who follow the chain of periods up to the first link, up to the first man; we have our tradition, our book, and, as witness to that tradition, as guardian of the book, an everlasting people. The priest cannot speak anywhere without calling to mind an eternal man, a Jew, who rises to say: Yes, it is true; I was there. — *The highest moral power*: the Church is chaste, and chastity is the beloved sister of truth. It is because we possess this virtue that we are steadfast. They know well what they do those who attack the celibate clergy, this crown of Christian priesthood. — *The highest social power*: the Catholic Church has carried to the highest level the respect for power by the people, and the respect of people by power. — But for that to happen, the Church needed a more general power: God granted his Church the great power of love, He gave her charity. And now, just how long will you work for passing things and fight against those that last? You repeat endlessly: We cannot allow the Church free rein because she will become too powerful. That is to say: we must stifle the persuasion that will dominate us in spite of ourselves. What else can you say that witnesses better to the divinity of the Church[25]?

No Church without unity. Evidently, the foundation of that unity on the shifting earth of the world must have been the object of significant work by God. The idea of the Papacy implies two inseparable correlatives: spiritual supremacy, temporal independence. — spiritual supremacy always visible, temporal independence always obvious. Unity without spiritual supremacy? A delusion! Supremacy without temporal independence, this means enslavement of truth locked in a single man, and that one man, handed over to the mercy of the emperor, to a republic, or to any other human power. — To the supremacy of St. Peter, instituted by Jesus Christ, there was need of a seat, Rome. But at Rome then and for three centuries, where was the independence? That could not remain the normal state of the Church. All at once, Caesar becomes a Christian, and with that (admire the work of Providence), with that, never again will a prince have his headquarters in Rome. There would be emperors in Ravenna and Milan; there would be kings of the Goths in Ravenna, kings of the Lombards in Pavia; in Rome, neither emperor nor king will rule. Is that not remarkable? Before long, the sovereignty of the Pope appears striking in the presence of Attila and of Genseric. Pepin and his Franks made of this moral sovereignty a temporal one. Later, in vain did the German emperors want to see the pope a simple vassal of the empire. Gregory VII resisted. He died in exile, defeated in appearance but rewarded in the future by the freedom of the Church, which had been the goal of his life. And yet, it is dangerous to flourish even with the help of justice and donations. One reaction disclosed itself and filled the last five centuries of history. Let us hope that it is reaching its end. The bark of St. Peter, if we are looking at one point in the span of centuries, often seems ready to disappear, and we are always ready to cry out: *Lord, save us; we are perishing!* But if we look at the span of the ages, the Church appears in all her power. Then we understand the words of Jesus during the storm: *O man of little faith, why did you doubt*[26]?

Next, the sequence of ideas leads us to examine the relationships between the Church and the temporal order. When the Church entered the world, she found only one authority, civil authority. Caesar was the Supreme Pontiff. Now, in entering the world, the Church had no less a demand than this: to raise, next to the civil power, a permanent purely spiritual power. This she did; and from then on, these two powers marched side by side, now supporting each other, now fighting each other, now indifferent.

But by what right was the power of the Church established?

The Church did not give itself its mission, but received it from on high. The mission of the Church is sketched by those celebrated words: *Go, teach all nations, baptizing them in the name of the Father, and of the Son, and of the Holy Spirit; teach them to keep the commandments that I have given you.* That is to say: Teach the truth, spread grace, see to it that virtue is practiced. Entrusted with spreading truth, grace, and virtue, the Church, cannot accomplish this mission except by using four means: unhampered preaching of the faith, freedom of worship, free administration of the sacraments, and free exercise of virtue. None of this can be accomplished without a clergy that ceaselessly announces the truth, calls for grace, arouses to virtue, and, consequently, without the unimpeded perpetuity of the priestly hierarchy. And so, when someone asks by what right the Church has refused to grant Caesar spiritual power, it is as if one were to ask by what right Christian freedom established itself.

No one can forget with what wavering of the voice, with what gleam of the eye, with what radiant pride of the heart, whose effects nothing else can produce, Lacordaire cried out: "By what right did Christian freedom establish itself? I reply, first of all, by divine right. It was not the Caesars but Jesus Christ who said: *Go and teach all nations.* We do not owe our freedom to the Caesars, we owe it to God, and we will not lose it because it comes from Him. The princes could well join together to struggle against the prerogatives of the Church, giving them disgraceful names so as to make them odious; we will let them speak and we will continue to preach the truth, to combat vice, to communicate the spirit of God. If they send us into exile, we will continue to do this in exile; if they throw us into prison, we will do it in prison; if they banish us from one kingdom, we will pass into another. It was said to us that, until the day when everyone will have to render an account of his deeds, we will not run out of earthly kingdoms. But if we are banished from everywhere, if the power of the Antichrist gets to spread over the entire face of the world, then, as in the beginning of the Church, we will flee into the tombs and the catacombs. Finally, if we are pursued even there, if we are made to mount a scaffold — in the very noble heart of man, we will find the ultimate asylum because we have not despaired of the truth, of justice, and of the freedom of the human race."

Moreover, the orator proved that Christian freedom comes from the natural law, since it is only the means to spread truth, grace, virtue — which cannot be ripped from man. With undeniable eloquence, he used to say: "Virtue! What rights could one have against virtue? Man is born for the good; this is more than his right, it is his duty. I wish to be humble, kind, chaste; who has any right against humility, kindness, and chastity? I wish to abandon the clothes of the rich and, out love, don those of the poor; who has a right against modest and friendly clothing? I wish to sell my inheritance and distribute it to the suffering members of Jesus Christ and of humanity; who has the right to place guards around a heart that opens itself and to forbid charity? ... Let us be frank, Gentlemen; we can quarrel about truth; here on earth, it is subject to the disputes of men. Then again, if Christianity were not free by reason of truth, it would be by reason of virtue."

Pursuing his demonstration, Lacordaire established that whoever attacks the Church attacks our freedom; I do not say only our political and civil freedom, but also our moral freedom, that which makes us men. Moreover, as regards the dignity of man, the establishment of the Church has been a benefit whose marvel is evident more than ever. With the establishment of the Church, civil power has lost control over human thought and is no longer master of divine laws. Religion subsists on its own, by its proper life and independence, counter-balancing by its influence all the excessive influences that would otherwise tend to prevail and to oppress the people. As for the debates that arise between two powers concerning sensitive matters, a source of understanding can be had through concordats. There is something remarkable in this, that the Church, not having an armed force at her disposal, can never coercively impose an injustice. Accordingly, there can be no reason for defiance or hatred against the Church because of her conclusive establishment in the midst of society[27].

Can we admit that the Church also possesses coercive power? In fact, no power can be imagined without sovereignty, that is to say, without being independent of those whom it governs. The coercive power of the Church is nothing more than the right to govern with independence the divine matters for which God has made her the depositor. It is in the nature of things that every wrong brings about woe to the one who commits it: this misfortune is the penalty. But is the penalty to be sterile vengeance? Not at all. The penalty must lead to the improvement of the guilty person and, at the same time, to reparation for the wrong; from this, it follows that, in the present order, the penalty is imperfect unless it be a mixture of justice and mercy. Now only the Church possesses the complete penalty, because she alone has the secret of penalties that foster rehabilitation. The first is the admission, the voluntary admission; the second is the penance. If one had come to say to Augustus, strolling in his garden with Horace or Mecenas: There is a man there with a beggar's bag and a walking stick, who says he was sent by God to listen to the admission of your faults, would not Augustus have taken this man for a fool? Well! That folly has prevailed. — As for excommunication, that penalty is simultaneously just and merciful; *just,* because every association rests on reciprocal obligations, and participation in the rights of the group presupposes participation in its duties; *merciful,* because without violence it can bring back the guilty. Besides, this is also the exercise of a high level of freedom. Whoever does not have the freedom to refuse his service is a slave. The Theodosius need to know that they will find some Ambrose who, seeing them covered with blood from Thessalonika, will wait for them in the doorway and tell them: You have soldiers, you can force open the doors of the temple, but if you enter, I leave. The freedom to leave, this is the first freedom of the man of heart; pity the one who does not have it!

One could object to Lacordaire that the Church, to have her laws enforced, accepted the collaboration of the secular arm. He answers, without bending history before the Gospel, nor the Gospel before history. First of all, he reminds us of St. Gregory the Great's words: "It is a new and unheard of preaching to demand faith by suffering!" Faith has to be embraced voluntarily and by persuasion; it cannot be motivated by violence. This is the teaching of the Church, defined by the Council of Toledo in a decree added by the Popes in the body of Canon Law. Nonetheless, is civil authority not able to use severity, not to convert, not to obtain the faith, but to prevent any and all exterior manifestation against the faith? In the Middle Ages, this was the law among European societies. Who does not notice how much this second question differs from the first? In fact, if civil society wishes to make the truth the fundamental law of the State, this is its right. Is it not the right of every society to set itself up freely under the yoke of certain laws? Really, if there is a lofty, strong idea, worthy of man, it is to adopt the truth as the fundamental law. Accordingly, the Church has accepted this order of things; she believed that unity was a benefit for the entire world as well as for herself. She rejoiced in creating with the State an empire wherein the differences between the powers resulted in a greater harmony and a more profound unity. She does not deny this. Were it only a utopia, it would still be an attractive wonderland. But the human passions that respected this state of affairs in antiquity, because religion was in error at the time, have attacked it in modern times because religion was untainted, holy, and true. The passions were victorious; civil society, profoundly divided, today rests on a completely contrary principle, the full and entire freedom of cults. May this freedom be more than an empty word, and the Church obtain from error the peaceful and full exercise of her spiritual rights, that is to say, the right to persuade the human race[28]!

I am not sure, but it seems to me that there was something more in those words; that there is in what we have just read a consequence, something of logic and something of theology. It seems to me that this teaching (very new, I agree) did not, after all, lack soundness, and that, however genuine it was at the time, it has not aged very much since then.

Much has been said that Lacordaire never converted anyone. Listen to a hearer of these first conferences, who later became a bishop. "Each year, now, below the arches of the cathedral of Paris, thousands of men, on Easter day, kneel at the holy table. Ask them what made them Christian. Many will answer you that the first spark that ignited their faith was the lightning that sprang from that man[29]." Listen to Lacordaire himself, on leaving for Rome in 1836: "I was disturbed by the sorrow in abandoning all those young persons, many of whom had offered me so much trust and attachment. I felt sorry for this beginning flock[30]." And later on: "Up to that point, my life had been spent in study and in argument; by the Conferences, it entered into the mysteries of the apostolate.... It was at Notre-Dame, at the foot of the pulpit, that I saw emerge a gratitude for which no natural quality could be the source, and which attached the convert to the apostle by bonds whose gentleness is as divine as their strength. I did not know all those souls attached to mine by the remembrance of a light *newly-found* or increased; every day, I receive more proofs whose warmth surprises me[31]."

And yet, however brilliant was the success of the Conferences of 1835 among men of the world, the elder clergy could not accustom themselves to this unprecedented preaching, to this unusual and almost lay method of treating Religion in a priestly pulpit. Without citing specifics, without directly attacking any propositions of the preacher, they protested in general terms against the inexact theology of his language. Strangely enough, he was reproached for having studied too exclusively the Fathers of the Church, while neglecting the latest oracles of the School, Bellarmine and Suarez[32]. He was accused especially for speaking of religious matters in a spirit that was *too modern*. He replied: "I know where I want to get in the soul of my hearers, and I do believe that I reach there sometimes. My audience feels the light, is disposed to receive it. With the attractive lines of scholastic architecture, while saying the same things, I would leave them indifferent. The day when I abandon my method, I will be a man lost[33]." He was speaking rightly; but it was not given to those men of yesteryear to understand him.

Jealousy, a spirit of rivalry, but especially prejudice (I know whereof I speak), played a great part in that chorus of outcries and accusations. The legitimists pursued in Lacordaire the shadow of *l'Avenir*. It was loathsome to them that a man emerged from that circle, a priest making public profession of indifference in matters of dynasty, could have gained any influence over minds. These were the people who obstinately set upon a few words of doubtful taste or of questionable accuracy, uttered in the boldness of a most captivating extempore, but also the most captivating ever. Lacordaire was thirty-three years old; he was too young and too ardent, he had too much vigor in his imagination, too many — I almost said involuntary — bursts of spirit to ever bare his flank to the ruthless ill-will of the enemies concerning his political direction.

It must be said to his credit, that, for a long time, de Quélen held firm against these attacks from whatever direction they came. He had attended in person those very controversial conferences and every time, he left delighted. The more fear he had about their success, the more he rejoiced over them. Moreover, he realized that he had the pleasure of having made a unique choice based on his own personal inspiration. How could the Archbishop of Paris not appreciate with indescribable satisfaction his immense cathedral — accustomed for fifty years to a solitude barely interrupted, now and then, by the official ceremonies of the Empire and of the Restoration — emerging from its widowhood, and floods of people storming its walls, drowning the base of its columns, hanging from its vast galleries[34]? This kind of crowd had not been seen at the foot of any pulpit since the days of St. Bernard. In attendance were men named Chateaubriand, Berryer, Lamartine, Tocqueville, and they were not among the ones who were little charmed or moved[35]. How could de Quélen, forced to go into hiding at the end of July 1830, officially denounced by revolutionary passions on 13 February 1831, how, I say, could de Quélen, seeing himself for the first time in the presence of a crowd, a crowd this sympathetic, not be transported, as reported by Montalembert, by a success that avenged him so nobly, by associating him with the popularity of this ascending glory? He was pleased to see his affection so well justified and to have hazarded so much without being mistaken. Still close to the days when he saw his residence demolished, with himself yet hidden within the narrow walls of a convent cell, he reappeared at Notre-Dame with the majesty of a bishop, surrounded by his people and making it understand, in a popular idiom, by an acceptable voice, the teachings of a religion vanquished yesterday by a monarchy of fourteen centuries and unable, it was believed, ever to recapture the empire of minds. This was a noble retaliation to the devastation of his residence[36].

On 23 April 1835, Lacordaire had just given his last conference. Following the final words of the Christian orator, the assembly went to kneel to receive the blessing of the premier pastor, the Archbishop, when he, getting up with a majesty that those who saw him only once will never forget, thanked the preacher whom "God has endowed with piety and eloquence, *and more importantly, with that virtue which makes priests: obedience*." He was not reluctant to call him publicly "that excellent, that faithful friend who brought consolation and joy to my heart[37]."

On that same day, Lacordaire received the following letter:

"My dear *abbé*,

"The course which, with the help of God, you have just provided in the Church of *Notre-Dame of France*[38] in such a brilliant manner, and I hope, no less beneficial, has led the chapter of Paris and me to engage with you bonds of a fraternity that is pleasant for a friend to arrange. By the power of the word, you have already taken, in a way, possession of the vast nave of the cathedral; its choir and its sanctuary will be available to you by the provisions which I attach[39]. I hardly need to tell you how happy I am, dear Lacordaire, to bring you closer to me, to have you associated with what is most venerable in the clergy of the diocese, and be the first to give you, with all the affection and the tenderness for which you know me, *salutem in osculo sancto*."

† HYACINTH, Archbishop of Paris

Nonetheless, the burdens of the Lenten series had shaken the constitution, at the time very fragile, of Father Lacordaire. The doctor prescribed salt-water baths and suggested Dieppe. Father passed the month of July there. Mme Récamier was also present; she paid very gracious attention to the *Conférencier* of Notre-Dame. He passed most of his evenings at her residence with Chateaubriand, the Duke of Noailles, Ampère junior, Ballanche. These last two had strongly criticized his break with La Mennais, but forgave him for it as soon as they got to know him. As for the author of *Génie du Christianisme*, he rightly flattered himself for having influenced most of the writings of his day; he could not miss recognizing in Lacordaire one of his most glorious pupils. He asked of him a sermon for the work of Marie-Thérèse, a rest-home founded by Mme Chateaubriand for invalid priests[40]."

On his return from Dieppe, Lacordaire found himself abruptly called to Burgundy to collect the last breaths of a blood-brother, about which he wrote a beautiful letter to Mme Swetchine[41]. A few days later, he set out for Cirey-sur-Vezouze, at the request of a rich family, that wanted him to oversee the education of one of their sons. It was there that one of the strongest and the most faithful friendships of his life was to be forged. It was there also that came to find him, for the first time, an incident that we will find again later, which I will save until then, the quarrel of *l'abbé* Bautain with de Trévern, bishop of Strasbourg.

A grievous sorrow awaited him in Paris. His mother had died, this mother who cherished Henri more than all his brothers, even though she had loved them all with daily devotion, 'steadfast and without favoritism, where action spoke louder than words.' A heart ailment of long-standing, but often slight, suddenly took a more alarming turn. Récamier was called, but in vain. The sickness could not be warded off; after six weeks of waiting without hope, Lacordaire saw his mother die in his arms[42].

The blow was terrible; it had as counter-balance, one of those sudden turn of events of which the life of Lacordaire had already given us more than one example. With his mother dead, it seemed to him that his ties with France were broken; accordingly, he resolved to retire to Rome immediately after his second series at Notre-Dame[43].

This series opened on 21 February 1836.

On could think, said a newspaper of the time, that the success of the conferences of 1835 was due in large part to the desire for new emotions which moved the idlers of an indifferent century to anything that promised to stir in them some string as yet not vibrating. Moreover, many persons expected that after a year and a winter, minds would have cooled from their original enthusiasm, so as to judge, by the reception of the preacher getting back to his pulpit, whether the impression he had produced was serious and long-lasting. The experiment was conclusive. Ten months apart, everything returned to its place, as if there had been only one week between the preaching of one year and that of another.

The orator treated the teaching of the Church, the sources of that teaching, Tradition, Scripture, Reason, Faith, the means of acquiring Faith; subjects of sovereign importance and inexhaustible riches. Standing before an audience that was in despair of religious truth, Lacordaire offered it Catholic teaching as the only teaching that had general knowledge of truth and of error, the complete knowledge of good and evil. He showed that Tradition is the link between the present, the past, and the future, and that any teaching that does not take Tradition into account is one without a future by the very fact that it has no past; a teaching without knowledge of the purpose of things because it ignores their beginning. He reminded listeners that Religious tradition everywhere came before sacred books, just as the spoken word preceded Scripture. Comparing books that are held sacred by this or that nation to each other, he showed the crushing superiority of the Bible to the collection of traditions without historical ties that we call the Kings, the Zens, the Vedas, the Koran. He inquired about who would dare to compare societies based on these books with those societies constituted by the Gospel, with Christian societies. He recognized that Reason must harmonize with divine testimony, whether traditional or fixed by Scripture; but he had no difficulty in proving that by affirming God, creation, the original fall, reparation, rewards and penalties of the other life, divine reason said nothing that the human mind could not testify to, to a certain degree. He was not at all embarrassed to admit that, if the mystery of good and evil has its bright side by which it is an object of knowledge, it also has a dark side, by which it is an object of Faith. It is appropriate that it be so in this life of trials, because if we had seen the totality of nature and of God, we would have had no virtue or reward in believing, and consequently, no glory of heart before God. That if supernatural faith is difficult, it is not because it is not an act of reason but because, in addition, it is an act of virtue; the question of divine faith is tied to the question of divine virtue, and it is because of the need for this virtue that faith frightens. In addition, faith is not only an act of the intellect but also an act of the will. Without the will, everything is impossible, faith like everything else, but no more than everything else. No doubt, the help of God is necessary to achieve faith, and that help is freely given by God. Yet He has given us the means to force His hand without obstructing His freedom: that means is Prayer. Pray, therefore, because this is not a vicious circle, because to pray it is sufficient to have an initial faith.

Here you have a brief summary of the Conferences of 1836. These Conferences led a notable skeptic at the time to say that Christianity is so lofty, and that the word of God seems to be so attractive and spiritual that one must have very little heart and intellect so as not to feel disposed to love them.

On 16 April 1836, Lacordaire ended his last conference with these words:

"I hope, Gentlemen, that I have inspired in you at least the good thought of your turning to God in prayer and to renew your contacts with Him, not only by your mind but also by the movement of your heart! It is hope that I carry with me, it is the wish that I harbor on leaving you. I leave into the hands of my bishop this pulpit of Notre-Dame well-founded henceforth by him and by you, by the Pastor and by the people. For a moment, that two-fold approbation shone over my head. Allow me to put that aside and find myself alone for awhile before my weakness and before God."

At those words, the Archbishop stood up, and using the Church's cry of joy in the pascal solemnity, said: "Yes! *Alleluia!* Praise God! And why would we not praise Him, why would you yourselves not praise him whom He has raised expressly for you, *His new prophet,* a preacher whose voice, more friendly than eloquent, reached your minds and moved in the depth of your soul that Christian sensibility that never was weakened, that is perhaps not weakened now, and never will be weakened!... But, we were telling you, Gentlemen, that here below we sing only on a melancholy tone. Alas! This sadness increases again because of the end of these Conferences. You have, indeed, heard this gentle minister say that he will be taken from us for a bit of time. *Despite the opposition of our heart,* he will carry his meditations to a distance. He will go to the Eternal City, at the foot of the tomb of the holy Apostles, to the feet of the Father of all the faithful, to make know to him what he has seen and what he has done... He carries along all our blessings, all our remembrances, all our interests. He will soon return to us laden with the blessings of that noble elder who presides over the entire Church. He will return with renewed enthusiasm, refreshed at the tombs of the Apostles, who were the first to spread the faith and to seal it with their blood.

"And yet, Gentlemen, we hope that, despite his absence, the pulpit of Notre-Dame will not remain mute. God will raise up new resources for us; we will hasten to receive them and to make them known to you.

"In the heart of his retreat, our cherished and eloquent preacher will meditate on the divine sciences. We know that it is in the depths of solitude that illustrious men and great saints are developed. As one eloquent bishop said: it is in deep solitude that St. John Chrysostom forged the thunder claps that he boomed so gloriously from the patriarchal pulpit of Constantinople."

In the document dictated by Lacordaire on his deathbed, he spoke briefly about the Revolution of 1836.

"After two years at Notre-Dame," said he, "I understood that I had not yet matured enough to provide the course in one sweep, but that I had need to collect myself, to terminate worthily the building I had begun. Accordingly, I asked the Archbishop for permission to resign so as to go pass some time in Rome. He was grieved by this move, told me I was making a mistake, that, on my return, I would not find the post of honor that I was moving away from, and that, if there was a certain advantage in interrupting my conferences, it was more than counterbalanced by the drawbacks. I did not acquiesce to his entreaties."

Without being rash, one can think that, despite all that he had received from God to bear with all opposition, one secret discouragement had slipped into Lacordaire's soul. His success inclined to exasperation at the opposition he faced. If, up to this day, in spite of long triumphs, there were — as attested by Castan[44] — in the highest ranks of the clergy, some men who were astonished that such language had been spoken and upheld in the most distinguished pulpits of France, if even today a part of the Church of France denies all the qualities and exaggerates all the defects, what must it have been like, in 1836, when the generation to which Lacordaire belonged and for whom he was especially speaking, was barely emerging on the stage of the world? "To utter a thousand words in which there is not one to find fault with, but to let slip one syllable that displeases, one that is not quite perfectly clear, someone will ignore what you have said well, but will be obstinately set on that syllable to try to draw from it something false or impious[45]." These words by a Father of the Church seem to have been written expressly against the opponents of Lacordaire. At the very moment when the conferences of 1836 were ending, those of 1835 were being denounced as heterodox in a public document by a Vicar General of Lyons, M. Cattet. A similar censure was being prepared in Toulouse. In Paris, a man who enjoyed a certain reputation, Cottret, bishop of

Caryste, threatened to publish two volumes toward the same goal. If here I am calling up items so deservedly forgotten, it is not because they are worthy in themselves of being recalled. One needs to be well acquainted with the reasons behind so serious a resolution as Lacordaire's decision in 1836 to withdraw, and to condemn, as they deserve, the prejudices that did not step back before the danger of also calling into question the continuation of the conferences of Notre-Dame.

"How can I let pass unnoticed," wrote Lacordaire, "that, in the pulpit, I will always say something that will displease a host of people, which, on their part, will be the object of attacks all the more passionate than they can be upright? Is it wise always to remain as a problem in the eyes of the public and the faithful? Can anyone acquire genuine authority, the authority needed by a priest, when honorable persons ask themselves whether you are or are not orthodox? Is it not better to live in isolation, to write rather than to speak? We are in need of a work that displays all the continuity of Catholic teaching in a manner that conforms to the thoughts of the time, that is to say, one that, by using certain analogies, is capable of making an impression on souls just as they are. In five or six years, I would have completed that work and endowed my reputation with a solid foundation; subsequently, nothing would have prevented me from getting into the pulpit and giving my life to all the works that might come up[46]."

These were, in 1836, Lacordaire's dreams. A brief stay in the holy city was a means to strengthen himself in ecclesiastical knowledge and to provide firm support for his ulterior apostolate. The brightness of the praises that De Quélen heaped on him did not lead him astray. The Prelate greatly cherished him as a person but distanced himself from his political ideas, coupled, as they were, with apprehensions regarding the status of his orthodoxy. He supported Lacordaire, but somewhat half-heartedly; he defended him without discouraging his adversaries. Lacordaire entertained the illusion that his voluntary withdrawal would disarm his opponents, that a few years of exile, and especially the approbation of Rome, would give prejudices time to abate and to die out. In that, he was mistaken. But as he had said — basically, his retreat to Rome would not to be what he expected; in the designs of Providence, it had a goal hidden even from himself, one that would not be revealed until much later[47].

ENDNOTES

1. Here, Father's memory fails him. At the time, Mme Swetchine was in St. Petersburg, which she left to return to Paris only on 4 March 1835. (*Life of Mme Swetchine*, by dc Falloux, p. 381)

There was, on Lacordaire's part a bit more hesitation than he indicates; but these are minutiae that ought not enter into History.

2. In the Saint-Germain district, whose opinion weighed heavily on the mind of de Quélen, no cleric enjoyed more authority than Lieutard. Founder of the Stanislaus College, he had instructed the sons of the most illustrious families France, and, under the Restoration, contributed to make and unmake some Ministers.

I was informed that de Quélen did not like Liautard, whom he did not wish to have as Vicar General. This would not have been a sufficient reason to set aside Lacordaire's explanation. I admit that the Prelate cherished Liautard very little; nonetheless he had to take into account the considerable influence of this cleric, and he was able to break with his hands the weapon he fashioned from the disgrace of Lacordaire. The two-fold advice given to Lacordaire to go to the Archbishop proves that the change in de Quélen's attitude toward his stand was already known by many people.

3. Affre, in his *Mémoires*, expressed the same opinion concerning the secret hopes of Lacordaire's opponents. (Castan, p. 75)

4. NOTICE.

5. Lacordaire, Œuvres, t. V, p. 410.

6. Lacordaire, *loc. cit.*

7. Lacordaire, Œuvres, t. V, p. 411

8. Preface to *Conférences de Notre-Dame*.

What Father says there about the deist phase of his life is perfectly applicable to the political phase.

9. Acts, 17:23.

10. Ozanam, letter of 16 May 1835.

11. Lacordaire: *Éloge funèbre de monseigneur de Forbin-Janson.*

12. Le Prince de Broglie, *Discours de réception à l'Académie française.*

13. Preface to *Conférences de Notre-Dame*.

14. To Lorain, 19 juillet 1834.

15. *Videmus Ecclesiam, credamus in Christum, quem non videmus; et tenentes quod videmus, perveniemus ad eum quem nondum videmus.* (Aug., serm. IX in dieb. Pasch.)

16. See Preface to *Conférences de Notre-Dame*.

17. Le Prince de Broglie, *Discours* cité.

18. 39th Conference, *De l'établissement du règne de Jesus-Christ.*

19. *Le Père Lacordaire*, par Montalembert. — Cf. Guizot, *Disc. à l'Académie française,* le 24 janvier 1861.

20. Preface, Conférences de Notre-Dame.

21. See Romans 10:14b: And how are they to believe in one of whom they have never heard?
22. Première conférence: *De la nécessité d'une Église enseignante et de son caractère distinctif.*
23. IIIe Conférence, *De l'autorité morale et infaillible de l'Église.*
24. Ve Conférence, *De l'enseignement et du salut du genre humain avant l'établissement définitif de l'Église.*
25. IIe Conférence, *De la constitution de l'Église.*
26. IVe Conférence, *De l'établissement sur terre du chef de l'Église.*
27. VIe Conférence, *Des rapports de l'Église avec l'ordre temporel.*
28. VIIe Conférence, *De la puissance coercitive de l'Église.*
29. De la Bouillerie, évêque de Carcassone, *Éloge funèbre du p. Lacordaire.*
30. To Mme Swetchine, 2 May 1836.
31. NOTICE.
32. Unpublished letter from a Sulpician, 27 May 1835.
33. Letter to Lacordaire, 24 June 1835.
34. *Univers*, 14 March 1835.
35. See letter of de Tocqueville to Lord Radnor, May 1835.
36. NOTICE.
37. *Univers*, 21 May 1835.
38. It was Lacordaire who, in one of his Conferences, had called Notre-Dame of Paris *Notre-Dame of France*.
39. The provisions of honorary canon of the Chapter of Notre-Dame.
40. This sermon was preached on 24 March 1836.
41. See Appendix XVIII, page 556, for an unpublished letter of Lacordaire to his blood brother, who was an unbeliever, to inform him of his entrance into holy orders.
42. On 2 February 1836. — Mme Lacordaire was 61 years old.

43. Lacordaire told me of this determination in a letter of 17 February, and he had fixed his departure for 15 April.
44. *Histoire de M. Affre*, p. 56,
45. St. Justin: Dialogue with Trypho the Jew.

St. Ignatius of Loyola, in his *Spiritual Exercises*, understood very differently the duty of Christians in relation to those who exercised the ministry of the holy word. "Supponendum est," said he, "*Christianum unumquemque pium debere promptiore animo sententiam seu propositionem obscuram alterius* in bonam trahere partem quam damnare. *Si vero nulla eam ratione tutari possit*, exquirat dicentis mentem... et si minus recte sentiat vel intelligat, corripiat benigne."

46. To Mme Swetchine, 21 December 1836.
47. NOTICE.

CHAPTER IX

LETTER CONCERNING THE HOLY SEE – BREAK WITH BISHOP DE QUÉLEN

Lacordaire at Rome and the Jesuits – Reception by the Pope – Cooling off by De Quélen – La Mennais publishes the *Affairs of Rome*: De Quélen wants silence; Rome engages Lacordaire to speak – *Letter concerning the Holy See*: De Quélen opposes the publication – Lacordaire writes about it to the Archbishop: he declares and justifies his resolution not to return to France for a long time – The Prelate announces his definite opposition to the *Letter concerning the Holy See* – Lacordaire withdraws its publication – The Pope approves his behavior – Cholera in Rome; new letter to De Quélen – Lacordaire comes to preach a series at Metz; he decided to have printed the *Letter concerning the Holy See* – Appreciation of this writing.

Lacordaire did not move at a distance without misgivings. "Never," he wrote to Mme Swetchine, " was I less ready to make a decision than this one. I left Paris with none of the eagerness to see the spectacles I have known (the Roman solemnities), convinced that I would not be spared boredom, knowing full well that I was abandoning rather natural opportunities to see my career get established, that I would never find friends over there, that I would *suffer from not opening myself up and from not loving* — and yet, impelled by an almost disastrous series of circumstances, and feeling that I had need of this respite to regulate my soul before God[1]."

He stopped as often as he could in his beloved Burgundy. He relived with deep feelings of melancholy and of religion the places where he had spent his early childhood: Dijon, whose quiet streets he loved, the church where his mother went to pray everyday and where he went to confession for the first time. He tarried two days at Aix, delighted with the warm reception by the archbishop, Mgr Bernet, later cardinal, a child of the mountains of the Auvergne, austere priestly figure, a man of yesteryear, who held nothing in common with him. And yet, when in Paris during the conferences of 1830, Bernet was taken aback by the timeliness of this new-style preaching, and was warmly attracted to the preacher. Lacordaire boarded a ship at Marseille, could not bear the sea, went ashore at Genoa and then directly by Siena to Rome, were he arrived on 21 May, the eve of Pentecost.

He was warmly recommended by Doctor Récamier to the Jesuits of Rome. Moreover, he carried a letter from Mme Swetchine to Father de Rozaven, assistant to the General for France, and the most open opponent, as is known, to the teachings of La Mennais. Mme Swetchine had known this priest in Russia; he was not unacquainted with her conversion. Besides, he must have been favorably disposed toward Lacordaire through the latter's *Considérations sur le système philosophique de M. de la Mennais*, which had received great approbation in Rome, especially among the most distinguished professors of the Company [of Jesus, i.e., Jesuits][2]. A fortunate happenstance had lodged Lacordaire very close to the *del Gesù* Church, where every day he celebrated Mass. Excellent relations developed quickly between him and the Fathers. The General, Father Roothan, an exceptional man, gave him a most cordial welcome. Father de Roazaven came to see him: everywhere, he expressed himself strongly against the censure of the Conferences of 1835 by *l'abbé* Cattet. At the *Gesù*, Lacordaire chose his confessor; he placed himself into the hands of Father de Villefort, former student at the Polytechnic School, exceedingly honorable, as saints always are. All that happened by itself, with no preconceived plan, as if most naturally in the world. Lacordaire wrote to Mme Swetchine: "Many people believe that I made a very skillful choice in attaching myself here to the Jesuit Fathers. Well! Not too long ago, perhaps such an action would have been impossible on my part, given my state of mind. A change in that state combined with my present position, to the degree that was necessary. This is the coincidence that surprised me and more than anything else reveals the action of God on the human mind in His relation with the destinies it has pleased Him to prepare for me. Indeed, it has always been impossible for me to make a decision or to do anything that was not in conformity with my convictions[3]."

For all that, everyone in Rome gave Lacordaire a perfect welcome: the Cardinal-Vicar (Zurla), the Cardinal Secretary of State (Lambruschini), the Ambassador of France (Marquis Florimond de la Tour-Maubourg), and finally, above all, Pope Gregory XVI. We have seen that Lacordaire arrived on 21 May: by 6 June, he had an audience with the Supreme Pontiff. When he entered, the Pope opened both his arms and joyously said: *Ah! L'abbate Lacordaire!* And while the conference-speaker at Notre-Dame kissed the feet of the Holy Father, Gregory XVI took his head in his hands, pressed it with affection while saying: "I know that, in you, the Catholic Church has made a significant acquisition. I remember a delightful room-full: *l'abbé* La Mennais was there, then the count de Montalembert, then *l'abbé* Lacordaire, and here, Cardinal de Rohan." And the Pope indicated with his finger the place each one had occupied. After this, he blessed Lacordaire in these terms: "I give you my blessing and I pray that God will strengthen you in the defense you have undertaken for the Catholic cause[4]."

This reception was all the more significant in that, a few days earlier, Gregory XVI had received the booklet of Cattet. He had found it to be distressing and, with a gesture of contempt, said to Cardinal Prince Odescalchi (the same who has since set aside the purple to become a Jesuit): "Here, I give you this as a gift!" The Pope said to the one who had given him the booklet: "It is a question of knowing: 1° if the propositions being attacked are in fact worthy of censure; 2° if the censure itself is more blameworthy than the propositions denounced[5]."

Cattet had gambled on misfortune. At that very moment, the *Ami de la Religion*, an organ known to the elder clergy, in response to two censures from Lyons, published two letters without rejoinders. They were unsigned, but Lacordaire easily recognized the benevolent intervention of Affre. From Toulouse, there were sent to the *Ami* some twenty propositions attributed to Lacordaire tarnishing them with falsified newspaper-clippings. The journal refused to publish them. The *Gazette de France*, edited at the time by de Genoude, had announced that the conference-speaker had been called to Rome to answer for his teachings. This time, the archbishop of Paris, under the official signature of Affre, Vicar-General, objected in these terms:

"We can affirm that Lacordaire has experienced nothing but opposition to the decision he had reached, *at the end of January* of this year, to go to Rome. It is certain that the Pope has *never* shown the *least* disapprobation, that even less had he given a thought to summoning Lacordaire to himself. It is certain, on the contrary, that this orator has made some ineffective entreaties not to preach the series this year, and that he agreed, while continuing his conferences, to some invitations that he could not possibly refuse[6]."

In his own hand, Bishop de Quélen wrote to Lacordaire: "I hope that your censors will accept the statement and that they will leave you in peace. You cannot doubt the happiness that I feel in knowing you are pleased. Enjoy this calm and return to us prepared to continue the wonderful struggle in which you have already shown so much enthusiasm and talent[7]."

One could perhaps find these words of the Archbishop somewhat cold, when compared with those he had publicly addressed to Lacordaire, under the arches of Notre-Dame. If we can believe the notes of Affre, he had just left for Rome when the feelings of the Prelate were completely changed[8]. Even though, at first, de Quélen carefully hid the fact, he remained hurt for not having been able to keep the brilliant orator in Paris. Affre did not doubt that the opponents of Lacordaire profited from the occasion to reawaken the early scruples of the Archbishop concerning the new preaching.

This immediate cooling, if indeed it did occur, was never suspected by Lacordaire. He was so sure about the heart of de Quélen that he did not hesitate to inform him of the deleterious effect produced in Rome by the persistence of the Prelate not to appear at the Tuileries. Gregory XVI could barely understand that the archbishop of Paris made it a point of honor not to grant to a royalty recognized by the Holy See the customary respects. De Quélen did no react to this indirect warning. He responded to Lacordaire: "With a word, someone may make me change my feelings and my demeanor, but I know that only obedience is able to bring about such a transformation. I hope to be ready to obey *when I am required*, because then I will have nothing to answer for. However, I do not think that one wants to come to that; it would be taking on a great responsibility. Silence, on the contrary, preserves everything[9]." It is possible that, on this point, de Quélen was more royalist than archbishop. But his attitude was fixed, and it was difficult for him to change impulsively without being reproached for insignificance and inconsistency. Moreover, at the end of that same year[10], he wrote to Lacordaire: "My position remains always the same; it seems to me that it will not change with the beginning of the following year (the solemnity of the new year). I believe that Religion is interested in my not changing my way of being. If I am given *orders* and if I am allowed to make them known *publicly,* no one will doubt my submission. Otherwise, at least here (in Paris) if one should do what ought to have been done for more than six years[11], my residence will be the same. Here, in a few words, is the plan I devised, the only one that can be followed without compromising Religion, it seems to me. As for the rest, be assured that nothing will suffer. I myself am in a more difficult situation, but I am destined to suffer. *Fiat! Fiat!*"

In the meantime, there arose an incident — which it was impossible for anyone to foresee — that resulted abruptly in a profound break between Lacordaire and de Quélen.

La Mennais was getting ready to publish his *Affaires de Rome*. Montalembert in vain pleaded with him not to do anything; unable to obtain this, he declared that this act completed their separation. Warned by his friend, Lacordaire was as troubled as he was about the publication. The first step both took after having been companions of La Mennais on his voyage to Rome in 1832, having been witnesses to everything, they could not lend the weight of their silence to a historical untruth, or at least presented on a day that would make the Holy See odious. Consequently, they had to protest with a public disavowal. Lacordaire had not forgotten the blame he incurred from many persons in 1834, for having attacked La Mennais in his *Consideration on the philosophical system*. "I know full well," said he, "the worldly advantages of silence in this present situation, but I am not as sure that remaining silent would not be dishonesty."

In this vein, he wrote to Mme Swetchine, who immediately referred it to the Archbishop.

Dominated, as always, by an excessive fear of anything that could arouse minds, the Prelate, on the appearance of La Mennais' book, hurriedly told the Internuntio Garibaldi, while pleading with him to make it known to Rome that "this diatribe called for silence only[12]." This was also his response to Mme Swetchine. Not doubting at all that this decision ought to be made by the Pope, whom he believed had been alerted in that sense by the internuntio. de Quélen said that Lacordaire ought to approach the Holy Father so as to learn whether the desire of Gregory XVI was in favor of silence or of speech[13].

Lacordaire was not at all embarrassed to follow this suggestion. On his arrival in Rome, he received from the Belgian Chargé-d'affaires, M. Blondeel, a most cordial reception. Immediately, the latter placed him in touch with the Assistant Secretary of State, Mgr Capaccini, who, without a doubt — after Cardinal Lambruschini — was the most important man in the pontifical court. From the very beginning, even before the work of La Mennais appeared, Lacordaire had confided to Mgr Capaccini his desire to protest against the book; the Roman Prelate encouraged his intention. When the advice of de Quélen became known, Lacordaire wrote to Mgr Capaccini, after being assured that the latter agreed to place his letter under the eyes of GregoryXVI, and would inform him of the response of the Holy Father. In that letter, dated 22 November, Lacordaire placed himself at the disposition of the Sovereign Pontiff, ready to maintain silence or to speak, according to what His Holiness judged appropriate. Moreover, Lacordaire requested that, in case a sign on his part was deemed necessary, the form it should take, and, for example, if the Pope would agree to have Lacordaire write him a letter, or if the Holy Father preferred a writing which, without attacking directly that of La Mennais, would set the actions and the status of the Holy See in their true light[14].

The response from Gregory XVI was not long in coming. He told Mgr Capaccini that he knew full well who Lacordaire was, but that there was no reason for him to receive any official document, as would have been his letter to the

Pope. "His Holiness thinks," added Capaccini, "that it is better for him to stay out of it completely. He asks nothing from you, but would find pleasant anything to which your enthusiasm moved you at this moment in the defense and the honor of the Holy See[15]."

Lacordaire had thought about it; as early as 26 November, he consulted Mme Swetchine about his intention of writing a *Letter concerning the Holy See*, addressed to those young persons who had attended his conferences at Notre-Dame of Paris. He felt that this was the better way to give his work moderate length, neither too long nor too short.

As soon as he received the Pope's answer, he went to see Cardinal Lambruschini and submitted his idea, which was immediately agreed to. This idea pleased Lacordaire because he found in it the advantage of defending the Holy See without saying a word concerning La Mennais. It was not to deny that he judged the latter's latest writing severely. "I have lost," wrote he, "the irritation that I had against this poor man *because of the troubles I suffered on his account*; I am unruffled by him as I would be by the most unknown man. But instead of having done what he did, I would rather be Ham[16]." He was no less determined to respect the memories that linked him to the great turncoat. "For a soul that has such enlightenment," he would say, "I feel a great yearning for resurrection, a holy pity. I feel this movement of a man who is disinterested in a calamity and in whom no passion obscures the clear view of the loss to the entire world when a privileged intellect falls. Alas! His charity was too far below his vision[17]."

Lacordaire had promised himself to write his *Letter concerning the Holy See* in less than two-months' time. Two weeks later, he had completed it[18]. It was addressed to a friend: on his own, the author had rejected "the young persons of Notre-Dame — as a somewhat prideful idea." The most difficult issue remained: obtaining the consent of his archbishop. Approved as he was in Rome, he could go without it, strictly speaking, but he did not wish to do so.

Now, while all this was going on in the holy city, Paris was under the impression we have seen, namely, that from every side, an opposition to the idea of publishing anything on the appearance of the book, the *Affairs of Rome*. In this frame of mind, de Quélen could only be vexed by the way things had gone at the Quirinal. On 20 December 1836, he wrote an extended letter to Lacordaire. In his view, there was no reason to bother with the pamphlet of La Mennais; it had met little success; so little was it talked about, that it would have been better not to say anything at all. There remained Lacordaire's idea: a letter concerning the Holy See, with no reference to *the Lammenais production*. On this point, Lacordaire had progressed too far (one can detect the Archbishop's grief) to abandon work on what he had promised; *but, as for publication, that will be something else.* The most prudent step would be for the author to send his work to Paris, allowing his friends the freedom to stop or to advance the work, *with full authorization to suppress whatever appeared necessary.* For example, "concerning the so-called Gallican ideas, an extreme nicety had to be kept so as not to provoke too much something that could become the subject of new discussions in our country. This must be carefully avoided — the enemy wanting nothing better than to see us divided — even if it involves only minor points that everyone does not understand well[19]."

When this letter appeared in Paris, everything was over in Rome. Lacordaire's manuscript was entrusted by the Chargé-d'affaires of Belgium to Cardinal Lambruschini, who, most likely, had placed it under the eyes of the Pope; only one line and a half ended up being deleted[20].

At about the same time, Gregory XVI received in a

private audience a holy bishop from the United States, Flaget, bishop of Bardstown. Turning the conversation to Lacordaire, the Pope admitted that he knew him, and that the young priest had already given much service to the Holy See and *would do more*. He knew that attempts had been made to harm him in the mind of the Pope, on the occasion of the conferences of Notre-Dame, but he was also aware of all the good these had accomplished, and that he counted on this faithful servant for the defense of Religion.

It was under the impression of joy and of confidence which authorized such words that Lacordaire had sent his manuscript to Paris. The principal goal of his trip (the complete rehabilitation of his orthodoxy by the highest doctrinal authority on the earth) was achieved beyond his expectations. A vacancy among canons was about to occur at Notre-Dame; everything seemed to favor Lacordaire's nomination, and that he would be recalled to the pulpit that he had left, to move upward with all the moral power that he gained from his sojourn in Rome. This brilliant prospect, however, did not fascinate Lacordaire. He believed in the protection of the Archbishop; but he feared, even with that support, even with that of the benevolence of the Supreme Pontiff — he feared, I say, to have to face anew the obstacles that he had avoided in the springtime. He asked himself whether it would not be worth waiting for five or six more years, and appear in France only after a major work that would express the entire Catholic doctrine with unshakable reliability, but at the same time, with an appearance favored by a large number of intellects[22].

The letter of de Quélen, dated 20 December, gave these fears unexpected strength, and showed that the Prelate was far from suspecting — so deep was the abyss (of which he was unaware) — the difference between Lacordaire's view and his own. The first response of the young priest was very quick, akin to unwarranted decisions. And yet, he did not immediately reply to the Archbishop. Addressing himself to Mme Swetchine, focusing on the only two objections presented up to that point by the Prelate, but strong in the conviction that he had already dealt with them satisfactorily, he asked that the publication should take place *without delay*, so that his writing maintain its quality of timeliness. "I see that as resolved," he added; "I would be greatly distressed otherwise." At the same time, he declared that he could not consent to have excised, without his approval, anything that could give offense in his *Letter concerning the Holy See*, and intimated that it was impossible for him to get involved in correspondence on this subject.

"Forgive me," Lacordaire continued, "if all that preceded sounds so unyielding. You are aware of my uneasiness regarding a conclusive decision that will put off or hasten my return. The letter from the Archbishop revealed to me the depth of the abyss wherein I would plunge myself. In it, he showed himself so fearful, so divided that it is impossible for me to return in the midst of a host of adversaries only to be so poorly supported. This would be to review fruitlessly all the issues, perhaps with less favorable opportunities. It would be to open myself to the task of the Danaides [see endnote 23], but my conscience would not compel me to make such a sacrifice.

"I owe a lot to the Archbishop, but not enough to turn over my career to him, hand and feet bound. He enjoyed some sublime moments on my account, but this is a burden under which he hunches over without wanting to, and which the future may make even heavier.

"Our clergy is divided into two parties: one wants the ancient Church of France with its teachings and its methods; the other believes that France is in an irreparable new status. I am the man who has not yet been recognized, but, in the end, possibly the man for that last group: one can feel it. The hatred for details, chosen from memories, join the intense dislikes of the parties.

"What is wanted is my fall; I know that all too well. For my part, I do not want to hand over my head to them. I vanquished them over there, by the ineffable grace of God; I have come to vanquish them here. I need to distance myself from both countries to allow my victory to rest; I need to grow older, to let time pass, to write a dependable work, to become better. These first ten years of priesthood passed very quickly and were too restless. I owe myself an extended seclusion."

Lacordaire revealed that he was going to find an asylum beyond the Po River[24].

To be sure, the Lacordaire of 1822 bubbled with excitement in this letter; he is not smothered; he is not completely crucified. He has an understanding of his worth; he also realizes what is vindictive in the antipathy of his adversaries, and especially of the strong hold they will always have over the prejudices — respectable in many ways — of de Quélen. He maintains control over himself, however, but he is too frank not to give hints about what he has on his heart.

Two days later, Lacordaire sought advice. Mgr Capaccini had told him: "I will see the Pope. He will know that if the booklet does not appear it will be the result of your obedience to your bishop; thus, you will have fulfilled on all sides your entire duty. Responsibility will fall completely on the Archbishop, and you will again earn credit."

That same day (5 January 1837), Lacordaire answered the Archbishop:

"I received the letter by which your Vicar General honored me in his letter of 20 December concerning a writing that he must at this moment have in his hands. At first glance, he will have learned that on my own I abandoned a subject that could entail some drawbacks, one that I had intended for the presentation and not for some secret motive of self-satisfaction. As for the essence of the writing, it has been studied by men who are in charge of Christian matters, and received the most complete and honorable approbation. Nonetheless, if the Vicar General raises objections against its immediate publication, or believes that certain statements are inopportune, I pray that he throw the manuscript into the fire, and that will end the matter. I do not wish to publish it without his consent, nor can I accept changes made at a distance from me, such as would transform the correct and free expression of my thought into a kind of piece written in an office by someone under orders. I have fulfilled my duty as a Catholic; I am about to complete it, as well as my duty as priest, by acquiescing to the decision you will make. Whatever it may be, I will be released from everyone; from you by my obedience; from the Sovereign Pontiff, by the knowledge that there will be obstacles, independent of me, obstacles that will have prevented me from upholding my word; from God, by my writing and by the sacrifice I will have made of it.

"Accordingly, I give the Vicar General complete authorization to decide as it will please him. I exclude only two impossible elements: a delayed publication in a daily too insignificant to uphold it, and changes that would have to take place only by correspondence that distance does not favor, and which, besides, would deal with points that are an extremely moderate expression of my convictions.

"I thank the Vicar General for the kind words expressed in his letter. I have been accustomed to them for a long time. I would hope that my gratitude could reach so far as to find me, one day, perfectly in tune with all the thoughts, all the ideas, and all the wishes of your heart. This is difficult at a time when men are so divided. I regret this profoundly; in the kindness of my heart, I am looking for the route that, completely and in everything, would lead me to the ultimate desire of your heart. If I should die without having been able to do so, your image will be no less dear and honored at that final moment; in heaven, I will breathe with greater calm in the hope that between my archbishop and myself there will no longer be any separation, no more doubts, no more opponents, but only he alone with that very noble thought about him that I have always harbored.

"Farewell, My Lord, allow me this very intimate expression, one that is in conformity with that state of soul in which I find myself on your account. You will meet many more men in the career that God has destined for you (I hope that it will be prolonged); but you will not encounter anyone who appreciated your glory more and in a more impartial manner than I have."

Up to that point, the letter was indeed praiseworthy. A language of such loftiness and of feeling was used so as to be understood by De Quélen, and indeed it was. The limits Lacordaire had placed on his submissiveness in no way displeased the bishop; he was very pleased with the feelings expressed to him at the end of this letter and touched to experience them in all circumstances[25].

But in Rome, Lacordaire did not have Mme Swetchine "to restrain him by the hem of his habit and to slow down his movements too sudden or too blunt." He lacked an individual who could fulfill the two conditions she did so completely, by her own admission, first by not being him, neither by the nature of his personality and background, nor by age, and secondly, to love him more than he loved himself. The sharp mind of Lacordaire had immediately understood all that lay behind the letter of de Quélen of 20 December: an enormous defiance of what the combined ultramontanism and the liberalism in the speaker of Notre-Dame could include in a writing concerning the Holy See, and the prejudice to prevent this demonstration, whatever form it took. Lacordaire, therefore, saw clearly all the clouds that he thought had dissipated forever, the clouds of 1833 and of 1834, the clouds that weighed so heavily on the conferences at Stanislaus College, continued to haunt the mind of his bishop, and that, should he return to Paris, the struggle would always begin anew. From this viewpoint, and in remembrance of the multiple proofs he never ceased to offer to the Church for five years — for which he received so little credit — an impetuous and irresistible indignation seized him. He despaired of the confidence that de Quélen had placed in him, and scorning all the latter's weakness, he believed that dignity required him to stay far from Paris and, from then on, no longer accept anything from the Archbishop, just as he believed in his frankness to make himself known to him without reservation. This is what he did, in these terms:

"My Lord, a few days have minimized the painful impression caused by your letter of 20 December last. I no longer write under the weight of that impression but with the calm of a man who has reflected on his place in so serious a matter; I ask you for the gift of allowing me to open my heart to you completely.

"When I resolved to leave France, about a year ago, I was not yielding to a casual desire for change. There are in matters natural endings that the intelligent man must recognize. You had called me suddenly, under an inspiration contrary to the your thoughts of the previous evening, to a magnificent battlefield. You had ordered me to remain silent at Stanislaus, but ordered me to speak at Notre-Dame. These are contradictions that do not reveal human weakness, but the power of instinct and of the heart. The life of great men is filled with similar deeds. Then, on two occasions, before three or four thousand men, you paid me a tribute that will never perish from my memory. Nonetheless, My Lord, all this success did not hide from me the dangers of my situation, the mistrust, the doubts, the jealousies, the political oppositions, the revisiting of the past — and I knew full well that within yourself, *I did not have adequate support.*

"Let us be frank, since I am approaching my thirty-five years and I need to make a choice. You have a personal inclination towards me; you like my sincerity, my disinterestedness, my faith, my humility; there is perhaps something in me that pleases you. You are certain that I will never be a heretic nor a schismatic, that I am passionately devoted to the Church. But there are in our two manners of being and of feeling, in our view of this time and of its remedies, a profound difference, brighter than the day. I am not your man, you belong to one period of time, and I to another, that is the truth. Consequently, My Lord, you cannot believe in me nor give me *the outright support that I need* against my adversaries, whose number and strong emotions I know all too well.

"What should a wise man do? He would withdraw. I have done that. I left quietly and deliberately, thanking my good fortune before it left me. The accusing writings that accompanied me to Rome, others that are ready for any opportunity[26], gave me proof that I had acted prudently. I dare to add that your letter of 20 December only confirmed my thought.

"And now, My Lord, I am unable and unwilling to return to where I was happy to leave; my decision has been made not to see France for a long time; I was waiting for the occasion to open myself to you.

"My greatest regret in making this definitive choice is that you might see in it some ingratitude towards you. I am in your debt for my having mounted the pulpit of Notre-Dame, and I will never forget that. But can I owe you for again plunging my life into ceaseless grief, for giving with my head bowed, in a situation that your arm was not strong enough to guarantee?

"I am like a stranger in your diocese, I hold no real office there. I do not even find that life for which the altar is in debt to the priest; moreover, without a modest inheritance — one quarter of which I have spent in the service of the Church — nothing, save the goodness of God, could offer me bread for the morrow. It is less that freedom which affects me, but rather the one which for me results in the moral impossibility for you to guarantee the honor of my priesthood. I received it from you without stain, I want to keep it that way. I no longer wish to expose it to the reproaches of those whom your very presence cannot hold back in their accusations. A moment will come when this solidarity would need to be clearly accepted or rejected by you; the danger of such a crucial alternative is too weighty for my head. You have done so much for me. It is time for me to stop myself respectfully, on my own, so as to spare your wisdom from the inevitable moment of your sacrificing yourself for me, or my sacrificing myself for you. Besides, my free time will not be lost; my conferences were simply the use of material that I have been collecting for ten years. Having it more complete and more precise, I will be able to use it in a format that will not lead to similar problems. If subsequently this publication disarms some more or less involuntary prejudices, if the years, in passing over matters and men, make the situation bearable, you will find me again, both faithful and better.

"Accordingly, it is not, My Lord, an irrevocable goodbye that I say to you. It is a separation as long as will be necessary, but one that leaves me with the hope of receiving again your blessing. While awaiting that happier time, I need to think about making my exile here more stable. I have already been busy in obtaining a chaplaincy that will soon be open at Saint-Louis-des-Français. Importantly, it offers lodging and 1,400 francs (admittedly a trifling sum). That, added to my inheritance, will more than suffice for my needs. I was never an ambitious person; I never dreamed of finding in the Church anything else than my daily bread; were I the greatest man in the world, I would not blush at receiving anything from the hands of the Church. I place my confidence in God, Who knows with what purity of intention I entered into His service, Who knows my heart and the difficulties of my career. I also place my confidence in you to interpret favorably the frankness of this letter and of the freedom of my resolutions. As for me, whatever happens, I will remember Notre-Dame and all the individual circumstances wherein I found in you the soul of a bishop[27]."

At first, de Quélen was incensed, then overwhelmed by this letter[28]. Never, neither near nor far, did the possibility of Lacordaire's expatriation cross his mind. Never had he been aware of what the one who wrote to him had suffered in silence in 1833, in 1834, and since. Never did he have any doubts about the true cause of Lacordaire's retreat to Rome. Given the mind set of the Prelate, it was a thousand times impossible for him to understand the impression given by his letter of 20 December. He could not place himself in the writer's position, nor feel like him the bitter disgust that appropriately fills a man of heart, pursued by a shadowy opposition as stubborn as it was imperceptible. Nonetheless, what suddenly was revealed to him was that the good nature and even the humility of Lacordaire had their limits, and that, without disobeying, he knew how to resist when he was in the right, without being too afraid of consequences, because he knew, because he had always remained poor, a powerful guarantee of independence. This bomb exploded on the eve of the Lenten series, before Father de Ravignan had appeared in the pulpit of Notre-Dame, at a moment when no one knew if he would have an audience and if his preaching would be successful. "What an embarrassing position Lacordaire has placed me in." cried the Archbishop! With whom does he want me to replace him[29]?" But at the same time, the Prelate was wounded to the quick by this forthrightness of language. "I am not your man; you belong to one period and I to another." These words and many others were simultaneously too startling in their truth and in an unaccustomed familiarity from the mouth of a priest speaking to his bishop for De Quélen not to be strongly shocked.

And yet, no one can deny that Lacordaire was speaking the truth, with no exaggeration whatsoever, when he thought that de Quélen could not *believe in him*, nor give him the *unlimited* support he needed. In fact, at the moment when he was writing what we have just read, the manuscript of his *Letter concerning the Holy See*, despite the high approval it obtained in Rome, could not find favor before the Archbishop of Paris.

Indeed, one is surprised by the evident insufficiency of the reasons alleged by the Prelate against the publication of that writing. He could not incriminate its teaching, His Holiness having forbidden all examination on this point. And yet, De Quélen used to say: "a great number of passages were noted and underlined as not presenting a clear enough meaning or one *in little harmony with the genius of our language*, to such a degree that it would be difficult for anyone undertaking to edit this work to take into consideration the many observations that had been made. The author himself would hardly have had the courage to *engage in a complete revision*. Nonetheless, it would be unfortunate if this writing did not radiate a certain luster; it would be an ever-increasing misfortune because of all the discussions that the pamphlet would arouse. The passage relative to Russia and to Poland was an indiscretion, in that it coincided with an amendment that was removed by the House of Deputies and that it could endanger the French Government with the Powers. The attractive and *agreeable* things contained in the *Letter*, the remarkable sections concerning the Holy See, do not appear to offset the troubles that could be feared from its publication. Besides, these passages will not be lost: they will serve with honor and advantage in other circumstances."

In summary, then, the work is badly written; it will not succeed, it will occasion discussions; moreover, the author did not show enough discretion for the Russian government; this is why the Archbishop of Paris could not assume responsibility for allowing the pamphlet to appear[30].

It is unfortunate for de Quélen's reputation that the *Letter concerning the Holy See* was published. It is assuredly one of the most eloquent and best thought-out writings that Lacordaire produced. After we read it and re-read the notice of de Quélen about this admirable production, Lacordaire's letter of 14 January 1837 is very amply justified.

On receiving this notice from the Archbishop, Lacordaire hastened so send a copy to Mgr Capaccini, who, without delay, passed it to the eyes of Gregory XVI. His Holiness wanted to convey personally to the author of the *Letter concerning the Holy See* his complete satisfaction about the behavior he showed in this whole matter. He received Lacordaire in a private audience, treated him with unlimited kindness, to the point of having him sit facing him during the entire session[31].

On the following day, Lacordaire wrote to the Archbishop:

"My Lord, it was on 2 February, the feast of the

Purification, that I received your letter of 18 January and the unsigned Notice that accompanied it. On the same day, those two documents arrived at the Secretariat of State, and on the following 5th, they were placed under the eyes of the Sovereign Pontiff. On the 9th, His Holiness was eager to receive me in a private audience and attest to his satisfaction about my behavior.

"I will not lay bare, My Lord, the feelings aroused in me as I read Your Grace's Notice intended to allow me to infer the reasons for your opposition to the publication of my manuscript. I refer to the letter that I wrote to you on 14 January of this year. By itself, it indicates that I am unable to remain in a situation that will unceasingly place me between its disgrace or the impossibility of acting according to my conscience. In Rome, I find peace, security, life, leisure, distance from intrigues, the means to serve the Church without exposing myself to catastrophes; what more can I hope for? I already have an assigned place at *Saint-Louis des Français* where I have to take up residence before the end of the month. Ready to separate myself from Your Grace without knowing whether I would ever see you again, I look backward, in spite of myself. I think of so many things that joined me to you and to those unexpressed but fundamental obstacles that always prevented us from understanding each other in the important depths of life. It is a consolation for me to leave you when all I needed was only a little patience to have you assure my career, at least under some significant aspects; it is something else to leave you, with the sacrifice that I offer you in a writing I pursued, a last pledge of my obedience and my respect. I ask you to burn those pages, condemned never to see the day, and to keep no copies: this is my will, and on this matter, I leave it to your word as a gentleman."

Does this mean that Lacordaire intended to consign to

nothingness, simply because it had displeased the Archbishop of Paris, a letter honored by the approbation of the Pope? Certainly not. To be sure, he was allowed to hope that publication had only been delayed. While awaiting a favorable occasion, he wanted to be the only one in possession of his work, and rightly so. He feared leaving a copy available to his enemies, in charge of the archives of the [Archiepiscopal] See, and quite capable of circulating in their circles incomplete and hardly faithful citations. This is what he wanted to keep from happening. As for the tone of the letter, I do not know whether anyone will see only pride in this; but even so, one may perhaps see that a pride expressing itself in this way does not come from a commonplace soul. Later, on examining himself before God, Lacordaire accused himself of having abandoned all restraints in these circumstances "in favor of a feeling of honor perhaps too human to be Christian." But he had the right to add that this feeling was not unreasonably human "so as to be *unjust* and not be understood by another man of honor[32]."

This could not have been said any better; and besides, this view of the matter is very secondary. Before asking oneself whether Lacordaire, in this current situation, exhibited sufficient humility, we need to know if, in his place, De Quélen, in the end, showed himself sufficiently just. Let us not speak of Lacordaire's relationship with La Mennais, at Rome in 1832, in Paris from 1833 to 1836; let us not speak of the startling proofs he gave on this point, nor of the significant services he had just offered in the pulpit of Notre-Dame; instead, let us look at his *Letter concerning the Holy See* for what it is, by isolating it from all those proofs and all those services. It was thirty-two years earlier that his *Letter* was written, thirty years since its publication. Posterity had already appeared for that writing; on this point, it can also be affirmed that posterity had arrived for de Quélen as it had for

Lacordaire. Well, I dare say that today, everyone would understand — I do not say approve of — the *veto* the Prelate placed on the publication of this pamphlet.

First of all, remember that it appeared barely eleven months[33] after the *veto*, and that none of its predictions, none of the apprehensions of the Archbishop came about. In fact, it won much success; it did not give rise to any disputes; may I add that it did not lead to any unfortunate repercussions from Russia? The outlooks were the same; nothing had changed, save that the opponents of Lacordaire no longer feared the penchant the Archbishop had for him as a person nor his reappearance in the pulpit of Notre-Dame. All this was enough to silence them in the presence of the new writing.

Moreover, it is strange today, at the distance we are from that past, to read again the *Letter concerning the Holy See*.

It opens with considerations about solidarity, a metaphysics perhaps too subtle but one of uncontested grandeur. It remains a tendency of superior minds to raise their thought to its most general expression then to descend from those heights to the field of historical reality. Moreover, the author is in a hurry to arrive at the unity of the Church, for which he offers a splendid page. He demonstrates the need to give a permanent and visible link to this unity, parent and governess. He presents its external conditions with an incomparably magnificent language, describes eloquently the geographic situation of Italy and that of Rome; moreover, he compares the two extreme links of eighteen centuries of Christianity, St. Peter under Nero and Gregory XVI at the Vatican, and asks himself what is the secret behind this considerable elevation of the Roman pontiffs. History replies: it is because in the world they have always been the faithful personification of justice. "What was it that founded all the great empires (which have all perished)? War, followed by victory and possession, which is to say, violence redeemed by time. If, on the contrary, you are looking for the source of the temporal sovereignty of the Holy See, you will see that it depended on four [three?] circumstances happening concurrently, that no foresight could have assembled: the weakening of the Empire of the East, which could no longer defend Rome against the Barbarians; the ambitions of the Lombard kings, who wanted to subjugate to their crown the progressive succession of two great men, Pepin and Charlemagne; and finally, the love that all the inhabitants of Rome bore toward the Sovereign Pontiff, whose children they felt they were, not only because of his duties but also because of his favors. As a result, in founding their proper State, the Popes enjoyed the glory of being accountable only for the salvation of their country. What had this prodigious transformation cost them? It had cost them eight hundred patient years of existence in justice."

To this angelic patience, the Popes almost always united a courage of bronze; and this is what Lacordaire admirably spotlights in a few pages, crowned by the momentous duel of Napoleon and Pius VII, the duel of genius and of influence against the faith. We know the results: the ashes of Pius VII rest below the dome of [the basilica of] Saint Peter, while those of Napoleon rest on a rock in the Atlantic.

But all of that is but a preface. Having reached Gregory XVI, Lacordaire faced one formidable obstacle, the one that La Mennais had formulated in his *Affairs of Rome*, and which has remained up to our days the most repeated commonplace topic of the anti-Christian press: does the contemporary Papacy understand its mission? Has it not failed against its past, spoiled its future by being of service to absolute governments? In this lies the crux of the debate.

Nothing is more current nor more valid than the response given by Lacordaire.

The war is in Europe, but where exactly? The war is not between nations, it is not between kings, it is not between kings and their people — the author of the *Letter* proved all of that. Where, then, is the war? "The war is greater than kings, greater than nations; it even lies between the two forms of human intelligence, faith and reason — faith having become a power through the Church, and reason itself having developed into a power, with its chiefs, its meetings, its chairmen, its rituals. War is being waged between Catholic power and humanist power, both of which contend for today's world on a much wider scale because both of them have reached a degree of internal and external force that no longer allows for combats on trifling and reformist matters but demands a resolution.

"The teaching of humanist power is that human nature is sufficient unto itself in all orders of things, for living and for dying. Having penetrated into the intellectual order, the absolute sovereign of his ideas; in the moral order, the final judge of his actions; in the social order, to recognize no other authority than the one he directly elected; in the material order, to conquer the elements and draw from them (for everyone, if possible) the only genuine happiness — this is the program of humanist power, this is the chart that it has planned for the human race. Success is evidently not attainable except by the destruction of Catholic power, which upholds absolutely opposite beliefs, sustained by the faith of fifty million men, and the beliefs of one hundred million other Christians separated by schism from the center of unity.

"Now, any teaching that does not wish to disappear must give immortality to man. Humanism which pushes God away — the only true infinite, who cannot multiply matter for the sake of sensual pleasure, nor make of the regularly established social order a vast ocean for all ambitions — is obliged to open to its creatures the bottomless pit of the future. The present is no longer regulation, it is a barrier to human destiny; everything that happens to existence is condemned by the sole fact that it *exists*: religion, royalty, fortune, anything whatever. TO BE *is to impede the human race.*"

In viewing things from this lofty perch, it becomes evident that it is not a question of the Holy See's embracing the cause of kings or of nations, but of upholding Catholic power against humanist power; a question unendingly complicated by the diversity of the elements that converge in favor of one power or the other. Accordingly, there are Catholic kings and humanist kings, Catholic ministers and humanist ministers, powerful Catholic lords and powerful humanist lords, Catholic bourgeois and humanist bourgeois. What was the duty of the Papacy if not to bring help, in everything and everywhere, to the Catholic element? Without adhering to any party, with no concern about the variable forms of governments, everywhere that humanist tyranny was restrained, the Holy See entertained friendly relations; everywhere the Holy See prevailed, it protested against the violation of the rights of the Church and of conscience. As regards those powers that lift up with one hand and tear down with the other, one that lays down the principle of humanism and pushes aside the consequences — equally arbitrary in both cases — the Holy See, while noting with bitter pain so deadly a contradiction, followed the Christian principle of respecting established powers, even when these were unfaithful to God.

At this point, Lacordaire had to explain the one act of Gregory XVI that La Mennais had identified as the most vulnerable, the brief addressed to the bishops of Poland after the taking of Warsaw, to exhort them to be resigned to the decrees of God. "Even supposing, which I do not believe," said the author in his *Letter concerning the Holy See*, "supposing that, in the hope of appeasing an irritated prince against a portion of his flock, the Pastor had been excessive in his language, I will never be convinced that Priam [last elderly king of Troy, killed on the altar steps - Trans.] performed an action unworthy of the majesty of a king and of the heart of a father, when he took the hand of Achilles while addressing to him these sublime words: "Consider the depth of my misery, since I kiss the hand that killed my son."

These are the statements that could not find favor with De Quélen and his Councillors. This is what the Prelate judged to be compromising as regards the Russian government. This is what he decided he could not allow to be published in Paris, in spite of the unqualified approval of the Sovereign Pontiff.

In fact, Gregory XVI wanted to have a handwritten copy of the *Letter concerning the Holy See*. Often, he read some passages to persons attending his audience and, pointing to the manuscript, he would say: "After this is published, the author will be even more famous[34]." Cardinal Lambruschini, at once theologian and statesman, assuredly far from being a revolutionary, was so pleased with this pamphlet that he went so far so to say that the *Letter concerning the Holy See* encompassed all his opinions[35]. What had struck him the most was the ingenious demonstration, clear and logical, that the war was, fundamentally, nothing other than between Catholicism and humanism[36]. But this opinion raised the question to a level that the eyes of de Quélen, it really has to be said, could not attain. Accustomed to blending the cause of the legitimate monarchy with that of God, never separating them in his thoughts, he found it impossible to conceive that one could abstract from the origin of a government to see only its attitude toward the Church. Whether he was aware of it or not, it was this way of looking at things that had shocked him much more than the trifles about which he complained in the writing of Lacordaire. Could he pardon the latter for citing Louis-Philippe as "*displaying* toward the Church some benevolent dispositions?" Only one line was in question, but this one line tainted the entire pamphlet for de Quélen[37].

Later on, we learned well that, on the part of Lacordaire, this had been a more or less farseeing impartiality and not flattery.

Basically, what separated Lacordaire from de Quélen was politics: the Archbishop remained a legitimist [royalist partisan - Trans.], Lacordaire had ceased being one; everything was there. Not that Lacordaire was a man to speak disrespectfully about "the ancients of the House of Bourbon[38]," Not that he saw in the inviolability of the heredity of the throne "an important and respectable principle[39]. But, on the one hand, he thought that this principle had been ruined in the mind of the majority of the French people and, consequently, no longer had any competence in our country. On the other hand, the legitimist feelings he had encountered in the clergy seemed to him to be tainted by a kind of idolatry, moreover tenaciously joined to the cause of Gallicanism — doubly odious to him — and by the spirit of servility that it fostered toward royalty as well as by the persecutions that the Gallicans waged to nourish this idolatry personally these past three years[40]. This is the truth. I am not debating this point of view, I am merely bringing it to light. I affirm that it was the truth Lacordaire held at that date. Up to that time, the occasion had not presented itself for him to explain it openly to de Quélen. The *Affairs of Rome* provided that occasion, unexpectedly; and so, he made the most of it.

One of the most remarkable traits of Lacordaire's personality was (I will never repeat it enough) a care for determined sincerity. It was a thousand times impossible for him to write his *Letter concerning the Holy See* without including his opinions. Nonetheless, he toned down their expression as much as he could; he did not elevate them into principles; he presented them only in an indirect and blamelessly tempered manner. Moreover, Cardinal Lambruschini, prejudiced as he was in favor of the principle of legitimacy because of his character and because of the general direction of his ideas, was in no way shocked. De Quélen was; this way of conceiving the duties of the Church in matters of politics, he believed ought not allow their display to any degree on the part of one of Her priests, even when approved by the Holy See. This is what disgusted Lacordaire. He did not disobey, but he experienced a demanding, irresistible desire to lay bare the very fundament of the situation between de Quélen and himself, to express the resolution in which he remained free concerning questions left free by the Church, and to remove from diocesan authority all hope and all thought of controlling him because of his need for it. He did not intend to break absolutely with the Archbishop, but he was not displeased to take away from him the longing to start all over again[41].

This is what clearly stands out in Lacordaire's correspondence in 1837.

"It is certain," he wrote, "that the most natural prudence required me to remain in the good graces of Mgr the Archbishop. But de Quélen represented the ancient Church of France, and had never aspired to anything else but to restore her with her ancient traditions: this was the foundation of his life and his hopes. How, then, could he accept a man who believed in many novelties? Do you think that, if I were ambitious, I would not long ago have known what I had to do? Well, my God, I would have to say only two words; but never will I utter them. At this moment, I am giving up my friends, my country, even my vocation as preacher, to my tastes, my memories. And why? To save my conscience, so as not to embrace ideas that I consider disastrous. What was it in my writings that wounded Mgr the Archbishop? Is there any child who would not notice it? Had I acquiesced to the ideas of Mgr the Archbishop, I could have, I know, gained everything; instead, I will be filled with disgust, half-way banished, uncertain about my life and my reputation all the way to the grave. Between these two alternatives, you preferred the first. You expected that with time and events, I would present enough proofs to earn confidence. In fact, with another personality than mine, this would have been possible. But since I am who I am, it is better to place me alone before everyone, as my body receives the arrows of hatred, living and dying as best I can. This fate pleases me because it is my duty to accept it, also because it is impossible for me, speaking sensually, *not to prefer sincerity above everything else*[42]. My strength is in the truth, as is my duty, and as are my pride and my satisfaction as well. Mgr the Archbishop thought he could dominate me because of my need for him and because of the gentle side of my being. For that to have happened, it would have been necessary for him to pay me more respect and to understand the value of men."

Here is the man. It was one of his sayings that "one can do nothing useful by being afraid of anything other than of error and of cowardice[43]. For him, these were not just words, they were also facts. In the very precarious situation he found himself at the time, living from the remnants of a very humble inheritance, with no position assured in Rome and no future possible there, anything else would have misled the

Archbishop. But it was that very consideration that stimulated him to an explanation for which he felt irresistibly moved by the dangers of the consequences it would entail. He believed that his dignity had been compromised. It was enough to keep him from looking ahead or behind, taking into consideration only what he believed was his honor — and this is what made him obstinate.

Needlessly did he feel that he was not approved by Mme Swetchine; needlessly, for during several months, she, Buquet, since then bishop of Parium, *l'abbé* Haffringue, Affre, gave him the strongest assurances of the favorable dispositions of de Quélen just in case he would consent to give to this Prelate mitigating explanations of the letter of 14 January. Needless was the effort to make his eyes brighten with the immediate prospect of becoming a canon at Notre-Dame, Lacordaire remained unmoved. As regards Paris, he felt an unimaginable interior remoteness; to leave no doubt about his determination, he arranged to have sold the furniture he left behind in the capital.

In he meantime, he made at St. Eusebius of Rome, with the Jesuits, a retreat that would have much influence on his subsequent decisions. But let us not anticipate the consequences of that retreat, so little suspected for a long time.

Nonetheless, the principal goal of Lacordaire's journey to Rome had been achieved beyond his dreams. Previously, Rome had been his weakness; it did not know him well enough. Even if suspected, one could easily enter. The welcome of the Jesuits, that of the cardinals in charge, that of the Pope, all had scattered the clouds. With success achieved, Lacordaire's sojourn in Rome no longer had a goal. Another year, without much advancement either in his studies or in his spiritual growth, would not have made him take a step toward the Sovereign Pontiff or toward public opinion. From another point of view, he found himself cruelly alone in the holy city. As he had foreseen, he suffered much in being unable to bare his soul and to love. No doubt, he was not without relationships; he had found again in Rome, M. Lacroix, the National Cleric of France, his former schoolmate at Saint-Sulpice, but now much older and especially belonging to an entirely different school than his own. He was very friendly with the Chargé d'affaires of Belgium, Blondeel; he was welcomed by the Borghese princess, née La Rochefoucauld, the most highly esteemed person in Rome, and by her young, friendly, and numerous family. But, in the end, he was lacking intimacy. "I have had too much weakness for loving," he wrote, "God is punishing me by isolation; he wants me to accustom myself to love Him alone." For a brief moment, he enjoyed the presence of Montalembert. But the departure of this very dear friend only made him feel more deeply the solitude of heart in which he left him. As we will see later, Lacordaire then took a lively interest in the proceedings for the canonical reestablishment in France of the Order of St. Benedict. But once this matter was settled, he felt that the will of God had been completely followed by his voyage and there was nothing left for him to do in Rome. He was offered the chaplaincy at Saint-Louis-des-Français, and for a moment, he was tempted to accept. But this favor (assuredly a slight one), coming from the Embassy of France, he felt would restrain his independence[44], to a certain extent, and he ended up declining the offer, being content to accept a small provisional apartment in that building. The Cardinal Vicar had proposed having him preach conferences to visitors in the church of St. Louis, and at first, the idea delighted him. But on reflection, he saw numerous obstacles: an Italian audience, which would understand nothing, an audience composed of Germans, Russians, English, which by reason of the diversity it would be impossible to move; finally, the possibility was crushed by the deep feeling he would have in engaging in a cold and false activity[45].

In spite of himself, then, his gaze turned toward France. There was his mission; there his power; of this he had a compelling intuition. He remained obstinate, however, in not wanting to yearn for Paris but he tried to persuade himself that the success of P. de Ravignan, at Notre-Dame, made his return pointless[46]. It is an indisputable fact, attested to by all his letters of that period, by his most personal outpouring of emotions, that he experienced great joy at this success. But, in the eyes of Lacordaire, Paris was not France. Why did not all cathedral churches have their conferences of Notre-Dame? Was this not a need of the times, a period, he used to say, when youth had no place to learn about religion and yet had an immense desire to know it? All his ambition was channeled to create in France this education that was missing everywhere[47].

Every day, his enthusiasm was dashed more and more concerning the location of the book [viz., Rome] whose composition was supposed to take up his time. All his friends dissuaded him from burying himself in a prolonged office life, always cold and less fruitful than action, especially in Rome, far from his home country[48]. "I do want to write," he would say, "but only after having collected material, after a useful and strong life, such as God had done to those whom He destined an activity for the salvation of souls. The first thing, therefore, is to *have a life*. Often the life of man is the reason to read his books. On this point, I am unable to control my instincts; they are innate and the past encourages me to follow them. Would I close myself up, for ten years, in an icy office to compose at leisure? Would I let time that was more appropriate for the word pass into a silence for which even my conscience would reproach me[49]?"

One favorable occasion came up. As he was leaving his retreat at St. Eusebius, a very kindly Providence brought to Rome another schoolmate of Lacordaire from Saint-Sulpice, Chalandon, today Archbishop of Aix. At the time, he was Vicar General of the bishop of Metz. Naturally, the two schoolmates conversed about the new and fruitful thought that occupied the mind of Lacordaire at the moment. This was how the idea sprung up to apply it immediately by conferences in the cathedral of Metz[50]. It was a question of starting as soon as Advent of 1837. "I would preach," wrote Lacordaire, "from Advent to Easter. The rest of the year would be devoted to study in the city where I will have preached, then to cultivate the souls who had more or less rallied to the faith. Every winter, I would go to another large city. In this way, I would avoid the newspapers of Paris and their absurd reporters; I would avoid the cliques of the capital, and be able to do much good[51]." At about the same time, overtures were made to Lacordaire at Lyons, by the pastor of St. Bonaventure, and at Bordeaux by the Archbishop, Donnet, today a cardinal[52]. The Bishop of Metz enjoyed priority; Lacordaire chose Metz.

He was preparing himself to leave Rome secretly at a rather early hour so as to pass the Alps before the snows came when cholera made itself known in the holy city; in a few days it had claimed thousands of victims. It would have been cowardly to leave under such circumstances; accordingly, Lacordaire placed himself at the service of the Cardinal Vicar who attached him as an auxiliary to the parish of St. Louis of the French. It was as a consequence of this service that he had the consolation of assisting at the death-bed of the artist Sigalon, painter of the beautiful copy of the *Last Judgment* by Michelangelo, which hangs in the School of Fine Arts in Paris. There was a rather sharp moment of alarm. Dom Guéranger, abbot of Solesmes, was in danger for twenty-four hours. Moved by this impression, Lacordaire suddenly decided to reconcile with his bishop. "When death shows itself to be close," he was wont to say, "and that at any moment one can be called before God, it is a very heavy burden to experience any disconnection with him whom God has given you as pastor and as father, even though there be a thousand reasons supporting his side, and that the heart be free of bitterness[53]."

This letter from Lacordaire to the Archbishop is dated 22 August.

"My Lord, cholera has arrived in Rome. Exposed, like everyone else, to be suddenly affected, I wish to carry before God a sincere heart united to my bishop, not only because of canonical obedience, in which I have never failed, but more because of an affection untainted by any haziness." Following a brief recapitulation, Lacordaire recalled the approbation given to his *Letter concerning the Holy See* by the Cardinal Secretary of State and by the Holy Father. It was because of the foreboding de Quélen had about the false situation in which he would find himself (believing himself obliged by his personal convictions to oppose a publication that Rome approved of and desired), that Lacordaire attributed the reluctance shown by the Prelate for this publication even before having seen the manuscript. "I immediately stopped my work," continued Lacordaire, "and even though, since then, the Supreme Pontiff had twice expressed the hope that it be published in a foreign country, I never thought of anything else other than keeping it enclosed in my briefcase. Yet, hurt by the judgment that had been made against my character, after thirteen years of frequent communications and so many ties made by the hands of Providence, I found it fitting to abandon myself to a feeling of honor, *perhaps too human to be genuinely Christian,* but not quite enough to be unjust and misunderstood by another honorable man. Time covered that over as it did everything else. It erased from old books newer writings and gave victory to the ancient, even though it thought of itself as the destroyer of everything that is old."

This letter remained unanswered for almost two months. On 15 October, de Quélen, believing that Lacordaire was still in Rome, sent him a few lines of congratulations for his care of the sick. He protested again that, to prevent the publication of the *Letter concerning the Holy See,* he had no other motives than those he had already expressed, especially nothing based on the divergences of political opinions. "You had sent me a document," said de Quélen, "and you left it so much to my judgment, regarding the fundament, the form, or the advisability, that you told me to throw it into the fire if I thought that it should never appear. I took you at your word and I simply used the right you offered me to use; that is all. If anyone *added* or saw something other, that was a mistake. A greater wrong if anyone interpreted and *called attention* to my behavior as based on reasons devised by the imagination.

"We have been assured," continued the Prelate, "that you intend to return to France within this year. Your steps are even counted and your projects recounted: to preach the following Lent in Metz, then travel in the South. I am unaware of those issues and therefore am unable to address them. All I can tell you is that you will always be received here as a friend, to whom I will always remain very devoted."

Is is not difficult to see that the new letter from Lacordaire had more than reopened the archiepiscopal wound. De Quélen could not help but be offended to hear himself saying that, foreseeing the approval of a document by the Pope, he had hurriedly taken the lead and placed it under suspicion without having read it. There was some hint of this in the letter of the Prelate of 20 December 1836; but, if the result of this letter, in any case, even if the work by Lacordaire would be approved by Rome, the archbishop of Paris remained absolute master of allowing or preventing its publication. The reason for this is that de Quélen rightly believed himself to be the better judge of the suitability of a publication destined for France. It does not follow, however, that the Archbishop had foreseen the pontifical approbation (he was far from seeing that), nor that he had thought, in this matter, to place his doctrinal authority above that of the Pope; that is an offensive supposition. Nonetheless, nothing justified de Quélen to suspect, as indeed he did, that Lacordaire had called Rome's attention to the fact that his behavior was based on the reason in question. This last suspicion was no less shocking nor less rash than the one about which the Prelate was complaining. Evidently, also, de Quélen was hurt that Lacordaire had not told him about his decision to reenter France and to preach in the provinces. And yet, all things considered, and being unable to prevent what was to happen, he decided not to make an open break with Lacordaire; and so, after six weeks of silence, he ended up writing the letter which we have just read.

Lacordaire received it in Metz. We find it hard to believe that he himself found it "very considerate and very cordial[54]." No doubt, he felt that this quarrel had lasted too long and that it was time to end it. He preferred to declare himself satisfied, even this easily, rather than to maintain a discontented attitude towards his bishop. Whatever the case may be, from that moment on, the feelings of the Archbishop for Lacordaire were irremediably changed[55]. He maintained appearances, but his confidence and sympathy never returned.

In the meantime, Montalembert pressed Lacordaire strongly to publish at last his *Letter concerning the Holy See*. The author continued to resist[56]. Finally, an incident that rocked all Germany and was the signal of a sudden and great awakening among Catholics, the armed abduction of the archbishop of Cologne, Dröste de Vischering, and his incarceration in a Prussian prison at the end of November 1837, seemed to Lacordaire a providential sign, in the presence of the new difficulties that this outrage created for the Papacy, that did not allow him to remain silent any longer about the truths contained in his document. Indeed, the occasion proved opportune. Gregory XVI had protested against the assault by the king of Prussia with a forcefulness that supported what was said in the Letter *concerning the Holy See* about the independence of the Pope in relations with imperious governments. Lacordaire, therefore, gave the order to publish this pamphet and forewarned de Quélen in a very simple yet very respectful letter. The Archbishop was not at all displeased[57].

Success was as rapid as it was notable; and it was well deserved. Like everything that comes from superior truth, the *Letter concerning the Holy See*, after thirty years, had lost none of its relevance. As it stands, even with its gaps, recognized from the start by the author[58], it is one Lacordaire's best writings. As he himself would say, it is not a treatise, it is a hymn, but a hymn in which, nonetheless, is found the answer to everything. "No," the author would cry out, "no; when I will no longer believe, when never a ray of divine grace has enlightened my understanding, I will still kiss with respect the feet of that man who, in a fragile pulpit and in a soul subject to all temptations, maintained very holy the dignity of my species and for one thousand eight hundred years allowed the spirit to prevail over force."

Is this not true also of the time of Pius IX as of the time of St. Peter?

In 1836, Lacordaire was speaking of Europe with foresight that is startling.

"War is not between kings," said he. "Something

warns them that the time is not ripe to enrich themselves with areas taken from their neighbors. It is not that ambition has been extinguished in them more than in other men, nor even that *their plans had been designed* for less difficult times. Prussia, for example, aspired to assemble Germany under its domination, because it is necessary that, sooner or later, German unity be constituted, and that Prussia deserves to inherit it all as much as Austria does. Russia is persuaded that whoever speaks a Slavic tongue or does not believe in the procession of the Holy Spirit, belongs to it by right, and that it is destined to rebuild in Constantinople the empire of the East, of which it will simultaneously be Patriarch and Caesar."

And elsewhere:

"Prussia marches at the head of European humanism whose political effects it abhors so heartily. What? It employs fourteen thousand men to produce humanism, and three hundred thousand men to prevent some of its repercussions? There is no proportion here.

"The disproportion between the body and the spirit of Russia is even more striking if we consider its intentions. What will it take to the Orient to establish it, to build it up from its ruins, which is even more difficult? It will bring a clergy impoverished to the bone because of its separation from unity [i.e., solidarity]. To that unfortunate country, that divine curse has not stopped pursuing a single day since they tore Jesus Christ apart in miserable disputes, Russia will present the very fruit of their crime to save them. It will heap schism upon schism, death upon death. It will tell them: Here is the cup by which you perished, let us sit at the same table, let us drink and be merry. I really understand the apparent advantage of a common error, when this error, still young, has not produced all its results, and that the first enthusiasm that it draws from its novelty subsists. But when the cadaver is dressed up, what can we give it, and what can we receive from it? Russia's need, at this point, is to be Catholic, and it will be so as soon as its sovereigns will allow.

The author crowns his prediction with the translation of an incomparable fragment from Isaiah about the expansion of truth and of unity on the earth, and ends with these words:

"Neither you nor I, dear friend, will see those marvels, reserved, if God is pleased, for love humiliated and unrecognized. We will see, on the contrary, sad spectacles: the good victorious over evil out of necessity, and evil regaining its control, *because the good will not be recognized in its own victory.*

"Too many disparate elements are mixed up and ground together. A century will not be too long for the disagreeable task of separating them, and we die before resting; yet this is not something about which we should complain.

"A few days ago, I was walking in the outskirts of Rome, near the catacombs of St. Lawrence. I was heading for a new cemetery, created within the old cemetery, and I was struck by an inscription at the gate: *Weep over the deceased, because he is at rest!* What did this mean? It was not difficult for me to figure out. Weep over the deceased because he has stopped doing well, because his hands can no longer give, nor his feet walk ahead of trouble, because his innards are no longer thrilled by the lamentation, and that his spirit, flown far away from the disputes of men, no longer opposes them by an act of humble and patient faith. Weep over the deceased because he has stopped, while the one who nourished him on earth with teaching and with the bread of life, his Lord and his Master, is yet subject to opposition. Weep over the deceased because the time for virtue is over and finished for him, because he will no longer add anything to his crown. Weep for the deceased because he can longer die for God. For a long time I rolled these thoughts around in my mind, maintained by the proximity to the martyrs and by that attractive basilica erected in the countryside to the memory of deacon Lawrence. I stared at the old walls of Rome before me and slowly returned to my lonely dwelling, happy to find myself, for a moment, far from my century, but without any desire of having been born in a more quiet one. Near the tombs of the saints and the martyrs, I heard this sublime warning: *Weep for the deceased because he is at rest.*"

For his part, Lacordaire was not at all resting. At the time when he was having these words published, he had begun to inaugurate at Metz the work of Conferences in the provinces.

ENDNOTES

1. 2 May 1836.
2. Letter to Mgr Lacroix, national cleric of France to Rome, 3 July 1834.
3. 25 July 1836.
4. To Mme Swetchine, 21 June 1836.
5. Unpublished journal of Mgr Lacroix.
6. This letter, addressed to the *Ami de la Religion* [newspaper], was reproduced in *L'Univers* of 8 June 1836. — The responses to Cattet appeared in the *Ami de la Religion* of 7 and 9 June [1836].
7. 9 August 1836.
8. Hist. of Affre, by Castan, p. 76.
9. Letter of 9 August 1836.

10. 20 December 1836.

11. Probably the restitution of the grounds of the archiepiscopal residence of Paris, after its demolition by the uprising of 1831. This site was requested by de Quélen but denied by the Government. In fact, the refusal made it difficult for the archbishop to make any public sign of reconciliation.

12. Letter of de Quélen to Lacordaire, 20 December 1836.

13. Letter of Lacordaire to Montalembert, 19 November 1836.

14. Lacordaire to Montalembert, 26 November 1836. – See also his letter of the same day to Mme Swetchine.

15. 29 November 1836, to Mme Swetchine and to Montalembert.

16. To Mme Swetchine, 26 November 1836.

17. To Montalembert, 19 November 1936.

18. Compare the letters to Mme Swetchine of 29 November and of 15 December 1836.

19. 20 December 1836.

20. Letter to Blondeel dated 20 December. See Appendix XIX, page 561.

21. This is a result of a letter from Buquet, today bishop of Parium, a letter written at the beginning of 1837.

22. To Mme Swetchine, 21 December 1836.

23. This refers to the fact that de Quélen (letter of 20 December) wanted "a free hand to delete what it seemed necessary to suppress."

= In mythology, the Danaides were condemned to keep filling a barrel without a bottom.

24. To Mme Swetchine, 3 January 1837.

25. Mme Swetchine to Lacordaire, 19 January 1837.

26. See *Correspondance de madame Swetchine, p. 115*.

27. 14 January 1837.

28. Letter of Buquet of 18 February 1837.

29. Letter of Buquet.
30. See the entire text of de Quélen: Appendix XX, page 562.
31. To Mme Swetchine, 10 February 1837. – Journal of Mgr Lacroix, 9 February.
32. Letter to de Quélen, 22 August 1837.
33. It was published at the end of December 1837. (*Correspondance ave Madame Swetchine*, p. 154.
34. Private journal of Mgr Lacroix, 24 February 1837.

On 30 January, the Pope had Lacordaire invited at the distribution of Candlemas (2 February) at the Sistine Chapel. As soon as he saw him Gregory XVI told the Master of Ceremonies: *Presto!* Then, His holiness handed over with his own hand to the author of the *Letter concerning the Holy See* a large candle that he ordered be kept aside expressly for him, while saying: *L'abbate Lacordaire, si!* (Same Journal, 2 February 1837.)

35. Lacordaire to M. de Quélen, 23 August 1837.

36. M. Blondel, Minister of Belgium in Rome, letter of 20 December 1836.
37. It was in that same year (1837) that Louis-Philippe, had proposed a project of law that granted freedom of secondary education. After the House of Deputies introduced an amendment against the Jesuits, the project of law was withdrawn.

At a date that could not be closer to the writing of the *Letter concerning the Holy See,* 12 February 1837, in an audience that he had granted to Montalembert, Gregory XVI lamented the attitude of de Quélen. He went so far as to say: "I am very pleased (*contentissimo*) with King Louis-Philippe; I wish all the kings of Europe were like him." And, based on this praise, the Pope recalled in detail the nomination of Guillon to the see of Beauvais, the resistance of Rome to that choice, and the declaration of Louis-Philippe who had no intention of constraining the conscience of the Holy Father. "Few princes would have dared to act in this way," added Gregory XVI.

We have to agree that the words of Lacordaire were far inferior to the praise of the Sovereign Pontiff given here by Louis-Philippe. The words of the Pope explain extravagantly those of the *Letter concerning the Holy See*. Lacordaire had written, in very reserved terms, as can be seen, what was thought in the upper reaches of the Vatican.

38. In his *Letter concerning the Holy See*, this is how he characterizes the princes of the elder branch.
39. To Mme Swetchine, 4 July 1837.
40. To Mme Swetchine, 4 July 1837.
41. To Montalembert, 20 November 1837.
42. To Mme Swetchine, 10 February 1837.
43. To Montalembert, 8 April 1837.
44. To Montalembert, 22 June 1837.
45. To Montalembert, 13 August 1837.
46. To Mme Swetchine, 3 March 1837. – To Montalembert, 28 February and 28 March. – To Chéruel, 28 February and 7 March.
47. To Mme Swetchine, 4 July and 8 November 1837.
48. To Montalembert, 15 July 1837.
49. To Montalembert, 13 August 1837.
50. To Mme Swetchine, 4 July 1837.
51. To Montalembert, 15 July 1837.
52. To Mme Swetchine, 8 August and 16 September 1837.
53. To Montalembert, 30 August 1837.
54. To Mme Swetchine, 18 December 1837.
55. Affre, cited by Castan, p. 76.
56. He was still resisting on 20 November, as can be proven by his letter of that day to Montalembert.
57. To Montalembert, 5 January 1838.

58. See his *Preface*.

Chapter X

Series at Metz — Dominican Vocation

Series at Metz: success and opposition – Episode: Bautain at Strasbourg; philosophical and theological quarrel between him and his bishop, de Trévern; pacifying intervention by Lacordaire – First signs of the latter's vocation to religious life – Development of that vocation – Voyage to Rome to inform the General of the Dominicans about his resolve to reestablish the Order in France; assent of the General – Publication of *Notice for the Reestablishment of the Order of Friars Preachers* – Lacordaire sets off with two companions to make his novitiate at a Dominican convent in Italy – Hippolyte Réquédat and the school of Buchez – Influence of Tommaseo on Réquédat: Dominican vocation of the latter – Difficulties aroused in Rome against Lacordaire's project; they are overcome; he enters as novice at the convent of La Quercia

Among the large cities of France, Metz has its particular characteristics. Filled with ancient memories, former capital of the kings of Austrasia, autonomous city in the Middle Ages, like all free cities of the Holy Empire, united to France since Henry II, it is a first-class district for war, with a large population of military men on duty and superior officers chosen from among them, since it is the seat of a scientific school, an extension of the Polytechnic School[1]. These many special conditions offered Lacordaire an audience of a new social standing. This expectation was not misguided. In the vast main nave of the attractive cathedral of Metz, a spacious section was reserved for men. From the first day, it was inadequate; what immediately caught the eye were the innumerable groups of epaulets, uniforms of all branches of service and of all grades who no longer feared to be seen at the foot of a Christian pulpit. The garrison and the schools comprised the largest part of this splendid audience: at least three-fifths of the attendants wore epaulets. And this was not the mood of one day: during four months, all these officers followed the conferences with as much attention as they had long ago for their catechism. The meeting was such that the University students had to request reserved places in front of the preacher. The crowd of women, however unequal the space allotted to them, and however extreme the rigors of the season, did not fall off for even one day. In short, there was as much eagerness as at Notre-Dame but much more calm[2].

The orator appeared in the pulpit with all the brilliance, all the conviction, all the influence of his young words, with no unevenness, no weariness from the informality[3]. His voice had grown strong; he had reached a point of forgetting himself, a degree of control over himself and and of accountability for his actions on others — such as he had not expected to achieve until after ten years[4]. Moreover, the audience was sincerely moved and the whole city experienced more or less the repercussions of that impression, but with rather diverging states of mind.

At the time, Metz had three newspapers and one magazine: it had its legitimist paper, its orleanist paper, and its republican paper. The first showed itself as the most sympathetic to the speaker; the second gave proof of justice but was cold; the third was openly hostile. The *Letter concerning the Holy See*, published on 1 January 1838, contained these words: "One could say that in France there were only monarchical parties [i.e., supporting the monarchy], unless one discovered at the bottom of society some kind of faction that considered itself republican, about which one lacks the courage to speak disparagingly only because it has many opportunities of chopping off our head in the interval between two monarchies." This phrase was not likely to earn for the author the good-will of the republican party. This party fired broadsides against him. On the other hand, it so happened that at the seventh conference, the Catholic orator was persuaded to treat of the significant religious break of he sixteenth century. He did so in irreproachable language and without partiality. Numerous and important in Metz (which has a Calvinist Consistory), the Protestants, in turn, published three booklets. The deists of Voltaire also published their own. This was the other half of Lacordaire's success. He had the good sense not to reply, whether by word of mouth or in writing; but this did not prevent the controversy from being prolonged in the newspapers. For all that, this debate was far from slowing down the increasing triumphs of the conferences of Metz. At the last one, held on Easter (15 April 1838), the preacher was due in the pulpit at one-thirty; by five o'clock in the morning, many places had already been occupied. After the sermon, a deputation — representing the elite of the city — came to offer the Christian orator some church-plate in gilt-silver, of great beauty, while placing in his hands a document on which can be read the names of General de Marguerie, one of the most remarkable conquests of the series; of Count du Coetlosquet, subsequently deceased on a pilgrimage to Jerusalem after having served as representative of the people in the Constituent Assembly of 1848; of many members of the royal court; of many superior officers, and of the Colonel commanding the School of Instruction for the Artillery and the Corps of Engineers.

Lacordaire was not able to receive this deputation in person, but before leaving Metz, he wrote to Count du Coetlosquet, compiler of the document, the letter that follows:

"Count, dear Sir,

"In my current inability to thank directly all the persons who offered me a testimony of their feelings, allow me to approach you to be towards them the spokesperson for my gratitude. 'I do not know,' said to her children the mother of the Maccabees, 'I do not know how you appeared in my womb, because it is was not I who gave you mind, soul, and life.' And neither do I know, Mr. Count, whence came so many friends of whom I was unaware. God only knows. He who has united all the worlds, He assembles easily some souls around another soul, however feeble it be. Accordingly, I attribute to His power and glory what I could be tempted to credit to myself; for the touching manifestations, I reserve for myself only the duty to understand the cost. I understand it quite keenly."

Lacordaire left in Metz some lasting traces of his apostolate: some notable conversions, for example, that of General de Marguerie, whom I just noted[5], along with an excellent undertaking, that of St. Vincent de Paul, which had as its first president an officer from the artillery. To establish a chapter of St. Vincent de Paul, a work of zeal completely in the hands of lay persons, was at the time a novelty as strange as Lacordaire's kind of preaching. Besides, one would have to have known the mind-sets in the provinces after 1830, to have noted to what degree Catholics were wrapped up as if buried due to the fall of Charles X, to realize how they were treated everywhere as vanquished and suspect, to what state of *individualism* and corresponding isolation they had fallen — that it required the influence of Lacordaire to group together in Metz some Catholics of all ages, of all conditions, with no concern for political parties (something unheard of in the provinces at that time), into an association of Christian resoluteness between men. This is what the missionaries in France had attempted almost everywhere following their missions, but under other conditions and often without continuance. Then again, the revolution of 1830 had not only dispersed their associations but also struck them with unpopularity. It was from this unpopularity, from this fall from grace that men of faith had to be raised up. Moreover, it was not excessive that all the prestige surrounding Lacordaire at Metz and the enthusiasm instilled in Catholics by the eloquent freshness of his language, made them spring up from under the earth and grouped them into an association.

Indeed, there were some shadows to that success. At Metz as in Paris, the elder clergy understood nothing about abstract generalities in which perhaps the preaching of Lacordaire delighted. This organizing of truth (this was the abusive use of a foreign word recognized in Metz) was suspect. The elderly bishop, at eighty-two years, former pastor at Lyons, was surely the man of the world least prepared and least sympathetic to this unusual kind of teaching. A very singular circumstance arose to worsen this natural state of things. In the mind of the Bishop and of his Vicars General, Lacordaire was to preach only in winter. A renowned preacher, Dufêtre, at the time Vicar General of Tours but who died as bishop of Nevers, had been chosen as early as August 1837, to preach the Lenten series at Metz in 1838. Lacordaire had been informed that the diocesan administration feared the simultaneous presence of two Christian orators in the same pulpit. But, by the end of February, the conferences raised such hopes, that interrupting them before Easter was unthinkable. From then on, impossible to avoid comparisons. Lacordaire got into the pulpit at one-thirty; M. Dufêtre preached in the evening. Indeed, the latter did possess considerable oratorical gifts, had an extraordinarily powerful voice, much richness of language and warmth. But he made the mistake of remaining in the conventional; the audience was not with him. Wounded to the quick, he could not remain silent. Lending his voice, a voice already accredited, to the muffled whispers of the elder clergy, he announced rather loudly that the preaching of Lacordaire required a separate pulpit, a separate audience, so as not to compromise by his proximity the simplicity and the formality of the apostolic minister. Moreover, he did not hesitate to disapprove of this kind of preaching as false and misplaced, especially in a pulpit like that of Metz, made famous by the oratorical beginnings of Bossuet. He even hinted that, despite Lacordaire's purity of intention, there slipped into his conferences some false, or at least very rash ideas. Indeed, one can imagine what echoes reverberated among the ranks of the elder clergy by these hardly confidential affirmations of Dufêtre[6].

In the eyes of the elders, the enthusiasm of the young priests for the conferences constituted an additional danger. Another new item introduced in Metz by Lacordaire, the Society of St. Vincent de Paul, also gave umbrage because of its organization of lay persons. The formula adopted by the elder clergy was that Lacordaire "was constantly *beside* dogma." The word was spread around that the elderly bishop of Metz had written about this to [Bishop] de Quélen, and had received a reply that satisfied him. As a result, in this city where Lacordaire had just done so much good, spiritual authorities seemed busy only at downplaying his memory[7]. And yet, the religious impulse resulting from the conferences of 1838 within the elite of the population of Metz, was such that, even several years later, one thousand two hundred men, from all intellectual classes of that population, joined together in the Eucharistic banquet — among them, a considerable number of students from the School of Instruction.

From another viewpoint, during this series at Metz, Lacordaire deserved much credit from the Church: more than any other person, he had hastened the end of the painful misunderstanding which, for six years, troubled a large diocese, that of Strasbourg. We will summarize the facts in a few words.

Eloquent disciple of Cousin (an oratorical master without rival in the teaching of philosophy), Bautain, apostle like him of spiritual teachings but deist, also like him, in the principal city of our studies, i.e., Strasbourg, created for himself a very considerable role. A legitimate success, to be sure, because as professor, he assuredly had few equals. He loved science, but science was unable to give him a satisfactory solution to the great problems of human life. "While he doubted everything, barely believed his own reason, not knowing what to make of himself or of others in the midst of the world[8]," Providence set in his path a superior woman, Mlle Humann, elder sister of a man whom we have seen as Minister, and esteemed Minister of the monarchy of 1830. She was an elderly person, who had made herself familiar with reading Kant and his disciples, but who had weighed them in the balance of Christianity and found them to be lightweights. Bautain liked to talk with her about philosophy; in return, she talked to him about religion. The day came, when following these rambling discussions, the deist found himself Christian, and a Catholic Christian. Never, wrote the convert, never was freedom of a man so fully respected, and never was it so completely conquered. Now this thought affected the heart of Bautain, who, having vowed his life to the defense of truth when it was still unknown to him, would not fail to spread it fully now that he had found it in the Gospel and in the Church. Soon, disregarding the offers of an immense fortune and of a political role[9], he became a priest of Jesus Christ. This occurred in 1828.

He was not alone to enter into the sanctuary; entering with him was a young judge, today one of the princes of the Roman Church[10], a student of the Polytechnic School who would later become Father Gratry, four Israelites of distinguished merit, won over by his lessons concerning the Christian faith[11], a medical doctor of great promise[12], two young gentlemen and the son of one of the most honored families in commerce of Strasbourg[13].

The bishop of that diocese, de Trévern, in his eighties, honorably known for a noted work of controversy against the Anglican Church, received with open arms these brilliant recruits; to their disinterested care, he hurriedly entrusted the minor seminary which, under their direction, quickly underwent a development without equal. But, by September 1831, complaints arose among the clergy concerning the philosophy espoused in that establishment: the professor was accused of denying the competence of reason in metaphysics. Jealousy was unfortunately not a stranger in those objections, well-founded as they were. The storm brewed and grew for three years. It finally erupted at the end of September 1834 with the publication of a pastoral letter by the Bishop of Strasbourg: *A Caution about the Teaching of M. Bautain*.

The Prelate had asked the professor six questions, to which the latter responded in writing.

The first of the six questions, and no doubt the principal one was this: " Do you believe that *unaided* reason is insufficient to prove with certitude the existence of the Creator and the infinity of His perfections?"

Here was the answer: " Not only do I believe that, but I have the deepest conviction, as Christian and as philosopher, that reasoning *alone*, without the light of faith, cannot offer me certitude concerning this first of truths[14]."

To be sure, the intention of Bautain was praiseworthy. The absolute sovereignty of reason is the preeminent illusion of our century. This is what had made Bautain an unbeliever. It was for that very reason that, in his eyes, one could never overreact against pride of the spirit. Besides, he did not expect to set reason aside but only to give it its proper place, second in line, as he did. It was with this viewpoint, but by an unfortunate borrowing from Kant's philosophy — to which he had long been attached — that Bautain, more philosopher than theologian, had presented his thesis: in the sphere of metaphysics, reasoning alone can do nothing, not even prove the existence of God. He was pleased to settle matters with one blow by demonstrating the metaphysical impotency of reason, with the presumption of private judgment; it seemed to him simultaneously pleasing and biting to see it overturned by the man who was seen as the greatest logician of his time. For another reason, Pascal had fallen, as we know, in a similar exaggeration that, in our day and under diverse viewpoints, captivates many Catholics. It is the honor of the Church to have always protested against this excess; always, in fact, did she claim, always did she maintain the rights of reason in the preliminaries to the faith. The danger of a contrary teaching appeared so great to de Trévern that he not only removed Bautain from the direction of the minor seminary but also from the ministry of the pulpit and that of preaching.

The consequences of these severities were regrettable. Struck with fruitlessness as priest, Batain was able to maintain, as member of the University, the fulness of his status and his advantages. He continued to teach philosophy in the Faculty of Letters with his usual brilliance and success. But he did more; with his disciples, he opened in Strasbourg a boarding school of secondary education, which immediately overflowed with students. All the while, the press intervened strongly for and against him. Minds were violently divided: almost the entire clergy followed the Bishop, while lay people, in great majority and with officialdom at their head, held for Bautain. Who does not feel that this was a predicament against nature, one that could not be prolonged without grave damage to the Church?

Basically, two worlds faced each other but were separated by an abyss. On one side, the spirit of routine, unable to adopt the view of the new disposition of minds and unfortunately not even taking it into account; on the other, the nineteenth century no less able to place itself in the shoes of the remaining men of the former Sorbonne, formed by scholasticism and nourished by a genuine superstition for that exclusive method of teaching. Is tangible proof needed? De Trévern was fully correct when he defended the prerogatives of reason in religious matters; but he appeared beneath his mission when, seeing the benefit of teaching philosophy in Latin, he prescribed as faultless text the *Philosophical Institutions* of Le Mans! It was this evident misunderstanding of the current needs of minds on the part of an old man — a worthy one, to be sure — and simultaneously, of the exaggerated importance, from his viewpoint, that Bautain gave to the efficacy of his philosophical method to return to the faith the men of this century — which explains especially the latter's resistance to the caution of his bishop.

A mediator was needed; one, in fact, offered himself in November 1835. Donnet, then coadjutor of Nancy, today archbishop of Bordeaux and cardinal, went to Strasbourg, devised a conciliatory formula and was able to have de Trévern approve of it. This document was signed by Bautain and by his followers. But the mediator had barely gone on his way that everything was nullified by the bishop of Strasbourg.

Other individuals stepped in, and many times, reconciliation was believed to have occurred. But jealous passions had strung together to attack a man who was their superior[15]; in December 1837, the misunderstanding was still there. It was then, on his own initiative, between two conferences in Metz, that Lacordaire during an intense cold spell crossed the Vosges mountains to reach Strasbourg.

Never had he experienced any strong liking for Bautain; their two natures were too dissimilar, I believe, for one of them to appreciate the value of the other. Nonetheless, struck by the secular reputation of Bautain, Lacordaire, before he even knew him, had generously attempted to draw him to Paris where de Quélen himself had sought him[16]. Later, Lacordaire judged the disciple of Cousin with extreme severity. About the orator, he would say like Mirabeau about Barnave: this is a man who speaks well, and yet has no divine spark in him. For all that, he placed the orator above the writer, even though he reproached both of them for their colorless style, a grave defect in Lacordaire's eyes. Moreover, he accused the priest of conceding too much to science, "which is merely secondary in the plan of Jesus Christ[17]." The professor, which is to say the eminent side of Bautain, was unknown to him. In the end, the philosopher, in the little he had read about him, seemed mysterious, methodical, selective. As for the fundament of his teaching, the speaker of Stanislaus had immediately noticed the same radical vice as that of La Mennais, even though his viewpoint, as Lacordaire recognized, was not the same. "Those two men," he said, "in their aversion to rationalism, wanted to place the faith on top, thereby reversing completely the ancient ordering of the defense of Christianity. The basis of Christianity lies in reason; by depriving reason of its genuine rights, one would later produce a frightful skepticism[18]."

Indeed, long before the cry of alarm by Bishop de Trévern, Lacordaire had predicted everything with most clear-sighted accuracy. He had seen with incredible pain the philosopher of Strasbourg isolating himself from the clergy, living in withdrawal with his followers, surrounded by their admiration, illogically creating for himself formidable obstacles, and engaging in a theological quarrel wherein he would necessarily lose[19]. Lacordaire was troubled all the more because, after all, the school of Strasbourg was, in France, the only Catholic school in existence. Why so? Because the influence of Bautain as preacher, although not first rank in his eyes, appeared no less worthy of respect — and also because the incident in Strasbourg complicated the general situation by providing the distrustful and lethargic mind with an additional excuse[20]. How could one console himself in seeing men of this quality wear themselves out in unproductive combat in which what was valuable in their ideas was almost hopelessly compromised by what was excessive in them[21].

Accordingly, the success (unfortunately too short-lived) of Donnet was for Lacordaire almost a personal satisfaction and a happy event in his own life. He disapproved strongly the futility of a supreme effort attempted by Bautain, in November 1837, to please his bishop.

"No one more than myself," he wrote[22], "rightly values purity of doctrine; I dare say that every day I become more jealous for myself. But charity in the appreciation of doctrine is the absolutely necessary counterbalance to theological inflexibility. The goal of the genuine Christian is to seek the truth in one doctrine and not the error, to do all he can to find that truth, to the point of blood, just as one plucks a rose from in between the thorns. The one who holds a low estimate of the thought of a man, of an honest man, of a man who has made visible sacrifices to God, that one is a pharisee, the only race of men that was cursed by Jesus Christ. The one who says of a man who believes to be working for the glory of God: of what value is man? Does God have need of witty men? That one is a pharisee. 'He removes the key to knowledge,' said Jesus Christ; 'he does not enter and he prevents others from entering.' Is there a Father of the Church who has opinions and even errors? Will we throw his writings out the window so that the ocean of truth be all the more unsullied? Oh! How holy is the man who fights for God; up to the day of an obvious heresy, one must carry his thoughts in a friendly heart."

Besides, in spite of all his reservations against the individual teaching of Bautain, Lacordaire believed him to be sincere, honest, devoted, beset by envy — a man who placed in the service of the Catholic cause his knowledge, his talent, his status. He felt he could not ask him to make an act of faith based on propositions formulated by a single bishop. But one avenue remained opened: to seek a decision from the Apostolic See. At the voice of Lacordaire, Bautain did not hesitate. Ten days after his conference with the preacher of Metz, the professor of Strasbourg was in Rome, carrying letters from Lacordaire for bishop Capaccini, for the general of the Jesuits, for the Princess Borghese, letters that arranged for Bautain most favorable receptions. Unfortunately, Cardinal Mezzofanti, who had been assigned as his examiner, fell sick and the matter dragged on.

In the meantime, Affre was called as coadjutor for de Trévern. From the convent of La Quercia, where he was making his novitiate as a Dominican, Lacordaire wrote impulsively to his friend to influence him in favor of Bautain. He succeeded without effort. This cleared the ways. Affre having been called to the see of Paris, the new coadjutor of Strasbourg, Ræss, did not wish to be any less agreeable than his predecessor: without requiring any other act of submission than a signature on the Donnet formulary, he lifted the suspension that weighed on Bautain, who, after all, had sinned only by an excess of faith, and allowed him to return into the pulpit of the cathedral.

But the quarrel had lasted too long; too many people had decided for or against. As soon as the honor of their priesthood was officially reestablished — while awaiting Rome's decision, that found them fully compliant. — Bautain and his friends no longer thought of leaving Strasbourg after having made their public peace with de Trévern, who was still alive. In fact, it was elsewhere that God called them to serve the Church. In the course of their life, amidst all the trials that attend Christian works here below, they were able to recognize the mysterious designs of Providence on them[23].

Lacordaire had been a generous instrument in their favor. But what was the immediate reward for that? The pulpit of Strasbourg, that had been offered to him before his visit to Bautain, was at the moment off limits to him. These obstacles, especially those of Metz, reawakened in the soul of Lacordaire the memory of the animosity shown against the conferences of Notre-Dame. They reopened wounds; they contributed to the appearance of a resolution that was nurtured in his heart for more than a year.

Lacordaire had always spoken with emotion about monks. On 8 September 1836, he wrote: "The spectacle of religious life is very touching. That large communal house, the silence, the elderly with their serious mien, so venerable, so admirably transformed by a prolonged interior life, the novices whose faces radiate all the charm of youth, embellished by the sacrifice they made to God, the meal, whose simple foods are seasoned with the reading of some edifying book — all of that touched me greatly[24]."

And a little later: "There is nothing so rare as a man who truly has the spirit of Jesus Christ and who knows how to make you share in it to the degree of your understanding and your calling. From that viewpoint as well as from many others, *the religious were very necessary* since the diocesan priests were too often turned away from the interior and divine life by their external occupations, and also by the influence of the times — which so easily penetrates the soul, without our realizing it — while we live with it[25]."

At the end of that same year, evidently already considering becoming a monk, he claimed in anticipation the freedom of religious enthusiasm. He wrote in his *Letter concerning the Holy See*: "When time will have done justice to the unfortunate theories that, while subduing the Catholic Church, deprived her of a large part of her social work, it will be easy to see what remedy to apply. Then, one will understand that the art of governing men does not consist in unleashing on them the freedom of evil by placing the good under faithful and dependable watch; one will liberate the good; one will say to men who are tired of secular worries: You wish to devote yourselves to God? Do so! You wish to withdraw from this world too brimming full, wherein minds are overloaded? Move apart. You wish to devote your fortune to comfort your dying brothers? Spend it. You wish to offer your life to the poor and to the insignificant? Teach them. You carry a name weighed down by three centuries of hate because your virtues appeared late in a world that was not worthy of them and you are not shocked at carrying it longer? Then carry it. All of you who wish for the good, whatever its form, who battle against pride and the rebellious senses, come and continue doing so. We have worn ourselves out in devising social forces, yet life has never fallen into our broken melting-pots. He who has life gives it away; he who has love, spreads it; he who has the secret, tells everyone! Thereupon, new times will begin, with a new overflowing of wealth; and wealth is not gold or silver, nor the ships that bring back from the extremities of the earth precious cargo, nor steam, nor railroads, nor anything that the genius of man can extract from the bowels of nature: wealth, if there be any, is love. From God to man, from earth to heaven, only love unites and fills everything; it is the beginning, the middle, and the end of things. He who loves understands; he who loves devotes himself; he who loves is happy; a drop of love placed on the scale with the entire universe will outweigh it, like what a storm would do to a bit of straw."

This was Lacordaire's state of mind at de Quélen's veto to the publication of the pamphlet. His first thought was to withdraw to a religious house: "I owe myself a long period of solitude. I have not yet told anyone but I will busy myself in searching for an asylum beyond the Po River, and I will be there after Easter for five or six years, even *longer, God willing... I need so little, and I hope that with time, I will need even less*[26]." M[me] Swetchine understood perfectly well what these last words implied: "an entire family of brothers, and at their head, a communal father to everyone[27]."

This sequence of thoughts dominated the mind of Lacordaire. "Oh," he wrote on 10 February, "if people only knew how much I love the peacefulness of obscurity, I would be less hated[28]."

In the meantime, at the end of March 1837[29], Father Guéranger arrived in Rome to request the reestablishment of the Benedictines in France. How could this coincidence not have struck Lacordaire? Father Guéranger also desired the revival in our country of the Order of Friars Preachers. He discussed it with Lacordaire and even told him that he had someone in mind to undertake just that. His hearer interrupted him to declare that he would willingly be that man. In the following visit, Lacordaire asked for information about the rule of life of the Dominicans. Father Guéranger told him what he knew about it and obtained for him a copy of the Constitutions of the Order. The following day, Lacordaire declared that he had read the entire work and found nothing there to trouble his mind[30]. Under the weight of serious thought, he felt the need to collect himself before God and to question Him in the silence of those pious exercises that were given the name *retreats*. Since having been ordained, only twice did Lacordaire have recourse to this powerful means of spiritual growth, and both times, said he, with little benefit. But in 1837, his soul was in an altogether different state. And so, he began a retreat with the Jesuits, under the direction of Father Villefort, at St. Eusebius, a small house with a church near St. Mary Major. This was May 4th, the feast of the Ascension; the retreat lasted up to the vigil of Pentecost. It was during these days of solemn recollection that Lacordaire felt himself clearly called to the monastic life and that he devised the formal design of reviving in France the Order of St. Dominic, just as Father Guéranger wished to revive that of St. Benedict[31].

Father Chocarne cited in their entirety the pages in which Lacordaire revealed all the thoughts that weighed upon his heart during that retreat at St.Eusebius. It is difficul to omit even one line.

"With my long stay in Rome giving me much time for reflection, I observed myself and studied also the general needs of the Church.

"As regards myself, already in my thirty-fourth year, a clergyman for twelve years, and having appeared twice with some brilliance in what had been attempted for the defense and the advance of Religion in France, I saw myself still alone, with no tie to any ecclesiastical institution; more than once the good-will of de Quélen had tried to make me understand that the ministry of parishes was the only one in which he could support me and train me. Now, I felt no calling for this kind of service and simultaneously, I also noted that in the actual state of the Church in France, no other door was open to the natural desire for security and stability that every reasonable man longs for.

"If, from these personal considerations, I crossed to the needs of the Church herself, it seemed obvious that, since the destruction of the religious orders, she had lost half of her forces. I saw in Rome the magnificent remains of those institutions founded by the greatest saints; on the pontifical throne, there sat, after so many others, a religious from the cloister of St. Gregory the Great. Even more expressive than the spectacle of Rome, history showed me, shortly after the exit from the catacombs, that incomparable series of cells, monasteries, abbeys, houses of study and prayer sown from the deserts of Thebaid *[region of ancient Egypt - Trans.]* to the extremities of Ireland, and from the perfumed islands of Provence to the frigid steppes of Poland and Russia. History recalled to me the names: St. Anthony, St. Basil, St. Augustine, St. Benedict, St. Columban, St. Bernard, St. Francis of Assisi, St. Dominic, St. Ignatius — as the patriarchs of those numerous families who, with their heroic virtues, filled deserts, forests, cities, encampments, and even the see of St. Peter. Under this resplendent pathway, which is like the Milky Way of the Church, I detected as creative principles the three vows of poverty, chastity, and obedience — keystones of the Gospel and of the perfect emulation of Jesus Christ. It was in vain that corruption — sometimes on one side, sometimes on the other

— had gnawed at these venerable institutions. There, when the flesh had died, the spirit gave life. Corruption itself was only the withering of enduring virtues, as we see in the forests where the axe has not penetrated, the fall of secular trees under the weight of a life which came from too far back to continue to resist old age. Should we necessarily have believed that the hour had come when these great monuments of the faith and those divine inspirations of the love of God and men would no longer be seen? Should we necessarily have believed that the winds of revolution, rather than being for them a fleeting penalty for their faults, had been, rather, the sword and the seal of death? As for me, I could not believe that. Everything that God has made is immortal in its nature; no virtue is lost in the world any more than a star is in the heavens.

"I persuaded myself that the greatest service to render to Christianity, in the times in which we were living, was to do something for the revival of the religious orders. Even though this conviction was for me the very light of the Gospel, it left me vacillating and trembling when I came to ponder how unworthy I was of such a sizable task. My faith, thanks be to God, was deep: I loved Jesus Christ and His Church above all created things. I had no cravings for clerical honors, and, even before my conversion to God, I never had a craving of any kind that involved ordinary objects on which the hopes of men attach themselves. I had loved fame before loving God and *nothing else*. However, nowhere in myself did I find anything to support my becoming a founder or restorer of an order. As soon as I considered those giants of piety and Christian strength, my soul felt crushed like a cavalry-man under his horse. I was prostrate, discouraged, and bruised. The very thought of sacrificing my freedom to a rule and to superiors terrified me. As the child of a century which hardly knew how to obey, I favored independence as my support and my guide.

How could I suddenly transform myself into a docile heart and seek only in submission a light to guide my actions?

"Subsequently, I was taken up with considering this: the difficulty of gathering men together, the diversity of temperaments, the holiness of some, the mediocrity of others, the fervor of these, the charm of those, minds with such opposed leanings: all of this, which is a consideration for religious communities even as for saints, is at once the most consoling and the most painful of burdens. After the trials of souls, those of the body came to mind. I was penniless in Rome, eating away the last remnants of a paltry inheritance. How to buy large houses, there to provide the needs of a group of religious as needy as I? Should I, then, relying on Providence, plunge into the risks of such a perilous endeavor?

"That was not all: external obstacles rose up before me like mountains. . . Would I have to wait for a similar tolerance from the French? Even though the laws of the revolution had taken only two actions: declaring that the State no longer recognized religious vows, and that it took away from communities their hereditary patrimony. Even though a vow is by its nature a free and imperceptible act of conscience and the common life is one of the natural rights of man — nonetheless, even within these limitations and under this formula, the government of 1830 was evidently little inclined to allow the religious orders to be reborn on French soil. It tolerated the Jesuits as a *fait accompli* and yet these religious led only a precarious existence, threatened at any moment by a change of opinion.

"Such an opinion was the last and most difficult obstacle to surmount. Concerning the religious orders, the State had preserved all the traditions of the Eighteenth Century but did not appreciate the fundamental difference between the communities living from hand to mouth by their labor, and those powerful societies recognized by the state, along with their holdings. No society, even literary or artistic, could be established in France without previous authorization; this extreme but accepted servitude provided an easy way to shield prejudices against attacks based on natural law or political right. What can you do when a country in which religious freedom, taken by everyone as a sacred principle in this new world, cannot protect in the heart of a citizen the invisible act of a promise made to God? What to do about this promise, whose very existence when torn from a bosom by tyrannical interrogations, is judged as evidence enough to deprive someone of the advantages of common law? When a nation has reached the point that all liberty seems to be a privilege of those who do not believe as opposed to those who do, can we hope to gain anything? Should we not rather despair because never more will equity, peace, or stability flourish, but only a civilization based on material progress?

"Clearly, my thoughts encountered everywhere nothing but stumbling blocks.... My sole resource was in the daring which aroused the first Christians, and in their unshakable faith in Almighty God. Christianity, I told myself, would not exist in the world were there no humble people, plebeians, workmen, philosophers, senators, the lowly and the great, to follow the Gospel despite all the laws of the Caesars. The cross has not stopped being folly, and *that which is weakest in God* has not ceased, according to the words of St. Paul, *to be stronger than all the forces of men.* He who would do something for the Church and who does not begin with this conviction — all the while not neglecting any means which circumstances allow him to use — will always be unfit for the service of God. The first Christians not only gave up their lives, they wrote, they spoke, they strove to convince the people and the emperors concerning the justice of their cause.

. . . There is always in the heart of man, in the state of minds, in the reshaping of opinion, within laws, in things and in times, a point of support for God. The praiseworthy skill is to find it and to use it, all the while placing the basis of one's courage and hope in the secret and invisible power of God Himself. . .

"As I encouraged myself by these thoughts, there came to mind that all of my previous life, *even my faults*, had prepared me for some access into the heart of my country and of my times. I asked myself whether I might not be guilty of rejecting these opportunities by a cowardice which would only profit from my inactivity, and whether the very grandeur of the sacrifice was not a reason to undertake it.

"After the general inquiry came the secondary one which was to decide to which order to give myself. . . Accordingly, I had to choose between the Company of Jesus and the Order of Friars Preachers, or rather, I did not really have to make a choice since the Jesuits, already existing in France, had no need of being re-established. The force of matters left me no doubt on this second point; facing the need to become a Dominican religious did, however, increase my fears and indecision. The material austerities of this Order appeared to me impractical, given our weakened bodies, as well as inconsistent with the labors of an apostolate significantly increased by the scarcity of missionaries and preachers. . . Nevertheless, in studying the constitutions of the order, I noticed that they offered resources against themselves. This latitude made me realize that there as elsewhere *the letter kills but the spirit revives*. I became interested in learning about the lives of St. Dominic and of some memorable saints who came after him as the sparkling mist of his virtues. The saints are the eminent individuals of the Church; on the high points of its history, they mark the summits human nature has reached. The more saints an Order has produced, the more obvious it is that the grace of God has been its foundation and gives it its permanence. All of this reassured me; and of the four elements which make up every religious institute — legislation, spirit, history, and grace — not one refused to that of St. Dominic its share in greatness[32]."

What we have just read is only a partial explanation of the choice made by Lacordaire. He became a Dominican because his goal was to revive in France the ministry of the apostolic word, and because, by nature, he was attracted by the very name: Order of Friars *Preachers*. It so happened that this order not only fit well with his goal, but also with his nature, because in it authority is granted by a vote and submitted to the control of a deliberative body, equally emerged from the election. Lacordaire lays stress on this in his *Notice for the reestablishment of the Friars Preachers*.

For all that, on his return to France, around the end of 1837, Lacordaire had not yet come to an irrevocable decision and kept his secret even from his closest friends. He returned to Italy with Dom Guéranger in October 1837 and tarried with him at the castle of Villersexel, where Montalembert resided, without saying a word about his monastic projects. On his return, everything went his way. We saw the success of his *Letter concerning the Holy See* and of the series in Metz. The future was very promising. Two major cities: Aix and Bordeaux; five cathedrals: Grenoble, Liège, Arras, Angers, Nantes, vied with each other in the hope of hearing him[33]. These requests met together from the most varied points of departure. Thus, the Bishop of Grenoble (Bruillard), and the Archbishop of Aix (Bernet) were former pastors in Paris. The Archbishop of Bordeaux (Mgr Donnet) belonged to the clergy of Lyons. The Bishop of Liège (Van Bommel) was singled out as the most open and most practical mind of Belgium. The Bishop of Arras, de la Tour-d'Auvergne-Lauranguais, could pass for the most perfect man of quality within the episcopacy. That of Angers, having reached the age eighty-three, referred to himself as the dean of the bishops of France. That of Nantes, De Hercé, had been, under the Restoration, a member of the Chamber of Deputies. The same desire had been evident in Strasbourg and in Marseille[34]. There could be no better proof of how Lacordaire had guessed correctly in offering to have the provinces participate in the work of apologetic conferences. It remained to be seen whether he would continue his work vested with the cowl of the honorary canon or the white habit of St. Dominic.

Having arrived in Paris at the end of April 1838, Lacordaire more or less opened himself on this point to those who cherished him. On this subject, he sounded out the bishop of Meaux, Gallard, confessor of Queen Marie-Amélie, a reconciling spirit who was known to be more open than others to an understanding of the matters of his time, and received an encouraging response[35]. The Prelate even showed himself disposed to open his diocese to future Dominicans[36], even though later on, he expressed totally opposite sentiments. At first surprised by a disclosure so little foreseen as that of Lacordaire's entering into religious life, Montalembert finally yielded to the reasons so eloquently presented by his friend[37]. Nonetheless, one has to believe that the encouragement was rather lukewarm since it left no lasting trace in Lacordaire's memory; he wrote in personal words that nowhere did he find approbation[38]. Mme Swetchine left him to act rather than supporting him. Most of the others saw in this project only an idle fancy. According to this one, the time for religious orders was passed; according to that one, the Company of Jesus was capable of everything, and so it was useless to try to resurrect societies that were no longer needed. A few saw in the Order of St. Dominic, having become so unremarkable in France on the eve of the Revolution, a decrepit institution — imbued with the ideas and forms of the Middle Ages, completely out of favor if only because it represented the Inquisition — counseled Lacordaire, if he wished to embark on a monastic adventure, that he should at least create something new.

The Abbot of Solesmes, however, was the exception. What he had obtained from Rome the year before spoke for itself, and allowed the hope for everything from that direction. Moreover, Dom Guéranger believed that the former preacher of Notre-Dame was quite the right person for the work intended and urged him to leave promptly for Rome[39].

It was at Solesmes that Lacordaire fixed his resolution. He came to engage in a retreat under the Abbot, in June 1838, with the idea of obtaining a final decision about his vocation to the Dominican life. This retreat lasted eight or ten days, concluding that he ought to enter into the Order of Friars Preachers. After having pored over in the abbey's library all the books that could enlighten him on the matter, he felt all the more confirmed in his calling and left for Rome. He was going there with the principal idea of making himself a Dominican and the secondary idea of re-establishing in France the Friars Preachers, if and when it pleased God.[40] "The only issue that frightens me sometimes," he added, "was finding myself insufficiently perfect." He was aware of many good qualities in himself, and especially a true gain in the fourteen years since he entered into the service of God. He considered himself unbiased, sober, not at all proud, more detached from the world and its agitations than ever, more capable of dying to himself, carried toward God by his mind and his heart, easily moved by divine matters; for all that, his life appeared to him as basically ordinary! But he reassured himself that he had never done anything with more calm and maturity[41]. He believed that this step was the untangling of his life, the result of all that God had previously done for him, the secret of the graces from on high, that of his trials and experiences[42].

Nonetheless, the disclosures of Meaux had been made known. De Quélen had been informed in general of Lacordaire's project by a person whom Gallard had spoken to in secret. The Archbishop though he had to bring it up to his council, with the result that the clergy began to understand what it was all about. Lacordaire felt that he could no longer delay in taking his bishop into his confidence. On 21 July, at his return from Solesmes where he had spent a month, he sought his leave from the Prelate. De Quélen received him sadly, the sorrow plainly evident on his face, like that of a wounded man, but more in his heart than in his pride[43]. The sadness of the Archbishop touched Lacordaire[44]. When the former had expressed his intention and manner of fulfilling it, de Quélen told him coldly: "Such things are in the hands of God; but His will is not evident."

But then the conversation became more lively. De Quélen took up again his old manner with Lacordaire and asked him to have copied for him, from the Dominican Convent of Santa Sabina in Rome, a painting representing St. Hyacinth, patron of the Prelate and one of the greatest saints in the Dominican family. Lacordaire took this opportunity to respond that if it was given to him to re-establish in France the Order of Friars Preaches, no doubt St. Hyacinth would be helpful to them. "Yes," replied the Archbishop, "and perhaps you are the one who will fulfill my dream." — What dream, my Lord? — What? You do not know about my dream? — No, my Lord. — Well! I will tell you what it was." And then, in a very charming manner, like a man suddenly changed, he related what we are about to read.

"I had been named coadjutor of Paris with the title of Archbishop of Trajanople. . . . During the night of the 3rd to the 4th of August, the eve of the feast of St. Dominic, when two o'clock rang on the Notre-Dame clock — at least, that's what it seemed to me — I believed myself transported into the gardens of the mansion, facing the small branch of the Seine which flows between the buildings of the Hôtel-Dieu [Hospital]. I was sitting in an arm-chair; after a few moments, I saw a great multitude gathering on the edge of the river, looking up. The sky was clear and cloudless, but then the sun appeared, cloaked with a black veil, from which some rays escaped, like flowing blood; its course was rapid: it seemed to be rushing to the edge of the horizon. Soon, it disappeared and all the people fled while crying out: 'Oh! What a misfortune.' Left alone, I saw the waters of the Seine swell up by an ebbing which came from the bank of the river and rose in waves into the narrow canal which it filled. Marine monsters swam in with the flow, stopped in front of Notre-Dame and the bishop's residence, then struggled to jump out of the river onto the quay.

"Then came a second vision: I was transported to a convent of religious women clad in black, where I remained for a long time. This exile over, I found myself in the same place where my dream had begun. But the archbishop's residence had disappeared and in its place there spread out in front of my eyes a flowery lawn. The waters of the Seine had resumed their natural course. The sun shone with its usual brightness. The air was fresh and as if scented by the fragrances of spring, summer, and fall blended together; it was a phenomenon I had never experienced in all of nature. While I was enjoying this scene with some kind of intoxication, I noticed on my right ten men all dressed in white; these ten men plunged their hands into the Seine, pulled out the marine monsters I had seen, and placed them, transformed into sheep, onto the lawn."

"You can see," added Archbishop de Quélen, "that this entire dream of 1820 has been accurately fulfilled. The monarchy, represented by the sun covered with a black veil, has fallen simultaneously with the self-confidence and revelry caused by the capture of Algiers. The populace had stormed Notre-Dame and my mansion; the mansion was destroyed and a grove of trees now covers the site. For a long time, I have lived and continue to live here, where I am talking to you, in a house of religious sisters dressed in black[45]. What more is left for my dream to reach its completion if not to see in Paris, those men dressed in white and occupied with converting its people?

"On the other hand, it is perhaps you who will bring those men here[46]."

Lacordaire was pleased to leave for Rome on such good terms with his bishop; he did not postpone his trip, following his saying that one should not delay the fulfillment of a thought that has sufficiently ripened. He left Paris on 31 July and traveled through Lyons, Chambéry, Turin, and Genoa, where he took a ship to Livorno. From there, he went to Florence, then made his way to Rome; he met with no one along the way so as to avoid explaining the purpose of his voyage[47]. He had written to the Princess Borghese, the only genuine friend he had in Rome, to inform her that he would go straight to her residence in Frascati, without stopping in the holy city wherein he did not wish to show himself before having informed Cardinal Lambruschini of everything by letter, and having obtained a meeting with him[48].

Never was a battle so quickly and so completely won. By 25 August, Lacordaire was received by Mgr Capaccini, who told him that the matter would encounter no obstacle. The attitude of the Jesuits was perfect. Cardinal Lambruschini, Cardinal Sala, Prefect of the Congregation of Bishops and Regulars, the Cardinal-Vicar (Odescalchi) appeared no less favorable[49]. The embassy of France voiced no objection. The Master General of the Friars Preachers, Ancarani — an honorable and saintly elder, who dreamed only of the reform of his Order — opened his arms to Lacordaire as to one who was heaven-sent. He immediately promised to future French Dominicans the convent where St. Dominic had lived, Santa Sabina, there to establish their novitiate, by themselves without being mingled, under a religious of Belgian origin, Father Lamarche, subprior of the Minerva (the principal house of the Order). After a novitiate of one year, the colony was to be brought back to France by Lacordaire, who, from the other side of the Alps, would be Vicar General of the Order with unconditional authority. He was empowered to found novitiates, houses for the professed, colleges for the education of youth ("one of the most pressing needs of France," he wrote), with dispensation from the public office for Fathers employed in these latter establishments, which was a significant but necessary innovation granted to us, Lacordaire would say. Thus, the French Dominicans would join together the life of clerics regular to monastic life. In his turn, Gregory XVI welcomed Lacordaire most cordially. Who has not heard of Roman dilatoriness and procrastination? In this case, everything was set up in eight days. Lacordaire could say like Caesar: 'I came, I saw, I conquered.'

In fact, on 15 September, he left again for France, carrying a certificate from the Master General who accredited the project in splendid terms, and who, ahead of time, approved of his course[50]. What had struck minds in Rome was that this project did not date from yesterday, that Lacordaire had mentioned it about fifteen months earlier to Father de Villefort, and that he had been able to keep his secret so admirably during those fifteen months. This prolonged nurturing along with the silence accorded him a distinguished air of maturity[51].

On his return, he tarried at Bologna to pray over the body of S. Dominic, then at Turin, to meet Silvio Pellico, that esteemed gentleman who bore very simply a name that had become so rapidly European. At Geneva, he wanted to greet that great athlete of the Church. Vuarin[52]. And yet, he kept mulling over the reasons for his resolution; his conscience reassured him that he could acknowledge them without reservations. The vexations first experienced in Paris were from then on next to nothing at all. "Never," he wrote, "had I so loved Paris, so felt the good that I could do there, nor received such tokens of esteem and confidence. My influence seemed greater than ever. It was precisely the feelings that I had about it that made me hesitate to fulfill the sacrifice that God demanded of me interiorly. My career, I told myself, is determined, my activity as preacher assured, why begin all over again? Without a doubt, also, the annoyances struck me as a reason for determination, albeit feebly. I called them to my rescue to assist the grace of God, to overcome my cowardice. In all of this, as God knows, I had only one battle: that of weakness in the presence of great self-sacrifice. I was happy, content, without cares, and I would drape over my shoulders, not so much a hard life, but a robe of wool, rather than the heavy burden of a family to raise and nourish. Here I was, with no obligations, going out to find some children who would ask me for bread. The selfishness in me said: 'Stop!' Jesus Christ told me: 'When glory and peace were proposed to me, I chose the life and the death of the cross.' My entire soul is contained in those final words.

"Today,' he added, "I have crushed the enemy; I no longer feel the shadow of human cowardice, and this is what assures me of success even more than the skills that I found. When I entered the seminary, fourteen years ago, I experienced the very same feelings: first of all a struggle in which I kept telling myself the same stories; then, having made my decision, a determination, a certitude that *no disappointment troubled for a single instant, not even one time.* To these two great stages of my life, I sacrificed a state achieved to a state uncertain — a state that pleased me to a state that frightened me[53]."

This is what he was repeating again on his deathbed: "Entreated by a grace much stronger than I, I finally made my choice, but the sacrifice was keen. Whereas it had cost me nothing to leave the world for the priesthood, it cost me everything to add to the priesthood the burden of religious life. Nonetheless, *in the second case, as in the first, once my consent was given, I experienced neither weakness nor regret*[54].

There was left the execution: he planned to spend the winter 1838 to 1839 to look for five young men of faith and courage, able to give themselves to each other, with boundless enthusiasm but also with genuine humility. With all his prayers, he sought some young men, some new men, who had not spent elsewhere their early ardor. Even before he left Rome, he felt that he had to make an initial appeal to souls by having these few words inserted in the *Univers* [a newspaper - Trans.]:

"At the moment, Father Lacordaire is in Rome. There, he busies himself with the restoration of the Order of St. Dominic in France, a thought he had long kept in mind. We have been informed that he experienced no difficulties, either on the part of the pontifical government, or of the part of the Dominicans, but, on the contrary, only universal approval. M. Lacordaire intends to return to France immediately, in order to gather a few men of deep and generous faith, and to return with them to Rome, where they will spend a year of novitiate in the convent of Santa Sabina, on Mount Aventine, placed exclusively at their disposition."

These lines appeared on 11 September 1838; unfortunately, by a blunder, they were printed in boldface, something that doubly displeased Rome, where secrecy and modesty in everything are prized. Lacordaire had to work hard to explain that in France the real power lay in public opinion, and consequently, this is what had to be won more than anything else. From this point of view, there was nothing better, at the outset, than to take a frank stand, giving oneself the benefit of the doubt for not having feared publicity, that, in any case, could not be avoided,. This tactic was successful; the announcement made by the *Univers* was reproduced in many papers without arousing hostile remarks. A Protestant paper, the *Semaine*, at the time the most important organ of French Calvinism, was the only one to express some disapproval, but in terms as restrained as they were honorable regarding Lacordaire. Under the Restoration, it had been the deceitful position of the Jesuits to have introduced themselves in an ambiguous manner, without daring to express their name openly. Lacordaire had firmly decided not to commit that error[55].

The opposition of the so-called Gallican bishops had been foreseen; it was not slow in making itself known. De Quélen welcomed Lacordaire graciously; but he wrote to the Pope and to Cardinal Sala, Prefect of the Congregation of Regulars, that he feared the restoration of an order destined perhaps to serve as a refuge and a bastion for the former friends of La Mennais. This was the frightening dread aroused in Rome and in France against the goal of Lacordaire — not without some success, as we will see later[56].

As for Lacordaire, he was not at all afraid. He defended himself in Rome by his letters and by acting in person in France. The Bishop of Meaux, Gallard, less out of sympathy for religious orders than for his hope of securing Lacordaire as preacher, proposed that he settle almost at the gates of the episcopal city, and in the meantime, pressed him to preach in his cathedral during the winter. He even arranged for Lacordaire to have a meeting with Barthe, at the time Keeper of the Seals and Minister of Cults. The latter voiced his objections but listened kindly to the answers, assuring him that the Government had nothing against him. This lack of prejudice on the part of Barthe was indeed something; it marked progress. The previous year, Louis-Philippe had said to Montalembert: "Are you quite sure that Father Lacordaire is not a *Carlist* [supporter of Charles X - Trans.][57]?" God does well what He does. It became clear that, without this partial rupture with de Quélen — which occurred, as we have seen, from the force of circumstances and that Lacordaire assuredly had never sought — nothing he attempted for a Dominican restoration in France would have been possible. Without that, however distant he was, basically, from the political sentiments of the Archbishop, it would have appeared that he remained his man, and as such, would have been treated by the Government as suspect, if not as enemy.

Lacordaire quickly felt that he could not move fast enough to present to France the plan he had devised to tell his country what the Dominicans were, to relate their history at that time very deeply forgotten[58]. With no further delay, he set about to compile his *Restoration in France of the Friars Preachers*.

The tone of the dedication of that writing was far from inferior.

"MY FATHERLAND,

"While you were pursuing with happiness and pain the formation of a modern society, one of your new children,

Christian by faith, priest by the traditional anointing of the Catholic Church, has come to claim from you his share in the freedoms you have won and that he himself has paid for. He invites you to read here the statement he addresses to you, and, with your knowing his wishes, his rights, his heart even, that you grant him the protection you will always give to what is useful and sincere.

"May you never, my fatherland, give up hope for your cause, but rather, overcome bad luck by patience, and outdo good fortune by fairness against your enemies; may you love God, Who is the Father of all you love; may you kneel before His Son Jesus Christ, the liberator of the world; may you not pass on to anyone the eminent office that you fill in creation; may you find servants better than I, but none more devoted."

This was the first time that a priest stood up in the midst of his fellow citizens while simultaneously laying stress on Rome and on the modern spirit. The attempt was bold: it was successful. Rome was not at all scandalized by the *liberal* attitude of the author of the statement; France was not shocked by his *monastic* way of life. "I address myself," said Lacordaire, "to an authority that is the queen of the world, that, from time immemorial, has repealed some laws, has passed others, on which the charters themselves depended, and whose decrees, one day misunderstood, ended up sooner or later being enforced. I turn to public opinion to ask for protection, and I ask for that protection even against itself, if necessary, because public opinion has within itself a wealth of resources, and its influence is very great since it knows how to change without ever betraying itself."

By placing himself in public like a man who has nothing to hide, Lacordaire had set himself immediately and strongly apart from all those who, in our days, have attempted something similar. As has been said, the authority whom he addressed was surprised by his deed and charmed by the frankness of his language; it found itself favorably inclined toward this uncommon man who had the gift of pleasing it while also having the courage to try everything[59]. Lacordaire could congratulate himself for having kept faith in his country. Neither at the rostrum, nor in the press was any voice raised to contradict his own.

And yet, he had deliberately attacked secular prejudices: he had supported the legitimacy of religious houses and defended the Inquisition. But he did this as a man who knew his times and did not ask the current to move upstream, back to its source. As we have seen, Lacordaire thought that, even in opinions, there is always a point of support for God. The expert skill, he used to say rightly, is to find that point of support and to use it while placing in the secret and invisible power of God Himself the principle of one's courage and expectations. In this, who cannot discern the point of support? It is the principle of freedom, boldly proclaimed, though not fulfilled, by the French Revolution, openly recognized by the Charter of 1830: freedom, which is to say: the right to do whatever does not harm another. On that score, freedom was invincible. A law could be passed to block it but no argument could be found to deny it.

This is how Lacordaire concluded:

"Never will the human race draw back to the past, however heavy be its troubles; but it will seek in voluntary associations, based on work and Religion, the remedy to the wound of *individualism*. I point out all the tendencies already made manifest on every side. If the Government, while keeping an eye on these generous tendencies, allows them the progress they seek, it will forestall major catastrophes.

"I believe, therefore, that I must act as a loyal citizen as much as a virtuous Catholic, by re-establishing in France the

Friars Preachers. If my fatherland allows it, it will take less than ten years for it to pride itself on this move. If it chooses not to, we will go establish ourselves on the frontiers, to some country more advanced toward the future; there, we will await patiently the day of God and of France. What is important is that there be some French Friars Preachers, that some of that generous blood flow under the ancient habit of St. Dominic. As for the territory, its turn will come; sooner or later, France will reach the predestined meeting-place where Providence awaits it.

"Whatever treatment my country reserves for me, I will therefore not complain about. I will continue to trust in it up to my dying breath. I even understand its injustices, I even respect its mistakes, not like the courtier who reveres his master, but like the friend who knows by what knots evil is tied to the good in the heart of his friend. These feelings have been ingrained in me too long for them ever to perish; even if I were unable to enjoy their results, they will, up to the end, be my guests and my comforters."

I lay stress on this attitude because not only did it bring about the originality of Lacordaire's public role, but also his success. Without a doubt, the *Notice for the Reestablishment of the Friars Preachers* is admirable; capable judges have thought that this was the author's best work. But what silenced the public's prejudice against monks was not the picture, however eloquent it was, that Lacordaire painted about the Order of Friars Preachers, nor the very attractive portrait of his patriarch St. Dominic, nor that long and splendid series of apostles, doctors, artists, in his train; it was none of that, it was the claim by the monks to the common right, to natural law, to the right of association under uniform conditions for everyone, under the ordinary supervision of judges, just as, in all civilized countries, legitimate responsibility falls upon every citizen.

"If we are asked," added Lacordaire, "why we have chosen by preference the Order of Friars Preachers, we will answer that it is the one which more closely fits our nature, our spirit, our goal — our nature, by its government; our spirit by its teachings; our goal by its modes of operation, which are principally preaching and divine learning.

"One single head, under the name *Master General*, governs the entire Order, which is divided into provinces. Each province, composed of several convents, has at its head a prior provincial, and each convent a conventual prior. The conventual prior is elected by the friars of the convent and confirmed by the prior provincial. The prior provincial is elected by the priors conventual of the province, assisted by a deputy from each convent, then confirmed by the master general. The master general is elected by the priors provincial, assisted by two deputies from each province. In this way, election is tempered by the need for confirmation, and in its turn, the authority of the hierarchy is checked by the freedom of the vote.

"One can detect an analogous reconciliation between the principle of unity, so necessary for authority, and the element of multiplicity, necessary also but for another reason. Indeed, the general chapter that assembles every three years is the counterbalance to the master general, just as the provincial chapter that meets every two years is the counterbalance to the prior provincial. Finally, the administration, however moderate it be by the election and the assemblies, is entrusted to the same hands only for a very limited time.

"Here you have the constitutions that a Christian of the thirteenth century gave to other Christians; assuredly, all modern charters, compared to those, would seem extraordinarily authoritarian."

The *Notice* appeared on 3 March 1839; on 7 March, the feast of St. Thomas Aquinas, the bright light of the Order of Friars Preachers; Lacordaire with two companions was taking the road to Rome to receive there the habit of St. Dominic.

Who were these two companions? One was a young pastor from the diocese of Versailles, who would not persist in his intent; the other, Hippolyte Réquédat, a young twenty-year old man, had just left Buchez's school.

It is appropriate for us to present a word about this school which gave three elite souls to the Dominican restoration, Réquédat, Piel, and Besson.

Beyond a doubt, Buchez was a man of great intellectual vitality and uncommon willpower. Born in poverty, he gained access to a liberal career only through marvels of energy, privations, and work. Having become a materialist and revolutionary at the School of Medicine of Paris, he joined the masons and, at age twenty-five, with three of his friends, established in France the *Carbonari* [an Italian revolutionary group - Trans.]. A member of all the conspiracies of the time against the Restoration, tried but acquitted as accomplice in the plot of Béfort, three years later he stopped plotting to join the socialist school of Saint-Simon, of which he became one of the directors in 1826. It was there that he learned how to give his studies an integrating and encyclopedic direction. Moreover, realizing the insufficiency of a simple philosophy to lead the human race, he set to work devising a set of beliefs that would replace Christian dogma in the world. Having become frankly a theist, Buchez labored entire months to have the school acknowledge the absolute spirituality of the Divine Being. Pantheism won out, and Buchez withdrew, predicting what would become of Saint-Simonism. After the explosion of 1830, when Bazard and Enfantin left the Saint-Simon society on

Taranne Street to devise a vast propaganda of public speaking and of the press, Buchez pitted one school against another. In his home, on Chabannais Street, he opened public discussions that won him fervent disciples; founding the *Européen*, he created a remarkable periodical that attracted attention. Indeed, in the nineteenth century, there was nothing more odd than this revival, almost in the public place, of schools of philosophy analogous to those of ancient Greece (Saint-Simonism, Fouriérisme, Buchézism), under conditions that had not been seen since the first ages of Christianity. One could imagine being in Alexandria, at the time of St. Justin, of Clement, of Ammonius Saccas, of Origen, and of Plotinus.

In the teaching of Buchez, as in his life, political thought occupied a prominent place. Ardently republican, brotherhood was his fundamental belief. Moreover, in his school, this was not a purely speculative notion, it was the highest duty. He wanted brotherhood to be confirmed by actions, that it be embodied by association. In Buchézism, association was the universal panacea. Besides, the school was highly spiritualist, and soon, no less highly Christian. The touchstone of the truth of a doctrine, in the eyes of Buchez, was morality. It was the moral consequences of materialism that converted him to theism. It was the moral teaching of the Gospel that, later, made him a Christian: as superior as it was new, such a moral teaching, according to him, could only be the work of divine revelation. Once on this road, he studied Christianity in history; he believed he found there the origin of all he admired and respected; he saw there why France was the eldest daughter of the Church; not only did he discover the proof but also the precise indication of the most fruitful scientific ideas: among others, the doctrine of progress, that explains so many things. As a result, he published his major work: *Essai d'un traité complet de philosophie, au point de vue du catholicisme et du progrès* [A complete treatise of philosophy from the viewpoint of Catholicism and of progress][60].

But let us not be deceived by this: the Catholicism of Buchez was but a rationalism that did not understand itself. In fact, it was nothing other than a personal notion of the mind, Buchez's particular manner of conceiving matters in the moral order and of unifying history. It was Catholicism, if you will, but a Catholicism lacking the teaching authority of the Church and participation in her sacraments. In a word, as has been said very wisely, it was reason self-enhanced — an independent research, taking a plan for social organization from the Gospel, as others were able to do with Plato[61].

Now, in the winter of 1837-1838, while Lacordaire was preaching at Metz, two disciples of Buchez were in Nantes: Hippolyte Réquédat and Louis-Alexandre Piel. Réquédat was only eighteen, Piel was thirty. A competition was held at Nantes for the construction of a new church: an unknown architect at the time, Piel boldly presented himself along with a plan in the style of the Middle Ages, and even more surprisingly, his plan won. The two followers of Buchez immediately became friends. Both were endowed with a rare shrewdness of mind: Piel, however, superior to Réquédat by the stronger quality of his intellect and by his acquired knowledge, Réquédat superior to Piel by his more lofty human qualities.

Chance, which is Providence in disguise, drew to Nantes, at that very moment, an Italian refugee with a rare scope of intellect and a greatness of heart even more uncommon, Niccolo Tommaseo — the same man we had seen in Paris as Venetian ambassador in 1848, subsequently heroic head of that republic with Manin. The fellowship of political ideas led him to look for Réquédat and Piel; before long, he was their teacher. Now Tommaseo was a fervent Catholic, and possessed a synthesis very superior to that of Buchez: the *Summa* of St. Thomas Aquinas. He opposed propaganda with propaganda. Nothing was more curious than the questions he was asked. "How does St. Thomas understand *progress*? What was his opinion about *material progress*? What were his thoughts about the rights and duties of revolutions?" Tommaseo had an answer for everything: Piel and Réquédat returned to Paris fascinated by the talent and the teaching of St. Thomas.

Unfortunately, the ardent and tender soul of Réquédat could not adapt itself for long to a simple theory of religion. A significant example had been given him: two other followers of Buchez, Roux-Lavergne, today canon of the Cathedral at Rennes, and he who was to become Father Besson, had recourse, as early as 1837, to the venerable pastor at Notre-Dame des Victoires, Desgenettes, who reconciled them to God. Réquédat followed the same path, and Piel did not delay in following him. Meanwhile, there appeared in *Univers* of 11 September 1838, Lacordaire's call for the restoration in France of the Order of Friars Preachers. This appeal found in Réquédat a ready heart. Already, in the reunions at Nantes, this fiery soul aspired to devote itself, body and goods, in the service of the neighbor. There remained to be found a kind of apostolate that would be appropriate for men born for action. The project of Lacordaire, that of a priest so sympathetic to the men of new times, seemed to answer in the nick of time the secret aspirations of Réquédat, and this is how God sent him to the restorer of the Order of St. Dominic in our country as his first disciple. Lacordaire has said that this victory was due to the *Notice*. In this matter, his memory was faulty. The day when Lacordaire left for Rome with Réquédat, 7 March 1839, the *Notice* was barely public[62]. The vocation of Réquédat, as we have seen, came from further back. "He came to find me," wrote Lacordaire. "No question was argued, no enlightenment requested, no fear expressed: he was a passenger ready to board my fragile vessel, who never even looked toward the unknown ocean whose waves he would cross. Later, souls like this one came to me, but none was more untainted and more enthusiastic, not one marked on the forehead by a more exceptional destiny. Réquédat had among all the others the glory of being my first companion, and death, in striking him shortly by an unexpected decree, left in my memory a virtue that nothing has tarnished."

Réquédat was wealthy and not yet twenty years old. On learning about his decision, Tommaseo uttered these words: "If M. Lacordaire's enterprise had achieved nothing else but to raise to such a height a soul like this one, that would be enough."

The farewell of Réquédat to his friend was this: "In one year, Brother Piel! I await you as the novice you will be."

The three pilgrims of St. Dominic arrived in Rome on Monday of Holy Week (25 March 1839). Their voyage had been a kind of continuous festival. At Lyons, one of the prelates of the Church of France, who more than others held on to the past, (Bishop) de Pins, had invited them to dinner. The Society of St. Vincent de Paul, directed by Ozanam, had given them a kind of ovation. But what awaited them in Rome was less clear.

As early as September, by a mind-set that is worth noting, Cardinal Sala, prefect of the Congregation of Regulars, generally little favorable to the Order of Friars Preachers, even less favorable to the person of Lacordaire, had shown himself opposed to the idea of allowing him to make his novitiate in the holy city. He had even talked about Bosco, near Alexandria, in the Piedmont region, convent in which the family of St. Dominic had saved or recovered something of the ancient enthusiasm. This blow was parried by the benevolent intervention of the Borghese princess. It is easy to understand that, this having been her initial step, Sala was especially hurt by the announcement made in *Univers* that the novitiate of the future French Dominicans would be held in Rome, "at the convent of Santa Sabina, *placed exclusively at their disposition.*"

There followed the letter of de Quélen to the Pope. The immediate effect was rather slight. Gregory XVI responded to the envoy of the Archbishop: "We are aware of these matters along with the difficulties Father Lacordaire will encounter; *he is a good priest whom we know and respect*; we have to leave him alone and see what will develop[63]."

But a few weeks later, there arose in France one of those crises among ministers, so frequent in parliamentary governments, when the conduct of the parties comes to divide the elective chamber in approximately equal factions. Seen from afar, in countries with autocratic regimes, these crises immediately appear to be the beginning of political dissolution. This is how the French crisis of 1839 (the coalition) was judged in Rome. As a consequence, the Cardinal Secretary of State, Lambruschini, counseled the General of the Dominicans to postpone for four or five months Lacordaire's taking of the habit. This counsel was in fact an order; the General hurried to inform Lacordaire by a letter that reached Paris on 2 March. Fortunately, as to what touched the interior situation in France, a Frenchman could, without foolish presumption, believe himself to be a rather good judge. Lacordaire's instinct told him that the hour for his plan had come and it was crucial that he hurry. Five days later, he and his two companions were, as we saw, on the road to Rome. From Paris, he had immediately written to the General to inform him that he was setting out.

The response reached Lacordaire at Bologna; it expressed a strong discontent and the firm determination not to allow continuation of the project to restore the Dominicans in France[64].

Fortunately, it was enough for Lacordaire to arrive in Rome to scatter the clouds. What was he seeking? The habit of novice, permission to test his monastic vocation in the ordinary manner. The canonical trial lasting one year, there was time for the political horizon to brighten. The General will then know, in a full understanding of the cause, whether or not he should authorize the attempt of a Dominican restoration in France. On the day when Lacordaire would be allowed to make profession, will he not be bound by the vow of obedience, and consequently entirely in the hands of the superiors of the Order? Accordingly, his entrance into the novitiate would in no way compromise anything. In any case, the French question remained fully set aside but unalterable. On that point, no rejoinder.

Besides, the *Notice* had reached Rome a few days before Lacordaire and had moved all minds in his favor. The elderly Father Olivieri, Commissioner of the Sacred Office, wept in admiration on reading the chapter about St. Thomas. Cardinal Pacca, Dean of the Sacred College and Secretary of the Congregation of the Inquisition, expressed, with an effusiveness uncommon in Rome, his complete satisfaction about the way in which Lacordaire spoke of the Holy Office. Moreover, the elderly cardinal joined in the legitimate concessions appropriate to make on this question, given the mind-sets. Three important men in purple, Cardinals Orioli, Castracane, Polidori (the latter an editor of the encyclical against La Mennais), praised highly the author of the *Notice*. Many others, however, whispered that certain sections relative to the present days were a bit bold. The Pope had this document on his desk when he received Lacordaire and his companions on 4 April 1839. Gregory XVI was greatly preoccupied by the crisis in France: è *una situazione*, he told them, *molto terribile!* [It is a very terrible situation!] Nonetheless, he gave full blessing to their generous plan. "It is a brave and noble project," said he to the Master General. "Let them march forward!"

The Master General decided that it was to the monastery of the Minerva, first convent of the Order of Friars Preachers, that belonged the honor of counting Lacordaire among the number of its novices. In conformity with the Dominican Rule, the postulant was presented to the Chapter of the community by the Prior, then admitted or rejected by the secret vote of the religious. He who distributed the ballots proposed to set the rule aside for this one time and to vote by acclamation, by raising the hand. This is how it was done; after which, Father Lacordaire was introduced, while hands clapped unanimously. Since the time of Blessed Reginald, no reception of a novice had given the Order cause for such great joy[65].

But in spite of all this, the concession had to be made to Cardinal Sala that the novitiate would take place outside Rome. It was in this same idea of deference and of prudence that instead of receiving the habit with appropriate solemnity in the church of the Minerva, the decision was made that Lacordaire and his companions would do so in an interior chapel, dedicated to St. Dominic. On these two points, a concession was made to a powerful influence, hoping thereby to disarm a secret hostility. Unfortunately, the uproar was only postponed, as we will see later.

Be that as it may, the solemn act of taking the habit took place on 9 April 1839. A few friends were present: Father Gerbet, the future Father Besson, the painter Cabat, Cartier, a Polish nobleman, Count Plater. Réquédat was an eyewitness;

M.Cartier was in a pious exaltation, embracing the Dominican religious and kneeling at their feet in gratitude for his happiness. Lacordaire, on the contrary, seemed admirably calm, accepting manfully and in a Christian manner, without troubling anyone, all the difficulties of the future. When he approached his friends in his white robe and his monastic crown [a haircut style - Trans.], he distributed among them, in friendly simplicity, the objects that would no longer serve him in the cloister. His heart overflowed. "The memory of my priestly ordination," he wrote, "is very much alive in me and I remember all the happiness of it; but what was missing at that first festival was found here in heady abundance — I mean to say, the outpouring around me of a wonderful fraternity. Never have I received such touching embraces[66]."

On the following day, the three French novices left for the convent of La Quercia, near Viterbo.

Endnotes

1. Bureau to apply for School of Artillery and Corps of Engineers.
2. Letter of 17 January 1837, published in l'*Univers* of the 23rd.
– This letter is from Falloux, Minister of Public Instruction and Cults, in 1849.
3. Same letter of Falloux.
4. To Mme Swetchine, 5 January 1838.
5. This conversation was not isolated: I have in front of my eyes proof that the Commandant of the Application Bureau, a colonel and head of a squadron of artillery, and a number of

others, swore to the consequences of that series. I cite these facts because it continues to be said that Lacordaire never converted anyone.

6. I have faithfully reproduced the proper expressions of the latter; I borrowed them from a letter by him to Lacordaire, dated 24 April 1838.

7. To Montalembert, 25 July 1838.

8. Bautain: The Morality of the Gospel, p. 75.

9. Humann offered him the hand of his daughter and his support in having him elected as deputy.

10. Cardinal de Bonnechose, archbishop of Rouen.

11. Théodore Ratisbonne, author of the life of St. Bernard and founder of the Congregation Our Lady of Zion; M. Goachler, subsequently director of Stanislaus College; Jules Lewel, superior of Saint-Louis-de-France, and his brother.

12. Adolphe Carl, subsequently dean of studies at Juilly College.

13. Messrs Eugène de Régny, Adrien de Reinach and Jacques Martian.

14. I have underlined the word *alone* because he had an important role, the principal one, in this controversy. Bautain asked that the word be stricken. The Bishop let it stand.

15. Lacordaire to Mme Swetchine, 9 January 1840.

16. To Foisset, 14 May 1833.

17. To Foisset, 26 May 1833.

18. To Foisset, 9 May 1834; four months before the *Avertissement* of D Trévern.

19. To Foisset, 9 May 1834. — To Mme Swetchine, 4 October, same year.

20. To Foisset, 15 October 1834.

21. To Foisset, 21 February 1835.

22. To Mme Swetchine, 9 January 1840.

23. Bautain: Christianity Today, letter XV.

24. To Mme Swetchine.
25. To Mme Swetchine, 11 October 1836.
26. To Mme Swetchine, 3 January 1837.
27. Answer from Mme Swetchine, 21 January 1837.
28. To Mme Swetchine, 10 February 18387.
29. To Mme Swetchine, 28 March 1837.
30. Letter to Very Rev. Father Dom Guéranger, abbot of Solesmes, of 5 September 1862. – I have to say that the Abbot dated all his conversations a little later, namely, after the ceremony of profession at Saint-Paul-Outside-the-Walls (16 July 1837). But his testimony having been given twenty-five years later, I believed I could correct the date of the meetings in question by reconciling his testimony with the affirmation that I find in a letter of Lacordaire, dated 25 July 1838.
31. Letter of Lacordaire to Foisset, 25 July 1838.
32. NOTICE.
33. In his correspondence with Mme Swetchine, Lacordaire mentions only four of those demands. I have before my eyes the letters of the seven prelates I name here.
34. To Mme Swetchine, 22 March 1838.
35. To Mme de la Tour Du Pin, 16 June 1838.
36. Letter of *l'abbé* Gerbet to Lacordaire, dated 30 May 1838. At the time, Fr. Gerbet was Vicar General of Meaux.
37. Notes provided by Montalembert, dated 20 June 1838.
38. NOTICE.
39. Lacordaire to Mme Swetchine 25 June 1838, and to Montalembert, I July.
40. To Montalembert, 1 July 1838.
41. To Mme Swetchine, 1 July 1838.
42. To Montalembert. 1 July 1838.
43. To Mme de la Tour Du Pin, 26 July 1838.
44. 25 July 1838, to Montalembert.

45. The Religious of Saint-Michel, rue Saint-Jacques, where de Quélen resided at the time.

46. NOTICE. In his Notice, Fr. Lacordaire gave as the date of de Quélen's dream the night of 3 to 4 August, vigil of the feast of St. Dominic. I believed I had to substitute this date for that of 5 October, which I saw in a letter of 25 July 1838, wherein Lacordaire retells the dream to Montalembert, barely four days after having heard it from the mouth of the Archbishop.

47. To Montalembert, 11 August 1838.

48. To Princess Borghese, 13 August 1838.

49. To Mme de la Tour De Pin, 14 September 1838. — To Mme Swetchine and the Princess Borghese, 27 August.

50. See Appendix XXI, page 565.

51. To Mme Swetchine, 27 August 1838.

52. To Mme Swetchine, 20 September 1838.

53. To Mme Swetchine, 14 September 1838.

54. NOTICE.

55. To the Princess Borghese, 3 November 1838.

56. To the Princess Borhese, 21 November 1838. — To Montalembert, 28 November. — Letter of Fr. Lamarche to Lacordaire, Rome, 8 January 1839.

57. On 26 December 1837. This describes a situation. Here you have the shrewdness of today's statesmen, when it is question of men and matters dealing with Religion.

58. To Montalembert, 4 October 1838.

59. Father Chocarne.

60. The sizable in-8° [in-octavo] volumes, 1839. – It should be understood that my intention is not to give a complete picture of Buchez' teaching, but only to show how this teaching was able to direct many minds, and elite intellects to Catholicism and even to monasticism.

61. Cartier, *Life of Father Besson*, p. 20. — The second chapter of this work contains the most clear, faithful, and gripping summary of Buchez' teaching that I know.

62. Lacordaire sent the first copy to Mme Swetchine on 3 March. The work was *announced* in *L'Univers* only on 11 March.

Amédée Teyssier, close friend of Piel and of Réquédat fully confirmed by report. (*Notice sur Piel*, 1843, p. 54-56).

63. Letter to Mgr Lacroix, Rome, 24 January 1838.

64. "Sono assai dispiacente ch V. S. illustrissima abbia intrapresso il viaggio anticipatamente e contro il mio sentimento. Questo viaggio e inutile, mentre sono *nella forma determinzaione che*, attese le circonstanze di Europa, *non debbasi mandare ad effetto il progetto di ristabilire in Francia in nostro sacro Ordine.*"

65. Testimony of Father Guilemoti, an eyewitness. – Letter of Réquédat, cited by Chocarne, p. 283, 1st edition.

Concerning Blessed Reginald, see Chapter XII in the *Life of St. Dominic*.

66. To Mme Swetchine, 13 April 1839.

CHAPTER XI

La Quercia — Santa Sabina — San Clemente

Beginnings of the Dominican project: Novitiate of the Father — Apostolate on the outside, confraternities in Paris and in Rome — Final contacts with Bishop de Quélen — Lacordaire professed; lecture at Saint-Louis — French college at Santa Sabina: Fathers Jandel, Piel, Hernsheim, Besson — *Life of St. Dominic* — Mgr Affre, archbishop of Paris — Voyage of the Father in France — *Lecture on the Vocation of the French Nation* — Death of Réquédat — Installation at San Clemente of the Father and his companions — Scattering — Secret reason for this step — Justice rendered to the Father by Gregory XVI

In the evening of Thursday, 11 April 1839, Lacordaire entered his room as novice. The fraternal eagerness of the Fathers of the Minerva had disappeared. For the first time, he realized that he was in a foreign area, in the presence of a life whose routine was unknown to him. He experienced a moment of weakness. It was cold. He turned his eyes towards what he had just left behind, he imagined sharply the life he had led, its positive advantages, friends tenderly cherished, days filled with conversations at once useful and charming, warm homes, the thousand joys of a life filled by God with so much external and internal happiness. For a moment, sacrificing all that, and everlastingly, seemed to him a heavy price to pay for the pride of a deliberate action. It is good, he himself acknowledged, that man lifts himself up or humbles himself under the hand of God like the billows of the sea and that the strongest characters realize their weaknesses. Lacordaire quickly vanquished that temptation by asking of Him Who can do everything the strength he needed. By the end of his first day, he felt that he had been answered; then, the consolations gradually filled his soul "with the gentleness of a sea that caresses its shores while covering them[1]."

    La Quercia is half a league from Viterbo, on the slope of the hill on which the city is built. Its name, which evokes the memory of La Chênaie, comes from an image of the Virgin, painted on a tile and long suspended on the trunk of an oak tree in the forest. Numerous miracles, accorded to the faith of those who had prayed at the feet of this image, inspired the idea of building, to protect it, a sanctuary that immediately became a place of pilgrimage, still visited in our days. To house the religious who would staff this sanctuary, a convent of rather grandiose proportions was built. The story is told that the Senate of Viterbo, divided on the choice of an Order to whom the convent would be offered, resolved to turn the keys over to the first religious who entered the city. Now, the first to arrive was a French Dominican, Martial Auribelle, Master General of the Friars Preachers[2].

    The monastery was laid out in two square cloisters, one of which, in the words of Lacordaire, was a masterpiece. The Church was large, simple, elegant, filled with *ex-voto* [memorials]. The surroundings were delightful. In the south, near the convent, rises the head of Mount Cimino; to the North, on the hill, the city of Montefiascone, of which Cardinal Maury was bishop; to the East, the Apennines; to the West, decreasing heights, falling to the sea, allowing it to be seen by anyone who goes up a little higher to catch a distant view. Within this framework, there spreads a rich valley whose pleasant farms receive new value from the abundant forests that cover the slopes of the Cimino[3].

La Quercia was one of those monasteries of Italy where the rule of St. Dominic was best observed. The master of novices, then in his sixties, Father Palmegiani, who died in 1863, was pleased to number among his spiritual sons not only Father Lacordaire, but also Cardinal Guidi and Father Jandel. In April 1839, this venerable elder had under his direction only five novices: Lacordaire, who had taken in religion the name Dominic; Father Bertaud, who had chosen for his patron St. Vincent Ferrer; Réquédat, who placed himself under the protection of St. Peter, the martyr of Verona; and two young Italians, who were a great delight to the three Frenchmen.

Lacordaire had refused the dispensation of six months of the novitiate offered to him by the General. His memory lives on at La Quercia as that of a model novice. The orator of Notre-Dame swept halls, drew water [from the well], trimmed the lamps. Never did he speak about himself and would not tolerate anyone who did so in his presence. One day, one of the Italian novices dared to ask him whether the crowds at his conferences were very large; Lacordaire pretended not to hear, and turning toward his neighbor, changed the subject in a tactful fashion[4].

Even from the privacy of his room as novice, he did not cease to fulfill a kind of apostolate on the outside [of the monastery].

At the moment he was to take the habit of Friar Preacher, he had received at the Minerva the visit of three Christian artists: the landscape painter Cabat, a young painter who accompanied him (Besson), and another friend of the arts who was a stranger to their friendship (Cartier). He had encouraged them to found in Rome a society of French artists, whose purpose was to sanctify each other as well as to prove that France still had children who held the faith of the Apostles. Before even entering La Quercia, Réquédat, for his part, had written to Piel about it in most pressing terms: the work, said he, will not be complete until it has representatives in Paris[5]. In his turn, Lacordaire himself recommended this work to Piel by urging him to take as cooperator a young painter, a student of Ingres, as Flandrin was, and from Lyons, as he was: Claudius Lavergne, a generous soul, who had enthusiastically embraced this attractive idea. At the same time, Lacordaire exhorted Besson to do the same in Rome, and pointed out a new helper, Hallez, who, since then, has very worthily profited from Christian art. In both areas, in Rome as well as in Paris, Lacordaire was asked for a set of rules. This document, dated La Quercia, 21 July 1839, opens with these words:

"Some French artists, touched by the spectacle the world presents, desired to contributed to its renewal through the Christian use of art; and since isolation, created by laws against nature, is today one of the major wounds that men suffer, they thought it appropriate to establish between themselves one of those associations called *confraternities* in the thoughtful and enlightened language of the Church. The rules that follow are the expression of that will which they had in their youth and which they hope to retain all their lives, to work together, under Jesus Christ and his Church, for the reclaiming of humanity.

"May it please God, unique source of things that last and that prosper, to bless their goal! If some souls, attracted to their profession, recover sufficient light to pass from a life of profit to a life of self-sacrifice, they will not attribute this to themselves, but to Him Who brings the dead to life, and whose hand, always extended, never tires from seeking hearts so as to refresh them — empty hearts to instill in them the taste for the infinite, broken hearts to offer them shelter from blows that are only transient.

"Moreover, they have placed his confraternity under the protection of St. John, because St. John — apostle, evangelist, prophet — of all the friends of Christ, was one of the earliest to penetrate into the mysteries of divine beauty and love, those eternal subjects of the contemplation of genuine artists."

Various obstacles delayed the flowering of the work until January 1840, at a time when it was established almost simultaneously in Paris and in Rome. In Paris, the founding members were Piel, Aussant, Victor Gay, architects; Duseigneur and Bion, sculptors, who, like Piel, emerged from the school of Buchez; Allonville and Lavergne, painters. In Rome, the confraternity consisted of twelve members, among whom were two boarders at the French school, Bonnassieux, sculptor of the colossal statue of Our Lady of France, and the musician Gounod. Their motto was the one St. Bernard had given to the knights of the Temple: *Non nobis, Domine*[6]!

The example was not an unprofitable matter: Christian medical doctors had their confraternity of St. Luke; lawyers reestablished with the breath of a totally new spirit that of St. Yves; painters set themselves apart under the patronage of Blessed Angelico of Fiesole [Fra Angelico -Trans.]. At the same time, men of letters united by a less notable link in an association that took the name of the apostle St. Paul. How distant this was from the wretched snicker of Voltaire and Jansenistic severity! Those who denied the benefits of the conferences of Lacordaire at Notre-Dame (1835-1836) assuredly have never read the letters exchanged between the members of the confraternities of which I speak. What faith! What vigor! What enthusiasm! What generosity of soul! What a deeply practical sense of Christian certainty! Those letters would do honor to the better ages of the Church. This is how Lacordaire refuted his opponents; he did as that Greek philosopher whose movement was denied: he marched on.

"Those confraternities," as Cartier said so well, "were the beginnings of the Dominican project. They prepared to serve as a family to the religious formed by Father Lacordaire on their return to France. They furnished the Order with numerous and precious recruits (Piel, Besson, Aussant, and still others). It is more unfortunate than I can say that they ceased to exist when the Third Order of St. Dominic was restored in France. This institution, approved by the Church and enriched with her blessings, had certainly been a more perfect religious group; but it was in the nature of things that there be degrees in the practice of the good and that, by preserving professional associations, which by that very fact required fewer conditions, attracted to themselves a greater number of Christians who could indeed exercise a wider influence on society."

This is what proves the vigor of the impulse given to the spiritualist reaction in medicine by the energetic prior of the confraternity of St. Luke, another former disciple of Buchez, Jean-Paul Tessier. The harshness of his polemic has led many to misjudge this mind of such rare ability. For all that, he did create a group of very remarkable doctors, and attached his name to the delayed but complete reintegration in science of the greatly profound teaching of St. Thomas about human nature. I do not overlook a complete opposite reaction that appeared twenty years later, under the impulse of and as a consequence to a political backlash: but if that retrenchment had prevailed in official teaching, the Thomistic School would not have been affected because it would not have been refuted; Lacordaire, even in death, would continue to protest by means of this school, fully provided for by the confraternity of St. Luke.

All this moved minds forward to the Dominican restoration; from various viewpoints, these confraternities were as many results of the *Mémoire* [Report].

Four thousand copies of this Report were printed. One thousand five hundred were freely distributed. Lacordaire sent it to Ministers, to the Peers of France, to Deputies, to Bishops, to Prefects, to the top Presidents, to procurators-general, and to all the newspapers. The author was not at all interested in selling a great number of them; what he hoped for was to have them read widely and quickly, in spite of the crisis in public matters. He spent nothing to have himself talked about in journals. The very silence of journals was already a success; it was astonishing that he remained silent in the face of the bold publicity of his actions. Having acted and spoken so loudly without causing outbursts was certainly a totally unexpected stroke of luck. No doubt, the vehement diversion brought about by the ministerial crisis, the assaults made on financial holdings, the riots that bloodied the streets, none of this jeopardized his good fortune. But the silence of the press did not any less prevent the Report from making its way into minds, while leaving time for public opinion to develop. The work pleased everyone; all the letters of the year 1839, all the memories of the period, are unanimous on that point. Even opponents agreed that the writing was impeccable; but, they added, this was only a plan; one had to wait and see the completed work.

The commendation that most pleased Lacordaire was that of [Bishop] de Quélen. He experienced such a sudden astonishment that immediately he wrote the Archbishop so as to ask him formally for the pulpit of Notre-Dame for the winter of 1841, on condition of appearing in the Dominican habit. This letter found the Prelate in a very serious state of health. As soon as he could respond, he assuredly did so in very affectionate terms, but far from the hopes entertained by Lacordaire. De Quélen had made long term commitments for Notre-Dame that he was unable to break. But had he been unconstrained, he still could not accept two years in advance, as a necessary condition, the obligation to have Lacordaire preach in the Dominican habit[7].

The Archbishop merely renounced all opposition to the restoration in France of the Friars Preachers. Frankly, on this point, he relied on the decision of the Supreme Pontiff. If the Dominican restoration had the approbation of the Holy Father, the work could find no obstacle on the part of the archiepiscopal authority in Paris. [Bishop] Affre assumed the obligation, with no quibbling, in the name of the Prelate, whom he defended vigorously on this occasion from the accusation of ill-will concerning the Dominican project[8].

A few months later, de Quélen had passed on to a better life.

Lacordaire honored the memory of the Prelate in words of fond sadness: "Unfortunate man," he wrote, "to whom I owe more than I can say, and whose faults helped me no less than his benefits." He could not overlook all that was missing to the Archbishop; but how could he not also remember what the Prelate had done for him, in spite of everything that separated them? From that time on, he never ceased speaking of de Quélen with filial gratitude — and rightly so.

Nonetheless, without losing sight in his room of the situation of Bautain, on whose resolution he continued to work with that tenacious spirit that leads to success, Lacordaire especially applied himself to prepare the fulfillment of his grand design: to restore in France the family of St. Dominic. Even then, he could see that the confraternities established through his impetus would be a ready nucleus for the future Third Order[9].

His first thought had been that a prompt return to France was one of the conditions necessary for success. Did he not have to hurry to profit from the effect produced by the *Mémoire* [Report] in that France which so quickly forgets? A number of important ecclesiastics and lay persons were pressing Lacordaire to allow them a share in his vocation; material resources were offered him with an eagerness that he was loath to discourage[10].

On the other hand, how to be equal to the task? Could one conceive of an Order composed of three religious? An Order implies the existence of a novitiate, to test the vocations, and a school of theology to round out the studies of the professed. Where to find the elements of these two equally indispensable institutions? Suppose that Lacordaire was prior, where were his professed members? If he opened a novitiate, where would he find his master of novices? Réquédat had pursued no theological studies; he was not ordained. Thus did Lacordaire see himself all alone, already crushed under the weight of the work. Why not say it: he himself felt unprepared; he, too, experienced a need to throw himself into St. Thomas, who was, after St. Dominic, the true founder of the Order, and who maintained its unity, knowledge, and customs[11]. Should not everything give way to the need to be completely Dominican, before initiating and perpetuating a new offspring in the family of St. Dominic? Now, to be fully Dominican it is not sufficient to know and to practice the regimen of the Institute, one must also be initiated into the core of learning of which it is the depository. The teaching of St. Thomas is the lifeblood which, by flowing into the veins of the Order, preserves its powerful originality. He who has not studied it deeply may be a Dominican in heart, but he is not a Dominican in mind[12].

This is what Lacordaire presented to the General while asking to spend three years in Rome, at the heart of the Order, to imbue himself in its methodically sound tradition. His ulterior project was to call several young men (in lay clothes, if needs be) to follow the courses of theology at the Minerva. He hoped that during their studies, many of those young men would receive Holy Orders, and that, on his return to France, they would have to undergo only one more year of spiritual novitiate to become Dominicans — active Dominicans at that, armed from head to toe with knowledge and with the priesthood[13].

This plan was immediately approved by the General; but, as an immediate consequence, it brought about the departure of one of the three French novices. Father Boutard had continuously suffered from the Dominican regimen and the air of Italy, although he fought courageously in the expectation of a prompt return to France. The modification of the original plan was a thunderbolt for him. He left the decision about his fate to Lacordaire, as to his spiritual father, and received from him the advice of returning to his country, so evident was it that this cleric would not survive a three-year sojourn in Italy.

Lacordaire was in no way discouraged. He plunged more than ever into his writing of the *Life of St. Dominic*, about which we will return.

In passing, we should note a fact, of not much importance in itself, but which perhaps causes astonishment, regarding the prejudices of the period, and which, from that viewpoint, is worthy of being known. At the end of 1838, the General of the Friars Preachers had written to Louis-Philippe to remind him of the feelings of sincere attachment to the crown of France which from time immemorial had distinguished the Order of St. Dominic. It took six months for a response to come but it was all that it could be. The letter of the King, dated 15 July 1839 and countersigned by Marshall Soult, assured "the honorable religious of the interest the monarch had in everything that could affect them; he was pleased to repeat the expression of his esteem and of his personal benevolence."

Relieved from that side, especially pleased to know that the Pope was reassured as regards Paris by these declarations, however vague they were, Lacordaire pursued strongly — in view of completing the goal he had proposed from the very beginning — the preparation of a decidedly French core of Dominicans. The Master General and the high administrators of the Order hastened to accept his views. Lacordaire could immediately count on only three novices, and yet this did not dismay him; he remembered that St. Dominic took twelve years to form sixteen disciples before seeing hundreds of religious fall at his feet "like ripe ears of wheat under the sickle of the reaper." He did obtain that he be placed, after his profession, at the convent of Santa Sabina on Mount Aventine, very renowned because of the prolonged stay of the holy patriarch whose biography he was in the process of writing. There, he would have as his prior his best friend, Father Lamarche, a Belgian Dominican, whose maternal tongue was French. The *French College* (this was the name given to the companions of Lacordaire at Santa Sabina) would occupy a separate corridor, which had its own chapel; it would follow its own regimen and exercises apart from others.

The day finally arrived. On Palm Sunday (12 April 1840), Lacordaire and Réquédat pronounced their vows with great joy, before a replica of the Madonna of La Quercia, painted by Besson and magnificently framed, thanks to the generosity of the Princess Borghese. The vows were received by the Master General, in the presence — Lacordaire said laughingly — of almost all the nations of Europe. In fact, half the religious of the convent were Italians, the other half Spaniards. In attendance were two saints: Princess Marc-Antoine Borghese, née Talbot, and Madame Albert de la Ferronnays; the first represented England, the second Germany, of which she was a native, and, if you wish, Russia, the adoptive country of her father. Madame Craven, née la Ferronnays, attended the ceremony with her husband, representing France. Réquédat bore the seraphic look shining in the portrait of St. Dominic by the angel of Fiesole [Fra Angelico - Trans.]. As on the day of his taking the habit, Lacordaire was serious and calm like a general at the beginning of a battle. The sermon was preached with much elegance and kindness by an elderly Dominican with the prophetic name, Father Sibilla[14].

The following day, the two new Brothers Preachers were on the road to Rome. Some Dominicans and French persons waited for them at the Ponte-Molle. The French entreated Lacordaire to preach at the church of St. Louis on Easter Sunday. He had a great aversion to this, being entirely unprepared for it; but on the very following morning, a letter from Mgr Lacroix, highest official cleric of France, insisted in the name of the ambassador, Count Septime de la Tour-Maubourg, thus making a refusal out of the question.

The sermon was given at four-thirty. It was the first time that Lacordaire spoke publicly in Rome and the first time also that he appeared in the pulpit wearing the Dominican habit. The crowd was sizable. The orator had chosen a significant text: *In mundo pressuram habebitis, sed confidite, Ego vici mundum.* [John 10:33] — In the world, you have tribulations; but be of good cheer, I have overcome the world.]. He had intended to show the logical, moral, and social value of the Resurrection: logical, in that only the resurrection can explain the mystery of death, that no other teaching was able to interpret; moral, in that it brings life from death by the power of sacrifice; social, in that it creates martyrs, the only spiritual power against physical force and against the tyranny of temporal powers. He said that the Resurrection was the triumph of Christianity. He explained that the dogma of the Resurrection assured that triumph in the order of ideas, in the order of feelings, in the order of power. — In the order of ideas, Christianity, while showing death as the consequence of sin, triumphed over pantheism, which held that death is only a phase of life; over Manicheism, which sees death as an expansion of life; over materialism, which professes that it is annihilation. — In the order of feelings, Christianity has taught and inspired sacrifice, thus overcoming the egoism, that ruled without counterbalance in antiquity. — In the order of power, Christianity triumphed through martyrdom.

In his conclusion, Lacordaire said that we were assisting at another triumph for the Church, her triumph over Protestantism and rationalism. He showed that Protestantism was dying after an experience of three centuries which revealed that it had nothing to offer in the order of ideas, nothing in the order of feelings and especially in the order of sacrifice, nothing from the social viewpoint, since it only kept dividing itself. He affirmed that the triumph of the Church was taking place principally in France, in that France which, after having saved the Church from Arianism by the sword of Clovis — after having saved her from oppression under Charlemagne, by creating the pontifical states — after having saved her from Calvinism by the League — went on to save her a fourth time by having her triumph over rationalism. "Gentlemen," Lacordaire said to his listeners, "you will be leaving Rome, which is the head and the heart of Christianity; but it is to return to our France, that is her right arm." In this statement can be seen the germ of a lecture of 1841 on the calling of the

French nation.

The reaction was enormous. This can be immediately ascertained by the liveliness of the conversations entered into by the listeners, barely outside the church[15]. There arose, Lacordaire wrote to Mme Swetchine, the same struggles as in Paris and in Metz: some approving, others furious. For almost two weeks, there was talk of nothing else in Rome. Whoever has lived in times of revolutions will very easily imagine what lighted coals amassed on the head of any preacher who dared to express this impassioned phrase: "the tyranny of temporal powers." The diplomatic corps, which was almost completely present at the feet of the pulpit, was moved beyond expectations. The Count of Spaur, Minister for Bavaria, cried out that thereby it was not resurrection being preached but insurrection[16]. Fortunately, there were in the audience a cardinal, four bishops, several prelates, some Jesuits, some Dominicans; it proved impossible to call attention in that sermon to even one statement that was theologically blameworthy.

Nonetheless, it was still indiscreet, I admit. Given the times, this denunciation against tyranny in a sermon about the resurrection awakened unnecessarily, in an audience as prejudiced as were the counselors of embassies, remembrances poorly suppressed concerning *l'Avenir*. Cardinal Lambruschini was not one to have a liking for Lacordaire. Not being able to find, in the reports given him, any canonical reasons for reproach, he remained silent; but the imprudence had dealt a blow, and later, Lacordaire would severely feel its effects.

For all that, the sermon did not produce immediate consequences.

The new Dominican requested an audience with the Holy Father, who treated him with extreme kindness, as usual. Nonetheless, Lacordaire understood clearly that, from then on, he had enemies in Rome, and that, without the support of the Pope, matters would no longer work in his favor as they had previously. With that exception, everything happened point by point as he had been promised. On 15 May, 1840, he lodged in the convent of Santa Sabina the young men who joined in his enterprise. They were six in number, namely, Réquédat, *Abbé* Jandel, later Master General of the Order, Piel, Besson, Hernsheim and a Pole by the name of Tourouski, who would not last.

Father Jandel was thirty years old, the son of an engineer in Nancy. Former superior of the minor seminary of his diocese, he had gone to listen to Lacordaire at Metz, received with delight his visit at Pont-à-Mousson, in 1838, and left for Rome towards the end of 1839, so as to become enlightened on his definitive vocation. He went to La Quercia to confer thoroughly with Lacordaire about it; he found the latter well disposed to receive him among his companions. But Father Jandel remained puzzled between the Order of St. Dominic and the Institute of St. Ignatius. A retreat he made at St. Eusebius, under Father de Villefort, put an end to his uncertainty. The pious Jesuit told him plainly that God was calling him to the work of Lacordaire and that he should immediately place himself at the latter's disposition. Even so, Father Jandel also wanted the personal advice of the Holy Father, who absolutely refused to make a decision. "The two Orders," Gregory XVI told him, "were founded by two great Saints; both of them furnished the Church with notable saints; both could offer her many others; I leave it to your choice, you are perfectly free in the matter." Jandel found sufficient encouragement in this response. On 17 December 1839, after the audience with the Pope, he wrote to Lacordaire: "You can make what use you like of me as if I had already made the vow of obedience." Nonetheless, with the agreement of his new superior, he agreed to preach the Lenten series of 1840 at the church of St. Louis of the French, while awaiting the profession of Lacordaire and the arrival in France of the neophytes who were giving themselves to his undertaking.

One was the cherished disciple of Buchez, the elder brother of Réquédat at the level of intelligence, Alexandre Piel.

We are already acquainted with him and we will get to know him even better. He was thirty-two, tearing himself away from a dearly beloved elderly father; he had resisted the influence and the objections of his master, renounced the protection of Guizot, his youthful dreams of glory, that church of St. Nicolas of Nantes which was to be the monument of his life. Why? To answer the call of God, to achieve the fulfilment of this saying: "Whoever, in my name, leaves his home or his father, will receive a hundredfold and will obtain eternal life[17]."

The other neophyte was a professor of philosophy at the Normal School, the prize-winner of a significant contest, in whom Cousin had placed great hopes. Charles Hernsheim was born in Strasbourg of Jewish parents. Baptized at a young age, he was not slow in denying all religion, in pitilessly making sarcastic remarks to his Catholic schoolmates, all the while concluding, like Pascal, that philosophy was not worth an hour of effort. He was in this state of mind when a terrible sickness threw him into an absolute collapse and into a kind of continuous torpor. Restored to life against all expectations and the limitations of medicine, when he regained his senses, he found himself once again a Christian. The terrors of the agony had nothing to do with it. Hernsheim himself was never able to explain how this miracle happened. The previous skeptic called for a priest, re-read the *Pensées de Pascal*, and took notice of the lives of the saints. It was then that he offered his resignation to the Ministry and returned to Paris in 1839, to await indications from Providence. The *Mémoire* [Report for the reestablishment] had just appeared. Hernsheim immediately thought of offering himself to Lacordaire. He was barely recovering, but he wrote: "I would rather die while *studying* religion than while *teaching* philosophy." Lacordaire replied as he did to all those who offered themselves to him that they had to await his return to France. A year devoted to reflection only strengthened Hernsheim's resolution. It was on 1 May 1840 that he boarded a ship at Marseille with Piel, and, on 16 May, entered with him at Santa Sabina. He was only twenty-four years old[18].

Besson was the same age. Born in Franche-Comté [a Department in SE France], brought to Paris by an indigent mother, he took residence with her at the house of the pastor of Notre-Dame-de-Lorette. "That generous man," relates Fr. Lacordaire, "had paid for the boy's placement in a boarding-school where he had little success. Often called to follow reason rather than his heart as regarded that student, the pastor replied with a kind of prophetic expectation: *Let us be patient; something tells me that this unruly student will one day be an instrument in the hands of God.* He held this presentiment so strongly that when dying, he left the mother a legacy of 40,000 francs." This was in 1833. One of the teachers of Besson, Mr. Roux-Lavergne, was also able to suspect the gifts that lay within him. Disciple and principal collaborator of Buchez, Roux introduced Besson to that school, composed especially of artists and physicians. Besson had known Piel and Réquédat; he became a convert, with Roux, somewhat before them. The masterpieces of Christian art spoke to his soul and the reading of the Gospel did the rest. Dedicated to painting by an irresistible calling, he had come to Rome at the end of 1838 to perfect himself in his art. We have seen how he was presented by Cabat to Lacordaire, who made of him the pivot of the confraternity of St. John the Evangelist in Rome. He had assisted, teary-eyed, at the ceremony of Lacordaire's taking the habit. Besson, wrote his historian (I should say 'witness', Cartier), participated with all his soul in this sacrifice, envying the fate of those who could thereby be the first to offer themselves. Later, he had gone to La Quercia, to copy there, at the request of Lacordaire, the miraculous Madonna which was to be, in France, the safeguard of the Dominican enterprise. After finishing this copy, Besson vowed to renounce painting if his mother gave him up by allowing him to embrace the life of Friar Preacher. His sacrifice, said Cartier, was no less than that of his mother, given that the facility to paint seemed to him to be one of the joys of Heaven. Finally, on Easter 1840, after the sermon of Lacordaire at St. Louis [Church], Mme Besson suddenly charged her son with following his calling. For two days, she never stopped talking to him about it, each time more resigned and more urgent. As Lacordaire used to say, he had only to bend down to pluck this beautiful flower. "He is, in fact," said he, "a miniature of Angelico of Fiesole [Fra Angelico - Trans.]: an incredibly pure soul, honorable, simple, with the faith of a great saint[19]."

What do you have to say concerning these beginnings of the Dominican restoration? What do you think of these three followers of Buchez and of that normal school graduate who became monks in 1840? All four were men of the new times, to the highest degree, men filled with the modern spirit, who completely drained the cup of rationalism and that of democratic beliefs. Moreover, there is no hint of a novel in those vocations. No disillusionment in love or in ambition. One by one, all four made their decision without the prompting of a priest, by a decision that was spontaneous, reasoned, unselfish. Let us get to the end: all four are now deceased, all four had been saints. In this, was the finger of God not present?

On 15 May 1840, Lacordaire, Jandel, Réquédat, Piel, Hernsheim, Besson, and Tourouski, took residence at the Dominican convent of Santa Sabina, under the very special conditions I have already mentioned. There, they followed a particular regimen, took their meals together, but separate from the religious, called each other 'brother', while preparing themselves for the Dominican life by practicing poverty, chastity, obedience, and mortification. Twice a day, they received instructions in theology from a Spanish Father[20].

The rector of the French college was Father Lacordaire. It was he who had set up the regimen and was the soul of that small circle. "A new life," wrote Cartier, "seemed to animate this old cloister, so highly celebrated by the approval Honorius III gave to the Order of Friars Preachers and by the extended residence of the blessed patriarch St. Dominic. A ray of hope and of revival lit up these impressive hallways, long forsaken. Moreover, one noticed, one points out like an auguring bough, the shoot that the previous year had grown at the foot of the orange tree of St. Dominic, during the novitiate of his previous historian.

On the morning of 16 May 1840, continued Cartier, Father Lacordaire celebrated Mass at Santa Sabina, in the very room of St. Dominic; at night, when the crowd of visitors had left, he gathered his companions in the chapel of the French college. There, he opened his heart to them and gave an exhortation that began with the words: "My brothers, we are gathered here for a task that is frightfully difficult."

There was no exaggeration in these words.

Lacordaire's plan, as we have seen, was to keep three of his companions at Santa Sabina to round out their education by the study of St. Thomas before they were to begin their novitiate. He even hoped that all of them would be ordained priests before their entrance into the Order of Friars

Preachers[21]. We will never sufficiently grieve that the catastrophe of San Clemente had brought to naught so wise a plan. The French college, lest we forget, was not a novitiate properly so-called; it was the ultimate preparation for the life of novice.

It was at Santa Sabina that Lacordaire put the finishing touches to his *Vie de saint Dominique* [Life of St. Dominic], entirely written at La Quercia. The approval of Father Cipoletti, former general of the Friars Preachers, consultant to the Congregation of the Index, was dated 26 July. The work, however, did not appear until December 1840, through the attention of the physician Amédée Teyssier, from Pézenas — not to be confused with the famous physician Jean-Paul Teyssier, prior of the Confraternity of St. Luke. Amédée Teyssier, whom his friends qualified as "protector of the Order of St. Dominic in France," was a man of faith and of heart who set himself as biographer of Piel. When the *Life of St. Dominic* appeared, it was received with great delight. "It is not simply an uncommon talent," cried Chateaubriand; it is a unique talent. It is stunningly beautiful; I do not know of any better one." On her part, Mme Swetchine wrote: "It is the most beautiful book of its kind of which I am aware. It is not only a masterpiece, it is a miracle because it is destined to bring about miracles. One could not praise too highly, in a painter with such a rich imagination, the extreme serenity of the brilliance. Especially on this point, the story of the battle of Muret is an exquisite study."

The *Life of St. Dominic* marks an era; it placed a seal on the hagiographic revolution so resolutely and so eloquently begun by the historian of St. Elizabeth of Hungary. The dryness of Tillemont, the false elegance of Marollier, the icy cold of Godescard, were no longer acceptable to anyone. Our century learned what a saint was. It read those biographies as they were written: with enthusiasm, with love, with a contagious uplifting.

The *Life of St. Dominic*, especially, brought about saints. A new school of hagiography was established.

In Paris, Lacordaire followed closely the publication of his book. He delayed so as to gather its fruits, to bring with him to Rome some select young men, to get in touch with a great number of others who could later help him. Besides, a significant event had occurred in the diocese of Paris: Bishop Affre had succeeded Bishop de Quélen. Lacordaire was impatient to learn for himself what he could expect from the new archbishop.

The nomination of Affre came about through rather odd circumstances. Several months before the death of Bishop de Quélen, [Bishop] de Trévern had obtained Affre as coadjutor, but Father Bautain, who feared that nomination, had been able to delay it long enough so that the future coadjutor of Strasbourg was still in Paris when the see of St. Denis became vacant. The requests of the metropolitan chapter placed Affre at the head of the chapter's administration. This is what led him to become Archbishop of Paris. At first, he was not being considered. But Cardinal de la Tour d'Auvergne, bishop of Arras, much desired by the government, remained inflexible in his refusals. Many names proposed were set aside by Thiers, at the time Prime Minister, because those names had the backing of another man: evidently, it was not convenient for the President of the Council that the Archbishop of Paris would owe his nomination to Molé. It was only after all these vain attempts, after all those fruitless struggles that, suddenly, thoughts fell on [Bishop] Affre. "Why," it was said, "look that far for what is so close to us? Surely what we especially need is an archbishop who will busy himself with the affairs of his clergy and not meddle with ours?" Considerations such as these brought to mind King Louis-Philippe. The passionate dislike of the Saint-Germain suburb for the candidacy of Bishop Affre put the finishing touches on his standing[22]. After some hesitation on his part, the Pope, in turn, yielded. Besides, this choice had been warmly presented to Thiers by Montalembert, who could not help but take into account the very continuous benevolence of Bishop Affre for the eloquent founder of the conferences of Notre-Dame.

The latter's [Lacordaire's] joy was great. He saw in the nomination of Bishop Affre — like the choice of bishops at the same date, that of Bishop Gousset for the see of Reims, for example — the unexpected dismissal of the school that so blindly persecuted the former friends of La Mennais. Bishop Affre held the modified Gallicanism of Bishop Émery. Thus, he held the theological opinions of that school while simultaneously repudiating antagonism against persons and extreme political animosity. That was something. "Theologically, Gallicanism was dead," wrote Lacordaire; "it lives on only in the political order (by the teaching of not abandoning royalty), and Affre was not a man of that Gallicanism. He had no hatred for the new institutions; he forgave inevitable happenings, even when these were not at all what is better. He entertained a desire for peace and reconciliation."

Tinged with political lukewarmness and perhaps with an after-thought of ambition in the eyes of de Quélen, Affre remained as member of the archbishop's council without being associated in a more active and direct manner in the administration of the diocese. This should not lead to any conjectures against him. If he lacked hostility, he was also untainted by any obligation and even of career advancement with respect to the government. He had a deep feeling of ecclesiastical dignity. Nonetheless, one must recognize that from the time of Affre, the bent toward this dignity is no longer the same. The attitude of de Quélen, as regards the new royalty was noble and proud, like that of a gentleman who does not stray from the virtues of his forbears. The attitude of Affre was firm, when needed, but without luster: an attitude enemy of noise; one avoiding display; without weakness, assuredly, but also with no resonance in his accent and in his voice; no echoing on the outside and consequently with no action on the inside, because under a regime of proclamations, like the one at the time, the Government pays attention only to opposition that embarrasses it, and consequently only if it is public. On this point, Affre was completely wrong concerning the scene and the epoch. In his relationships with a monarchy spawned from the conspiracy of newspapers, and, consequently, entirely subordinate to public opinion, he embodied the circumspect demeanor of Saint-Sulpice, just like the habit of extreme secrecy required in matters of absolute governments[23]. This misreading of the new conditions of the episcopacy in France was doubly unfortunate. Deprived thereby of external advantages so richly provided to de Quélen, clumsy and at a loss in his behavior, lacking any facility in public speaking, dull in his style, Affre — by condemning to obscurity the merit of his episcopal independence — ended by invalidating all his prestige. It was a serious mistake.

What would he be like for Lacordaire? From the first day, the latter had said: "Affre could only be more just. He will not give himself over, feet and hands bound, to a clique. *He wishes to be and to let be.* He will fell the need to act and consequently not rebuff enthusiastic and talented men raised up by Providence. He will not hate his era because of its miseries. He will allow himself to be seen and to be approached. He will attempt to repair the dissension among the clergy of Paris. But he is a Gallican; he does not like the religious orders unless they are absolutely submitted to the bishop. Perhaps some day I will complain about him more than I did about de Quélen. No matter. I am pleased for those whom he will help; as for me, Providence will settle things as it will. Finally, at least he is a man who will say *yes* or *no*, and on whom you can count for one or the other[24]."

A better evaluation could not be had. In everything, Affre knew how to be himself; this is what he wanted to be in regard to his clergy as well as toward the government. This is what he wanted to be towards Lacordaire. He received the latter as a friend, but remained a bishop in his stand, without succumbing to any impulse, without undergoing any pressure, not even that of public opinion.

Besides, at bottom, Lacordaire had not come simply for Affre. He was anxious, above all, to make his presence known in the heart of France. "This return," said he, "will prove my complete liberty; it will demonstrate the confidence of my Order; it will give new proof that the reestablishment of the French Dominicans is not a figment of the imagination. Our vesture will be seen. It will only be a preparation for our voyage of the following year, when *I count on reappearing in the pulpit wearing our habit*[25]."

In this sense, the attempt was fully successful. Lacordaire had brought with him only his Dominican habit and an overcoat. He had decided to wrap himself up when necessary, but he did not wish to give up his garb. This was bold but frank, just like his character. Entering France by the bridge of Beauvoisin, he therefore crossed the Dauphiné, the Lyonnais, Burgundy [districts of the country – Trans.], wearing the cowl that no Frenchman had seen in fifty years. Here and there, some marks of astonishment greeted him. Two or three times, in Paris, those elements of surprise revealed a somewhat aggressive character. He paid no attention, but continued to accustom the public to seeing him, just as he accustomed himself to be seen before the public, under the protection of a forgotten past. As

497

Father Chocarne said so well, the enemies of yesteryear did not have time to think about their grudges grown cold; all of them yielded to the curiosity of the fact. Everyone wanted to see that ghost of another age, a monk, a son of Dominic the *inquisitor*. The government showed no irritation. Barely arrived in Paris, Lacordaire dined in habit at the home of the Keeper of the Seals, Martin (from the North Department), with the archbishop of Paris, the archbishop of Bordeaux, the Internuntio and more than forty guests[26]. During the meal, Bourdeau, at one time Minister of Justice under Charles X, leaned over to his neighbor and said to him: "If, when I was Keeper of the Seals, I had invited a Dominican to my table, the following day the Chancery would have been burned down."

The contradiction noted by Bourdeau was simply misleading. To be sure, the hatreds had not been extinguished; they simply no longer had the same hold on public opinion. From then on, the Revolution was consolidated. Under Charles X, a cowl would have seemed a harbinger for the former regime; under Louis-Philippe, it could only be a sign of confidence in the relative appeasement of irreligious passions and in the respect of all for the liberty of everyone. Does it not mean something (this is what has been long forgotten) that the man who, at that moment, personified the revival of monasticism, was precisely the man of France least suspected of dreaming of a return to the past — was precisely Lacordaire?

It was not enough to dine at the Chancery; there was need to take possession of the pulpit of Notre Dame while wearing the cowl. This was indeed accomplished on 14 February with a sermon on charity for the poor visited by the Society of St. Vincent de Paul. Thus do we find this organization in all the important pages of the life of Lacordaire. As early as seven o'clock, a large group of young men huddled together at the foot of the pulpit. At ten o'clock, there was no more room in the long nave. At eleven, the side naves, including the chapels on the right and on the left, were filled. At twelve-thirty, the Archbishop, taking his place in the churchwarden's pew, saw assembled in the cathedral an audience of ten thousand persons. At his side, the Prelate had the Minister of Justice and of Cults, with ambassadors, peers of France, members of the Chamber of Deputies, Chateaubriand, Molé, Guizot, Berryer, Lamartine, while many others lay hidden in the assembly, in the midst of a crowd that overflowed to the door of the sanctuary. At one o'clock, the Friar Preacher rose up, with his head shaved, his white tunic; for an hour and a half his improvised talk held this entire multitude captive and attentive, albeit trembling with emotion.

The subject was *the religious calling of the French nation*. The new monk, as he himself said, wanted to envelop with the popularity of ideas the boldness of his presence. The effect was stunning. Using history in this way was a significant novelty in a Catholic pulpit! Moreover, there was an excitement in this struggle with the unknown, with uncertain success, given in this way by Father Lacordaire for a cause at once Catholic and personal — a drama in the solemn inauguration of the Order of St. Dominic at Notre Dame of Paris, in the reappearance in the pulpit of that forbidden garb, in the presence of the Keeper of the Seals of the July Monarchy. All of this constituted a surprising boldness, and all of this was a complete success.

But it is the misfortune of revolutionary times that the most inoffensive matters be unceasingly distorted by the passionate interpretations of parties. In 1841, Lacordaire found himself facing the rule of the bourgeoisie. He did not flatter it, he was unable to flatter; but could he not recognize that it was the bourgeoisie that governed France? He did not go beyond that. Here are his words: "God said to the bourgeoisie: you wish to reign, then reign. You will learn what it costs to govern men, you will judge whether it is possible to govern them without my Christ." He added, it is true: "Do not lose hope in a class that is the foundation of modern society, and whose access to power, highlighted by so many important facts, is no doubt tied to the general plan of Providence." This was enough for a portion of the legitimist party [royalist partisans - Trans.] to thunder against the preacher. Who would dare, in the pulpit, to name the bourgeoisie? Was the bourgeoisie not Louis-Philippe? Could Louis-Philippe fit into the general plan of Providence? All this from a revolutionary, all this from an *orator*? The word was disseminated for a long time. We need to remember these things because they reveal the passions of the times. Have they really been extinguished?

Lacordaire took no offense and did not allow himself to be distracted from his project. The writing to which I allude was from a long-time friend; the son of St. Dominic did not cancel his friendship. Besides, Lacordaire did not lack compensations. Newspapers, reviews of most diverse viewpoints, even Protestant flyers, vied with each other in praising his latest talk. All sought to obtain a sermon from him: Lille, Orléans, which at the time had as bishop the most reserved man of all, Cardinal Morlot, wished to hear him. The Archbishop of Bordeaux (Mgr Donnet) offered him a house and property, two leagues from his episcopal city. And, what was worth even more, on March 1, Lacordaire set out again on the road to Rome, taking with him five new companions, among whom were an architect, Louis Aussant, and a lawyer, today Father Bourard.

He had left only four at Santa Sabina: Piel, Besson, Hernsheim, and Jandel. Réquédat has passed to a better life on 2 September 1840. He had suffered greatly from the lungs during his novitiate at La Quercia; three and a half months of apparent health led to the belief that he was cured; but from the end of January, he struggled against the disease with courage, with patience, with the resignation of a saint. On the day when he pronounced his vows, he had joyfully offered his life for the re-establishment of the Order of St. Dominic in France. Arriving at the end of his earthly trial, he received the final sacraments in a state akin to rapture. On 2 September, in the arms of Piel, he went to sleep in the Lord in a death more gentle than the most peaceful sleep. "Death," said Lacordaire, "thereby gave us his consecration and chose from among us the soul that was the best prepared and the most worthy of ascending toward God to speak about us. Later, similar souls came to me but none was more undefiled and more enthusiastic, no one imprinted on the forehead with such a rare destiny. Above all others, he had the glory of being my first companion. In striking him unexpectedly, death left of him in my memory a virtue that nothing could tarnish. I had never seen anyone arrive so quickly at such a full supernatural perfection. I had already met some men much better than I; but this one, more than any other, gave me a fresh understanding of my inferiority. We buried this gentle and strong young man in the very church of Santa Sabina, in a modest brick tomb with the inscription [in Latin - Trans.]:

> Here the Lord awaits
> Father Peter Réquédat
> of the Order of Preachers,
> a youth of pious memory.
> whom death untimely called,
> in the year of salvation 1840,
> on the restoration of St. Dominic in France,
> so that the news of the work would ascend
> in its first fruits
> and with its consent.[27]

The trial was painful; it was endured in a Christian manner. The brother of Réquédat, by adoption, Piel, wrote to a mutual friend: "God has kept Brother Peter in the Order of Friars Preachers because there is only one family of St. Dominic on the earth and in heaven, where we hope the Good God has placed him. He also has kept him in our friendship, because there is only one separation, that which comes from sin. Let us accept this sacrifice which God demands of us and implore Him to forget, to delete our faults, in memory of the virtues of him whom He took from us[28]." Piel added: "Could a better Frenchman die for the reestablishment of the Friars Preachers in France?"

It was from the blow of that death that Father Lacordaire, with his usual abruptness, made the decision of coming to France, to display the habit of St. Dominic and to recruit apostles. Hardly returned to Rome after having been very well received in Turin by King Charles-Albert — whom he found reading the *Life of St. Dominic* — and by Count Solaro della Margarita, his chief minister; after having received in Genoa the manly encouragement of that vigorous and generous elder, Cardinal Tadini, Lacordaire wanted to go to La Quercia to bring a memorial ciborium from Réquédat to the Madonna. During the trip, he was stricken with an unknown illness and had to spend the night at Viterbo in a hotel bed, from which he was carried to the convent where he had fulfilled his novitiate. After ten days of the breaking out in boils from head to toe, that caused worry about his days, Lacordaire remained master of the battlefield. It was, he said, the greatest assault he ever underwent in his life. It is worth noting that, on his return to health, his constitution — up to that time, fragile — grew in unusual energy: it was almost a transformation.

On learning of Lacordaire's illness, Pope Gregory XVI was greatly downcast and expressed his desire to see him again.

Consequently, the Father was anxious to find himself in Rome, where he returned, still ailing, on Wednesday of Holy Week (7 April 1841). But he did not enter Santa Sabina; he took up residence with his companions at San Clemente. Immediately, he got them busy following chant lessons, which he assiduously attended, making heroic efforts to sing the scale, without ever being able to distinguish a tone from a semi-tone nor to appreciate the value of the notes. At the same time, he was giving them lessons in Sacred Scripture and glosses on the conferences of Cassian which lifted them up with unutterable enthusiasm.

What was San Clemente?

On the long street that, from the Coliseum, rises to St. John Lateran, we see a rather small church which, by its antiquity and its notable primitive arrangements, is one of the most venerable monuments and at the same time, the most surprising one of the holy city. Erected, if one believes tradition, on the very site of the house of the senator Flavius Clemens, of the family of Vespasian; — depository of the body of St. Clement, third successor to the prince of the apostles, and that of St. Ignatius of Antioch (so great a pope and so great a martyr); — moreover, enriched by relics of Sts. Peter, Paul, Polycarp of Smyrna, as well as the remains of Blessed [St.] Cyril, apostle of Moravia, of the Slavic lands, and of Bohemia; — well-known by great memories, since it was in this basilica that pope Zozimus, in 417, pronounced the condemnation of Celestine, disciple of Pelagius, and that Paschal II was elected sovereign pontiff in 1099; — decorated with a major work by Mosaccio, one of the renovators of painting; — cherished, among all the sanctuaries of Rome, by those who favor the worship of Christian antiquity, because it has retained, more than any other, the original basilica pattern; — since Urban VIII, this small church belonged to the Order of Friars

Preachers. In 1841, it was transferred to the Irish Dominicans, whose contiguous convent they still occupy. They were the ones who recently discovered the subterranean church, from the time of Constantine, and several centuries older than the current church.

Can you believe it? In 1841, the guardians of this sanctuary thought of abandoning it because the convent, they said, required extensive repairs, and they lacked the funds for them; they also gave as an excuse the *aria cattiva* [offensive air]. A fortunate event revealed their secret to Father Jandel, at the time a simple postulant in the Order of St. Dominic. Immediately, he conceived the idea of acquiring San Clemente forever for the future province of France. Piel ran with this idea. It was promptly reported to Father Lacordaire in Paris, who strongly approved of it. He preferred to use the offerings that he had obtained for his work to repair and embellish a house that would belong to the Dominican Province of France, rather than to Santa Sabina, which was the property of the Province of Rome. He smiled at the thought of settling in his own place, on his return to the holy city, in a manner determined, independent, and stable. For his part, the Master General quickly gave his assent. Piel remembered that he was an architect. The General got to work with a speed that was not, according toCartier, a Roman custom, and the convent, repaired at the expense of Father Lacordaire, was quickly ready to receive its new guests. Were installed the copy of the Madonna of la Quercia and another painting by Besson, the resurrection of Lazarus, a symbol it would seem of the resurrection of the Order in France. A Belgian Dominican, whose mother tongue was French, Father Lamarche — subprior at the Minerva and fully devoted to Lacordaire — was appointed prior at San Clemente; Father Henrique, a Spaniard, was to be master of novices.

Before moving any further, Lacordaire sought the approbation of the Sovereign Pontiff. He requested an audience, which he obtained on 19 April 1841. Gregory XVI received him with affectionate familiarity. *Ecco il predicatore!*, cried he. Then he poured out his heart with very paternal abundance. "You Frenchmen," said he, smiling, "you are bold, [you are] entrepreneurs; we do not have the same temperament. We must always keep in mind the future, a long future; a misguided attempt has infinite repercussions." In this way, the Pope seemed to go beyond the reproaches made to the Apostolic See about his forbearance concerning many matters arising from the crises of the day. Always with the same smile, he added: "I believe that, despite your stay among us, you still have the French spirit." Lacordaire replied: "I hope, Holy Father, that with the years I will lose all that remains of extreme in my character." Gregory XVI was enchanted. He gave Father the assurance that he would immediately approve all that the Congregation of Discipline of Regulars would propose to him regarding the restoration of the Friars Preachers in France[29].

Lacordaire, as we have seen, was impatient for San Clemente to be erected as the French novitiate. He was fully confident; it seemed to him that matters had progressed in giant steps for the previous four months. He did not, however, lack opponents. Always dominated, always blinded by the fear of a European cataclysm and by the remembrance of 1831, in which the revolutionary spirit had played such a large part in the heroic awakening of Poland, Cardinal Lambruschini had a momentary idea of denouncing to the Congregation of the Index ten lines from the *Life of St. Dominic* concerning the infamous persecution of the Catholic Church along the borders of the Vistula. He did not deny the facts. "That is true," he would say, "all too true; but one ought not to irritate the wound." A few days of reflection led him to recognize that, in this case, orthodoxy was not an issue, the *Index* had nothing to do with the ten lines in question. The *Diario* announced publicly the sale of the book in a Roman bookstore. Nonetheless, it was certainly appropriate to take into account and to be alarmed by this bent of mind of the Cardinal Secretary of State. It was he who, in January 1839, had tried to have postponed for six months Lacordaire's taking the habit, which led the Father to say on 28 April 1841: "I see what little it would take for everything to collapse around me[30]."

In fact, the catastrophe was imminent. The following day (29 April), Father Lamarche was informed that the Congregation of Discipline of Regulars could not authorize the establishment of a French novitiate since there was no longer a province of France and that there was not even one French community. The reason seemed to warrant no reply. Yet, we are surprised in that the General of the Friars Preachers had never doubted that such an authorization was perfectly possible.

Upon this first notice, Lacordaire did not hesitate to counsel a Polish candidate, whom he had brought from France at the insistence of Prince Adam Czartoryski, not to risk remaining with him. Nonetheless, the number of his companions remained stable; Providence was seeing to it. A pious and charming young man from Alsace, "who had dreamed of art and of legends on the banks of the Rhine," not having found in Paris instruction in keeping with his aspirations, had come to Rome to study the painters of the Middle Ages. He who was to become Father Danzas had known Besson at the Confraternity of St. John the Evangelist and liked him fondly. He had come to say goodbye when suddenly, Besson asked him to remain.

The cardinals declared that the future novices of San Clemente were free to choose some novitiate, even that of the Roman Province of St. Dominic; but these, in agreement with the Master General, opted for La Quercia. They even began a novena to prepare themselves. The old basilica, on that occasion, was decorated with flowers and foliage. Joy reigned in all hearts. But, in the very middle of that retreat, on 5 May — the feast of St. Pius V — a new order from the Discipline of Regulars commanded the French of San Clemente to separate into two groups and to proceed to two different novitiates. What is even more significant: it ordered Lacordaire to remain alone in Rome and explicitly denied him the direction of one or the other band[31].

The blow was sharp; it was received and endured with decidedly supernatural peace, mildness, and faithfulness. Lacordaire communicated the orders of the Congregation to his small flock: all behaved admirably, not one was discouraged. It is written in the *Imitation* that it is indeed a significant matter among many to suffer injustice without complaining: *magnum valde si silens portaveris*. At San Clemente, everyone obeyed, everyone remained silent. The retreat continued and was completed in the greatest calm, to universal edification. The old Spanish prior who had been placed at San Clemente declared to the Master General that he had never seen young men comparable to these Frenchmen[32].

The words and the behavior of Father Lacordaire, on this occasion, were admirable. "Never," wrote to me someone who saw him a few moments after the order of dispersion was transmitted, "never will I forget the self-control and the calm he displayed. He was neither shocked nor beaten down. It is only today that I understand what holiness I witnessed at that moment." As always, Lacordaire found reasons to persuade himself that what was happening was for the best. The air of Rome, in summer, was unhealthy; outside of Rome, the French would experience a better climate, free from visits, more distant from the world, and more entirely occupied with their vocation. It was a question of dividing themselves between La Quercia and Bosco, a convent built by Pius V, not far from Alexandria, very near France. Now, observance at La Quercia was mild, the master of novices excellent, the Fathers very sympathetic; at Bosco, the Piedmontese Dominicans were austere: all the better. At Bosco, the future novices would prepare themselves and become habituated gently to the severities they promised each other before their arrival in France. After all, the separation was to last only one year. During that year, Father Lacordaire would return to that beloved France to level the roadways, perhaps even to acquire a convent to establish there a novitiate of studies. Having given his companions the message, Father invited them to reflect on it seriously and to come to see him in his room, one after the other, to inform him of their final decision, adding that they had contracted no engagement, that they were perfectly free to leave, that thanks be to God, he had some money left over and that he was ready to grant to those who would return to France the funds needed for the voyage[33].

The retreat over, the decision of each one made known, all of them bound themselves to it by receiving the Body of Jesus Christ from the hand of the Father; he made his farewells to them at the feet of the altar. Everyone was weeping. As for him, his face was radiant as in his better days. Everyone took from the altar the name he would bear in the cloister. Then, the men were separated into groups: the Brothers Jandel, Hernsheim, Aussant, Bourard, and Roy-Lafontaine, left on 11 May for La Quercia, where they took the habit on the 13th, day of the conversion of St. Augustine. Thirty-six hours later, there set out toward Bosco the Brothers Piel, Besson, Bonhome, Danzas, and David. Not one complaint, not one murmur. "We came here," said they, "to become Dominican, let us be that; God will show us, in His good time, what we will have to do." As for Lacordaire, prepared by all his past life to suffer injustice, never had he experienced anything with such forbearance. Yet the first impression had been sharp; barely a half hour later, there came a light by which he saw clearly the goal of Providence in this affliction, pleased with himself to have recovered the freedom to take up again his ministry in France[34].

Nonetheless, there remained a mystery in this; if the first decision of the Discipline of Regulars was easy to justify, how to explain the second? At first, the French government was suspected; but soon, there came from higher up other information. The *abbé* de la Bouillerie, son of the Intendant General of the civil list under Charles X, welcomed under that title by Cardinal Lambruschini, went to see him, opened himself to him about his desire to return to France. "Marvelous!," said the Secretary of State. "To be sure, one can do good in France. But a loss for that country is the group of young men who got together, with Father Lacordaire as chief, since they dream of nothing else but the separation of Church and State." On hearing these words, de la Bouillerie was troubled and responded timidly that, for all that, the Father is a good priest. "Oh," replied the Eminence, "not everyone thinks that way. I was sent a brochure... I have received letters... Don't you see: Lacordaire and de la Mennais are all of a piece[35]?"

The full answer to the enigma was not long in coming. On 8 July, Father Modena was attending an audience of the Holy Father. Spontaneously, the Pope expressed his complete satisfaction in the perfect obedience of Lacordaire, protesting that the decision taken in the matter of San Clemente was based on certain circumstances from which no solid evidence could be found concerning the French novices or their master. A few days later, Father Buttaoni, Master of the Sacred Palace, was in his turn at the audience. Gregory XVI inquired about Lacordaire. Buttaoni, who was aware of the previous conversation, did not hesitate to express his surprise about what had taken place at

San Clemente. At that, the Pope opened up *like a bandbox*. He stated clearly that the Cabinet of Vienna had sent him a booklet, printed in Paris in 1840, under the title: *The French Clergy in Rome*, by Georges Dalcy. In this booklet, Lacordaire was praised to the sky but presented as the successor of Father La Mennais, persisting in the latter's projects, more intelligently, however, much more cleverly than he, and consequently with better chance of success — side-stepping difficulties, shifting, introducing ideas, becoming more timid or bold, according to circumstances. On reading this communication from Vienna, he, the Pope, thought it his duty, out of prudence, not to allow such a spectacular move as the establishment of a French national novitiate in Rome itself, absent a canonical reason. Besides, His Holiness had declared himself perfectly content with all Lacordaire's behavior, having nothing, nothing at all, against him[36].

And so, Father Lacordaire received without delay the reward of his virtue. Never had his position in Rome been better, especially in the mind of Gregory XVI. Lacordaire asked his closest friends to maintain the most absolute secrecy about the pressure exerted by Vienna in this matter. It was not disclosed until after his death by papers he left behind. "It is necessary," said he, "to save the honor of the Holy See; whatever advantage we might have gained in knowing that everything came from Austria, we owed to God the sacrifice of our silence. He blessed this silence up to today; let us keep it longer, [even though] now it would be so expedient for us to break it in conversation. We owe it to the Holy See to take part in its difficulties, even at our own expense[37]."

But what should we think of Metternich, and how to overlook the words of Chesterfield: "Go and see, my son, by what kind of men the world is governed!" Here was one of the highest men of State, one of those paramount pillars of

European public order, a man, who for thirty years, had a strong hand in the most important matters of the civilized world — here he is taking the word of a hare-brained individual, an unknown (indeed, who has known Georges Dalcy?). Here he is, for a trivial fantasy (and what a fantasy), placing all its impact on Cardinal Lambruschini. And for what? To prevent ten Frenchmen from taking the Dominican habit *in Rome*. Let those ten Frenchmen make their novitiate in two groups, separated especially from Lacordaire, and Europe will have escaped from a great danger. On that score, Cardinal Lambruschini stirred himself up; and what happened is what we have just seen. Enough! The future came for both men alike as well as for the politics which they represented. What could have been more useless! As we have seen, they often impeded the good. What, in fact, did they save?

End of Book One.

ENDNOTES

1. To Mme Swetchine, 13 April 1839.
2. To the Princess Borghese, 21 December 1839.
 - The main altar at the church of La Quercia is placed at the base of the oak tree and below the image.
3. To Mme Swetchine, 13 April 1839.
4. Testimony of Father Palmegiani. (Chocarne, p. 247, 1st edition.)
5. 7 April 1839. (Chocarne, pp. 281-282, 1st edition.)
6. Ps. 115:1. "Not to us, O Lord."

7. Letter to Bishop de Quélen, 20 June 1839.
8. Letter to Mme de Vauvineux to Lacordaire, 16 April 1839.
9. To Montalembert, 4 February 1840.
10. See the letters to Mme Swetchine 9 October 1838, 3 July, 22 September and 17 December 1839, 1 March 1840.
11. To Montalembert, 4 February 1840.
12. To the Master General, 25 January 1840.
13. To Montalembert. 4 February1840.
14. An idea of this sermon can be gained from a letter of Mme Albert de la Ferronays to Montalembert (*Récit d'une Soeur* [Report from a Sister], 1st edition, pp. 275 and 276. -

See also Cartier, *Le R. P. Besson* [Reverend Father Besson].
15. I speak according to a dependable witness, Ernest Naville, who was attending this sermon and who kindly shared with me the notes he wrote that very night in his tourist logbook.
16. Journal of Mgr Lacroix.
17. Mt 19:29.
18. See *Father Hernsheim*, biography by Rev. Fr. Danzas, 1856. The following details, not to be found in that work, are taken from two letters of Hernsheim which are in our possession.
19. To Mme Swetchine, 13 May 1840. — With no qualms at all, I borrowed from the attractive book of Cartier the major lines of the life of Fr. Besson.
20. To Mme Swetchine, 13 May 1840. — I have before me the text of the regulations of the French college of Santa Sabina, dated 16 May 1840.
21. Letter of Besson to Dr. Tessier, cited by Cartier,
pp. 90 and 91.
22. The nomination is dated 26 May 1840.
23. This judgment appears severe. The heroic death of Bishop Affre forever elevates him before posterity, and rightly so. Nonetheless, we can find in the book by Castan, p. 93, how

much the Prelate systematically disdained any *public* protest of the episcopacy.

24. To Mme Swetchine, 8 July 1840. - To Montalembert, 9 June.

25. To Mme Swetchine, 4 November 1840.

26. To Foisset, 14 January 1841. — In his *Notice*, Lacordaire places this dinner at the Chancery on 15 February, but the letter that I cite, confirmed by the postmark, resists strongly that error of memory.

27. To Mme Swetchine, 24 July and 30 September 1840. — *Notice*, ch. VI — *Notice about Piel,* p. 131.

— The remains of Réquédat and those of Piel were returned to the Province of France and piously interred at the convent of Flavigny (Côte-d'Or), on 21 July 1869.

28. To Dr. Am. Teyssier (from Pézenas), 23 September 1840.

29. To Montalembert, 20 April 1841.

30. To Mme Swetchine, *Correspondence*, p. 274.

31. To Montalemebert, 11 May 1841.

32. To Mme Swetchine, 11 May 1841.

33. Testimony of Fr. Bourard.

34. To Mme Swetchine, 11 May.

35. 4 June 1841, to Mme Swetchine; 7 June, to Montalembert.

36. To Mme Swetchine and to Montalembert, 19 July 1841.

37. To Montalembert, 19 July 1841.

APPENDICES

(Supportive Evidence)

Trans. note: footnotes are incorporated into text, within brackets.

Appendix I [Intro., endnote #12]

— *"The entire correspondence of Napoleon shows that in his eyes the bishops were nothing other than ecclesiastical prefects."*

This is what he wrote from Saint-Cloud on 1 *prairial* year XII (21 May 1804):

"Mr. Portalis, Counselor of State,

"The situation of priests in the Department of Deux-Sèvres arouses all my attention. This part of the diocese of Poitiers is the one that functions most badly. It will take time before the bishop can be installed. *It is my wish that you CONFER the administration of this diocese to another bishop, for example, that of Meaux.* HE WILL BE GRANTED THE AUTHORITY NECESSARY, and he will use *all the means of his position* to strengthen the people of good faith, bring back those who have strayed, *have punished* and [made to] shudder the evil ones."

"NAPOLEON"

This letter is in the archives of the Empire. It was published in *Correspondance de Napléon* [Correspondence of Napoleon], in-4 [in -quarto] edition, No. 7767.

We see that there was a bishop named by Napoleon, instituted by the Pope, but who was not yet *installed*.

Under these circumstances, given that the installation of the bishop would take time, the Emperor ordered his Minister of Cults *to confer the administration of the diocese to another bishop*, to whom Portalis would *grant* the necessary authority.

The ecclesiastical delegate of the Minister will the use the means of his position (what scorn behind these few words!) to obtain the result desired by the Emperor. This concerns not only the means of persuasion. The ecclesiastical *delegate* must have the evil ones *punished*, which is to say, those who would not bend to the government's politics of conciliation in favor of priests who were steeped in schism.

Does this not resemble very much the mission Napoleon could have given to a commissioner of the imperial government?

The letter we just read is not an isolated document. The work of Haussonville leaves no place for doubt as to Napoleon's way of seeing things. I call attention especially to the overbearing tone by which, in 1811, he required the immediate resignation of the bishop of Séez.

Appendix II [Intro., Endnote # 13]

— *"Not only bishops but also pastors . . . have to bind themselves by oath to report to the Government all that would be plotted to the detriment of the State."*

Here is what I found in the *Correspondance*, book IX.

No. 7,366

To Citizen Portalis, Councillor of State, charged with all matters dealing with cults.

"Paris, 16 *frimaire*, year XII (8 December 1803)

"Citizen Portalis, Councillor of State, there are two movements in the Vendée [region of France]. *I am amazed at not having received news from the bishop of Orléans.* Nonetheless, it appears that the head of the movement are Forestier and several other individuals *who trusted in him*.

"Bonaparte"

As we can see, the First Consul is amazed that the Bishop was able to ignore the effort of Forestier, *who trusted in him*, and after having received the trust, he had not denounced to the Government the chief from Vendée. What other meaning can be given to the letter? — Four days later, on 12 December, Bernier wrote and Bonaparte thanked him in these terms:

No. 7399

"To the Bishop of Orléans (Bernier)

"Paris, 24 *frimaire,* an XII (16 December 1803)

"Sir, Bishop of Orléans,

"I have received your letter of the 12th, that the Councillor of State Portalis gave me. I *thank you for the details that you provided concerning the Vendée.* I recognize the zeal *for which you have given ME proof MANY TIMES...*

"I was relieved to see that the first opinion I had of the troubles that have just occurred were in agreement with your thoughts. But it is no less true that there are four hundred destitute persons without residences, poor subjects formed by impunity in the license of civil wars, and of whom it would be urgent to rid the country. *I would like you to give me a list of them so they can be arrested.*

"I am also led to believe that seven individuals who landed at *l'anse du Repos* (Côte des Sables-d'Olonne) were seen in the midst of the assembly. Signs of correspondence were made between the English fleet and Saint-Hilaire and

516

Sallertaine. Let me know your opinion about those villages, *pastors, notable persons*, that you would believe *capable* of such correspondence.

"BONAPARTE"

Let us continue:

No. 7419

"To Citizen Portalis.

"Paris, 30 *frimaire*, year XII (22 December 1803)

"Write to the bishop of Orléans to ask him for information concerning the man named Lecoq and to learn what kind of man he is.

"Tell him I think that Préjean is in the West; let him find out if he can HAVE HIM ARRESTED.

"BONAPARTE"

No. 7507.

"*Proposals to make to a former chouan [Breton pro-royalist insurgent] through the intermediary of the Bishop of Orléans.*

— It is in these terms that the editors of the *Correspondance de Napoléon* summarize item 7507.

"Citizen Portalis, Councillor of State,

"I wish that you write to the Bishop of Orléans that my intention being to have in Paris an agent who knows the Chouans perfectly, I thought that the man named Barbot, former head of the Chouans, would do. He would profit very secretly in Paris from a salary and would be in a position to discover suspected men from the West who would be here.

"BONAPARTE"

The letters that we have read apparently escaped the eyes of [Father] Theiner. If he knew of them, he would not have written this:

"That Bernier had *sometimes* felt the pressure of Bonaparte, we could *easily* presume... If Bernier seems at times to bend before the will of Bonaparte, it is always, of course, in the interest of Religion... The acts of Bernier, when better known, will justify him completely, we hope, from the odious accusations of which he was charged (*Histoire des deux Concordats*, tome 1er, p. 89).

"I acknowledge that Father Theiner here considers Bernier only as negotiator of the Concordat. But who does not feel that a bishop who lowers himself to the point of making himself a police agent, under the conditions we have just seen, is a man capable of all servility and all cowardice?"

Unfortunately, Bernier was not the only prelate who did not blush at giving to the Emperor this kind of service. The Bishop of Vannes, Mayneaud de Pancemont, was in the same position. On 12 April 1805, Napoleon wrote to his Minister of Police (Fouché):

"I had someone ask the bishop of Vannes from whom he received the secrets he gave me. Here are the names. Have some information collected... But do not have interrogated or compromised in anything these individuals or the Bishop. (*Corresp. de Nap*, tome X, n° 8573.)"

Father Theiner was shocked that the gratuities given to Pancemon appeared suspect to d'Haussonville. Not one of the rewards given by Napoleon was not an act of politics on his part. To be convinced of this, it is sufficient to read the series of his letters addressed to Portalis on the subject of the sums that Napoleon had distributed to the prelates and the priests with whom he was pleased.

As for the episcopal denunciations, they were not limited to inform the Government of plots against the Emperor. We see, Barral, the Archbishop of Tours, denounce a community of Poitiers, The Ladies of the Christian Institution, as being under the influence of the Fathers of Faith. Napoleon was quick to thank him for this and to transmit the denunciation to the Minister of Police (14 September 1806). — *Corres. de*

Nap., tome XIII, n°s 10779 and 10780.

Appendix III [Intro., endnote #19]

" From that, as regards the Church of France, I saw with my own eyes a situation brought lower than could be expressed."

The bishop of Meaux, Barral, in good terms with the court as we have seen in Appendix I, had an eye problem. It was a question of receiving treatment from an oculist. But the Organic Articles forbade a bishop to leave his diocese with permission from the Government.

In book VII of the *Corres. de Napoleon*, we read this:

N° 6,262.

The Bishop of Meaux requests permission of the First Consul to spend some time in Paris so as to treat an eye problem.

Answer

"Paris, 6 fructidor, year X (23 August 1802).

"I will be pleased to see him stay in Paris where he will busy himself no less with matters of his diocese.

"BONAPARTE"

Can we believe that this interpretation of residence imposed on bishops by law keeps their position perfectly intact?

Appendix IV [Intro., endnote #23]

"A special report from Portalis to the Emperor was needed to avert the storm for the first time."

This report to the Emperor was dated 14 May 1807. It can be read in the collection entitled: *Discours, Rapports et Travaux inédités sur le Concordat de 1801* [Unpublished talks, reports, and works about the Concordat of 1801], by Jean-Étienne-Marie Portalis, Minister of Cults, p. 579 ff.

The event that had given rise to this report is perfectly described in a letter of Portalis to the Minister of General Police (Fouché), contained in the same collection, p. 586.

"Paris, 17 March 1807.

"Sir, and dear Colleague,

"When Your Excellency wishes to give some directive to the Ministers of Cults (Portalis admitted, as we can see, that the Imperial Police could have some *directive* to give to priests), it does me the honor and the friendship of informing me in advance. I profit from his knowledge and we work for the good. The Prefect of Police of Paris thought otherwise; last Saturday (14 March), he sent word to the Police about *abbé* Frayssinous, for no reason, no motive and even with no excuse.

"I add that the conversation of this magistrate with this cleric disturbed me as much as it surprised me.

"I will offer Your Excellency some details.

"For several years, the *abbé* Frayssinous has given a course in religion. His conferences were held in a private chapel, situated beside the church of Saint-Sulpice. I invited him to transfer them into the church itself; a public teaching can never be suspected.

"Consequently, since this year, *abbé* Frayssinous holds his conferences on Sunday in the church of Saint-Sulpice. He regularly has a numerous and brilliant audience. Cardinal Maury heard him twice, much to his satisfaction. Public servants, persons of all classes, habitually attend the conferences of *abbé* Frayssinous. I myself have attended, as the Prefect of Police must know. All of this should have reassured that magistrate sufficiently against mysterious reports based on foolishness and malevolence.

"Nonetheless, without notifying me and not thinking that the matter would fall under my prerogatives, he took it upon himself to cite the *abbé* Frayssinous to the police, so he could be interrogated about his lectures and even to set forth for him a mandate of topics. This cleric was very surprised when the Prefect of Police reproached him for preaching bigotry and superstitious practices, but never about military conscription, the glory of the Emperor, and that of our armies. These reproaches prove that Frayssinous did not allow himself anything that could compromise public tranquility and provide an occasion for the Prefect of Police to display his zeal. And so, why turn this cleric over to the police? The move was disturbing: one ought to respect the character of a man about whose intentions nothing could arouse suspicion.

"How did the Prefect of Police dare to reproach *abbé* Frayssinous for never having spoken of the glory of the Emperor and that of our armies? In three different lectures, Frayssinous spoke of the tribute of admiration and of gratitude we owed to His Majesty, and of the degree of glory to which the French nation had been raised by the distinguished deeds of our armies. I attended one of those lectures: a magistrate of the police, despite his care and vigilance, could be surprised or misled when it is a question of deeds that occur in secret and in mystery; but it is inexcusable for him to be poorly informed about a public lecture, given on a Sunday in a church, in the presence of an audience of almost four thousand persons. The blunder is all the more unfortunate in that it provoked on his part a step that the malevolent could abuse. His Majesty does not need forced respect; only the unfortunate and the enemies of all order would be able to refuse him the awareness that his genius, his victories, and his benevolence demand pressingly from Europe and from the world.

"The second reproach against Frayssinous was that he preached bigotry, superstitious practices, and that he stirred up youth. I am unaware of what this reproach could be based on. Frayssinous is a praiseworthy and enlightened individual. When he was summoned by the Prefect of Police, he had only spoken about the great truths of natural religion. He had presented Christianity only as the most admirable system of religion that could be given to civilized nations; it was not yet a question of worship, nor of devotion, or of simple practices of piety. The Prefect of Police would do well reeducate all the agents who make similar reports, or at least, not to take them as judges of lectures they had not attended.

"As for military conscription, Frayssinous did not talk about it because he was not to bring it up in *lectures entirely off the subject.* A cleric would be giving evidence of bad intentions and of malevolence if he spoke at random about conscription when the topic did not naturally come up in the one being treated. One could then suspect an informer of wanting to make the law offensive or to give credit to false rumors of outrageous spite that attempt to spread to the public that our armies were cut to pieces and that, consequently, several new calls for conscripts would be made. If Frayssinous, whose purpose in his conferences was simply to offer proofs in favor of religion, was so clumsy or so badly advised as to speak out of turn concerning a matter completely foreign to his plan, *I would call for his suspension* by the Archbishop of Paris.

"All the bishops in their pastoral instructions, all pastors in their sermons, all clerics in their sermons, have preached, as they should, the sacred duty of conscription.

"*I have invited them by printed notices,* and it was with enthusiasm that they answered this appeal. Your Excellency knows this; I confidently ask for his testimony.

Never has conscription taken place with so few obstacles than in the last two calls for conscripts; our newspapers give credence to all of Europe of the eagerness of the nation to participate in the vast undertakings of the most eminent of princes. Is it in such a moment that there would be need to have recourse to absurd measures that would serve only our enemies and would slander the nation?

"I believed, Sir and dear colleague, that I needed to place under your eyes all that concerns the order to have Frayssinous appear. If the Prefect of Police had been pleased to consult Your Excellence, he would certainly not have attempted a measure that would serve only to disgust an esteemed cleric, discourage all those who, like him, in genuine disinterest, seek to be useful, and to inspire disdain for religion and its ministers.

"Besides, since clerics can truly serve the public good, we should refrain from ordering what they are to say. Lectures suspected of having been dictated by a magistrate would make no impression on minds and hearts. *The magistrate can, in silence and without fanfare, direct the ministers of worship*; but if he tips his hand, authority can no longer expect any real help from religion.

"Who, better than Your Excellency, knows the wise maxims of conduct and of governance? Accordingly, I dare to recommend that the Prefect of Police, in delicate matters such as these, show more caution and prudence, and not to take me as an outsider in matters that His Majesty has entrusted to my immediate direction."

Appendix V [Intro., endnote #24]

"The Master accepts their flattery; but as for the rest, he harshly imposes silence on them."

CORRESPONDENCE OF NAPOLEON — Book XIV
No. 11,629
"To Mr. Fouché
"Warsaw, 14 January 1807.

"It is easy to see that the *Journal de l'Empire* and the *Mercure* are not moved by a proper spirit...

"These two newspapers make use of religion to the point of hypocrisy. Instead of removing the excesses of the exclusive systems of some philosophers they attack philosophy itself and human learning... This cannot continue.

"I have nothing to say about political opinions: one does not need to be a genius to see that, if they dared to speak, their opinions would not be any more sound than those of the *Courier français* (a newspaper suppressed by the Police).

"NAPOLEON"

APPENDIX VI [Intro., endnote # 32]

"The Emperor ordered to be inserted an entire chapter in which LOVE of Napoleon (yes, love) *was commanded, under penalty of eternal damnation.*"

Here is the chapter in question:
LESSON VII
- FOLLOWING THE IVth COMMANDMENT
"Q. — What are the duties of Christians toward the princes who govern them, and what do owe, in particular, to

Napoleon 1ˢᵗ, our Emperor?

"A. — Christians owe the princes who govern them and we owe in particular to Napoleon 1ˢᵗ, our Emperor, *love*, respect, obedience, fidelity, military service, taxes, etc., etc.

"Q. — What must be thought of those who would fail in their duty towards our Emperor?

"R. — According to St. Paul, they would be resisting the plan established by God Himself, and become worthy of *eternal damnation*."

It is not out of place to warn that what has preceded is totally foreign to the catechism of Bossuet. On the duties of subjects towards the Prince, the catechism of Bossuet has only one word. Here is the text:

"Q. — What else does the IVᵗʰ Commandment prescribe for us?

"A. — To respect all superiors, pastors, *kings*, magistrates, and others."

There you have the true teaching of the Church.

APPENDIX VII [Intro., endnote #37]

"As answer, he placed in the Bulletin of the laws of the Empire what he called the Concordat of Fontainebleau."

Here are the terms of the act:

"At the Tuilleries Palace, 13 February 1813

"Napoleon, by the grace of God and the Constitutions, Emperor of the French, King of Italy, Protector of the Confederation of the Rhine, Mediator of the Swiss Confederation, etc., etc., to all present and to come, greetings.

"The Concordat of Fontainebleau, whose tenor follows, is published as law of the Empire:

TENOR OF THE CONCORDAT.

"His Majesty the Emperor and King, along with His Holiness, wishing to bring an end to the differences that have arisen between them, and to provide for the difficulties concerning numerous matters of the Church, have agreed to the following articles, intended to serve as basis for a definitive arrangement:

"Art. 1. — His Holiness will exercise his pontificate over France and in the kingdom of Italy in the same manner and with the same procedures as his predecessors.

"Art. 2. — The ambassadors, ministers, chargés-d'affaires of the powers to the Holy Father, and the ambassadors, ministers or chargés-d'affaires that the Pope could have with foreign powers, will enjoy the immunity and privileges enjoyed by the diplomatic corps.

"Art. 3. — The properties owned by the Pope *that are not transferred* will be exempt from all types of taxes: they will be administered by his agents or chargés-d'affaires. Those that would be transferred will be replaced up to the amount of two million francs of revenue.

"Art. 4. — Within the six months following notification of the nomination by the Emperor to the archbishops and bishops of the empire and of the kingdom of Italy, the Pope will fulfill canonical regulations, in conformity with the concordats and in virtue of the present indult. A preliminary notice will be made by the metropolitan. Following the expiration of the six months without the Pope having granted the appointment, the metropolitan, or in his absence, when it is a question of the metropolitan, the longest serving bishop of the province will proceed to the appointment of the bishop named, in such a manner that the see would never be vacant for more than one year.

"Art. 5. — The Pope will make nominations, whether in France or in the kingdom of Italy, to ten sees, that will subsequently be designated unanimously.

"Art. 6. — The six suburban bishoprics will be restored; they will be nominated to by the Pope. The existing goods will be returned and measures will be taken for goods that have been sold. At the deaths of the bishops of Anagni and of Rieti, their dioceses will be united to the six sees, in conformity with the agreement that will have been reached by His Majesty and the Holy Father.

"Art. 7. — As regards the bishops of the Roman States, *absent from their dioceses because of circumstances,* The Holy Father will be able to exercise in their favor his right to give them sees *in partibus* [in other areas]. He will grant them a pension equal to the revenue they previously enjoyed, and they could be placed in vacant sees, either in the Empire or in the kingdom of Italy.

"Art. 8. — His Majesty and His Holiness will agree, at an opportune time, on the reduction to be made, if necessary, to the sees of Tuscany and the country of Genoa, as well as for the sees to be established in Holland and in the Hanseatic departments [NW Germany - Trans].

"Art.9. — The Propagation Office, the Penitentiary, the Archives, will be set up where the Holy Father resides.

"Art. 10. — His Majesty exonerates cardinals, bishops, priests, lay-persons, who incurred his disfavor as a result of current events.

"Art. 11. — The Holy Father supports the above resolutions in consideration of the actual state of the Church, and in the confidence inspired by His Majesty that he will grant his commanding protection to the many needs religion has in the our times.

"Fontainebleau, 25 January 1813.

"*Signed*: Napoleon, Pope Pius VII.

"We inform and ordain that the presents, endowed with the seals of the State, inserted in the *Bulletin of Laws*, be transmitted to the Courts, the Tribunals, and to the administrative authorities, to be inscribed in their registers, to observe them, and to have them be observed; and that the High Judge, Minister of Justice, be entrusted with publication.

"Given at our palace of the Tuilleries, 13 February 1813.

"*Signed*: Napoleon

"*Seen by us, Arch-Chancellor of the Empire,*

"*Signed*: Cambacérès

"By the Emperor:

"*The High Judge, Minister of Justice*

The Minister Secretary of State

"*Signed*: Duke de Masssa

"*Signed*: Count Daru"

BULLETIN No. 490

Imperial decree relating to the execution of the Concordat of Fontainebleau.

No. 7,067

"At the Tuilleries Palace, 25 March 1813.

"Napoleon, Emperor of the French, King of Italy, Protector of the Confederation of the Rhine, Mediator of the Swiss Confederation, ete., etc.

"We have decreed and do decree what follows:

"Art. 1. — The concordat signed at Fontainebleau, that regulates Church matters, and that was published as law of the State on 13 February 1813, *is obligatory for our archbishops, bishops and chapters*, WHO WILL BE HELD TO CONFORM TO IT.

"Art. 2. — As soon as we will have summoned [someone] to a vacant see and have made this known to the

Holy Father in the manner set by the Concordat, our minister of cults will send a dispatch of the nomination to the metropolitan, and if it is a question of a metropolitan, to the oldest bishop of the ecclesiastical province.

"Art. 3. — The persons whom we will have named will present themselves to the metropolitan, who will make the inquiries required and address the results to the Holy Father.

"Art. 4. — If the person named were in some ecclesiastical exclusion, the metropolitan will make this known immediately; in the case when no reason for apostolic exclusion would exist, if the appointment is not made by the Pope within six months of notification of our nomination, in terms of Article 5 of the Concordat, the metropolitan, assisted by the bishops of the ecclesiastical province, will be held to make the said appointment.

"Art. 5. — Our imperial courts will be aware of all matters known as appeals or abuses, as well as all those that could result from the non-execution of the laws of the concordats.

"Art. 6. — Our High Judge will present a project of law to be discussed by our Council, which will determine the procedure and the *penalties applicable in these matters.*

"Art. 7. — Our ministers of France and of the kingdom of Italy are charged with executing the present decree, that will be inserted in the *Bulletin of Laws.*

"*Signed*: Napoleon
"By the emperor:
"The Minister Secretary of State,
"*Signed*: Count Daru

APPENDIX VIII [Intro., endnote #39]

— *"Who is not aware that the students of the major seminary, numbering 236, of whom 40 were deacons and sub-deacons, having refused to assist at a Mass by the intruder whom Napoleon had named bishop of that diocese, were expelled and incorporated as a body into a training corps where they served until the fall of Napoleon?"*

The fact was officially verified. In the *Bulletin of laws* of the kingdom of France, for the year 1814 (at No. 2 of the collection), we find the following:

"Paris, 9 April 1814.

"The provisional government, informed that the seminarians of the diocese of Ghent, numbering 236, of whom 40 deacons or sub-deacons, were led to Wesel, in the month of August 1813, to be placed in the artillery.

"Decree that they be immediately freed.

"Members of the provisional government.

"Signed by: Prince DE BÉNÉVENT, Duke D'ALBERG, François de JAUCOURT, General Count de BOURNONVILLE, *abbé* MONTESQUIOU."

APPENDIX IX [Chapter I, endnote #1]

Extract from the Register used to learn of individual births in the town of Recey-sur-Ource, in District One of Côte-d'Or, during year X.

"No. 16. — Birth of Jean-Baptiste-Henri LACORDAIRE.

"From the twenty-second of the month of *floréal*, year

ten of the French Republic, birth registration of *Jean-Baptiste-Henri Lacordaire*, born at Recey, the twenty-second day of the month of *floréal*, year ten, at seven o'clock of the morning, son of Nicolas Lacordaire, health officer residing at Recey, and Ann-Marie Dugied, married at Recey on the eight of the month *ventôse*.

"The sex of the child was recognized as masculine. First witness, Nicolas Morisot, residing at Recey, Department of Côte-d'Or, a baker by trade, forty-one years old; second witness, Claude Bailly, residing at Recey, Department of Côte-d'Or, ... by trade, fifty-five years old. From the request made by citizen Nicolas Lacordaire, I drew up this present act.

"Signed.

"*Signatures in the register*: MORISOT, BAILLY, and LACORDAIRE.

" Verified, according to law, by me,

Luc-Jean-Baptiste Rouhier,

mayor of the town of Recey,

"undersigned, acting as public officer of the civil state.

"*Signed* ROUHIER, mayor."

Extract from the register of baptisms and marriages of the parish of Lucey, Faverolles and Saint-Broint.

No 5 in the REGISTER

"In the year one thousand eight hundred two, the thirteenth day of the month of May, by us, serving the town of Lucey and its dependencies, canton of Recey, district of Châtillon-sur-Seine, Department of Côte-d'Or, was baptized *Henri-Jean-Baptiste*, son of Nicolas Lacordaire, physician at Recey, and of Anne-Marie Dugied, his wife, who had as godfather Jean-Baptiste Bougueret, represented by Jean Tridon, and as godmother Henriette Dugied, represented by

Jeanne Degond, Tridon's wife. Done at Lucey, the said day, month, and year. Signed in the register Le Blond, serving Lucey.

"Certified in agreement with the register by us, serving Lucey, Faverolles and Saint-Broint, undersigned, today three February one thousand eight hundred fifteen.

"*Signed*: BUROT, pastor of Lucey."

APPENDIX X [Chapter II, endnote #6]

"Nothing more tender nor as well written as these two letters, written at the age of twenty-three by Lacordaire, to one of his classmates at Saint-Sulpice, one to keep him in the seminary, the other to encourage him to remain faithful to God after he would have left."

See: www.worksoflacordaire.com for translation of both letters.

Here you have the ecclesiastical vocation that was suspect by the directors of the seminary of Saint-Sulpice. This suspicion lasted at least two years, without diminishing. It is enlightening to stress this example — not, of course, to diminish the legitimate admiration surrounding the Company, nor to reduce the memory of Father Garnier, who at the time was Superior and the confessor of Henri Lacordaire — but to allow for deep reflection on the priests who have such a heavy responsibility to open or to close for young seminarians access to the sacred orders.

APPENDIX XI [Chapter III, endnote #26]

— *Guizot has rightly given to Catholicism this testimony that it is a notable school of respect. No one has earned a share in that praise less than La Mennais.*

By chance, I have extracted from the correspondence of La Mennais the following:

"28 March 1825

"I experience every day something that I would have thought impossible: an increase in disdain for the men of this time. I would have never thought that human nature could fall so low; it has surpassed my guesses and *my hopes*. In vain did I search my memory, I have found nothing that compares, even at a distance, with the spectacle offered to us by the Chamber of Deputies (1825). This is certainly something new under the sun. Never has a degradation so ludicrous or a corruption so stupid been seen. I challenge the future to believe the *Moniteur* [a newspaper] of this year; there is no official character that could make likely such baseness and such idiocy."

"3 July 1825

"Now listen, small and great,
Listen to the sad story
Of two knights of writing,
Who for their shameless misdeeds,
Were hanged simultaneously.

"One was Gascon by birth [de Villèle]
Well-versed in obscure language
          [a book of spells?]
That placed him so low in glory,
As well as the Breton lawyer [Corbière],

His obliging companion.

"Having come, alas!, and so cheerlessly,
Having come to the feet of the scaffold,
The clerk read them the sentence;
After which, with penitent heart,
The went up, kissing each other.

"I find something quite touching in this fraternity of the scaffold."

"17 July 1825

"Near the Tuilleries garden
There lies a very obvious lumber-yard
[the House of Deputies]
Where four hundred rotten logs
Are currently for sale.
The seller tells whoever approaches him:
'Who wants some logs at a low price?
But, of course, my friends,
They are sold only by the cord!'"

"Mr. De Villèle seems to have arranged for himself, at the expense of France and of the colonists, a retreat in Haiti. Residing there are the *three percent* of morality and of politics. I have no doubt that Religion also has its own, if we can believe the bishop of Hermopolis. The next session will be the most curious scene of this grand display called the *representative*."

"13 November 1825.

"Another tavern: the French Academy, where it will depend only on you to surprise the Duke of Montmorency, removing his boots on his arrival. He and his followers having many beds available at the Hospital for Incurables, one could not help but agree that it is a precious acquisition for the Academy."

"21 January 1827.

"In no way do I fault you for not having before your eyes the spectacle of all the passions, all the folly, all the baseness offered at this moment by the capital of the descendants of Hughes Capet. Are any means left to express what one feels on seeing so shameful and so foolish a degradation? The *three powers of the State,* as they are called, seem to be a direct emanation of overflow of Might, from Sainte-Pélagie and from Charenton." [Insane asylums - Trans.]

"5 January 1829

"You are quite right in reproaching me for my wrongs against Tisa [the favorite dog of Mme de Senfft]: but also I have to deal with so many other animals! Portalis, Foutrier, Vatimesnil, all those *beasts of prey,* made me neglect that poor animal, si mild and so faithful."

"30 March 1829

"I am quite feeble, but that does not prevent me from conversing with the Bishop de Quélen. La Mennais had just published his *Première lettre à ce prélat* [First letter to that prelate]. By now, you must have received a *First Letter* to be followed by several others, as the song says. I hope that His Excellency will be pleased, otherwise the next one will be very difficult. I harbor some hope that His Excellency will have our correspondence read at the sermon; this encourages me greatly.

"The singing has already begun in another key. It will be something else in a year or two. Do you want to know their history? It is that some people (the Bishops) do not want to march. *Pan!* [Slap / bang]. A kick on the behind! This will move them a hundred paces."

La Mennais wrote the above to a woman, M^{iss} de Lucinière.

Léon Boré, professor of foreign literature at the Faculty of Letters of Dijon, heard La Mennais, before his fall, speak of the bishops of France: "I tell you that no one can make *those people* move except with sizable kicks on the behind. And here is a famous one that I give them there!" said La Mennais. on making the gesture.

"22 January 1830
"We await the opening of the Houses to give you some news... I know of nothing so disgusting as our present state; it is a war of bugs and spiders."

Enough, no?

Unfortunately, this style, more than contemptuous, started a school: the more we treat its opponents from top to bottom, the better we believe to serve the truth. This is something new in the Church.

Appendix XII [Chapter VI, endnote #40]

= Letter of Pope Gregory XVI to Father Lamennais in Latin and in French.
Translation of the French:
>>>To our dear son, Father La Mennais
>>>GREGORY POPE
>>>XVIth of the name

Dear son, greetings and apostolic blessing.

What we had anticipated of your fidelity to us and to the Apostolic See, we find with joy that you have finally shown by a humble and simple declaration which you took care to transmit to us by our venerable brother Bartholomew, Cardinal Bishop [Pacca] of Ostia. We bless the Father of lights, from Whom we have received this great consolation, Who, as we truly express with the Psalmist, rejoices our soul in proportion to our many sorrows.

Thus, the depths of our paternal charity, dear son, open for you with all possible tenderness. We praise you in the Savior that you have obtained a true and full peace by the gifts of Him who saves the humble in spirit and who drives away those whose wisdom follows the principle of the world and not the knowledge that comes from Him. Indeed, the most illustrious and genuine victory, which triumphs over the world and which will attract to your name eternal glory, is that you did not allow yourself to be distracted by human considerations and by obstacles and plots of enemies, and that you made every effort to arrive there where you were called by the voice of the most tender father, according to the rules of wisdom and of truth.

Continue, then, dear son, to obtain for the Church similar subjects of joy on the roads of virtue, of docility, and of faith, and to use the gifts of talent and of knowledge that you enjoy so eminently, so that others will think and speak unanimously, following the teachings traced in our Encyclical. Our happiness has already increased because of the care that you have taken so that our son Gerbet, one of your disciples, give to that subject a praiseworthy declaration, that we have received. Consequently, we wish to have him find here a particular witness of our benevolence.

We cannot conceal that the enemy will again sow tares. Nonetheless, have courage, dear son, and remain firm in your sacred resolution. Seek refuge *where*, as Pope St. Innocent proclaims, there rises *a rampart for everyone; where are found security, a port protected from the stormy waves, a treasure of goods without number.* There, attached to the rock that is Jesus Christ, you will engage with courage and assurance the battles of the Lord so that the sound teaching will flourish everywhere and that Catholic peace will not be troubled by any novelty or any system tinged with the most seductive allegations.

Here we make an end to this letter which we send to you as witness of our hopes for you. We ask only one thing from God, who dispenses all goods, and is the object of our most ardent prayers: that by the intercession the Most Holy Virgin — our hope, our guide, and our teacher on days of difficulties and of storms — to confirm what He has done. Moreover, as a foreshadowing of so powerful a help, we give you, with all our heart, our apostolic blessing.

Given at Rome, at Saint Peter, 28 December 1833, in the third year of our pontificate.

APPENDIX XIII [Chapter VI, endnote #45]

— *"... Unless it is that he has become as eminent as he was good."*

On the full sincerity of Lacordaire in his support of the Encyclical of 1832, I find in a certain number of persons doubts so obstinate that I believe I need to confirm his letter to Bishop de Quélen by unequivocal extracts from his most personal correspondence.

The letter to de Quélen is dated 13 December 1833. On the following day, Lacordaire wrote to Montalembert:

"The Encyclical of the Holy Father, to which I ask you to adhere, according to the formula contained in the Brief to the

Bishop of Rennes, does not contain the teaching that you reject.

"It is not a question of becoming a supporter of Emperor Nicolas or enemy of the freedom of the world and of the Church.

"The Encyclical decides against l'*Avenir* [a newspaper] on only five matters:

"1. That there is no need for a regeneration of the Church;

"2. That freedom of the press in matters of religion is not a normal state; that this freedom spreads error and troubles in minds and that censure belongs to the Church, following previous decrees of Supreme Pontiffs and of the Fifth Lateran Council;

"3. That one must submit to established powers, which is not to say that there is never a case when the people may free themselves from an unjust power, but only that these cases are not the rule, and that today there reigns in Europe a spirit that, *in combating against all authority without distinction,* makes of the actual situation a state of war, in which servitude is established under the mask of freedom.

"4. That the alliances of Christians with men who have no religion, under pretext of obtaining freedom of the Church, are condemnable actions because impiety is basically enemy to the liberty of the Church, as is proven by the example of France and even that of Belgium.

"5. That the Church and the State are naturally united.

"There you have all that the Encyclical had to say. Not one of the points cannot be embraced by men who are friends of their country and of genuine freedom. De Maistre never said anything else.

"Are you fully persuaded that freedom of the press is the oppression of feeble minds by stronger minds, and that God, in bending all minds under the authority of the Church, did not do more for the GENUINE freedom of humanity than the writings of Luther, Calvin, Hobbes, Voltaire, than the *Constitutionel* or the *Tribune du Mouvement* [both newspapers]? Has it really been demonstrated to you that freedom of the press will be the ruin of European freedom and of literature? Do you not see to what depths the latter has fallen in France, and on the other hand, the little genuine liberalism there is in our country after forty years of revolutions? Could you respond that the prophecy of Jean-Jacques Rousseau on printing will not come to pass, namely that we would be obliged to destroy it as a dark secret? Can you not believe that a country can be free without having hundreds of young persons who have left college come to indoctrinate it every morning? *Besides, in the Encyclical, it is not a question of the political press*, of the right to speak on public matters, *but of writings against morality, against faith and common sense.* In any case, the question is very deep; assuredly a Christian can believe that, by divine inspiration, the Pope knows more than he does on the future of Society.

"As for submission to powers, is it so difficult to believe, after all we have seen, that force that overturns only leads to force that builds in blood and on cadavers? Did Poland perish by any other cause? In other times, would Christianity not have come to its aid? And in France, what are the Poles doing today besides revealing that everywhere, among one hundred there are a few Catholics, and the others are false liberals, oppressors of freedom?

"My friend, the Encyclical is immortal and I will tell you why. Because it has uttered a prophecy, the highest and the most important, concerning the future destinies of the world; it has predicted that freedom, power, the good, the beautiful, the letters, and the arts will be revived here below only by means of the Church, and that all enemies of the Church are but despots that the earth will one day reject with abhorrence.

"What deceives you is that you take an artificial state that results from liberalism itself, like the one that the Sovereign Pontiff approves and glorifies, while at the same time he himself declares in a most forceful manner at the beginning of his letter, that the Church *is held in bondage*; and he means by that kings and people just as well. The Encyclical is admirable even under this aspect, in that it does not remain silent about the evils that arise from all sides. She condemns despotism of the Courts as well as that of journalists; but she does not wish, that on the pretext of avoiding the one, we throw ourselves on the mercy of the other.

"I am convinced that today, in the House of Peers, there are not ten men who agree with what the Encyclical decided, given that what it decided is so natural and social."

One could detect some exaggeration in this manner of praising the pontifical act of 1832. And yet, evidently Lacordaire does not dream of diminishing or evading its authority. Here, he does not address himself to ecclesiastical authority, whose benevolence he might have an interest in obtaining. He writes to his closest friend, who, for his part, has not yet adhered to the Encyclical, and regarding which nothing obliges him to insist in this way, unless it be his most complete conviction.

In another letter, he explains the attitude of Gregory XVI concerning the various governments of Europe.

"One should not confuse the Encyclical with the series of acts flowing from Gregory XVI. In the Encyclical, it is a question of neither Poland, nor Russia, nor Belgium, nor France, nor the United States, but only of the bondage of the Church, on the one hand, and the remedies to that servitude indicated by the *Avenir* [newspaper] on the other. One should not confuse the Encyclical with the other acts of the Pope as if you were asked to hold to ALL the acts, effects, as they are, of the needs of the times. Besides, we should not judge the Vicar of Jesus Christ too severely, as he fought against a disorganized society, with no solid support except in God. With the social order turned upside down, and no throne being stable, no institutions being basically more Christian, the Church — the only society in existence today — finds herself as in the time of the Caesars, less indifferent, perhaps, because there remains some ruins from the ancient order. She does not get aroused, then, for a political cause; she is neither legitimist nor republican. She acknowledges the facts; insofar as she can, she pours balm on the wounds of society. Everywhere she still has influence over minds or over princes, she uses it; where she has none, she remains silent or groans. If Poland had been victorious, and she had acted as in Belgium, on the level of religion, which is not clear that she would have, the Pope would have treated Poland as Belgium. If, having been victorious, the impious would have prevailed, the Pope would have condemned Poland according to the degree of its impiety, just as he approved and condemned simultaneously the complex situation of the revolution of 1830 in France, an event advantageous to the Church because anarchy did not triumph, but disadvantageous in other respects. With Poland vanquished, the Pope reminded it of the example of the Christians of the early centuries, when humanity carried the burden of a very different tyranny. When there will be some flattery for Nicolas in the Briefs of the Pope, it will again be necessary to forgive a father who can do no more for the salvation of his children than by flattery and prayer." [To Montalembert, 4 January 1834]."

"By a strange fantasy, it has been imagined that in the Encyclical, Rome condemned freedom in itself and thereby all the hopes of people.

"For the Pope to condemn freedom, he would have had to express clearly that the people *had no right* to it; that they belonged to the sovereign like a flock of sheep to its master; that *absolute power*, without laws, without brakes, is the only Christian government; that even the Church depends on princes in its faith, its morality, and in its worship. But, in good faith, is there a word about that in the Encyclical? The Pope rises against absolute freedom of conscience and against freedom of irreligious and immoral writings: is that to destroy freedom or to establish it?

"As for his conduct regarding princes, do you not see that the Pope is in a frightful position? He has no support from people, none among liberals. Not only do princes have force, but in fact, they preserve the only remnants of order that subsist in society. Are you saying that the Pope should separate himself from everything; that he pour new wine into old skins, to use a Gospel expression? In this, is there not an abyss impossible to fill for the moment? The Church is patient, like God, because she is immortal. You think as a being of a single day; the Church acts as a being for all time. This is why I let myself be led by the Church and not by my feeble outlook, led by the Church in all matters that she expresses as teaching. In the entire history of the Church, you will find only one universal act of the Holy See on general questions, an act sent to all the bishops, received by them, approved by their obedience or their silence, that encountered opponents.

"As to what you see in the Encyclical, neither the Pope, nor the bishops, nor anyone has seen it. Thus, you will have the recognition of being troubled because of the phantoms in your mind." [To Montalembert, 3 February 1834].

At the same period, Lacordaire wrote:

"I am a victim in all its most contradictory meanings, but I do not complain; I deserved it. All I hope for is that some day someone will see the bottom of my heart. If it will not be seen in this world, it will be seen later." [To Montalembert, 17 April 1834].

His biographer would consider himself pleased if finally Lacordaire were seen as he always was since his return to God in 1824, submissive to the Church like a child, mild like a son towards the Holy See; *neither republican, nor middle-of-the-road, nor legitimist*, a stranger to all parties, superior to all of them, even though he had compassion for all the distress [to Montalembert, 17 April 1834]; intending to be involved only with matters relating to God, but by those matters, a delayed and future happiness of peoples [same letter]; and by that, prompt to allow himself to be surprised by generous ideas and feelings that give energy to the soul and dignity to human life.

Appendix XIV [Chapter VI, endnote #67]

Here is Lacordaire's final judgment about La Mennais.

"La Mennais was uncompromising, unable to grasp something that had two aspects and never to return to the aspect that he had not seen at first.

"His only change was to pass from an absolutist idea to a liberal one, and from Catholicism to an absolute skepticism. But this two-fold revolution was not achieved progressively; it was achieved abruptly under the Empire by a violent passion: the first time because the Episcopate and the monarchy party (read the royal Government) had abandoned him; the second time, because the Papacy had declared itself against him.

"Apart from these striking changes, *abbé* La Mennais never knew how to transform himself. His thoughts, like the fate of Jupiter, were inflexible. It was this lack of flexibility that prevented him from understanding that the Pope could be right about him, and from grasping the nuances where his condemnation ended. Indeed, he was condemned; and so, everything was lost, and a chasm opened at his feet. This was the least effective disposition against himself that one could imagine. A child's reason would have resolved the issue whereas La Mennais' reason was failing. I tried a thousand times to have him understand that time was in his favor, that he had only to remain silent, that victory was close behind lost battles: this was a language unintelligible to him. He failed for lack of power and not by excess of force, but by a lack of power that no seminarian would experience.

"His character was good-natured and mild. He attached himself, he looked on youth in a fatherly manner. One would have thought of him as a simple and honest father of a family. Nonetheless, he liked criticism to excess; he looked for words that could crush an enemy. His tenderness knew no forgiveness.

"In the later times that I saw him, when his soul was troubled by the waning of his party and the abandonment of Rome, I caught him in dark and fearful moods; he reminded me of Saul. At the end of 1832, after having accompanied him to *La Chesnaie,* I left him only because of the sorrowful impression caused by the sight of him. *I recognized a downfall as if it had already happened.* This vision is still with me twenty-five years later; after that, nothing surprised me about the depth of his fall. By his character as well as by his mind, he could stop himself only where nothing falls any further.

"His life had been poorly prepared: no regular education, no studies directed by a hierarchical authority; a room, some books, the reading of everything that came to his hands, *the early abandonment of his individual temperament,* a few weeks, at most, at a seminary. Fundamentally, in theology, he did not know some very common matters, such as, for instance, the basis for the distinction between nature and grace. *This initial fault of his intellectual formation* left him with gaps that would never be filled. When, at *La Chesnaie*, he read to me the philosophical explanations of the dogmas of creation and of the Trinity, I had the keen and enduring impression that he was in manifest opposition with all that I had been taught. In a word, he was ignorant, but in very good faith, he believed that he was defending Catholic truth by attacking it. His intellect, faulty in itself for lack of flexibility, had not found in life points of support capable of helping him. He was a confused man on all sides; on the day when his genius was to weaken, it was inevitable that he was to experience the greatest fall yet to be seen. All heretics stopped at a point that seemed to be the truth for them; La Mennais found no such fixed point in himself. Not even error could save him." [Letter to Foisset, 23 December 1858].

May I be allowed, in my turn, to have the last word on La Mennais? He did not pass by like an insignificant meteor; he is especially the one whom it pleased God to use to bring about one of the greatest moral revolutions of our time, the dissolution of Gallicanism in France. Unfortunately, however, by no claim did he possess what alone has legitimate authority among men: precision of intellect. From many points of view, however, he deserves painful sympathy: he was a very sick man, and his sickness bears a well-known name: hypochondria. This is the only explanation for his letter of 25 June 1816 to his brother (*Œuvres inédites*, publiées par Blaize, t. 1, p. 263) [Unedited works]. There was also something unhealthy about that infatuation with his individual thought that lost him. Alas, what moral disorder attracts less sympathy than pride? This pride, after all, combined with Breton obstinacy, led him to die as an outcast. His demise imprinted on my memory an indelible and sinister mark from a Christian viewpoint. Here is a man whose remembrance will always bring about shuddering. *Qui se existimat stare, videat ne cadat.*[Therefore let anyone who thinks he stands take heed lest he fall. - I Cor 10:12]

Appendix XV [Chapter VII, endnote #29]

"On a single day, he will show himself roused because of it.

On 21 March 1834, Lacordaire wrote to Bishop de Quélen:
"My Lord,

"I have in mind all that Your Grandeur was good enough to tell me last evening. I understood, by the efforts that were taken with you against me, that I was again beholden to you.

"It will soon be ten years, My Lord, that I was introduced to you in your episcopal residence. You received me as your diocesan priest by adoption, you took me at your expense during my entire stay at the seminary, you gave me the early proofs of an affection that never wavered. I was young and ignorant of the most common matters of Christianity; my conduct at the seminary naturally experienced it. It was a mixture of innocence and imagination, difficult to appreciate by men with an admirably simple and regulated life. You hoped better of me than anyone else; it was your arm that sustained me. Cruelly wounded by the suspicions that I did not deserve, I wished to bury my life in the depths of cloisters, to associate with a body famous by its disgraces and fated to suffer new ones. It was you who kept me from that with a tact so pleasing it could have come only from your heart. When after two or three years of ministry in which you sought to ascertain my tastes, I was unable honestly to associate my feelings and my thoughts to the most common ones in the clergy of France, it was again you — forgetting what I owed you — who allowed me to move to a different diocese. One revolution changed the face of everything. I attached myself to a man about whom you had lodged complaints, I served him; our project having collapsed, along with my individual convictions, I returned to you. I found you unchanged; you did not display offensive distrust of me; you did not ask for my history; you took me on my word. This is what I owe you; it is a lot for ten years. It is even more since up to now my life has been useless for your glory and your flock. On your part, it is an unexplained benevolence, from its having been complimentary. Nonetheless, this you did show, My Lord; never will that thought fade from my memory.

"Yesterday, when you were speaking to me, I again recognized you; you have fought in my favor more than a thousand others who would not have had the courage or the will to do so; but it is beyond your abilities to support me to the end. My fate is sealed. An immense force is in play against those who took part in the works of a celebrated school, and even though some may be unjust or ungrateful on my account, and although I have done everything to prove my obedience to the Church, nonetheless, I honor the resistance of which I am victim. It is the result of a painful fear aroused in the depths of consciences. I will not defend myself against it. I was denounced in Rome more than one month before the lecture that I delivered last Sunday, a lecture taken out of context against me today. Rome was alarmed [I know nothing about these alarms in Rome; I do not doubt that this was a very dangerous rumor, spread by the opponents of Lacordaire; the proof is that, later on, the matter is never brought up]; that was sufficient. I am not strong enough to cope with the storm.

"As of today, my conferences are done with. I would willingly have continued them a few days longer if I could handle the spontaneity, given the feelings from the blow I was dealt. I terminate them with no regret other than that of the good they were beginning to produce. From now on, I have no possible career. I have nothing else left but to pass in humble peace the days God has destined for me, and to make those men blush who harassed me without knowing me, in their unrelenting mistrust. Let others justify this hostile caution, let others make themselves respected by accepting the battle. As for me, it is not possible. If one day, during one of those storms in which the bark of Peter reels, and in which the disciples are agitated by the danger, the Church has need of a poor servant forgotten in the hold and unknown, he will attempt to rekindle in her bosom the stifled remnants of her youth. If he is able, he will bring to the feet of God, whom he had not served, an apology, perhaps, touching on his outcast and lost talent, without his ever having complained about it."

APPENDIX XVI [Chapter VII, endnote #31]

"Lacordaire wrote to the prelate, to announce his resolution to close the conferences of Stanislaus — a guarded but resolute letter."

"Paris, 14 April 1834

"My Lord,

"Yesterday, I put an end to the conferences that I had been giving for three months at Stanislaus College. [On receiving the letter of 21 March, Bishop de Quélen urged

Lacordaire to continue his conferences; accordingly, they were extended up to Good Shepherd Sunday (13 April 1834).] The genuine draining of my strength and the need to invigorate myself in the work of meditation are the reasons that I put forth to justify my retreat. The actual reason was already known by a great number of persons who had learned about it from *abbé* Rauzan. [Superior of the former *Missionaries of France*, who became the Fathers of Mercy.] I believe that only the Government was upset and will be disturbed by this decision. As for me, my Lord, I have already had the honor of telling you, I am not pulling back because of the innuendos or menaces of the Government. I would take it as cowardice or an offense against Jesus Christ to bury my word as priest to comply with the misgivings more or less confirmed by the powers of this world. If I turn aside from my duty in the holy pulpit, it is up to my bishop to judge. If he believes me innocent and that civil authority alone pursues me, it is up to me to defend myself before the courts. I have learned from my ancestors in Christianity that I should never be afraid to appear before them. And so, I withdraw, my Lord, over and against your will, and only your will, knowing full well, besides, that it is not at all fear of the Government that pushed you to act and that you consulted no one else but yourself.

"What exactly are the faults for which I am reproached, I do not know. I have spoken before respectable priests; not one was able to call attention in my presentations to the slightest fault in orthodoxy; if certain words were uttered in a language a bit too modern, they were swallowed up by everything else. Not knowing either my failings nor my opponents, nor what is expected of me, I remain silent, as child of the Church. I place my confidence in God, Who sees in the depth of hearts and helps those who have on earth no other support than a righteous conscience."

APPENDIX XVII [Chapter VII, endnote #48]

I believe it my duty to cite the entire letter of 31 October 1834 that opens to the light of day the depth of Lacordaire's soul as well as the situation at the time. Unless I am mistaken, this letter is admirable.

"My Lord,
"I come to complain about you to you. Twice I had the honor of discussing with you the revival of my conferences at Stanislaus College: the first time at the seminary of Saint-Sulpice, on 3 October last; the second, at the former Biron mansion, the following 10 October. The first time, these were your words: 'I will tell you what I think; I want you not to speak during the Sundays of Lent, not because I am jealous of your talent but because it is better not to set up rivalries.' And since I agreed with your wish with the sincerest grace in the world, you immediately added: 'Nonetheless, I ask you for some time to reflect.' Eight days later, I returned to see you and you expressed your apprehension that taking up the conferences again would lead to fears that boiled down to two: the division of minds and the possibility of a troublesome intervention on the part of the Government. I fought these fears with much calm and respect. As long as it not a question of orthodoxy, what is the division of minds, and what work since the origin of Christianity has not divided them? You yourself have cited the text of the Gospel regarding sermons of Jesus Christ: *Some said he is honorable; others: not so, but he was beguiling the crowds.* I called as witnesses all the priests at Stanislaus College, who approved of my teaching, and on the impossibility of my opponents to cite anything against me except for isolated phrases in which orthodoxy was in no way compromised, and could only be objected to because of some

impropriety in their expression. As for the Government, I bid you not to do anything unless you could assure me positively that it saw or had seen something objectionable in those religious meetings. The conversation ended with these words from you: 'Besides, I give you my word, I am unable to do so; go, examine, consult.' This, My Lord, is how matters took place. From those two conversations, I naturally found proof that the conferences at Stanislaus College offended you, but that, nonetheless, since no positive reproach could be laid against me, you left me free to continue my work.

"However, My Lord, on Monday last, 27 October, *abbé* Rauzan, former superior of the Missions of France, on leaving a conversation with you and speaking of my conferences with *abbé* Buquet, director of Stanislaus College, said, in no uncertain terms, that you did not want the conferences to resume, that you had forbidden me to do so, and that he learned this from you yourself. Those words, My Lord, place me in a very serious situation because, based on your word, I have affirmed to anyone who asked that you had left me free to resume the conferences — and it is affirmed, in your name, and with your word, that this is not the case at all. Allow me, Bishop, to ask of you a favor that touches my honor, the dignity of my priesthood, and the direction of my life, that, in a response, you deign to state my position clearly and inform me of your decision.

"Last winter, I terminated my conferences, not because of an order from you, but because of friendly observations you made to me, and because of uneasy remarks of the Government, it as said — uneasiness in which I place no credence, as I had the honor of expressing to you in writing, but that I did not wish to verify. On the one hand, I valued giving Your Excellency proof of my respectful submission, and on the other hand, you left me clearly with the hope of continuing my work unimpeded the following year. Besides, I did feel that my position, regarding the matters in which I had been involved, were not as clearly outlined, and that the Church, before granting me full confidence, had a right to expect from me something more decisive. Since then, the occasion has arisen, and I did what assuredly ought to have removed from all reckless suspicions the desire to attack me. [Allusion to the *Considerations on the System of de la Mennais*.] — The publication of this work, which I falsely blamed in Chapter VI, p. 262, par. 1, above], is sufficiently justified by what we have just read. So doggedly suspected, Lacordaire had thought it necessary to give new evidence of his irrevocable break from La Mennais. Accordingly, he had determined to publish the *Considerations* to burn his boats more and more. The obstinate injustice of his enemies had forced his hand. Today, therefore, I am on new ground because of the circumstance I mentioned, and also because since time has moved to another year, it is no longer a question of a temporary cessation of my teaching, but a question of knowing if that teaching will continue or be definitively ended. As I see it, this is a question for the public. I was never able to prevent it from being asked, this is the absolute power of events. It is up to you, My Lord, to decide, and I beg Your Excellency to do so in a manner that, if it leave me free, I have, at least, proof of your will; if it does not leave me free, I have some thinking to do before God to decide which part is the better one to press.

"If you leave me free, My Lord, I will begin my conferences again without a doubt and immediately, in spite of the suspicion they cause you. It is my duty to express to you the reasons for this resolve; I will do so all the more in that they will help to enlighten your conscience about the decision I am seeking.

"If someone told me: You are not orthodox, you

express some odd teachings; — if someone told me: all the priests who have heard you give testimony against you; — if someone told me: ecclesiastical authority was present at your teaching and condemns it; — if someone told me: here is the philosophical system, political or religious, that we reproach you for; — if someone told me: you speak as a ranter, you dishonor the word of God, you have neither eloquence nor ecclesiastical knowledge, no feelings of propriety for the flesh; — if someone were to tell me that, My Lord, my response would be very simple. In reply, I would say: the priests heard me, the ecclesiastical authority present accused me of supporting such a false or dangerous system, well, I condemn it; should I decide to support it anew in the pulpit or in writing, I agree that I should be deprived of the Christian word; I am incapable of all preaching, well, I give it up willingly. That, My Lord, would be the end of the matter, were it presented as I have just expressed it. But, is that the case? I spoke for three months, every Sunday, before twenty to thirty priests, to an audience of more than eight hundred people, composed of men from all political parties, many of whom were heartily opposed to me: what did they attribute to my teaching? Did they find something against it by imagination or by ill will? Four or five phrases, isolated from the others, that they spread in salons, exaggerated, distorted, without being able to extract any kind of teaching or system with substance. Not to mention groundless insinuations, vague fears about the Government, phantoms; these are crushing troubles because no suitable reply for them can be found, given that they amount to nothing. Do you, My Lord, wish me to remind you in detail what is less obscure in all that, and that I respond to it? Gladly will I do so.

"I have been reproached for having wished to destroy the conferences of Notre-Dame. — Bishop, you know my conferences began one month before those of Notre-Dame, and you had given me express permission to undertake this task. If my work rivals yours, one would have to say that one parish is a rival to another, that the holy word is rival to another holy word, and that there could not be two men or two things from God under the same heaven. So little did I intend on getting involved in such meanness that I immediately agreed not to speak during Lent, as soon as you made you wish known. If the conferences of Notre-Dame did not enjoy the success that they ought to have had, this is not due to me but to the failure of the institution that does not allow the public to get interested in seven or eight men who arrive successively to open for it a discourse on generalities. I say this frankly because this is the thinking of everyone, even of your orators; one must have the courage to speak the truth to those who are not unworthy of hearing it.

"I have been accused of preaching republicanism. — By a grace of God, for which I thank Him, the Republic always seemed to me to be nonsense and tyranny; never did I desire or defend it. No day passes that I do not laugh about it by the fireside. Is it therefore allowed to slander persons with so little awareness of who these others are? One of the reason for my break with a famous and unhappy man was precisely because of my dislike of his republican delusion. It is true, once I did use the words 'Christian republic' to characterize Christianity; but I used it following St. Augustine's *City of God*; one could just as well accuse another of being republican for having spoken of the *republic of letters*.

"I have been censured for arousing uneasiness even in the Council of the King, and, on this matter, letters were sent to *abbé* Rauman to frighten him. — Well, I met with Guizot, two weeks ago on 18 October last; I saw him to find out, finally, how far the meanness of my opponents and their contemptible plots could go. What did Guizot, in the presence of the Count de Bastard, peer of France, tell me? He said that never did the Government entertain any discomfort regarding the conferences of Stanislaus College; that his colleagues had never complained about them, and that he himself, as Minister of Public Instruction, saw them with the greatest satisfaction. Furthermore, he assured me of the only protection he could offer to an ecclesiastical work, namely, complete security.

"I have been blamed for upholding in the pulpit the philosophical views of La Mennais. — I have given such a cutting denial of that it is useless to bother about it any further.

"I have been accused of compromising Stanislaus College by attracting a crowd of all kinds of strangers. — In the testimony of the heads and of numerous clerics of that house, in their eagerness to request anew my conferences, lies the proof that I did not harm the establishment. In their gratitude, I have a reward that makes me feel all the more how trifling are the grounds alleged against me, in that complaints have been made to a house that for so long echoed with praise for me and desired to hear me anew.

I have been accused of causing divisions in minds. — What man is there, what task is there that never had adversaries? Can we prevent three or four men from spreading suspicions against another or against a work that displeases them; and is more needed, for a crowd of other men, who neither saw nor heard the matter at hand, nonetheless repeat boldly that the man is a heretic and his work worthy of condemnation? The Academy of St. Hyacinth has brought about more divisions than the conferences of Stanislaus: was this a reason to abandon and to dishonor it? Ah! My Lord. A benefit that we should owe to those who have no protection would be to crush them while saying that this is our good pleasure, rather than to charge them with imaginary crimes! If some phrases in my talks were improper or exaggerated, did I not request that they be corrected? Was it not your duty, My Lord, to support me at the beginning of a career so beneficial and difficult? Could you not have selected some trustworthy men and send them to learn for themselves to what degree I lacked precision in the expression of my ideas, and up to what point those defects jeopardized the totality of my preaching? No one came from you; never did the concerns of my heart reach all the way to you. After ten years of my sojourning in your diocese, you know neither my soul, nor my voice, nor my manners, nothing at all about me except what has come through the channel of antipathy or of jealousy. This us how seeds of talent are stifled, for lack of sympathy, of a bit of love, of a bit of foreshadowing that forgives something in the present in favor of the future.

"Accordingly, I resume my conferences, if you allow me to be free, My Lord, because the accusations against them were worthless, and, if one had to remain silent before so little, the last valet who overheard a word while in the next room and repeated it in the living room would become master of the world.

"Another reason for my decision is that the conferences are the one ministry possible for me, and in withdrawing from them, I would be withdrawing from all priestly service. I know myself, I have studied myself, I have engaged in experiments, my vocation lies only there. I have entered the clergy for that or for nothing. I will not be made into a pastor, a confessor, a preacher; I have only one gift and if I do not use it, I will be reduced to nothing as a priest.

"Moreover, I am in such a situation that my entire reputation depends on taking up my conferences. These are being awaited to learn whether the Church, through the mouth of my bishop, places confidence in me or not, whether she believes in my sincerity or not. Already, from the four corners of France and even from abroad, the rumor is being spread that I will never again climb to the pulpit, that you have silenced my speech, that I am destined to suspicions, to curses — that after having obtained from me what was desired, I would be set aside like a tool that was used for a certain purpose, then destroyed. Such is my condition before the world and before the Church. It is a serious and decisive condition. I have served the Church in a situation that belongs to her history; I served her at the expense of my feelings, with a heartbreak that only God knows, at the risk of my reputation in friendship, in integrity, in the most generous feelings of man. I have served her with no hidden motives; as reward, I ask neither for riches nor dignities, matters in which I am unskilled, should I ever have the misfortune of wanting them; all my life, I will remain content in my humble functions in the convent, and will not ask you to get me out. But I demand of the Church, in the person of my bishop, that she have confidence in me, that she give honor to my priesthood. If she does not, I will have to think things over.

"My Lord, I am over thirty-three years old; had I remained in the world, I would be in a position of respect when I spoke of myself or of others; it is not right that, having sacrificed my life for the Church, I be the plaything of the lowest intrigues and of the ill-will of some party that will not forgive me for not having dedicated to it my existence and my priestly consecration. My Lord, I demand justice from you; I lay claim to the only possession of the priest, the only honor of the priest, the freedom of the evangelical word, the freedom of preaching Jesus Christ until such time as it has been established that I lack divine orthodoxy — which is he highest matter of all, and which, God willing, I will never betray, and least not obstinately."

APPENDIX XVIII [Chapter VIII, endnote #41]

"Paris, 28 December 1826

"I do not know, dear brother, whether I need to reveal to you my irrevocable admission to the clerical state; it was last Saturday that it took place and I received the orders to which are attached the vow of perpetual chastity and that of reciting the breviary every day.

"I accepted this commitment after more than two years and a half of examinations and reflexions. In other centuries, you would have congratulated me; today, you will forgive me. Thus do thoughts of men change. What used to be surrounded with respect by all classes, what the most admirable geniuses sought to make their talents more holy for themselves and for others, what made Bossuet, Fénelon, Vincent de Paul, has become of little value in this generation. I am unaware of what the future holds for its judgment; time is impartial and we will no longer be around when the issue will be judged. Luckily, the heart is separate from the mind, and the separation of ideas does not outweigh the separation of feelings. Friendship and esteem come from the heart. It is the heart that judges actions, that appreciates attachments, that knows what we owe of respect to the beliefs of men, even when we do not share them. In that general division which brings about, in Europe as in America, that two knowledgeable men do not agree on two ideas, you took the side of the party of new times, while I took the one of former times. 'I bound myself to what I found stronger, more striking, more extraordinary in this world, to the only religion that is trustworthy,' said a deist Englishman not long ago; he moved many to Catholicism. More and more, experience has proven to me that I had made a sound choice; Christian life confirmed for me Christian dogma. After that, what more can you ask for? If we cannot shake hands in church, we must do so on the porch and socialize between the two camps.

"This year is the last one that I will pass in the seminary. It will have been three months in May since I entered; time did not seem long. I am now overwhelmed with work and yet, my health is better than ever. I need to be exceedingly occupied, to have my imagination filled; resting my head tires me to death.

"Farewell, my dear brother; I kiss you like a friend and wish you a happy year."

APPENDIX XIX [Chapter IX, endnote #20]

"Lacordaire's manuscript (Letter to the Holy See) had been transmitted by the Chargé-d'affaires of Belgium to Cardinal Lambruschini, who most likely, placed it under the eyes of the Pope; only one and a half lines had been removed."

This is what is attested to by the letter we will now read:

"December 1836

"My dear Lacordaire,

"I have the honor of transmitting to you the manuscript that you communicated to the Secretary of State. Cardinal Lambruschini and Bishop Capaccini are more than satisfied with the way in which you treated this delicate question.

"What especially pleased them was the demonstration simultaneously clear, ingenious, and logical, that the battle is now only between Catholicism and rationalism.

"Nonetheless, my dear Lacordaire, when I gave

assurance from you that you desired that we not spare you the slightest observation, I was charged with asking you to delete two or three words on page 11, second paragraph, lines 5 and 6. While *everyone acknowledged the truth of your assertion*, it was feared that, in the current circumstances, this admission on your part could be misused.

"I write this note to you hastily, my dear Lacordaire, because I absolutely do not have time to go see you before three o'clock; I believe I should not lose a moment.

"Believe me to be your sincere and devoted friend,
"Blondel Van Culenbrœck."

APPENDIX XX [Chapter IX, endnote #30]

"Briefly, the work is badly written; it will not be successful, it will bring about discussions; besides, the author did not have sufficient discretion for the Russian government. This is why the Archbishop of Paris cannot take responsibility on himself to allow this booklet to appear."

Here is the note of Bishop de Quélen.

"We have read very carefully the *Letter to the Holy See*, come from Rome and addressed to a friend. Despite the benevolent presumption of the author, the subject and the goal of this letter, it is impossible to take upon oneself the responsibility for its publication by way of printing. One does not believe himself bound to dwell on considerations that struck him and which rather counsel silence.

"1. Assuredly, there can be no question here of passing judgment on the teaching contained in this Letter. It is sufficient to know that, as has been assured, it was placed under the eyes of the Holy Father by the Cardinal Secretary of

State and by his assistant: on this score, the approbation of His Holiness would prohibit all discussion. Accordingly, observations and criticisms can only deal with the purpose of the *Letter*, on its style and on the effect it is meant to produce.

"2. The purpose the author intended for this *Letter* no doubt is not to treat authoritatively of the Holy Apostolic See, of its prerogatives, of the wisdom of its conduct at all times; such a plan would have been too limited. But it appears evident that the author, believing himself obliged to make a new profession of faith on the occasion of the latest writing of La Mennais, wished to satisfy what conscience and honor seemed to require of him. The *Letter* does not appear to achieve perfectly the goal intended. The thoughtfulness and the caution used by the writer in the *Letter* will not quiet certain spirits but instead will give them a new field in which to repeat their accusations and their attacks against him whom they only want to see, even though unjustly, as a former follower under the influence of his first teacher. Up to now, the author of the *Letter* has done more than enough to counter those slanderous assertions. It is believed to be better for him to remain wrapped in absolute silence than to break it only half-way.

"This purpose is again strengthened by the different writings that have appeared against the author of *Affairs of Rome*, and that, having attacked him more openly, more rigorously, perhaps too emotionally, would present too great a contrast between the *Affairs* and the new *Letter*. Besides, we should realize that the libel entitled *Affairs of Rome* caused less sensation here than we would have expected. It is perhaps better to let it sleep rather than to expose ourselves to arousing new responses and new attacks.

"3. The style of this *Letter* will also offer ample material for criticism. Metaphysical thoughts, treated in a subtle manner, expressed in sometimes obscure terms, will be too strong a reminder of what was found to be blameworthy in the conferences. A large number of passages were pointed out and highlighted as being insufficiently clear or poorly harmonized with the genius of our language. It would be difficult to find someone willing to assume the task of revising this work, given the numerous observations that have been made; it is hardly possible for the author himself to summon the courage to recast it almost in its entirety.

"4. The result of these observations is that the effect of the *Letter* would be completely other than the one desired. It would really be unfortunate for this writing to spread a certain scandal. The indifference with which it would be received by the public would become a calamity ever increasing from all the discussions it would provoke.

"5. The fate of things in this world, already so inconsistent, races forward in our time with greater rapidity. A few days are enough to change ideas and situations. Since the arrival of the *Letter*, there has occurred here a modification remarkable enough to require a reworking of the passage dealing with Russia and Poland. An additional article, brought to the House of Deputies by a new and unexpected majority would be able to influence our political relations with foreign countries. Would it really be prudent that in this circumstance, a priest, distinguished by his talent, already acclaimed — in a way, from the pontifical throne — sent to France, the center of Catholicity, a writing that, without his consent and against his intentions, would appear to sympathize with efforts that could compromise the French Government with the powers, under the aspect of a generous impetus of patriotism and freedom? At least, it is to be presumed that the passage in the *Letter* that has some relation to Poland would be taken, interpreted and commented according to the meaning of those who would drum up support for themselves among the clergy. [I do not understand this well, but I transcribe faithfully this last phrase. - remark by Foisset]

"6. The noble and pleasing things contained in the *Letter*, the remarkable sections on the Holy See that we lament being unable to achieve immediately, do not appear to counteract the drawbacks that we could fear from its publication. Besides, those passages will not be lost; they could appear with honor and advantage in other circumstances. If this judgment were found to be too harsh, its cause would need to be found only in the rocks found on all sides around which we are obliged to navigate, but also in the affectionate jealousy with which we wish to preserve all the reputation of our young friend, and to manage, like an expensive perfume, the resources that the Church of God can assure herself by her means, her frankness, and her virtue."

"Paris, 18 January 1837."

APPENDIX XXI [Chapter X, endnote #50]

Here is the text of the document in question:
- *The full Latin text is given, along with the French translation.*

We

FATHER ANGE-DOMINIQUE ANCARANI

Professor of theology, Master General
and Servant of all
the Order of Friars Preachers

To [Father]

JEAN-BAPISTE-HENRI LACORDAIRE

Honorary Canon
of the Cathedral of Paris

GREETINGS

It has finally received great relief, it is almost terminated, the sharp pain that had penetrated our soul, on seeing the Order of our Holy Patriarch Dominic, still exiled from the fair country of our Europe where it began, even though it has spread elsewhere to the extent of the Christian universe. In fact, we learned recently about an eminent man who had already deserved much from the Catholic Church, that the Father of Lights had inspired you with the pious and fervent goal of courageously devoting all your efforts to reestablish the holy institute of Friars Preachers in the country where St. Dominic had set the groundwork six centuries ago. We have learned (God be pleased to grant our eager wishes for the success of that undertaking!), we have learned with great joy that several companions, some great-hearted men, recruited from among your countrymen, would be ready to enroll, following you, and to vow their life to our Order.

Blessed be God the Father of Our Lord Jesus Christ Who consoles us in all our trials! This is why we give thanks to the very merciful giver of all benefits and address our most fervent prayers to Him so that He allow us, as soon as possible, to begin a work so marvelously appropriate to increase the glory of God, to bring salvation to the faithful, and to insure its success in the heart of a very Christian kingdom.

Courage, then. May your role and that of your companions, may your enthusiasm, your efforts, the splendor of your teaching and of your virtues, bring to life and rebirth from its ashes an Order that has left so many noble examples and so many contributions of untainted science regarding divine matters as well as human ones; an Order that was the honor, the influence, the ornament not only of the Church — but also of civil society.

As for us, we will dedicate with enthusiasm and resoluteness the fortunate beginning and the increase of so important a work — not only our wishes, but also our advice, our management, our authority, and all the means of action that could depend on our administration.

May the God of all goodness bless this excellent undertaking. May the holy Patriarch who brought the family of Guzman to the light of day and who preserves it be benevolent! We pray earnestly for your success and that of your companions. In addition, we address this letter to you with love as a faultless proof, not only of our joyful assent but of our complete cooperation.

Given at Rome in our convent of the Minerva, on 14 September 1838.

Father Ange Dominique ANCARANI,
General of the Order of Friars Preachers.
— Father Mariano SPADA, Master of Theology,
Assistant to the General.

End of the Appendices to Book One.

END OF BOOK ONE

Made in the USA
Charleston, SC
06 June 2014